BARTOS AND MESTON ON THE SUCCESSION (SCOTLAND) ACT 1964

BARTOS AND MESTON ON THE SUCCESSION (SCOTLAND) ACT 1964

6th Edition

David Bartos, LLB (Hons) (Edin.), FCIArb

Advocate, Chairman Faculty of Advocates' Trusts Fiduciaries and Executries Bar Group (TrustBar)

and

Michael C. Meston, MA, LLB (Aberd.), JD (Chicago)

Late Professor of Scots Law at the University of Aberdeen

W. GREEN

 THOMSON REUTERS

First published 1964.
Second edition 1969.
Third edition 1982.
Fourth edition 1993.
Fifth edition 2002.

Published in 2015 by W. Green, 21 Alva Street,
Edinburgh EH2 4PS
Part of Thomson Reuters (Professional) UK Limited
Thomson Reuters (Professional) UK Limited (Company No. 1679046). Registered in
England and Wales. Registered office: 2nd Floor, 1 Mark Square, Leonard Street, London
EC2A 4EG.

Typeset by LBJ Typesetting Ltd
Printed and bound in the UK by Ashford Colour Press, Gosport, Hants

No natural forests were destroyed to make this product; only farmed
timber was used and replanted.

A CIP catalogue record for this title is available from the British Library

ISBN 978-0-414-01938-6

To Clare, Mark and Thomas

To Doris

PREFACE TO SIXTH EDITION

The Succession (Scotland) Act 1964 was revolutionary in substituting most of the law of intestate succession with a new code and placing the executor as the key figure in the transmission of an estate from the deceased to those inheriting it. The bare terms of such a far-reaching Act could scarcely be understood without a reliable and scholarly text explaining how the individual provisions were to function and the extent of the changes from the previous law. The first edition of this book more than amply satisfied this requirement. It and its four succeeding editions, bearing the hallmark of Professor Meston's expertise, became the port of call for practitioners, academic lawyers and students seeking answers to questions both practical and theoretical. Passages of the book have been cited with approval by the courts. During the course of its 50 year evolution, the book expanded to provide an account of testate succession and Scots international private law in relation to intestate succession.

For many years it was thought that reform of the 1964 Act was imminent and hope was raised by the publication of a second Scottish Law Commission *Report on Succession* in 2009. However, thoughts of imminent reform were dashed and it was decided that notwithstanding this, the extent of ad hoc changes to the law of succession since the fifth edition in 2002 were such that a new edition was merited. Professor Meston commenced work on the sixth edition but this was brought to a halt by his untimely death in early 2013. Shortly thereafter I was approached by the publishers W. Green with an invitation to complete the work.

Naturally I had used the book on many occasions having relied on it in research for numerous opinions and litigations over the years. Perhaps as a consequence of my litigation background, I felt that one drawback in its use was the separation of the guide from the actual wording of the Act. This necessitated not merely a need to look at two different places when using the book but also had a tendency to draw attention away from the all-important wording and structure of the Act itself. In this respect the book was out of line with modern commentaries on codifying statutes. It seemed that the book would benefit from a re-structuring which would place guidance on the Act as a commentary on the individual provisions of the Act itself. Having co-authored a work on the recent Arbitration (Scotland) Act 2010, that work appeared to be a suitable model to follow. W. Green agreed to these changes to the structure of previous editions and I took on the mantle of reviewing, revising and updating Professor Meston's classic work.

The law in general is constantly changing in response to the changes in society and the law of succession is no exception. The years since 2002 have seen the creation of civil partnerships, and the granting of discretionary rights of succession to cohabitants upon intestacy, not to mention substantial increases in the limits for spouses and civil partners' claims for prior rights. Internationally there has been the EU Regulation on Succession which even though not applicable as part of Scots law may have effect on the recognition abroad of confirmations and Scottish courts' judgments on succession. There has also been a regular stream of case law. On both the procedural and substantive side there have been a number of changes to the succession to crofting tenancies. It has been attempted to take all of this, and more, into account.

There have now been two Scottish Law Commission *Reports on Succession* since the 1964 Act. Whether and to what extent their suggested reforms to the law of intestate succession will be reflected in legislation is anyone's guess. However, the opportunity has been taken to comment on certain important features of the proposed reforms or, in the case of special destinations, proposed lack of reform. Other proposed reforms are mentioned in the text dealing with the current law.

In the latter part of 2014 the Scottish Government published a *Consultation on Technical Issues Relating to Succession* which sought views on changes to "technical" aspects of the law of succession, many of which had been highlighted in the 2009 Scottish Law Commission Report. This has resulted in the publication of the Succession (Scotland) Bill just as this edition is about to go to press. Nevertheless, the likely changes have been anticipated in the text, although the reader is advised to check that (a) the reforming Act is in force; and (b) the wording of that Act.

Section 29 of the Family Law (Scotland) Act 2006 introduced discretionary rights of succession to cohabitants on intestacy but for some reason the draftsman eschewed the logical approach of amending the 1964 Act. Accordingly it was felt that to retain the book's comprehensive coverage in relation to intestate succession the wording of s.29 and a commentary thereon should be included. This is in Part III.

The revision of this book has proved to be more time consuming than originally thought. In reviewing the text my admiration and respect for Lord McLaren's definitive nineteenth century work *The Law of Wills and Succession* has only increased and I would like to record a debt to that work in particular, so much of which is still relevant. Nevertheless, Scots law remains in great need for a modern work combining the depth and width of that treatment. In the meantime the hope is that this book can provide the reader with some bridge between Lord McLaren and the present day.

I have sought to retain as much of my co-author's text from that edition as possible and, in particular, passages that have received judicial approval. However, significant revision has been required, both to accommodate the new format and particularly where there has been legislative change. It is a great personal regret not to have met my co-author and an even greater pity not to have had the opportunity to discuss a number of difficult issues with him that have cropped up during the writing of the book. These related to new matters. Any differences of view between myself and Mike Meston in relation to his existing text have been almost as rare as hens' teeth. Professor Roddy Paisley of Aberdeen University kindly provided the beginnings of Mike's manuscript for this sixth edition together with some opinions which he intended to use. These have disclosed additional case law which has been incorporated into the text. My debt to my co-author remains immense.

Frank Fletcher of Harper Macleod (formerly Bird Semple) took the trouble to read the whole manuscript and made many valuable suggestions. While a pleasure, the reviewing and writing process suffered numerous interruptions due to the pressure of advocacy and tribunal work. This has been tolerated with the patience of Job by Janet Campbell and Alan Bett, and my House Editor, Lauren McIndoe, all of W. Green who have also made suggestions. I would also like to record my gratitude and thanks to the staff of the Advocates' Library the resources of which have been invaluable.

The aim of the book remains to provide a guide to the 1964 Act, now supplemented by s.29 of the 2006 Act, the common law of intestate succession, and the law on other ancillary matters that the practitioner is likely to encounter. There are also chapters dealing with debt, forfeiture, testate succession and will substitutes.

Any errors or infelicities in the text remain my own and any suggestions for improvements will be gratefully received.

I have tried to state the law as at March 1, 2015.

DAVID BARTOS

PREFACE TO FIRST EDITION

The purpose of this work is to state and to explain the substantial changes in Scots law made by the Succession (Scotland) Act 1964. The main effects of the Act are in the law of intestate succession, but there are very important provisions making completely new arrangements for the property consequences of divorce and a number of provisions affecting testate succession and inter vivos deeds. Taken together, these changes amount to the most important reform of Scottish private law in recent years.

It is hoped that this book will provide a guide through the provisions of the Act which will be of assistance to practitioners and to students and others concerned with the law of succession. An attempt has been made to present a complete picture of the law of intestate succession in Scotland, with a new Table of Heirs and some illustrations of particular situations in the Appendices. Those parts of the previous law left in existence, e.g. in the field of legal rights, are considered, albeit briefly, along with the changes made by the Act. In relation to the other topics dealt with by the Act, comment has been limited to the specific changes made. Any suggestions for improvement will be gratefully received.

Although the Act will not come into force until September 10, 1964, the text has been written as if this had already happened.

My thanks are due to my colleagues for the willingness to act as guineapigs on whom ideas could be tried out, and in particular to Professor D.M. Walker and Professor J. Bennett Miller who suggested valuable improvements.

Faculty of Law   M. C. MESTON
University of Glasgow
July, 1964.

CONTENTS

Contents

Contents

Contents

PART II

PART III

APPENDICES

TABLE OF CASES

TABLE OF UK STATUTES

TABLE OF ACTS OF THE SCOTTISH PARLIAMENT

TABLE OF STATUTORY INSTRUMENTS

TABLE OF SCOTTISH STATUTORY INSTRUMENTS

TABLE OF ABBREVIATIONS

1823 Act	Confirmation of Executors (Scotland) Act 1823 (4 and Geo. IV, c.98) as amended
1858 Act	Confirmation of Executors (Scotland) Act 1858 (21 and 22 Vict. c.56) as amended
1868 Act	Titles to Land Consolidation (Scotland) Act 1868 (31 and 32 Vict. c.101) as amended
1900 Act	Executors (Scotland) Act 1900 (63 and 64 Vict. c.55) as amended
1924 Act	Conveyancing (Scotland) Act 1924 (14 and 15 Geo. 5, c.27)
1964 Act	Succession (Scotland) Act 1964 (c.41); the 1964 Act has been amended as indicated in the commentary
1968 Act	Law Reform (Miscellaneous Provisions) (Scotland) Act 1968 (c.70)
1986 Act	Law Reform (Parent and Child) (Scotland) Act 1986 (c.9) as amended
1990 Act	Law Reform (Miscellaneous Provisions) (Scotland) Act 1990 (c.40)
1995 Act	Requirements of Writing (Scotland) Act 1995 (c.7); as amended by Land Registration etc. (Scotland) Act 2012 (asp 5)
2006 Act	Family Law (Scotland) Act 2006 (asp 2); as amended by the Cross-Border Mediation (Scotland) Regulations 2011 (SSI 2011/234)
EU Succession Regulation	Regulation (EU) No.650/2012 on jurisdiction, applicable law, recognition and enforcement of decisions and acceptance and enforcement of authentic instruments in matters of succession and on the creation of a European Certificate of Succession [2012] OJ L201/107
European Convention	Convention for the Protection of Human Rights and Fundamental Freedoms signed in Rome, November 4, 1950 and set out in Sch.1 to the Human Rights Act 1998 (c.42)
Forfeiture Act	Forfeiture Act 1982 (c.34)

OCR	Sheriff Courts (Scotland) Act 1907 (7 Edw. 7, c.51) First Schedule (as substituted by the Act of Sederunt (Sheriff Court Ordinary Cause Rules) 1993 SI 1993/1956 (as subsequently amended)
RCS	Act of Sederunt (Rules of the Court of Session 1994) 1994 (SI 1994/1443) Sch.2 (as amended)
Succession Act	Succession (Scotland) Act 1964 (c.41); the 1964 Act has been amended as noted in the commentary
Succession (Scotland) Bill	Bill introduced by the Scottish Government to the Scottish Parliament on June 16, 2015
1990 Report on Succession	Scottish Law Commission, *Report on Succession* (HMSO, 1990), Scot. Law Com. No.124 which also contained a draft Bill ("the 1990 Report Bill")
2009 Report on Succession	Scottish Law Commission, *Report on Succession* (HMSO, 2009), Scot. Law Com. No.215 which also contained a draft Bill ("the 2009 Report Bill")
2014 Scottish Government Consultation	Scottish Law Commission, *Consultation on Technical Issues Relating to Succession* (Scottish Government, 2014)
Anton (2011)	A.E. Anton, *Private International Law,* by P.R. Beaumont and P.E. McEleavy, 3rd edn (Edinburgh: W. Green, 2011)
Bankton	Andrew McDouall, *An Institute of the Laws of Scotland in Civil Rights* (Edinburgh: Kincaid & Donaldson, 1751)
Bell, *Principles*	G.J. Bell, *Principles of the Law of Scotland,* edited by W. Guthrie, 10th edn (Edinburgh: T. & T. Clark, 1899)
Currie on Confirmation (2011)	*Currie* on *Confirmation of Executors*, by E.M. Scobbie, 9th edn (Edinburgh: W. Green, 2011)
Gordon on Scottish Land Law	W.M. Gordon and S. Wortley, *Scottish Land Law,* 3rd edn (Edinburgh: W. Green, 2009)
Erskine	J. Erskine of Carnock, *An Institute of the Law of Scotland in Four Books*, 8th edn (Edinburgh: Bell & Bradfute, 1871)
Johnston on Prescription and Limitation	D. Johnston, *Prescription and Limitation,* 2nd edn (Edinburgh: W. Green, 2012)
Mackintosh Committee	Committee on Inquiry established by the Secretary of State for Scotland and chaired by the Hon. Lord Mackintosh which

issued a report entitled *Law of Succession in Scotland* (HMSO, 1951), Cmd.8144 ("the Mackintosh Committee Report")

Meston's   Professor M.C. Meston, *Meston's Succession Opinions,* edited
Succession   by D. O'Donnell (Edinburgh: W. Green, 2000)
Opinions

Wills &   The Hon. J. McLaren, *The Law of Wills and Succession as*
Succession   *Administered in Scotland*, 3rd edn (Edinburgh: Bell & Bradfute, 1894)

PART I

CHAPTER 1

INTESTATE SUCCESSION IN SCOTLAND BEFORE SEPTEMBER 10, 1964

The Succession (Scotland) Act 1964[1] came into force on September 10, 1964. It **1–01** does not purport to be a code in itself, for it adopts the device of requiring succession to be regulated by the provisions of the Act and by

> "any enactment or rule of law in force immediately before the commencement of this Act which is not inconsistent with those provisions and which, apart from this section, would apply to that person's moveable intestate estate, if any."[2]

Nonetheless, when read with the subsequent amending legislation, it does in fact state most of the law relating to intestate succession in Scotland (together with various other topics) and it was certainly the first attempt to set out intestate succession as a coherent body of rules.

Despite the passing of over 50 years since the Act came into force on September **1–02** 10, 1964, an understanding of the previous law remains useful. This is particularly true for succession to heritage, for it can happen, particularly in farming or other rural property, that the title to land still remains with a person who died before the Act came into force. In such a situation, the older law is necessary to guide one through possibly several generations of inheritances in order to provide a good title to a purchaser.[3] Sections 27 to 50 of the Titles to Land Consolidation (Scotland) Act 1868,[4] dealing with service of heirs (to heritable property), were repealed by the 1964 Act in relation to the estates of persons dying after the commencement of the Act. It was expected that there would be very few cases of this sort, and that services of heirs of persons dying before the commencement of the 1964 Act would form a minuscule and vanishing jurisdiction of the Sheriff of Chancery, to whom the whole jurisdiction over services was transferred.[5] Sections 27 to 50 of the 1868 Act together, with by implication s.43 of the Conveyancing (Scotland) Act 1874,[6] were revived in 1980 by s.6 of the Law

---

[1] (c.41).
[2] s.1(1).
[3] See, e.g. *Meston's Succession Opinions*, No.8, pp.17–18.
[4] (31 and 32 Vict., c.101)
[5] See the commentary on s.35.
[6] (37 and 38 Vict. c.94).

Reform (Miscellaneous Provisions) (Scotland) Act 1980[7] for the limited purpose of enabling an heir of provision of a last surviving trustee of heritage to establish his heirship and thus his entitlement to become a trustee.[8] Sections 27 to 50 of the 1868 Act were repealed finally for all purposes by the Abolition of Feudal Tenure etc (Scotland) Act 2000 which replaced service of heirs with declarators of heirship which may be granted by the Sheriff of Chancery.[9] New rules of procedure also required to be established.[10]

1–03   The system of intestate succession in Scotland prior to the passing of the Succession (Scotland) Act 1964 was one based on common law (which itself derived partly from feudal law and partly from canon law) with a succession of piecemeal amendments contained in a variety of statutes. The general principles were tolerably well known, but the exceptions and special statutory provisions were such that difficulties could be experienced in applying them to practical situations. There was a fundamental distinction between succession to heritable (immoveable) property and moveable property.

Intestate succession to moveable property

Fragmentation of approach

1–04   Three different sets of rules had to be considered before the precise division of a particular estate could be established. These were first, the preferable right to the first £5,000 of a deceased's estate given in certain circumstances to the surviving spouse, secondly, the legal rights of spouses and children, and thirdly, the ordinary law of intestate succession. These three sets of rules had to be considered in that order, and if all were applicable, the preferable right would be deducted from the estate to which legal rights applied. Then the entitlement to legal rights would be applied and deducted, leaving the balance subject to the ordinary law of succession. A person succeeding under the law of intestacy as heir at law to heritage was, however, normally barred from sharing in the moveable estate.[11] An exception was where he was also heir to the moveables and chose to collate the heritage with the moveables under the principle of collation *inter haeredes*. This is discussed further below.

Statutory preference of the surviving spouse

1–05   This right was created by the Intestate Husband's Estate (Scotland) Acts 1911 to 1959.[12] Despite the title of the Acts, the right applied in favour of a husband in his wife's estate as well as vice versa. Where one spouse died intestate and without

---

[7] (c.55).

[8] *Skinner, Petitioner*, 1976 S.L.T. 60. Where the destination appointing the heir of provision is in favour of the "heirs" of the last trusteee, the heirs are likely to be those in terms of s.2 of the 1964 Act (*MacMillan, Petitioner*, 1987 S.L.T. (Sh. Ct) 50).

[9] Abolition of Feudal Tenure etc. (Scotland) Act 2000 (asp 5) s.68 and Sch.12 para.8(11).

[10] Act of Sederunt (Chancery Procedure Rules) 2006 (SSI 2006/292).

[11] *Law v Law* (1553) Mor. 2365.

[12] (1 and 2 Geo. 5, c.10); (9 and 10 Geo. 5, c.9); (3 and 4 Geo. 6, c.42) s.5; (7 and 8 Eliz. 2, c.21). The figure was raised from £500 by the 1959 Act.

lawful issue, the surviving spouse had an absolute right to the first £5,000 of the free estate, with interest at four per cent, from the date of death until payment, taken rateably from heritage and moveables belonging to the intestate. If the intestate's total estate was less than £5,000, and the conditions were satisfied, the surviving spouse took the whole estate. If the deceased's intestacy was only partial, the surviving spouse had this right in the intestate element of the estate but had to deduct from the £5,000 any legacy left to him or her. The "prior rights" created by the 1964 Act have obvious similarities of approach.

Legal rights of spouses and children—Moveable property

After allowance for any statutory preference, the next point was the "legal rights" of the surviving children, known as "legitim", and of the surviving wife, known as "*jus relictae*", or surviving husband, known as "*jus relicti*". Legal rights were, and remain, indefeasible rights, in the sense that they cannot be overriden by the will of the deceased. The origin of legal rights in moveables in Scotland seems to have been in a Norman system of common family ownership of property,[13] and in theory a testator had no power to deal with any part of his moveable estate other than the one-third or one-half included in what was known as "the dead's part". **1–06**

If both children and spouse survived, the legal rights of the children amount to one-third of the net moveable estate (shared equally between them) and the legal rights of the spouse amount to the same amount. This leaves one third of the net moveable estate ("the dead's part") open to disposal either by will or upon intestacy, by the other rules of intestacy. If only children or spouse survive, the legal rights of either amount to one half of the net moveable estate (shared equally between the children if there is only legitim). This scenario leaves one half of the net moveable estate as the dead's part. **1–07**

In calculating the amount of legitim to be divided between a number of children, the doctrine of collation *inter liberos* was applied whereby a child claiming legitim who had received an advance (e.g. gift setting him or her up for life, or in business or dowry or similar payment made upon marriage) could be required by the other legitim claimants to collate the advance with the legitim fund in order to calculate the amount that would be paid to the legitim claimants.[14] Legitim claimants who had received collatable advances would have the sum of these set off against their claim for legal rights but would not be required to set off any interest on such advances. In addition, a claimant who was the heir at law in respect of heritable property could only claim legitim if he collated the heritable property with the moveable property into a single pool under the principle of collation *inter haeredes*. That pool would be distributed according to the law of intestate moveable succession.[15] **1–08**

Prior to the commencement of the 1964 Act, "surviving children" had to be literally interpreted for the purposes of legal rights. There was no representation **1–09**

---

[13] J.C. Gardner, *The Origin and Nature of the Legal Rights of Spouses and Children in the Scottish Law of Succession* (Edinburgh: W. Green, 1928), pp.42–45.
[14] *Coats' Trustees v Coats*, 1914 S.C. 744; 1914 2 S.L.T. 2.
[15] McLaren, *Wills & Succession*, i, 150; and see paras 1–24 to 1–26.

in legitim, and thus only those of the immediate children of the deceased who survived him were entitled to it. The issue of predeceasing children could not in any circumstances represent their parents in claims for legitim, nor could they have independent claims in their own right.

1–10   Legal rights could, of course, be evaded by transactions during the deceased's own lifetime, e.g. by making a gift of the fee of his whole estate inter vivos and reserving only a liferent, which left nothing at his death on which legal rights could operate.[16] Of more importance from the point of view of intestate succession was the fact that legal rights might be excluded, either by an express discharge granted by the party prospectively entitled[17] to the deceased, or by exclusion in the deceased's antenuptial marriage contract.[18]

Intestate moveable succession—The general common law rules

1–11   These rules applied to the estate left after any statutory preference and legal rights had been deducted. Instead of using either the civil law or the canon law system of computation of degrees of relationship through a common ancestor, Scots law used (and to some extent still uses) a modified version of the parentelic system. This system employs the principle of lines of succession, so that the whole of the first line from the deceased must be exhausted without finding a surviving heir before any member of the second line can take. Thus the claim of any member of the second line, however close by a system of degrees, is postponed to that of any member of the first line, however remote. Within a particular line, the order of priority is determined by the number of steps from the head of the line.

1–12   In the version employed in Scotland the first line consisted of the children and other more remote lineal descendants of the deceased. In the absence of such descendants, the succession opened to the second line, consisting of the collaterals (siblings) of the deceased and their descendants. Note that the second line did not (and does not) commence with the parents of the deceased as in a true parentelic system such as that in Germany. Failing successors in the categories of descendants or collaterals, the succession opened to ascendants.

1–13   Intestate moveable succession operated on the different principle that all surviving members of the class nearest in degree to the intestate should share equally in his moveables, as "next of kin". This at least was the common law principle, although it was subject to various statutory modifications. The general rules of propinquity to the intestate were the same as in intestate heritable succession, but the special rules of primogeniture and preference of males applied to heritable succession in order to select the one member of the class to take the whole, did not apply to moveables. Further, since the principle at common law was that only the next of kin, i.e. the *surviving* members of the class nearest in degree to the intestate, could succeed, there was at common law no representation in intestate moveable succession of any person who predeceased the intestate.

---

[16] *Campbell v Campbell's Trustees*, 1967 S.L.T (Notes) 30.
[17] *Melville's Trustees v Melville's Trustees*, 1964 S.C. 105.
[18] *Panmure v Crokat* (1856) 18 D. 703; *Dunbar's Trustees v Dunbar* (1902) 5 F. 191; *Galloway's Trustees v Fenwick*, 1943 S.C. 339.

Thus at common law, the next of kin, even if the class consisted of only one person, took the entire moveable succession in preference to any number of people in the next or remoter degrees of propinquity.[19] However, a person who was the heir at law to heritable property was generally barred from claiming as next of kin as well as a legitim claimant unless he opted to collate *inter haeredes*.[20]

Statutory amendments to the common law rules

The various statutory amendments to the common law of moveable succession **1–14** had the effect of creating a dichotomy between the next of kin identified on the common law principles and the heirs *in mobilibus*, i.e. the persons who actually took the moveable estate. As a result of the changes, the heirs *in mobilibus* became a class including the next of kin, but not limited to the next of kin. The three major statutory changes were the introduction of representation in moveables to a limited extent, improvements in the position of the parents of the intestate, and the grant of limited rights in favour of collaterals of the half blood uterine.

Representation in succession to the free moveable estate was introduced by s.1 **1–15** of the Intestate Moveable Succession (Scotland) Act 1855.[21] Apparently copying a provision of the English Statute of Distribution of 1670, the 1855 Act limited the principle of representation to descendants and collaterals (siblings) of the deceased. The moveable estate in which representation became possible was defined as "the whole free moveable estate on which the deceased . . . might have tested".[22] As it was well established that a testator had power to test only on the dead's part, and not on the part of his estate subject to legal rights, the result of this definition was that the 1855 Act did not extend representation to legitim. When the succession opened to ascendants and their collaterals, representation was no longer applicable. Thus, after the introduction of representation in 1855, grandchildren could not share in legitim along with surviving children, but could share with them in the dead's part by representation. Nephews and nieces could share by representation along with surviving brothers and sisters, but one survivor of the class of uncles and aunts would take the whole free moveable estate in preference to cousins by virtue of his position as next of kin at common law.

The improvements in the position of the parents of an intestate were effected by **1–16** the 1855 Act and also by the Intestate Moveable Succession (Scotland) Act 1919.[23] At common law the father of an intestate ranked next after the intestate's collaterals and before his own collaterals, forming in effect a special class of next of kin. The mother of the intestate had no rights as such. Presumably in recognition of the oddity of treating the second line of succession as preferring collaterals to parents, s.3 of the 1855 Act gave the father an extra right to share in moveables in a situation where the succession would not otherwise have opened to him. It provided that he was to have one-half of the moveable estate in preference to

---

[19] *Ormiston v Broad* (1862) 1 M. 10.
[20] See paras 1–24 to 1–26.
[21] (18 and 19 Vict. c.23).
[22] Intestate Moveable Succession (Scotland) Act 1855 s.9.
[23] (9 and 10 Geo. 5 c.61).

brothers and sisters of the deceased or their descendants. The mother's position, finally contained in s.1 of the 1919 Act, was effectively a right to represent the predeceasing father, so that if the father had predeceased the intestate, the mother took over his right to one-half of the free moveable estate in preference to collaterals or to the whole free moveable estate if the intestate left no collaterals.

1–17 At common law collaterals of the half blood uterine (sharing the same mother) had no rights of succession to moveables, although the half blood consanguinean (sharing the same father) had full rights postponed only to collaterals of the full blood. Section 5 of the 1855 Act gave uterine collaterals a right limited in all circumstances to one-half of the moveable estate (the balance went to the Crown if there were no other heirs). This right applied only if the intestate died without issue, without collaterals of the full blood or of the half blood consanguinean, and predeceased by both parents.

1–18 There could be considerable difficulty in the application of these various piecemeal statutory modifications of the common law. For example, the Intestate Moveable Succession (Scotland) Act 1855[24] gave the deceased's father in certain circumstances a right to one-half of the intestate's "moveable estate." That phrase was defined by s.9 as "the whole free moveable estate on which the deceased . . . might have tested, undisposed of by will." The Intestate Husband's Estate (Scotland) Act 1911[25] gave to the widow of a man who died intestate and without lawful issue a prior right to the first £500 out of his estate. The deceased might clearly have tested on this £500, even though he did not in fact do so. Thus it was difficult to establish that the £500 was meant to be deducted before the father took one-half of the balance under the 1855 Act, although that was the only sensible course. The difficulty was not resolved until the passing of the Intestate Moveable Succession (Scotland) Act 1919,[26] which deemed any sums due from an intestate's estate to the surviving spouse not to be estate on which the intestate might have tested.

Representation of pre-deceasing heir to moveable property

1–19 Similarly, when the 1855 Act first introduced the concept of representation in intestate moveable succession[27] it did so in the broad general form that

> "the lawful child or children of such person so predeceasing shall come in the place of such person, and the issue of any such child or children, who may in like manner have predeceased the intestate, shall come in the place of his or their parent predeceasing, and shall respectively have right to the share of the moveable estate of the intestate to which the parent of such child or children, or of such issue, if he had survived the intestate, would have been entitled."

This broad assertion of the principle of infinite representation among descendants did however use the term "next of kin" to describe the person predeceasing the

---

[24] (18 and 19 Vict., c.23) s.3.
[25] (1 and 2 Geo. 5 c.10).
[26] (9 and 10 Geo. 5, c.61) s.4(1).
[27] s.1.

intestate and this use of a technical term led to the remarkable decision by the Court of Session in *Turner v Couper*[28] that representation was not in fact complete among descendants, and commenced only at the nearest class of descendants in which there were any surviving members. This peculiarity still bedevils our law and should be reformed to avoid the enormous variations in benefits which occur under the present law through the accident of whether or not a single member of a previous generation happens to have survived the deceased.[29]

Intestate succession to heritable property

Destinations and three sets of rules

Technically, heritable property subject to a special destination could form part **1–20** of intestate estate. In that event the special destination would take effect in precedence to the rules of intestate succession. Once any special destination had been taken account of, three sets of rules required to be applied. First, the preferable right to the first £5,000 of a deceased's estate given in certain circumstances to the surviving spouse had to be considered, secondly, the legal rights of spouses and thirdly, the ordinary law of intestate succession. These sets of rules had to be considered in that order, and if all were applicable, the preferable right would be computed first and the appropriate sum of money deducted from the estate. Then the entitlement to legal rights would be applied and deducted, leaving the balance subject to the ordinary law of succession. The statutory preference of the surviving spouse described under reference to intestate moveable succession applied to intestate heritable succession also. The law relating to special destinations has not altered greatly since the 1964 Act came into force and is considered in the commentary on s.36(2).

Legal rights of spouses—Heritable property

After allowing for the spouse's preferable right, next the "legal rights" of any **1–21** surviving wife, known as "terce" or of any surviving husband known as "courtesy" required to be dealt with. These legal rights were indefeasible rights, in the sense that they could not be overriden by the will of the deceased. Indeed until 1868[30] it was not possible to deal with heritable property in a will. Both of these legal rights were in the form of liferents. This meant that they were consistent with the rights of succession to ownership under intestacy. The origin of legal rights in heritable property in Scotland seems to have originated from an Anglo-Saxon influence, in the case of terce, and from an Anglo-Norman source in the case of courtesy.[31]

---

[28] *Turner v Couper* (1869) 8 M. 222.
[29] M.C. Meston, "Representation in Succession" (1995) 1 S.L.P.Q. 83, 83–92 and see the commentary on s.6.
[30] Titles to Land Consolidation (Scotland) Act 1868 (31 and 32 Vict., c.101) s.20.
[31] Gardner, *The Origin and Nature of the Legal Rights of Spouses and Children in the Scottish Law of Succession* (1928), pp.46–58.

1–22   A widow's right (terce) gave her a liferent of one-third of the heritage owned by her husband at the date of his death. (Note the important difference from the Anglo-American concept of dower which could apply to land owned by the husband at any time during the marriage.) Even after the removal of some peculiarities deriving from a rule that terce existed only in heritage in which the husband was infeft (had a registered title)[32] certain items of heritage were still not subject to terce, e.g. the principal mansion house of an estate, feuduties[33] and minerals.[34] The practical value of the right was usually negligible, being to one-third of the net income after payment of local rates, interest on heritable debt, etc. The corresponding right of a widower (courtesy) was a liferent of the whole of the heritage belonging to the wife at her death. It has been said that it was awarded to the husband more as father of an heir than as husband of an heiress, for it applied only if a live child had been born of the marriage, and that child was at some time the wife's heir.

Intestate heritable succession—The general common law rules

1–23   These rules applied to the estate left after allowance had been made for any statutory preference and legal rights. Intestate heritable succession operated on the principle of picking out the one individual who would succeed as heir at law to all the heritable property of the deceased. This was based on the necessity under the feudal system of preserving the unity of landed estates so that the appropriate military services might be rendered, but in certain circumstances in which the succession opened to females, a group of females might be regarded as a collective heir and were known as "heirs portioners". The principles on which the heir at law was selected were as follows:

(1)   The succession opened first to lineal descendants of the deceased.

(2)   In the absence of descendants, the succession opened to collaterals (siblings) of the deceased and their descendants.

(3)   In the absence of descendants or collaterals, the succession opened to ascendants of the deceased. Emphasising the importance of direct blood relationship in this system, and also the feudal preference for males to perform military services, this meant that the mother and maternal relations were excluded and ascendants meant the father, whom failing the father's collaterals or their descendants, whom failing the paternal grandfather or his collaterals or their descendants, and remoter ascendants *ad infinitum* on the same principles.

(4)   Preference of males applied in any given category. If there were one son and several daughters, the one son took the whole of the heritage. Only if there were no males in that category did females succeed. Thus, if the deceased left only daughters, they could inherit the heritage, but they took it as heirs portioners, which meant that they were a kind of

---

[32]   Conveyancing (Scotland) Act 1924 (14 and 15 Geo. 5, c.27) s.21(4).

[33]   *Nisbett v Nisbett's Trustees* (1835) 13 S. 517.

[34]   *Grosset v Grosset*, 1959 S.L.T. 334.

collective heir at law. Heirs portioners shared the heritage equally *pro indiviso*, except that any indivisible items of heritage went to the eldest daughter as her *praecipuum*. The main examples of indivisible items were titles of honour and the principal mansion house of a landed estate with its garden and ornamental policies.

(5) Primogeniture was used as the principle to select the one male descendant of a given category to succeed as heir at law, i.e. the eldest son had this position. Primogeniture did not however apply among collaterals, so that the selection of the one brother of the deceased (or the brother of his lineal paternal ascendant) was done according to the rule "heritage descends" so that heritage would pass to the next younger brother of the deceased and in the absence of any to the next eldest brother. Primogeniture also did not apply to succession by females, except to the extent that items regarded as indivisible fell to the eldest heir portioner.

(6) Representation was unlimited in every degree of intestate succession to heritage. This rule of genuine representation was entirely different from the position in moveables (and indeed is entirely different from the present day position—except for titles of honour). Any descendant, however remote, and whether male or female, of someone who would have been entitled to inherit if he or she had survived could stand in that ancestor's shoes. It did not matter if the whole of an intervening generation had died. Thus if the eldest son predeceased the intestate, his issue, however remote, could represent him and take in preference to the second son of the intestate. Primogeniture and preference of males operated to select the person to act as representative, but even if the representatives were a class of females they were still preferred to the second son of the intestate. If sisters would have inherited as heirs portioners, their children took their respective shares. It did not matter if all the sisters had predeceased the intestate. The issue of each still took the share which their mother would have taken, and did not divide the estate per capita among all the grandchildren. Note that this genuine representation was entirely different from the rules of succession to moveables, and the fact that there was genuine representation in heritage seems to have been totally ignored in the modern law.

(7) Exclusion of the mother and all maternal relatives was complete in heritable succession. While the child was heir to its mother, the mother and anyone tracing relationship through her could never be the heir at law of the child.

(8) The full blood excluded the half blood in all degrees of succession. This meant that any collateral who shared both parents with the deceased took in preference to any collateral sharing only one parent with the deceased. However, if there were no collaterals of the full blood, or their issue representing them, the half blood consanguinean could inherit. This meant that collaterals sharing the same father with the deceased could inherit in these circumstances. The complete

11

exclusion of the mother and maternal relations in heritable succession had the consequence that collaterals of the half blood uterine (sharing the same mother with the deceased) were completely excluded from the succession.

(9) The rule that heritage descends was applied in cases where the succession opened to brothers of the intestate or of his lineal paternal ascendants, but was not applied where sisters succeeded collectively. Although the intestate might have had elder brothers, the rule of descent pointed out the next younger brother to the deceased as his heir at law. Failing that brother (or his issue by representation), the next brother down the line was entitled. Failing younger brothers, or their representatives, or if the intestate was himself the youngest of three or more brothers, the succession opened to the immediate elder brother in preference to the eldest.

(10) The Crown, as *ultimus haeres*, was entitled to the heritage of anyone dying intestate without other lawful heirs entitled to the succession. The Crown's interests were, and still are, represented by the Queen's and Lord Treasurer's Remembrancer, a position which is now part of the functions of the Crown Office.

The process by which the heir at law proved that he was the heir at law and obtained a judicial declaration to that effect was service of heirs. Until 1964 all sheriff courts had jurisdiction in services. This process has now been centralised with the Sheriff of Chancery in Edinburgh. For the cases in which it is necessary to obtain a service (or the equivalent) in respect of deaths prior to 1964, the process has been centralised with the Sheriff of Chancery in Edinburgh.[35]

Collation *inter haeredes*

1–24   Collation *inter haeredes* was a doctrine which arose as a result of the existence of different rules of succession applying to heritable and to moveable property respectively. In mixed estates with both heritage and moveables, it qualified the separation of the two lines of succession by permitting, in appropriate circumstances, the massing together of the heritage and the moveables and the distribution of the combined fund by the rules normally applicable to moveable property only. Accepting the inequality which arose from giving all the heritage of an intestate to his heir at law, the object of collation *inter haeredes* was to make some show of equality in the distribution of the intestate's moveable property.

1–25   A person succeeding as heir at law to the heritage was normally barred from sharing in the moveable estate.[36] However, provided that he was a member of the class entitled to succeed to the moveables of the intestate (which was not always the case)[37] he could choose to throw his heritage into a common pool with the moveables and to take his proportionate share with the other heirs *in mobilibus* in

---

[35] See commentary on s.35.
[36] *Law v Law* (1553) Mor. 2365.
[37] *McCaw v McCaws* (1787) Mor. 2383; *Colville's Judicial Factor v Nicoll*, 1914 S.C. 62.

the composite fund. He had a completely unfettered option and, naturally, a decision to collate would normally be made only when the heir's share of the combined fund was more valuable than the heritage to which he succeeded as heir at law.

However, if there was no heritage, no question of collation could arise. Collation **1–26** was a doctrine applicable only to mixed estates, and if the estate was wholly moveable the heir at law simply took his appropriate share of moveables along with the other heirs *in mobilibus*. He was excluded from sharing in the moveables only so long as he actually took heritage from the intestate's estate. Equally there could be no collation if there were no other heirs *in mobilibus* to share the moveables. In that situation he simply took the whole estate, heritable and moveable, since there was no one with whom to collate.

Proof of death and of survivorship

The law of succession prior to the 1964 Act began with the usual problems of **1–27** establishing that the deceased had in fact died and that potential beneficiaries had survived. Then, as now, the rules of succession depended on proof of the death of the person whose estate was being divided. In most cases this prerequisite is so obviously satisfied that it is seldom considered beyond the steps necessary to obtain a death certificate, but in cases of disappearance proof of the fact of death and of the date of death can become matters of considerable difficulty.

Actions were available, both at common law and under the Presumption of Life **1–28** Limitation (Scotland) Act 1891,[38] for settling the question of death and the date on which it occurred.

The common law action was based on a general presumption that human life, **1–29** once shown to have been in existence, continued until the extreme limits of human age. It was never completely clear what those limits were, but they seem to have meant that life was presumed to continue until the missing person would have been between 80 and 100 years old.[39] The effect of this was that the onus of proving an earlier date of death fell upon the persons propounding it, and if no clear evidence of earlier death could be produced, the result was that the missing person had to be regarded as still alive and 40 or 50 years might have to elapse before the missing person's property could safely be distributed on the basis of his or her death.

The statutory action under the 1891 Act solved some of the problems by intro- **1–30** ducing the seven-year rule. The statutory procedure came to be widely used and the result usually was that, in the absence of fairly cogent evidence pointing to an earlier date of death, a missing person was presumed to have died exactly seven years after he was last known to be alive.[40] However, the Act dealt only with property, and did not affect other issues such as the continued existence of the missing

---

[38] (54 and 55 Vict. c.29) repealed by the Presumption of Death (Scotland) Act 1977 (c.27).
[39] Stair, IV, xlv, 17, nineteenthly; Bankton, II, vi, 31; *Secretary of State for Scotland v Sutherland*, 1944 S.C. 79.
[40] Presumption of Life Limitation (Scotland) Act 1891 s.3. If he reappeared, the missing person had a right to recover his property for a period of 13 years from the registration of title to it or the transfer of possession, as appropriate: ss.6 and 7.

person's marriage. Conversely, dissolution of marriage on the ground of presumed death under the Divorce (Scotland) Act 1938[41] had no effect on the succession to the missing person's property, and in theory it was necessary for the representatives of the missing person to raise a number of separate actions to establish death for different purposes.[42]

1–31   Closely linked with the question of establishing the death of the owner of the property in question is the problem of establishing that the beneficiary survived the date of the previous owner's death. Again this requirement is so obviously met in most cases that it is not considered, but problem situations can arise in which the issue is by no means clear. The problem which caused the greatest difficulty was that arising out of the common calamity. There was, until the passing of the 1964 Act, no presumption of survivorship in such cases. The approach taken was that, unless a potential beneficiary could be affirmatively proved to have survived the deceased, he had no claim to succeed.[43] Thus if, for example, a husband and wife died intestate in a common calamity without proof that one survived the other, the result was that neither set of representatives could claim their predecessor's share of the estate of the other. The practical result was much the same as if the husband had predeceased his wife and the wife had also predeceased the husband, but in fact predecease was not established either. All that was established was that neither had been proved to have survived the other. Thus if two persons, whether or not they were spouses, died in an incident in which there was no proof of survivorship by either of them, and left wills in each other's favour, neither could be proved to qualify as a beneficiary in the other's estate. Equally, however, neither could be proved to have predeceased the other, so that even if the wills provided for an alternative disposal in the event of the "predecease" of the other, the alternative could not be used either and the result would be intestacy.[44] Under s.31 of the 1964 Act this is still the case when the common calamity involves husband and wife, but there is now a presumption of survivorship for other cases. See further the commentary on s.31.

1–32   Once these preliminary questions of death and survivance had been considered, the rules of division discussed above came into play.

---

[41] (1 and 2 Geo. 6 c.50).
[42] Scottish Law Commission, *Report on Presumption of Death* (HMSO, 1974), Scot. Law Com. No.34.
[43] "Survivance is in every case a matter of proof, and . . . when a claimant whose claim depends upon proof of survivorship is unable to establish the fact of survivance, his claim necessarily fails." *Drummond's Judicial Factor v Lord Advocate*, 1944 S.C. 298, per Lord President Cooper at 302.
[44] *Ross's Judicial Factor v Martin*, 1955 S.C. (HL) 56.

CHAPTER 2

THE 1964 ACT

The background

The main policy of the alterations made by the 1964 Act was one of taking **2–01** account of changing social conditions. The previous law was framed in such a way as to be relevant mainly to the large landed estate and, although modifications had been made from time to time, it still bore the marks of the feudal system in which these landowners might be called on as such to provide military services. Changed conditions, however, demanded a different approach. This change had taken place over many centuries. For example the valuation roll for Aberdeenshire in 1674 displayed a much larger number of small landholdings than the equivalent valuation roll for 1548 when Mary Queen of Scots (or her advisers) anticipated an invasion by England.[1] By 1964 not only had the typical estate containing heritage left by a deceased person changed from a large landed estate to a much more modest estate, but there had been steady progress in the equalisation of the sexes and a growing feeling that a surviving spouse, especially a widow, was not properly catered for by the law of intestate succession.

All this meant that the law of intestate succession in Scotland was completely **2–02** out of touch with the expectations of a large section of the population. Many a solicitor was abused, or suspected of improper dealings, by disappointed relatives who found that they were to get no share of the estate. It was not easy to justify the privileged position of the heir at law to his younger brothers. It was not easy to tell a mother that she had no right to her deceased child's heritable estate and that it might go to the Crown rather than to her. Even if, as an act of grace, the Crown did make a gift of the heritage to her, she rightly would consider that the fact that this was necessary, let alone the expense, was ridiculous. It was not easy to tell the cousin who had nursed the deceased for years prior to his death that, because the deceased had made no will, the whole of his moveable estate went to his Aunt Jemima in Timbuktu, and that, devoted or not, the cousin got nothing. And in particular, it was not easy to tell a widow that the amount of capital which she had to live on after her husband's death might be substantially less than she had expected. Many a widow imagined that the whole estate of her husband automatically passed to her on his death and was disappointed when the truth emerged.

---

[1] M.C. Meston, *The Aberdeen Sheriff and Commissary Court Style Book 1722* (Stair Society, Vol.47).

2–03   The reforms therefore attempted to bring the law of intestate succession into line with modern post-war conditions. In the well-known phrase of the Mackintosh Committee Report

> "we have throughout kept in view the principle that when a man dies without a will the law should try to provide so far as possible for the distribution of his estate in the manner he would most likely have given effect to himself if he had made a will".

2–04   It is probably true that no general provision for intestacy can provide a result which will be that most likely to have been selected by every deceased person, whatever the size of his estate. Fears were expressed in Parliament as to the effect the Act would have on larger estates, but it was pointed out that intestacy was far commoner in small estates than in large ones. Thus, although ideas as to what constituted a "small" estate varied widely, the Act was framed with the medium to small estate in mind.

2–05   Figures obtained from a survey of confirmations granted in 1961 were quoted in the House of Lords to illustrate the proposition that the Succession Act had to be mainly concerned with the smaller estates. Of 26,943 confirmations granted in 1961, 17,273 (or approximately two-thirds) were cases where wills had been made. Only 9,670 (approximately one-third) were intestacies. Of the 9,670 intestacies only 32 were estates with a gross value over £25,000, and in only five cases was the heritable portion of an intestate estate valued at over £10,000. Intestacy was thus rare when the estate was large, and extremely rare when there was substantial heritable estate. As this would suggest, experience since 1964 has allayed fears that the Act would cause wholesale subdivision of country estates and farms.

2–06   Even these figures do not give the full picture. Although there were 26,943 confirmations in 1961 there were 63,928 deaths in Scotland in that year. For many years the annual number of deaths in Scotland had been stable at around 63,000 (which is almost the same as the number of deaths in 1855). Thus although deaths in a given year need not necessarily lead to confirmation in that year, the proportion of confirmations to deaths in any year gives useful evidence, being set against a relatively stable number of deaths. Some of the deaths will have been of persons whose estates were wound up elsewhere, but that should be counterbalanced by deaths elsewhere of domiciled Scots. Allowing for these factors, there were therefore in 1961 approximately 37,000 cases, over and above the 27,000 in which confirmation was granted, in which it must be assumed that the estate was so small that confirmation was not obtained.

2–07   A survey carried out at Aberdeen in the mid-1980s produced similar results. In the five years from 1980 to 1984, the Scottish average of confirmations as a proportion of total deaths was about 43 per cent. This conceals variations between different parts of the country. In Aberdeen and Stonehaven sheriff court districts, confirmations averaged around 50 per cent of relevant deaths, with the obvious conclusion that in other areas the proportion was less than the national average of 43 per cent. It is rather startling to the solicitor accustomed to winding up estates and obtaining confirmation to realise that only about two-fifths of the persons who die in Scotland leave estate of sufficient value to be worth the expense of obtaining confirmation of an executor.

It seems probable that there is a correlation between the proportion of estates in **2–08** which confirmation is obtained and the proportion in which there is a will. Although not yet fully established, it seems that there is a higher proportion of testate to intestate confirmations in areas where the proportion of confirmations to deaths is also higher than average. Put crudely, more confirmations seem to equal more wills. If this correlation exists, then there seems to be a strong possibility that the deaths in respect of which no confirmation was obtained will include a high proportion of intestacies. Although the estates may have been small, the rules of intestate succession would still be of importance. The figures clearly indicate the need for the law of intestate succession to be relevant to the small and very small estate rather than to the large estate.

These figures also cast doubt on the frequently quoted ratio of one-third intes- **2–09** tacy to two-thirds testacy. Although the figure is not readily verifiable, it may be true that about 66 per cent of confirmations are in respect of testate estates. However, if one makes the heroic assumption that not more than one-fifth of the 57 per cent of people whose deaths do not lead to confirmation will have left any testamentary provisions, the result would be a true figure of about 39 per cent testacy to 61 per cent intestacy.

The abolition of the old regime

In order to bring the law into harmony with changed conditions, the 1964 Act **2–10** effected a variety of changes. First, there was a greatly reduced emphasis on the importance of heritage in succession. While the distinction between heritage and moveables in succession was not totally removed, the privileged position of the heir at law was. Apart from the special case of titles and coats of arms, he no longer has any rights which are not shared by the other heirs. Scotland cannot reasonably be accused of undue haste in making this change, for it was one of the very last countries in the world to abolish the special rules of succession to land.

Similarly, there was a substantial reduction of the feudal emphasis on direct **2–11** blood relationship through the male line. This showed itself in various ways. The position of the surviving spouse of an intestate was substantially improved, partly by changes in prior rights, and partly by being for the first time included in the list of heirs to the free estate after providing for prior and legal rights. Previously, whatever rights a surviving spouse might have had in the other's estate, he or she was never an heir of the other, and this change represented a substantial breach in the doctrine that succession depends on direct blood relationship. So also did the grant of full rights of succession to adopted children in the estates of their adopting parents. Despite pressure in Parliament, however, stepchildren were not given rights of succession. In this situation the principle of blood relationship was apparently too strong to be overcome.

In addition to the widow's increased rights, there were other changes in the **2–12** position of women. The preference for males disappeared with the abolition of the need to look for the one member of a given class to take the heritable estate as heir at law and the substitution of the principle that all members of a class share equally in the whole, but equating the sexes was carried further. The mother, and relations through her, were given the same rights as the father and the relations through him, and this had effects such as giving collaterals of the half blood uterine exactly the same rights as collaterals of the half blood consanguinean. Bringing in the maternal relatives substantially widened the potential field of research into the family tree but was clearly necessary in the interests of justice and logic. From the viewpoint of the 21st century it is difficult now to believe that an argument was presented against the Mackintosh Committee Report on the basis that "it is contrary to all Scottish feeling for heritage to go out of the family to which it belongs".

2–13   Another consequence of the assimilation of heritage and moveables is the virtual abolition of the status of heir at law. Apart from the restricted items excepted by s.37, where the status is still relevant, the heir at law and his anomalous privileges vanished from the law. Among other changes consequential on the partial assimilation of heritage and moveables, the 1964 Act empowered minors[2] to dispose of their heritage by will as they already could in respect of their moveables.

2–14   The doctrine of collation *inter haeredes* was also abolished by the 1964 Act. For some time after the Act, collation remained relevant in cases where the heir at law succeeded to the tenancy of a croft and had to collate the value of that tenancy in order to share in the moveable estate.[3] However, crofting tenancies, formerly excluded from the operation of the Act, were brought within its scope by Part II of the 1968 Act. Thus the heir at law no longer has, as such, any right of succession to crofts, and collation *inter haeredes* disappeared in that situation also.

The order of applicability of rules of succession

2–15   Under the 1964 Act, as under the old law of intestate succession, there is a fragmentation of approach in deciding how a particular estate is to be divided up. After payment of the deceased's debts and any other liabilities and charges to which his estate is subject, there are under the Act three sets of rules to be considered in their proper order, before the final division can be established. These have now been supplemented with cohabitees' claims under s.29 of the 2006 Act. The sets of rules and their order[4] are:

(1)   prior rights under s.8(1), (3) and then s.9;
(2)   legal rights under common law as read with s.11;
(3)   cohabitee's claim under s.29; and
(4)   the residuary rules under s.2.

Prior rights and the residuary rules are discussed in the commentary on the relevant sections of the Act. Legal rights are discussed in Ch.4. Cohabitees' claims are discussed in the commentary on s.29 of the 2006 Act in Part III of this book.

---

[2]   Being girls over 12 years and boys over 14 years of age (superseded by the Age of Legal Capacity (Scotland) Act 1991 which introduced a common age of 12 years).

[3]   M.C. Meston, "Collation of Crofting Tenancies", 1965 S.L.T. (News) 209.

[4]   ss.1(2), 10(2) and 9(6)(a); and s.29(2)(a) and (10) of the 2006 Act (asp 2).

Agricultural property

The special administrative provisions for agricultural units which appeared at **2–16** one stage of the Succession Bill's history were eventually dropped. The purpose was to ensure as far as possible that farms would be kept in the ownership of a single member of the family. The provisions were highly complex and seemed likely to cause many practical difficulties in operating them. It was also pointed out in the House of Lords that, from a survey of the estates of persons dying in 1961, intestacy was extremely rare among those with heritable estates of over £10,000 (of 9,670 intestacies recorded, only five involved heritage of over £10,000 in value). As £10,000 even then represented a very modest farm, there seemed to be no real substance in the fears that, without special provisions, farms would be split up, or pass out of the family's hands altogether. From the figures, the vast majority of farmers regulate the succession to their farms by will. In any event it would be extremely unlikely that a farm would be subdivided on intestacy, for the economic facts of life would dictate its continuance as a unit.

Similar reasoning led to crofting tenancies being brought within the scope of **2–17** the 1964 Act by the 1968 Act: see the commentary on s.37.

Administration of estates

With the virtual abolition of the heir-at-law and heirs portioners, the automatic **2–18** transfer of heritable property to the heirs entitled to succeed to heritable property on intestacy was replaced with the enhancement of the role of the executor. The general policy enacted in Part III of the 1964 Act is to extend the administrative competence of an executor to virtually[5] the whole of the estate of the deceased. This is to enable the executor to act as a central administrator with the duty to ingather the estate of the deceased, to pay off the debts of the deceased, and to distribute in accordance with the law of intestate or testate succession as appropriate. The detail of these changes and the appointment, confirmation and function of an executor is discussed in the commentary on ss.14 to 22 of the Act.

---

[5] Heritable property subject to survivorship destinations being the principal exception.

CHAPTER 3

DEBTS

General

3–01 Before any estate is available for distribution to beneficiaries, whether under a will or on intestacy, there must be deducted from the gross estate any debts incurred by the deceased and any liabilities to which his or her estate is subject. It is from the balance after these items have been deducted that the beneficiaries take their inheritance. Even though a surviving spouse and children are sometimes classed as creditors in respect of their legal rights in a competition with others having ordinary rights of succession, this does not entitle them to participate in the gross estate along with genuine creditors. They are limited to sharing in the net estate after deduction of debts and liabilities. Thus in a competition with true creditors those entitled to legal rights are ordinary beneficiaries.[1] The special privilege of an illegitimate child of being regarded as a true creditor for aliment was removed by the 1968 Act.[2] Thus all the rights of succession are in the net estate after satisfaction of debts and liabilities.

3–02 There is no obvious limit to the way in which a deceased person may have incurred liabilities falling to be paid out of his estate. Contractual obligations, for example debts on the deceased's own account or guarantees of the debts of others, may be liabilities of the estate. So also may delictual claims arising from wrongful acts by the deceased.[3] However, typical examples of debts which commonly have to be paid or allowed for before division of the estate are outstanding loans secured over the deceased's house, local council tax, suppliers' accounts, funeral expenses and the expenses of administration of the estate.

3–03 A creditor seeking recovery of a debt must, if necessary, sue the executor, if one has been confirmed. It is for the creditor to take action against the executor within six months of the death. If he does not do so, there is a risk that the executor will have distributed the estate to the beneficiaries. If that occurs, while the creditor will not have a claim for payment against the executor in a personal capacity, the debt is not extinguished. Instead the creditor must raise an action against the executor to constitute the debt,[4] and in the same proceeding seek repayment (repetition)

---

[1] *Naismith v Boyes* (1899) 1 F. (HL) 79 per Lord Watson at 82.
[2] (c.70).
[3] A right of indemnity against such liability under an insurance policy will be part of the estate which will have vested in the executor under s.14 upon confirmation thereto.
[4] *Clelland v Baillie* (1845) 7 D. 461.

of the distribution by the beneficiary to the executor or directly to himself.[5] The liability of the beneficiary to the creditor is based on the doctrine of passive representation of a deceased's liabilities[6] and extends to the value of the inherited asset. In this context an heir of provision under a special, typically survivorship destination, counts as a beneficiary of the heritage acquired under the destination and can be liable directly to a creditor up to the value of the heritage.[7] Generally speaking a creditor can seek to recover a debt from any part of the estate, including that vested under a survivorship destination. However, if a creditor wishes to recover a debt from any heritable property he must follow a specific order of recovery.[8] Thus a heritable creditor must look first to the secured heritable property (if any) before turning to unsecured property in the residue of the estate (heritable or moveable), and then only to other heritage covered by special destination or special legacy. The situation where a debt is secured over both heritable and moveable property is discussed below.

If no executor has been confirmed the remedy for the creditor is to raise an **3–04** action to constitute the debt *cognitionis causa tantum* calling all of the known heirs or legatees. Once the creditor obtains decree he can then have himself confirmed as an executor creditor. For confirmation as an executor-creditor see *Currie on Confirmation of Executors*.[9]

Classification of debts as heritable or moveable and incidence of debts

Although there has been an assimilation of heritage and moveables for some **3–05** purposes, it is still necessary to classify debts as either heritable or moveable. Not only must there be a precise value for the moveable estate from which the legal rights of spouses and issue are due, but the prior rights of a surviving spouse may also be affected.[10] The prior right in s.8 of the 1964 Act to the deceased's interest in the matrimonial home is "subject . . . to any heritable debt secured over the interest". Thus the benefit taken by the surviving spouse is directly reduced by the whole amount of any debt which can be classed as both heritable and secured over the deceased's interest.

The result is that the liabilities of the estate must still be allocated to heritage and **3–06** moveables under the old principles regulating the liability *inter se* of heir and executor. Section 14(3) of the 1964 Act expressly preserves all the rules by which any particular debt falls to be paid out of any particular part of the estate. These have the general result that debts secured[11] over heritage are payable out of, or form a

---

[5] *Armour v Glasgow Royal Infirmary*, 1909 S.C. 916 (a true beneficiary's claim).
[6] *Wills & Succession*, ii, 1280.
[7] *Baird v Earl of Roseberry* (1766) Mor. 14019; 5 Br.Supp 927; 3 Pat. 651. This case was not cited in the wrongly decided case *Barclay's Bank v McGreish*, 1983 S.L.T. 344 which has in any event been overruled by *Fleming's Trustee v Fleming*, 2000 S.C. 206; 2000 S.L.T. 406.
[8] See in detail, *Wills & Succession*, ii, 1319–1320.
[9] *Currie on Confirmation* (2011), paras 6–76 to 6–114.
[10] e.g. 1964 Act ss.8(6)(d) and 9(3).
[11] These can include charging orders under s.23 of the Health and Social Services and Social Security Adjudications Act 1983 (c.41) which act as a modified standard security in respect of sums due to a local authority in respect of the provision of residential accommodation. The modification is in the Charging Orders (Residential Accommodation) (Scotland) Order 1993 (SI 1993/1516).

deduction from, the value of first the heritage over which they are secured and then from other heritage[12] while all other debts are payable primarily out of the moveable estate.[13]

3–07 The effect of these rules on creditors' claims has been mentioned. Principally, however, these rules of law allocate liability for the debt as between the beneficiaries' interests in the estate. The importance for prior rights and legal rights has been mentioned already. Allocation of debts also has an effect on legacies of testate estate and property passing under special destination.

3–08 Arrears of rent are unsecured obligations and so the moveable estate is primarily liable to bear these.[14] Usually the liability for rent goes with the assignation of the tenancy. However, in a case where the liability to pay rent was stated to be of the deceased tenant, his heirs, executors and successors "conjunctly and severally" it was held that while the deceased's interest in the lease had transferred to his heir the moveable estate bore the rent for the remaining duration of the lease.[15]

3–09 If the moveable estate is insufficient to meet the debts, heritable estate must be resorted to. This is subject to the important point that where there is testate estate, special legacies[16] do not suffer abatement on account of debts until intestate estate (in the event of partial intestacy) and all other legacies are exhausted and such a rule is displaced only with a very clear indication in the will on the part of the testator.[17] Deeds of variation (also known as deeds of family arrangement) can also displace the general rule.

3–10 Ultimately, however, even heritable property subject to a specific legacy or special destination must be realised to meet any debts still outstanding. An executor or heir of provision has a right of relief against the other where he has settled a debt which is partly to be borne by the deceased's property held by the other. Thus where an executor has required to sell heritable property subject to a specific legacy in order to pay a creditor of the deceased, the executor has a right of relief against the heir who has taken heritable property under a survivorship destination. The relief is to ensure that the debt is borne by both items of heritage in proportion to their respective values.

Debts for which the creditor holds both heritable and moveable securities

3–11 One aspect of the general rules which has achieved a new significance in a number of cases is the method of dealing with debts for which the creditor holds both heritable and moveable securities. It was not uncommon and can still occur that a bank or insurance company which provided a loan for the purchase of a house took both a heritable security over the house and an assignation of policies of assurance on the life of the borrower. In such a situation if the borrower dies,

---

[12] *Bell's Trustee v Bell* (1884) 12 R. 85.
[13] See *Wills & Succession*, ii, 1305; and Wilson, *Law of Debt*, 2nd edn (Edinburgh: W. Green, 1991), para.29.10.
[14] *Wills & Succession*, ii, 1307. See also the special provisions for the liability of legatees of crofting tenancies in s.10(4E) and (4EA) of the Crofters (Scotland) Act 1993.
[15] *Burns v Martin* (1887) 14 R. (HL) 20.
[16] See para.6–100.
[17] *Greig's Trustees v Greig* (1854) 16 D. 899 at 903.

the lender will be very generously secured, as the life policies will frequently be sufficient by themselves to pay off the debt. Nonetheless, the situation remains that there is a heritable debt secured over the house at the time of death. Assuming that the house is one in which the deceased's spouse is ordinarily resident, the result would be that the value of the surviving spouse's prior right to the house would be reduced by the whole amount of the heritable security if no account could be taken of the creditor's concurrent moveable security.

Thus, as was also the case between heir and executor before the 1964 Act it is **3–12** necessary to apportion the debt between heritage and moveables so that only the appropriate proportion of the debt is classed as a heritable debt. The heritable element is therefore the same proportion of the total debt as the proportion between the value of the heritable security held by the creditor and the whole value of all the securities held by the creditor. If the heritage held in security is worth £100,000 and the moveable security is worth £50,000, only two-thirds of the debt is a heritable debt.[18] Very difficult questions arise if a life policy assigned in security is a joint one on the lives of two spouses. Depending on the precise terms of the policy, there can arise a debt due by the estate to the survivor of half of the proceeds of the policy.[19] This is on the basis that the survivor's interest in the policy has been used to meet a debt due by the deceased.

Unusual debts

Apart from the ordinary run of debts met with in most estates there are some of **3–13** rarer occurrence. One which appears nowadays to be rarely invoked is the right of a surviving spouse to aliment till the first term for payment of her provision from the estate after the deceased's death. As stated by Erskine[20] and in *M'Intyre v M'Intyre's Trustees*[21] this is a right available to a widow only,[22] the purpose being to provide funds for her maintenance until her provisions, either on intestacy or under a will, become payable. It would seem, however, that s.4 of the Married Women's Property (Scotland) Act 1920[23] gave a surviving husband a reciprocal right—if he was indigent—until it was repealed. Any such alimentary rights are specifically saved by the 1964 Act. Section 37(1)(c) provides that nothing in the Act is to

> "affect any right on the part of a surviving spouse to claim from the representatives of his or her deceased spouse payment of aliment out of the estate of that spouse".

---

[18] *Graham v Graham* (1898) 5 S.L.T. 319. See also *Meston's Succession Opinions*, No.40, p.117.

[19] G.L. Gretton, "Life Policies and the Law of Succession" (1988) J.L.S. 141.

[20] Erskine, I, vi, 41.

[21] *M'Intyre v M'Intyre's Trustees* (1865) 3 M. 1074. See also *Barlass v Barlass's Trustees*, 1916 S.C. 741.

[22] It is arguable that a court would require to offer this to a widower or surviving civil partner in order to comply with the anti-discrimination provisions of art.14 of the European Convention (Human Rights Act 1998 (c.42)).

[23] (10 and 11 Geo. 5, c.64)—repealed by the Family Law (Scotland) Act 1985 (c.37) Sch.2.

In view of the bereavement benefits which have been made available by the State, it may be that it will rarely be necessary to invoke this right, but it could still be of importance given the level of such benefits and the potential for their restriction or abolition in the future. In both its 1990 and 2009 *Reports on Succession*, the Scottish Law Commission proposed the abolition of the aliment.[24] The justification of the Commission appeared to be that an executor could be relied on to make payments to account of the inheritance to the spouse. However the Commission did not take account of the restrictions on executors making payments in safety from ordinary creditors during the first six months after death nor the very real effect on a widow or widower's cash flow that might be caused by a loss of income from the deceased and consequent hardship. It is hoped that the Scottish Government will not implement the proposal.

3–14   Another unusual debt is that of the expenses connected with the birth or baptism of a posthumous child. This is mentioned by McLaren[25] who cites the authority of Erskine[26] and two early cases in *Morison's Dictionary*.[27] Erskine explains this as an aspect of the lack of a fund for the subsistence of the widow and her family. One can also regard this as a liability incurred by the deceased husband by fathering the child, and it is certainly consonant with reason that the expenses should be treated as a debt due from his estate. Again, in view of the existence of the NHS, the point will rarely be of much importance nowadays, but if, in the case of complications, the mother were to be in a private nursing home for a lengthy period, the sum involved could be substantial, and could make a considerable difference to the shares to be taken by the beneficiaries from the estate.

3–15   The right of the deceased's widow (but not, apparently, widower)[28] and family to a reasonable allowance for mournings on a scale suitable to the family's social position is a debt of the estate. Erskine,[29] Bell[30] and McLaren[31] all refer to the cost of mournings as a debt, while Bell goes so far as to treat it as a privileged debt payable even although the estate should be insufficient to meet the claims of the deceased's creditors. The right to mournings is due to be abolished as anachronistic in the Succession (Scotland) Bill on the basis of the proposals of the Scottish Law Commission.[32]

Taxation

3–16   The principal tax that may require to be paid by executors from the estate as a debt of the deceased is inheritance tax.[33] Aside from this there may be a liability

---

[24] *1990 Report on Succession*, recommendation 56; *2009 Report on Succession*, recommendation 75.
[25] *Wills & Succession*, i, 127.
[26] Erskine, I, vi, 41.
[27] *Countess of Caithness v The Earl* (1767) Mor. 431; and *Sheddon v Gibson* (1802) Mor. 11855.
[28] See fn.22 above on art.14 of the European Convention.
[29] Erskine, III, ix, 22, 43.
[30] Bell, *Commentaries*, i, 679.
[31] *Wills & Succession*, i, 127; see also *Sheddan v Gibson* (1802) Mor. 11855.
[32] *1990 Report on Succession*, recommendation 54; *2009 Report on Succession*, recommendation 75.
[33] Inheritance Tax Act 1984 (c.51) s.200(1)(a), with the limitation in s.204(1)(a) of liability to the extent of assets received by the executor. This can be relevant where heritage has passed under a survivorship destination.

to pay income tax on the deceased's income prior to death. In addition while transfers upon death to beneficiaries are exempted from capital gains tax[34] if executors require to dispose of capital assets as part of their administration of the estate (e.g. to meet inheritance tax or other debts), then they may become liable to pay capital gains tax. It is important to note that the beneficiaries are deemed to have acquired the assets for a consideration equal to the market value at the date of death.[35] The reader is referred to specialist works on these taxes for a detailed explanation of their workings.[36]

At this stage it should be noted that any inheritance tax and interest thereon **3–17** payable by an executor which is attributable to the value of property in the United Kingdom which has vested in the executor is, unless the deceased showed a contrary intention in his will, treated as part of the general testamentary and administration expenses of the estate.[37] That being the case, like any ordinary unsecured debt it falls to be paid out of residue in the first instance rather than any special legacy.[38] Where the tax is not payable by the executor as an administrative expense, for example because it relates to property not vested in him (e.g. heritable property subject to survivorship destination, or property outwith the United Kingdom), but nevertheless the executor pays the tax, the executor will have a right of relief from the legatee or heir to the property to which the value of the tax is attributable.[39] This is important to ensure that heirs under survivorship destinations or persons inheriting property outwith the UK do not escape their fair share of inheritance tax.

A Scottish executor should not use Scottish estate to pay a revenue or taxation **3–18** claim of a foreign government given that such claims are unenforceable in Scotland.[40]

Deeds of variation or family arrangement

It is possible for beneficiaries whether testate or intestate to re-arrange the **3–19** succession to the estate by means of a deed of variation, which is sometimes known as a deed of family arrangement. Alternatively there may be a deed of disclaimer executed unilaterally by a beneficiary. Such deeds are made usually for reasons of (entirely legitimate) inheritance tax avoidance. If such a deed is executed within two years of the death and in compliance with the requirements of s.142 of the Inheritance Tax Act 1984, the effect will be that inheritance tax will be due, if at all, as if the variation has been effected by the deceased or the disclaimed benefit had never been conferred.[41] Such a deed may be executed even after the estate has been wound up and distributed to beneficiaries although it is preferable for it to be

---

[34] Taxation of Chargeable Gains Act 1992 (c.12) s.62(1)(b).
[35] Taxation of Chargeable Gains Act 1992 s.62(1)(a).
[36] e.g. *McCutcheon on Inheritance Tax*, by Withers LLP, Aparna Nathan and Marika Lemos, 6th edn (London: Sweet & Maxwell, 2013).
[37] Inheritance Tax Act 1984 s.211(1) and (2).
[38] Inheritance Tax Act 1984 s.211(3) and *Cowie's Trustees, Petitioners*, 1982 S.L.T. 326.
[39] *McCarthy's Executors v McCafferty* Unreported December 16, 1999; [2000] G.W.D. 14–549 (heir under survivorship destination liable to relieve executor from liability for inheritance tax paid by executor).
[40] *Scottish National Orchestra Ltd v Thomson's Executor*, 1969 S.L.T. 325 at 330.
[41] Inheritance Tax Act 1984 s.142(1)(b).

executed at the earliest opportunity, bearing in mind the requirement to pay inheritance tax in order to obtain confirmation. A deed of variation executed within the two year period can have a similar effect in relation to capital gains tax.[42] A deed of variation or disclaimer can be executed after two years from the date of death, but it will not have the retrospective effect for the purposes of certain taxes as set out above and may indeed have other tax consequences. However, it can be a useful way to settle a dispute between beneficiaries.

3–20   A potential difficulty may arise where the succession has taken place by means of a survivorship destination.[43]

Insolvent estate

3–21   If an executor discovers, or should have discovered, that the estate is absolutely insolvent, an executor acquires the duty to petition for sequestration of the estate or the appointment of a judicial factor and to do so within a reasonable period. The sanction is that any intromissions with the estate after the date by which the petition should have been presented render him liable to the penalties of vitious intromission[44] even although he has obtained confirmation from the court.[45]

---

[42] See Taxation of Chargeable Gains Act 1992 s.62(6)–(9).
[43] See C. Anderson, "Survivorship destinations and section 142 of the Inheritance Tax Act 1984", 2007 S.L.T. (News) 241.
[44] See para.S14–24.
[45] Bankruptcy (Scotland) Act 1985 (c.66) s.8(4).

CHAPTER 4

DEATH, SURVIVORSHIP AND FORFEITURE

Death and survivorship

General

The fundamental nature of the law on these points remains as before the 1964 **4–01** Act.[1] Death must be proved before there can be succession. The onus of proof lies on the person seeking to establish succession. Death certificates are sufficient, though not conclusive, evidence of the death, and an action is now available under the Presumption of Death (Scotland) Act 1977[2] for fixing the date of death in cases of missing persons who are thought to have died or have not been known to be alive for a period of at least seven years. For further information the reader is referred to the undernoted works.[3]

Equally any person who is alleged to have been a beneficiary must be affirma- **4–02** tively proved to have survived the deceased. The onus of proof lies on the person relying on the death or survivorship, and the consequence of failure of proof is the failure of that person's claim on the estate.

Common calamities

The 1964 Act effected a very valuable change in establishing survivorship. **4–03** Section 31 deals with situations where "two persons have died in circumstances indicating that they died simultaneously or rendering it uncertain which, if either of them, survived the other". Such circumstances are frequently called a "common calamity" although that label appears nowhere in the Act. The commentary on s.31 provides detailed analysis of that provision. Reform has been proposed in the *2014 Scottish Government Consultation* which is noted in the commentary.[4]

---

[1] See para.1–29.
[2] (c.27) as amended by the Civil Partnership Act 2004 (c.33) Sch.28(4) para.45(2) and (3); and the Marriage and Civil Partnership (Scotland) Act 2014 (asp 5) Sch.1 para.2.
[3] *Greens' Annotated Rules of the Court of Session* or *Parliament House Book*, Vol.2 (Edinburgh: W. Green), notes 50.1.1–50.6.3; and *Macphail's Sheriff Court Practice*, edited by T. Welsh QC, 3rd edn (Edinburgh: W. Green, 2006), paras 20–06 to 20–15.
[4] See para.S31–12.

Testamentary condition of survival

4–04   It is common to find that a legacy in a will is made conditional on the legatee surviving the testator by a specified period of time. At present there may be a lack of evidence to establish survivorship by the relevant period of time and uncertainty may result. The Scottish Law Commission in its *2009 Report on Succession* proposed that in the event of "uncertainty" whether the legatee did survive for the period specified by the testator, the legatee should be deemed not to have survived for the period. This would be a very valuable provision if the deemed non-survivorship was made conditional on it not being possible to establish on a balance of probabilities whether the legatee survived for the period or not.[5] It features in the *2014 Scottish Government Consultation* and may well appear in the Bill that is to follow.

Posthumous children

4–05   A different question of survivorship arises in connection with posthumous children. Under the 1964 Act there are references to survivorship in ss.2(1)(a), 9(1), and 11(1) in connection with free estate, prior rights, and legitim respectively. Wills frequently refer to a beneficiary being "survived by issue". The question is whether a child born after the death of a parent counts as such a survivor.

4–06   In *Elliot v Joicey*[6] a testatrix appointed funds to be held in a trust for her children after her death and upon the death of any one of them:

> "In the event of such child of mine leaving any issue him or her surviving [a share of the funds] in trust for such child of mine absolutely".

It was held that the deceased child did not "leave issue him surviving" when his only child was born posthumously. This was first on the basis that whether the deceased left issue surviving him must be assessed at the date of death of the testatrix. Secondly, while it was acknowledged that a posthumous child could benefit from the fiction of having been alive on that date ("*Qui in utero est, pro jam nato habetur, quoties de ejus commodo quæritur*") the fiction applied only for the purpose of enabling the child to take a benefit to which, if born, it would be entitled. In *Elliott* the child ("issue") did not obtain a benefit under the provision requiring survivorship and therefore the fiction did not apply. Lord Macmillan noted that on the facts of that case the child would still have a claim for legal rights from the moveable estate of his late father.[7]

4–07   In the vast majority of cases, and in particular cases arising under the 1964 Act, there is clear benefit to the child in holding that it survives, and thus the fiction should be adopted. The maxim *qui in utero est pro jam nato habetur* is of very

---

[5] In order to avoid arguments over "uncertainty" such as existed in *Lamb v Lord Advocate*, 1976 S.C. 110.

[6] *Elliot v Joicey*, 1935 S.C. (HL) 57.

[7] *Elliot v Joicey*, 1935 S.C. (HL) 57 at 71.

long standing[8] and gives the posthumous child the same benefits as one born before the parent's death, providing it is born alive.[9] The consequence of prenatal death is that the child is treated as never having existed.[10]

Until recently this meant only that it might be necessary to wait for up to nine **4–08** months after the death to determine the division of an estate, but the courts have not yet had to face the problem of how to administer an estate when a child is born by the use of frozen sperm some years after the father's death. Complications do arise from the use of modern technology. In one instance a widow gave birth to two children by artificial insemination using her husband's sperm after his death. The second child was born in 2002 fully two years after his death.

At least three issues arise in connection with such cases.[11] First, the maxim **4–09** relies on the child being *in utero* at the time of the husband's death. Therefore such a child may be seen as having only one parent, namely the mother. Secondly, is it appropriate or equitable for posthumous children born many years after their parent's death to be deemed to have been alive at the death with the consequence that beneficiaries may be forced to repay inheritances? The prescriptive period of five years for claims of repetition (repayment) may provide some limited comfort. The solution here may be to provide for a time limit for claims to take advantage of the posthumous birth akin to the time limit for the bringing of claims by cohabitees under s.29 of the 2006 Act.

The third issue is that of executors concerned at the possibility of being liable **4–10** for wrongful distribution through omitting children not even conceived at the time of their father's death although the whole estate had already been distributed to those in existence or *in utero* at the time of his death. The solution here may be to make provisions protecting the executors similar to those in s.24(2) of the 1964 Act or s.7 of the 1968 Act.[12]

Forfeiture and the unworthy heir

In order to qualify as a beneficiary in the division of an estate, it may not always **4–11** be enough for the person apparently entitled under the rules of testate or intestate succession to establish that he survived the deceased. In certain situations, the person otherwise entitled to succeed may be passed over because of some factor making it inappropriate that he should succeed to that particular deceased. The theoretical basis of this disqualification, and therefore the precise area of its application, is not entirely certain, but considerations of public policy are clearly involved in a determination that an heir is so unworthy that he ought not to be permitted to inherit.

---

[8] See Roderick R.M. Paisley, "The Succession Rights of the Unborn Child", 2006 Edin. L.R. 29.
[9] *Cox's Trustees v Cox*, 1950 S.L.T. 127; 1950 S.C. 117.
[10] Bankton, 1, xlvii; J. Walker, *The Law of Intestate Succession in Scotland* (Edinburgh: Hodge, 1927), p.10.
[11] For more detail see the discussion in Paisley, "The Succession Rights of the Unborn Child", 2006 Edin. L.R. 29.
[12] See paras S14–30 to 14–32.

Homicide

4–12   The main situation for invoking the disqualification arises when the potential beneficiary has killed the person whose estate is being distributed. There is statutory provision in the Parricide Act 1594[13] disinheriting anyone convicted by an assize (jury) of "slaying" a parent or grandparent, together with the children of the convict but the Act is limited to these relationships and applies only to those entitled to succeed to heritable property on intestacy.[14] The result of a disqualification is clearly spelt out in the Parricide Act, namely that neither the killer nor his or her children can inherit the heritage and the heirship passes to collaterals.[15] Given the existence of the common law the Succession (Scotland) Bill proposes the repeal of the Parricide Act.

4–13   It seems, however, that there is also a more general rule of common law *ob turpis causa non oritur actio*[16] that a person who has culpably killed another cannot benefit from the death that he has caused and is debarred from succeeding to that other's estate. A rule of this nature is well established in England, where it has been formulated as:

> "The principle can only be expressed in that wide form [that it includes manslaughter]. It is that a man shall not slay his benefactor and thereby take his bounty"[17]

Although it was generally accepted in Scotland that there was also a general disqualification at common law, and estates were indeed wound up on this basis when one spouse killed another,[18] there was little direct authority. Public policy demanded that the same approach be taken to killing the deceased, and the sheriff court case of *Smith, Petitioner*[19] for the first time held that a wife convicted of culpably killing her husband was barred from taking any benefit in his estate. The degree of culpability was not high, but was sufficient to bring in the forfeiture. Since then several cases have confirmed the existence of the common law rule.[20]

4–14   In *Burns v Secretary of State for Social Services* in connection with the claim for a widow's social security benefit by a claimant who had been convicted of culpable homicide, it was held:

> "It is a recognised principle of the jurisprudence both of England and Scotland that a person may not benefit from his own crime. This is the

---

[13] (c.30); (12 Mo. c.224).

[14] Bankton, II, ccci, 30; and 1964 Act Sch.2.

[15] Erskine, IV, iv, 47.

[16] *Smith, Petitioner*, 1979 S.L.T. (Sh. Ct) 35 at 36. This dictum is also echoed by Erskine where he writes that "what is given *ob turpem causam* must be restored if the turpitude was in the receiver and not in the giver" (Erskine, III, i, 10).

[17] *Hall v Knight and Baxter* [1914] P. 1 at 7.

[18] e.g. the estate involved in *Garvie's Trustees v Still*, 1972 S.L.T. 29.

[19] *Smith, Petitioner*, 1979 S.L.T. (Sh. Ct) 35.

[20] *Burns v Secretary of State for Social Services*, 1985 S.C. 143; *Paterson, Petitioner*, 1986 S.L.T. 121; *Cross, Petitioner*, 1987 S.L.T. 384; *Gilchrist, Petitioner*, 1990 S.L.T. 494; *Hunter's Executors, Petitioners*, 1992 S.L.T. 1141.

general rule but it is not an absolute one. Not every crime will require the general rule to be applied to deny a claim for benefit. In particular, as was pointed out by Salmon L.J. in *Gray v. Barr* [1971] 2 Q.B. 554, 581 not every kind of culpable homicide will necessarily result in the application of the general rule."[21]

The claimant was found to be barred from her claim but nevertheless the Inner House left open the possibility that there may be rare cases where the culpable homicide did not involve an intent to injure which might entitle a court or tribunal to not apply the principle of public policy underlying the common law rule. This appeared to move away from the case law which indicated that the degree of moral turpitude or culpability in culpable homicide or manslaughter was immaterial.[22]

Despite the strength of the principle of unworthiness, it is interesting that a **4–15** power to exempt from the forfeiture was introduced soon after the existence of the forfeiture was formally recognised in Scotland. The Forfeiture Act 1982[23] was introduced as a private member's bill and became law in a form which leaves many questions unanswered. Except in cases where the killer has been convicted of murder, a court is given power to "modify" what the Act calls "the forfeiture rule". It has not been clear whether power to modify includes power to exclude the rule totally, and in Scotland the courts have proceeded on the assumption that it does not.[24] However they have been prepared to go so far as to remove all practical difference between modification and exclusion by awarding the killer the whole of the deceased's heritage and 99 per cent of his moveables.[25] In other cases the modification has been to specific items of property or to 80 per cent of the estate.[26] In deciding on whether and if so to what extent there should be modification the court must be satisfied that having regard to the conduct of the offender and of the deceased and any other circumstances which appear to the court to be material, the justice of the case requires it.[27]

In its application to Scotland the Forfeiture Act runs into another problem in **4–16** that it enables relief from the "forfeiture rule" which is defined as the "rule of public policy" and not to the statutory disqualification created in Scotland by the Parricide Act 1594.[28]

---

[21] *Burns v Secretary of State for Social Services*, 1985 S.C. 143 at 148 per Lord President Emslie (First Division).

[22] *Re Giles* [1972] Ch. 544 followed (obiter) in *Smith, Petitioner*, 1979 S.L.T. (Sh. Ct) 35.

[23] (c.34).

[24] The Succession (Scotland) Bill proposes to introduce a power to exclude the common law rule entirely.

[25] *Cross, Petitioner*, 1987 S.L.T. 384. In *Cross* no account was taken of the Parricide Act, although a son had killed his father, but it may be that the culpable homicide of which he was convicted did not amount to "slaying" for the purposes of the Parricide Act. The *1990 Report on Succession* of the Scottish Law Commission proposed replacement of the Parricide Act with new statutory provisions but both the *2009 Report on Succession* and the *2014 Scottish Government Consultation* suggest mere repeal.

[26] *Paterson, Petitioner*, 1986 S.L.T. 121; *Gilchrist, Petitioner*, 1990 S.L.T. 494.

[27] Forfeiture Act 1982 s.2(2).

[28] Forfeiture Act 1982 s.1(1).

4–17   An application for modification of the common law rule can be made to either the Court of Session or a sheriff court having jurisdiction and that by petition, summary application, or as part of an ordinary action.[29] While s.2(3) of the Forfeiture Act provides that if a person has been convicted of unlawful killing an application must be brought before the expiry of three months beginning with his conviction, there is no time limit for the bringing of civil proceedings for declarator of unlawful killing.[30] The Succession (Scotland) Bill proposes that the period be extended to six months and that a period where the conviction was being appealed should not be counted.

4–18   At common law the result of forfeiture may be unclear. There is English authority that if the share of an unworthy legatee falls into intestacy it will be distributed according to the law of intestacy[31] and will not fall to the Crown. However where a will contains provisions for persons inheriting following the predecease of the killer, those provisions will be ineffective[32] given that the killer did not actually predecease the deceased. The Succession (Scotland) Bill contains a proposal[33] that an unlawful killer who incurs forfeiture is to be treated as having predeceased the deceased for the purposes of succession to the estate and any destination of trust property.[34] This could make legacies conditional on the killer predeceasing the deceased, effective.

4–19   It can occur[35] that an unlawful killer is appointed and confirmed as executor and distributes the estate to *inter alia* himself before he is either convicted of the unlawful killing or a declarator of unlawful killing or the equivalent civil remedy is granted. Indeed the estate may have been gifted or sold on to a third party long before the unlawful killing is affirmed by a conviction or decree. A question may arise as to the remedies of the persons who, following the conviction or decree, discover that they may have acquired vested rights to succeed to the estate on the basis of the unlawful killing.

4–20   If the estate has not yet been distributed there is the possibility of an action of delivery or count reckoning and payment, or interdict against the executor.[36] If the estate is heritable and has been sold by the apparent heir or legatee to a third party who has purchased in good faith as to the killer's apparent innocence it will be irrecoverable from the third party.[37] If the estate is moveable there may be greater scope for recovery at least until s.17 of the 1964 Act has been extended to moveable property.[38] Equally if the estate has been transferred by the apparent heir or legatee without receiving value in exchange (e.g. by means of a gift) it may still

---

[29] *Paterson, Petitioner*, 1986 S.L.T. 121.
[30] Where the standard of proof may be lower: see *Rehman v Ahmad*, 1993 S.L.T. 741 at 745.
[31] *Re Callaway, deceased* [1956] 2 All E.R. 451.
[32] *Hunter's Executors, Petitioners*, 1992 S.L.T. 1141.
[33] At para.3.37 of the *2014 Scottish Government Consultation* following recommendation 63 of the *2009 Report on Succession*.
[34] See also, for Ireland, the Succession Act 1965 (No.27) s.120(5) and, for Germany, Bürgerliches Gesetzbuch (BGB) § 2344.
[35] For a modern example see *Tannock v Tannock*, 2013 S.L.T. (Sh. Ct) 57.
[36] Interim interdict may be possible upon the homicide charge being made by the police.
[37] See commentary on s.17 of the 1964 Act.
[38] The *2014 Scottish Government Consultation* proposes such an extension (para.3.42) and is implemented in the Succession (Scotland) Bill.

be recoverable from the possessor on the basis of unjustified enrichment. There may be a remedy against the executor for wrongful distribution but it may be subject to the defence of honest and reasonable conduct available to an executor under s.32 of the Trusts (Scotland) Act 1921.[39] The *2014 Scottish Government Consultation* contains a proposal to provide a fuller defence to executors-dative, although the relationship with s.32 is left unclear.[40]

Other unworthiness

As between husband and wife another disqualification could at one time arise **4–21** under the Conjugal Rights (Scotland) Amendment Act 1861.[41] Property acquired by a wife after she has obtained a decree of judicial separation passed on her intestacy as if her husband had then been dead.[42] In effect this created a statutory unworthiness of husbands (though not of wives). The disqualification ceased if the spouses resumed cohabitation.

A similar result is achieved where a share of heritable property is owned *pro* **4–22** *indiviso* by one spouse subject to a survivorship destination in favour of the other spouse. Section 19 of the 2006 Act[43] provides that if there is subsequently a divorce or annulment of the marriage before the death of the owner, the heir under the destination is deemed to have predeceased him or her and is thus disentitled under the destination. In contrast, divorce or annulment of marriage has no effect on wills under Scots law.

---

[39] (11 and 12 Geo. 5, c.58), extended to executors-dative by s.20 of the 1964 Act.
[40] para.3.41.
[41] (24 and 25 Vict. c.86) repealed with effect from May 4, 2006 by the 2006 Act (asp 2).
[42] (24 and 25 Vict. c.86) s.6.
[43] (asp 2) due to be re-enacted in the Succession (Scotland) Bill.

CHAPTER 5

LEGAL RIGHTS OF THE SURVIVING SPOUSE
AND OF DESCENDANTS

5–01 Traditionally, by virtue of a common law going back at least to the Regiam Majestatem[1] in mediaeval times, a person's estate has been seen as divided for the purposes of succession into (1) the part subjected to the legitim of his or her issue (sometimes known as the "bairn's part"); (2) the part subjected to the *jus relictae* or *jus relicti* of his or her spouse; and (3) the remainder, known as the "dead's part". Only with the dead's part[2] did a person have the absolute power of making a will and granting legacies of it. The rights of the issue and spouse in first two parts came to be known collectively as "legal rights". This description highlighted their absolute nature in the absence of their renunciation or discharge, as for example in a pre-nuptial or other contract or upon the election of a testamentary legacy. So strong were the legal rights that upon the death of a person the sums, if any, due under them came to be seen as debts owed by the estate to the issue or spouse postponed only to the ordinary debts of the deceased, including any taxation liabilities, and taking precedence over any claims for the making over of a legacy to a legatee or any claims of the next of kin[3] upon intestacy. Duty towards one's children and spouse were seen as taking precedence over a personal preference expressed through a legacy in a will. This was also reflected in the system under which in a divorce an "innocent spouse" was entitled to legal rights from the estate of the "guilty spouse" on the fiction that the marriage had in effect come to an end by the death of the "guilty spouse". That rule was removed by the 1964 Act.[4]

5–02 The nature of legal rights as debts of the deceased person's estate which vest upon death in the issue or spouse and which, in the absence of discharge or renunciation, an executor must satisfy has been clearly established and remains the law.[5] The use of the terminology of "claiming" legal rights has sometimes caused confusion leading to a suggestion that the rights do not vest until they have actually been paid, but this is clearly wrong. Even an estranged spouse who survives by only one minute has a vested right to *jus relictae* or *relicti*. Where there is

---

[1] Erskine, III, ix, 15.
[2] Restricted to moveable estate only until the Titles to Land Consolidation (Scotland) Act 1868 (c.101) s.20.
[3] The spouse was not one of the next of kin: see Ch.1.
[4] s.25.
[5] *McMurray v McMurray's Trustees* (1852) 4 D. 1048; *Earl of Dalhousie v Crokat* (1868) 6 M. 659 at 666.

estate available for the payment of legal rights, the executor must satisfy such payment or have or obtain a valid renunciation of legal rights. An example of the latter after death is where a legatee elects to take a legacy under a will in preference to legal rights. Regrettably, one of the authors has come across cases where executors have distributed estate to legatees without any discharge or renunciation from the legal rights holders, typically issue. Such conduct could render the executor personally liable to settle the legal rights. Legal rights are entitlements to fixed fractions of the value of the moveable estate of the deceased at the time of his death. Consistent with their nature as debts of the estate, legal rights confer no entitlement to particular assets of the estate.[6] Legal rights are subject to the long negative prescription of 20 years[7] and this is something that should be borne in mind by an executor.

Purpose of legal rights

The principal function is to ensure that at least some of the wealth of the **5–03** deceased remains within the family regardless of the claims of legatees under a will who may be wholly unrelated to the deceased. Given that wills can be forged, or obtained from an incapax testator or procured through facility and circumvention and undue influence, legal rights provide protection from such conduct also, which can be difficult to prove for anyone seeking to challenge the will.

Order of priority of legal rights in intestate succession

In their application to intestate succession, legal rights are exigible from the **5–04** moveable estate available after any prior rights under ss.8 and 9 of the 1964 Act have been satisfied.[8] This explains the origin of the term "prior rights". They require to be settled prior to the legal rights.

If the deceased is survived by a spouse the practical result of the postponement **5–05** to prior rights may be that legal rights are of no significance. If the composition and size of the deceased's estate are such that the prior rights of the surviving spouse are greater than the value of the estate, the whole estate passes to the surviving spouse and there will be no legal rights.

The legal rights available

The legal rights which are available to the deceased's surviving spouse and to **5–06** his descendants are exigible from his moveable estate only, and the moveable estate in question is that remaining after satisfaction of any prior rights. It is therefore still essential to classify property correctly and to allocate debts to heritage and to moveables.

The legal right of a surviving wife is *jus relictae* while the corresponding **5–07** right of a husband is *jus relicti*. They are identical in all but name and entitle the

---

[6] *Cameron's Trustees v Maclean*, 1917 S.C. 416.
[7] Prescription and Limitation (Scotland) Act 1973 (c.52) s.8 and Sch.1 para.2(f).
[8] s.10(2).

surviving spouse to one-third of the deceased's moveable property if the deceased is survived by qualified descendants or to one-half of the moveables if there are no such descendants. The emergence of an entitlement to legal rights upon partial intestacy many years after the death is immaterial to the fractional entitlement.[9]

5–08 The legal right of descendants (not merely immediate children of the deceased as was the case before the 1964 Act) is known as legitim. If the deceased parent has left a surviving spouse, the descendants share a legitim fund consisting of one-third of the available moveable estate of the deceased parent. If the deceased left no surviving spouse the legitim fund to be shared among the descendants consists of one-half of the moveables.

5–09 In other words, in an intestate moveable estate, there are three possible units of division of the moveable fund for succession purposes. These units are:

(1) surviving spouse's share—*jus relicti* or *jus relictae*;
(2) descendants' share—legitim (bairn's part);
(3) dead's part—this, along with any heritage not required to meet prior rights, passes on intestacy under the rules of succession to the free estate contained in Part I of the Act.

If the intestate was survived by both spouse and issue, the moveables available to meet legal rights are split into three parts, one part to each of the units of division. If the intestate was survived by a spouse, but not by issue, or conversely was survived by issue but not by a spouse, the available moveables are split into two parts, one being dead's part and the other being the surviving spouse's share or the legitim fund for division among the issue. To the legitim fund there may require to be added (collated) advances made by the deceased to the issue (or the issue's predeceasing claimant) under the doctrine of collation *inter liberos*. This is discussed below.

5–10 The legal rights formerly exigible from the heritage of a deceased person were abolished in respect of any deaths occurring on or after September 10, 1964.[10] However, the opportunity was not taken to extend legal rights to the whole estate. Despite strenuous efforts in Parliament during the consideration of the Succession Bill, the government insisted on retaining the distinction between heritage and moveables for the purposes of legal rights. Consequently the abolition of terce and courtesy means that there are no legal rights—as opposed to prior rights—in a deceased's heritable property.

Interest on legal rights

5–11 Interest is payable on the ascertained amount of the legal rights from the date of death until paid.[11] Although there is little theoretical discussion of the basis for

---

[9] *Mill's Trustees v Mill's Executors*, 1965 S.C. 384.
[10] s.10(1). These are discussed in Ch.1. See George Gretton's "Letter to the Editor", 2001 S.L.T. (News) 318 for a case in which courtesy was still applicable.
[11] *Hardie v Kay's Trustees* (1823) 2 S. 187; *Minto v Kirkpatrick* (1833) 11 S. 623.

payment of interest, it is well established that it is payable.[12] In only two of the reported cases[13] has interest been refused altogether and these may not be safe authorities on which to rely given that in neither case does the court appear to have had a full citation of the authorities finding interest due from the date of death. Usually interest is due at common law on a contractual debt only from the date of a judicial demand for payment[14] through the raising of court proceedings against the debtor, although there are exceptions to this. The distinction between the standard contractual debt and legal rights is that in the contractual situation a creditor can raise proceedings for payment immediately on the debt becoming due and unpaid and trigger the payment of interest thereon. In the case of legal rights, however, while the debt vests and becomes due on death, it is not possible for the claimant to raise an action for payment, at the very least until the expiry of six months to allow ordinary creditors to make claims on the estate and even after that time it may not be safe for the executor to pay the legal rights. Regardless of the underlying rationale, it is well established that the date from which interest runs is the date of death.[15] Despite the terms of the decision in *Young v Young*,[16] interest on legal rights in succession does not depend upon unreasonable delay in payment. In *Kearon v Thomson's Trustees*[17] interest was awarded from the date of death even although it was expressly held by Lord President Cooper that the legitim claim had been promptly complied with by the executors and no objection to their administration had been raised.

The rate of interest is at the discretion of the court,[18] taking account both of **5–12** prevailing rates and of the interest actually earned by the estate in this period. Factors such as that substantial parts of the estate may not be in a state of productive investment at the time of the deceased's death mean that the rate of interest to be awarded will be somewhat below the current going rate for commercial investments. Delay by the executor in making payment where there is no question of an election of a legacy in preference to the legal rights might justify a rate equivalent to that in any other wrongful withholding of a just debt[19] although in *Kearon* the First Division reserved its view on what would be an appropriate rate in such circumstances. If the legal rights holder were to receive a higher rate of interest, such as the judicial rate on account of the delay in payment, that would suggest that the difference between the expected rate of interest on investment and the judicial rate of interest should be borne not by the beneficiaries of the dead's part but by the executor personally. The Scottish Law Commission has recommended[20] that future legislation should remove the uncertainty of the present discretionary

---

[12] *Wills & Succession*, i, 125.
[13] *Wick v Wick* (1898) 1 F. 199; *Young v Young*, 1965 S.L.T. (Notes) 95.
[14] *Elliott v Combustion Engineering Ltd*, 1997 S.C. 126.
[15] *Gilchrist v Gilchrist's Trustees* (1889) 16 R. 1118 per Lord Fraser (Ordinary) at 1120. See also *Russel v Attorney General*, 1917 S.C. 28; *Sanderson v Lockhart-Mure*, 1946 S.C. 298; *Kearon v Thomson's Trustees*, 1949 S.C. 287.
[16] *Young v Young*, 1965 S.L.T. (Notes) 95.
[17] *Kearon v Thomson's Trustees*, 1949 S.C. 287. The rubric to the report at 1949 S.L.T. 286 is misleading in this respect.
[18] *Kearon v Thomson's Trustees*, 1949 S.C. 287. There is a comprehensive citation of earlier authority in Lord Cooper's opinion.
[19] *Ross v Ross* (1896) 23 R. 802 at 805 per Lord McLaren.
[20] *1990 Report on Succession*, the 1990 Report Bill cl.7(6) and para.3.28.

rate by specifying a fixed rate and that in the circumstances in 1990 the figure of seven per cent then (and currently) payable in respect of prior rights should be adopted. Unfortunately this sensible recommendation appears to have been over-looked in the *2009 Report on Succession* which is regrettable.

Persons entitled to legal rights

5–13   *Jus relictae* and *jus relicti* are available only to a surviving spouse or civil partner,[21] there being no representation of a predeceasing spouse or civil partner at any stage in the division of an intestate estate. Legitim was originally similarly restricted to the surviving children of the deceased and any posthumous children of the deceased.[22] The only provisions permitting representation are those in ss.5 and 6 of the 1964 Act dealing with the free estate (which expressly do not apply to spouses or civil partners) and those in s.11 dealing with legitim which is available to issue only.

5–14   The introduction of representation in legitim was a major change effected by s.11 the Act. Legitim ceased to be confined to surviving children. This remedied what was widely regarded as one of the major anomalies of the law prior to the Succession Act. In a situation such as the following:

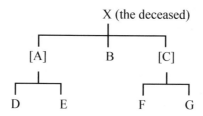

B, the surviving child of the intestate, used to take the whole legitim fund to the exclusion of D, E, F and G, the issue of predeceasing children. While s.1 of the Intestate Moveable Succession (Scotland) Act 1855 had introduced representation of the rights of next of kin in relation to the dead's part in the event of intestacy, the definition of "moveable estate" in s.9 of the 1855 Act prevented any represen-tation in relation to legal rights and preserved the common law position.

5–15   The Mackintosh Committee recommended the introduction of infinite repre-sentation in legitim and so far as this was done, it was done by s.11 of the 1964 Act. Section 11(1) makes the general provision that where a person dies prede-ceased by a "child who has left issue" who survive the deceased, and the child would, if he had survived the deceased, have been entitled to legitim out of the deceased's estate, such issue shall have the like right to legitim as the child would have had if he had survived the deceased. "Child" refers to an immediate child of the deceased, and, in respect of deaths occurring on or after November 25, 1968, includes also an illegitimate child,[23] but it was not until deaths occurring on or after December 8, 1986 that "issue" could include an illegitimate descendant.[24]

---

[21] Civil Partnership Act 2004 (c.33) s.131 (in force from December 5, 2005).
[22] *Jervey v Watt* (1762) Mor. 8170.
[23] The 1968 Act s.11. Repealed by the 1986 Act Sch.2.
[24] See paras S2–13 to S2–16.

In itself, s.11(1) would have the effect of requiring a division of the legitim fund **5–16** *per stirpes* into as many parts as there were children of the deceased, irrespective of whether any of the children had survived. However, s.11(1) is subject to s.11(2).[25] Briefly, s.11(2) provides that there is a division *per stirpes* at the level of the class nearest in degree to the deceased of which there are surviving members.

If the deceased's children predecease him, but he is survived by grandchildren, a situation such as the following may arise:

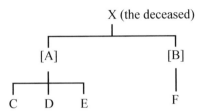

In this situation C, D, E and F are the class nearest in degree to the deceased of which there are surviving members. By virtue of s.11(1) they are entitled to legitim. As they are all of the same degree of relationship to the deceased, the effect of s.11(2)(a) is that the legitim fund is divided among them equally, i.e. a per capita division. The division is not one-half to A's family and one-half to B's family, but a division into quarters at the level of grandchildren. A's children have benefited substantially by the fact that both A and B predeceased their grandparent X.

However, take a case where the claimants are not all of the same degree of relationship to the deceased, for example:

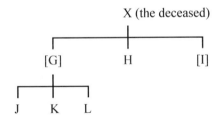

Those entitled to legitim are the child H, and the grandchildren J, K and L. The class nearest in degree to the intestate of which there are surviving members is the class of children, H being the survivor. The division of the legitim fund is therefore *per stirpes* into two parts, there being two children either surviving or represented by surviving issue. Of these parts, H takes one, giving him one-half of the legitim fund, and the other part is divided equally between J, K and L, giving them one-sixth of the fund each.[26] It seems anomalous that the accident of whether or not a member of the previous generation survives should make such a dramatic difference to the shares taken.

---

[25] See the commentary on s.6; and M.C. Meston, "Representation in Succession" (1995) 1 S.L.P.Q. 83.
[26] s.11(2)(b).

5–17   Legitim was formerly confined to surviving legitimate children related by blood to the deceased, but beginning with the Succession Act important changes have now been effected. Adopted children were given full rights of succession (including legitim) in the estates of the adopting parent or parents.[27]

5–18   Illegitimate children, by an even more far-reaching series of provisions, now have the right to legitim in the estates of both parents. The first step came in the 1968 Act[28] which added a new s.10A to the Succession Act. The result then was that in the division of the estates of its parents dying on or after November 25, 1968, an illegitimate child had exactly the same right of legitim as a legitimate child. A decree of affiliation and aliment established paternity for this purpose unless the contrary was proved.[29] There were, however, anomalies even after the 1968 reforms, as a grandchild which was illegitimate could not represent its predeceasing parent to obtain legitim from the estate of a grandparent.[30] The full assimilation of the position of the illegitimate child to that of the legitimate child finally came in the 1986 Act.[31] In the succession to persons dying after the commencement of that Act on December 8, 1986 no distinction is made between legitimate and illegitimate children (except for succession to titles and arms) and in particular, all grandchildren will be able to represent their predeceasing parents for the purposes of legitim in the estates of their grandparents. For practical purposes, illegitimacy has now been abolished. A declarator of parentage (which requires "sufficient evidence") establishes paternity.[32]

Property subject to legal rights

5–19   Legal rights are exigible from such of the moveable estate owned by the deceased at the time of his death as is available after deduction of the appropriate proportion of any surviving spouse's prior rights. With the abolition of terce and courtesy, there are now no legal rights in heritage. For property outwith Scotland at death see Ch.7.[33]

Property owned by the deceased

5–20   One perennial problem is whether particular assets were *in bonis* of the deceased at the time of his death, as only such assets are available for legal rights. In *Beveridge v Beveridge's Executrix*[34] a question arose over a Treasury gratuity paid to the legal representatives of a deceased civil servant. This was held to be part of the moveable estate subject to legal rights, despite the argument that the deceased had no enforceable right to the sum and thus it could not have been *in bonis* of the

---

[27] s.23(1). Titles of honour etc. are however excluded; s.37(1)(a). See, in general, the commentary on s.2 in relation to "Descendants".

[28] s.2.

[29] The 1968 Act s.11. Repealed by the 1986 Act Sch.2.

[30] The "issue" who could represent their parents were defined by s.36(1) of the Succession Act as lawful issue, however remote, with the result that an illegitimate child could not claim the legitim to which its parent would have been entitled by survivance.

[31] s.1. Section 10A was repealed by Sch.2.

[32] The 1986 Act s.5(3).

[33] para.7–27.

[34] *Beveridge v Beveridge's Executrix*, 1938 S.C. 160.

deceased at his death. In *Drysdale's Trustees v Drysdale*[35] a question arose over funds held by inter vivos trustees in a partly revocable inter vivos trust. On the wording of the trust it was held that the deceased had retained a radical right in the funds which were therefore *in bonis* of the deceased at his death.

Property subject to legal rights can emerge many years after the death of the **5–21** testator. An example of this is where a legacy of liferent and fee and the fiar or fiars predecease the liferenter.[36]

Heritable property and deemed heritable property

The distinction between heritage and moveables for the purpose of legal rights **5–22** remains almost completely unaffected by the 1964 Act.[37] Land, buildings, things annexed to,[38] and growing in, or on, land, are heritable.

The right of a purchaser under a concluded contract for purchase of land, or a right **5–23** of pre-emption or contracts giving an option to purchase are heritable.[39] A right of a beneficiary under a trust to a fund comprising solely heritable estate or to a share of such a fund is heritable.[40] A rather peculiar case is the position of tenancies at will. Although the special position of the Kindly Tenants of Lochmaben is abolished by s.64 of the Abolition of Feudal Tenure etc. (Scotland) Act 2000[41] there would appear to be no similar abolition of the tenure (if it is a tenure) of tenants at will. It would seem that this form of tenure must also be heritable for the purposes of legal rights.

There are also certain points worth notice in connection with debts secured over **5–24** heritable property. A heritable security is moveable in the general succession of the creditor "except that in relation to the legal rights of the spouse or of the descendants, of the deceased, it shall be heritable estate".[42] As there are now no legal rights in heritage, this means that investment in heritable securities is not subject to legal rights at all. It is strange that the anomaly was not removed when the new standard security was created by the Conveyancing and Feudal Reform (Scotland) Act 1970,[43] and even more strange that it should have been continued by the Abolition of Feudal Tenure etc. (Scotland) Act 2000.[44]

It is surely nonsensical to preserve classification of a given type of property as **5–25** heritable for some purposes and moveable for others, the more especially as the distinction between heritage and moveables is abolished for the purpose of succes-

---

[35] *Drysdale's Trustees v Drysdale*, 1940 S.C. 85.
[36] *Mill's Trustees v Mill's Executors*, 1965 S.C. 384.
[37] See *Gordon on Scottish Land Law*, Vol.1, paras 1–01 to 1–34.
[38] See *Scottish Discount Co Ltd v Blin*, 1985 S.C. 216 at 233.
[39] *Arbuthnot v Arbuthnot* (1773) Mor. 5225; Hume, IV, 558–559. The authors are indebted to Professor Paisley for bring the Hume reference to their attention. The debt owed to the seller is however moveable (*Arbuthnot* (1773) Mor. 5225; and *Macnicol v Macnicol*, Faculty Collection, June 16, 1814).
[40] *Learmonts v Shearer* (1866) 4 M. 540; *Watson v Wilson* (1868) 6 M. 258. But note the special position of heritable securities.
[41] (asp 5).
[42] Titles to Land Consolidation (Scotland) Act 1868 (31 and 32 Vict. c.101) s.117, as amended by the 1964 Act s.34 and Sch.2 and substituted by the Abolition of Feudal Tenure etc. (Scotland) Act 2000 Sch.12(1) para.8(15).
[43] (c.35).
[44] (asp 5).

sion to the free estate after prior rights and legal rights. The only thing that is achieved by this chameleon-like nature is confusion and uncertainty as to how the executor should deal with a heritable security in allocating funds to meet a surviving spouse's monetary prior right under s.9.[45]

5–26 Personal bonds may also be in an anomalous position. At one stage of the Succession Bill's progress it was proposed to repeal the Bonds Act 1661 c.32.[46] That Act made personal bonds moveable in the succession of the creditor, unless they excluded executors or contained an obligation to infeft. When the difficulties which would have arisen from such a repeal were pointed out, the proposal to repeal was dropped and the Act remains in force. The snag is that the part of the Act which should have been repealed, namely the reference to bonds excluding executors, also remains in force. Executors can no longer be excluded, inasmuch as they now administer both heritable and moveable estate, but nonetheless, it would seem that a personal bond which purports to exclude executors still becomes heritable in the creditor's succession, at least after the first term of payment of interest has arrived, and is thus not subject to any legal rights.

5–27 Finally Erskine mentions that rights *tractus futuri temporis* which are of such a nature which cannot be at once paid or fulfilled by the debtor but continue for a number of years with a yearly profit to the deceased creditor without relation to any capital sum or stock, are deemed to be heritable.[47] However it is difficult to see what rights could be covered by such a definition since the profit in yearly annuities or pensions which he gives as examples are at least in modern times, all dependent on a sum of capital invested[48] or in some way tied to it, should they not terminate at the creditor's death.

Moveable property and deemed moveable property

5–28 Things capable of movement and most incorporeal rights are moveable. Assets which have been held to be moveable for the purpose of legal rights include insurance policies on the deceased's own life,[49] or taken out by him on the life of another,[50] the deceased's vested right in the succession to heritable bonds[51] and certain bonds and debentures of statutory bodies deemed to be moveable in the statutes of their incorporation.[52] An interest in a partnership is moveable, and this can have dramatic effects when farms are involved. If the deceased owned a farm and was in partnership solely for the purpose of working the farm, the farm itself is clearly heritable and not subject to legal rights. He will normally have

---

[45] See paras S9–23 to S9–24 and Appendix 2, example 5.
[46] APS c.244.
[47] Erskine, II, ii, 6. This somewhat esoteric concept refers primarily to regular payments to a creditor although not related to any particular capital sum. An annuity is the standard example. See *Meston's Succession Opinions*, No.35 for an example where an "annuity" was probably not a true annuity qualifying as having a tract of future time.
[48] As in *Hill v Hill* (1872) 11 M. 247 where Lord President Inglis described this as a "somewhat forgotten area of the law".
[49] *Muirhead v Muirhead's Factor* (1867) 6 M. 95.
[50] *Chalmers's Trustees* (1882) 9 R. 743. The actuarial value was used.
[51] *Borland's Trustees v Borland*, 1917 S.C. 704.
[52] *Robertson's Trustees v Maxwell*, 1922 S.C. 267.

granted a lease of the farm to the partnership which includes himself. However if he has allowed the farm to become partnership property,[53] his interest in the partnership is wholly moveable,[54] even if it mainly represents the value of the land which he had conveyed to the firm. He has no direct interest in the individual assets of the partnership.[55] This can substantially increase the value of legal rights claims in his estate.

Conversion from heritable to moveable and vice versa

Heritable property which has been sold but where the seller has died before **5–29** the settlement[56] of the sale is converted to be moveable[57] for the purposes of legal rights. Such a conversion occurs also where a testator directs an executor or trustee to sell heritable property after his death.[58]

A *pro indiviso* share of heritable property which has been subjected by another **5–30** *pro indiviso* owner to an action of division and sale but the defending owner has subsequently died before the settlement of the sale is also converted to moveable property.[59] The position may be different where the deceased was the pursuer in the action of division and sale as the critical requirement for conversion appears to be that at the time of death the deceased was bound to convert the heritage in question to moveables but had not yet done so. A decree of adjudication for debt converts a moveable debt into heritable property.[60]

Voluntary acts by a guardian, trustee or judicial factor or general attorney of the **5–31** deceased do not affect the succession to the deceased's estate.[61] Thus unless the sale of the ward's heritage is completely unavoidable (for example for the maintenance of the ward),[62] a merely prudent sale by the guardian or other representative does not effect conversion of the heritage into moveables for the purpose of legal rights.[63]

Moveable property subject to special destination

Legal rights are exigible from bonds with a special destination but in settling **5–32** legal rights executors should secure payment first from the residue, if possible, before realising the bonds.[64]

---

[53] A recorded or registered title in the name of the partnership or partners is not necessary for a transfer to the partnership: see Partnership Act 1890 (53 and 54 Vict. c.39) ss.20 and 21; *Munro v Stein*, 1961 S.C. 362; and *Gordon v Inland Revenue Commissioners*, 1991 S.C. 149 at 160 per Lord President Hope.

[54] Partnership Act 1890 (53 and 54 Vict. c.39) s.22.

[55] G.L. Gretton, "Who owns partnership property?", 1987 Jur. Rev. 163.

[56] i.e. delivery of the disposition, typically in exchange for the price.

[57] *Heron v Espie* (1856) 18 D. 917; and *Macfarlane v Greig* (also known as *Stewart v Macfarlane*) (1895) 22 R. 405 at 408 per Lord McLaren.

[58] *Buchanan v Angus* (1862) 4 Macq. 374 (HL).

[59] *Macfarlane* (1895) 22 R. 405; and *Howden, Petitioner* (1910) 2 S.L.T. 250.

[60] Erskine, II, ii, 14.

[61] *Macfarlane* (1895) 22 R. 405 at 409 per Lord McLaren; *Turner v Turner*, 2012 S.L.T. 877.

[62] *McAdam's Executors v Souters* (1904) 7 F. 179.

[63] *Laurie's Trustees v Stewart*, 1952 S.L.T. (Notes) 20; *Kennedy v Kennedy* (1843) 6 D. 40; *Moncrieff v Miln* (1856) 18 D. 1286.

[64] *Farmer's Trustees v Farmer*, 1917 S.C. 366.

Property outwith Scotland

5–33   The reader is referred to Ch.7.[65]

Reform

5–34   It will be seen from the above that the rules for whether an asset is heritable or moveable can be somewhat random in their application for the purposes of legal rights. The sensible answer would be to apply legal rights to the whole estate, thereby completely abolishing the distinction between heritage and moveables for all purposes of succession. The Scottish Law Commission proposes just such a reform in both of its Reports on Succession[66] and it is to be hoped that legislative time will speedily be found for change. The new "legal share" proposed by the Commission will take the form of percentages of the whole estate and this is greatly to be welcomed. It would then be possible to ignore all the oddities of classification of property in the law of succession.

Date of valuation of property

5–35   The value of the moveable estate is normally that shown in the Confirmation, less the moveable debts of the deceased. However, if the value actually realised after proper administration with due despatch is different from the value in the inventory, it is that realised value which will be used for calculation of legal rights. It is important that the administration has been carried out with all due (or appropriate)[67] speed.[68]

Collation *inter liberos*

5–36   Where a claimant for legitim has received any advances of the appropriate type during the parent's lifetime, other claimants for legitim may require him to add the amount of the advance to the legitim fund calculated in the ordinary way from the estate owned by the parent at death. The total of the legitim fund plus the advances is then available for distribution among those entitled to legitim. The person who received the advance is required to impute his advance against his rateable share of the collated[69] fund of legitim including advances. This is known as the doctrine of collation *inter liberos* (between children).

5–37   If the claimant for legitim is representing a predeceasing claimant, he can be required to collate not merely the advances made by the deceased to him but also

---

[65] See paras 7–26 to 7–27.

[66] See Ch.8.

[67] *Warrack v Warrack's Trustees*, 1934 S.L.T. 302 where the executors were held to have been entitled to hold onto investments during the great depression with the court commenting "no trustee in his senses would have thrown the estate upon the market" (at 305 per Lord Pitman (Ordinary)).

[68] *Russel v Attorney General*, 1917 S.C. 28; *Alexander v Alexander's Trustees*, 1954 S.C. 436; 1954 S.L.T. 342. In *Alexander* the realised value was so much lower than the original valuation that legal rights calculated on the original figure would have been greater than the whole estate.

[69] i.e. "stuck together".

"the proportion appropriate to him" of advances made by the deceased to the predeceasing claimant.[70]

There must be more than one claimant for legitim before the collation can **5–38** come into play at all. If, as might arise when the deceased has left a will unfavourable to only one of those entitled to legitim, and only that person claims legitim, collation cannot arise. The claimant simply takes his or her rateable share of the legitim fund computed in the estate owned by the deceased at his death and advances are not taken into account at all. Collation is an equitable doctrine for the actual distribution of the legitim fund and can be invoked only by actually competing claimants for legitim.[71] Thus if one child has received substantial advances and is subsequently omitted from the parent's will, a situation could arise in which that child could also claim a share of the legitim fund, without collating, if the other children prefer their legacies under the will. This is so even if the size of the advances had been such that if there had been collation, the child with the advances would have had to pay money back to the fund for the other children. Depending on values and the other provisions of the will, the remedy might then be for the other children to reject their testamentary benefits and also claim legitim, whereupon the "advanced" child would be likely to withdraw.

Equally, claimants for legitim cannot require other persons who are entitled to **5–39** legitim, but are not claiming it, to collate advances made to them. *Coats's Trustees*[72] was an unusual case in which the sole claimant for legitim was actively seeking to collate the advances made to her in order to benefit by collation of the much larger advances made to others who were not claiming legitim. The attempt failed.

It should be noted that the necessity under this doctrine of collating any **5–40** "advances" which may have been made to one or more children of the deceased means that it is not appropriate simply to divide the whole estate remaining after *jus relictae vel relicti* equally among the children. There may be a different division of the legitim fund from that applicable to the free estate.

The purpose of the doctrine is to preserve equality in the division of the legitim **5–41** fund when more than one of the persons entitled does in fact claim legitim, and one or more of the claimants has received certain types of advances during the parent's lifetime. It can act as an anti-avoidance device to deter alienations of moveable estate by the deceased in order to avoid a legitim claim.

An example may illustrate the result more clearly. A dies intestate, leaving a widow B and three children, C, D and E.

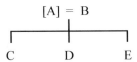

---

[70] s.11(3). See the commentary thereon.
[71] *Coats's Trustees v Coats*, 1914 S.C. 744 overruling *Nisbet's Trustees v Nisbet* (1868) 6 M. 567.
[72] *Coats's Trustees*, 1914 S.C. 744.

A's net estate amounts to £305,000 in value, consisting of the matrimonial home valued at £200,000, its furniture and plenishings valued at £15,000, and other moveable estate valued at £90,000. By virtue of her prior rights, B, the widow, receives the house and its furniture, etc., plus £50,000. Thus the estate available to meet legal rights is £40,000, all moveable. The legitim fund is therefore £13,333, there being both widow and children.

5–42   During his lifetime A had given his child C an advance of £4,000 to enable him to set up in business. This being one of the types of advance covered by the doctrine of collation *inter liberos*, C is required to collate his £4,000 as a condition of claiming legitim. Thus the total value of the fund to be divided among the children as legitim is £17,333, being the £13,333 computed in the ordinary way in the estate owned by the deceased at his death, plus the advance of £4,000. Of this total, C, D and E each are entitled to £5,777 as their share of legitim. In C's case the £4,000 advance already given to him is set against his share of the combined fund, so that he receives only £1,777 from the £13,333 available on A's death, and D and E receive £5,778 each. If A would have earned interest on the £4,000 during his lifetime, such interest would not fall to be collated.[73]

5–43   If inter vivos payments qualifying as advances are large enough the result can be that the beneficiary of the advances will receive nothing from the estate as legitim[74] and could even have to make a payment into the legitim fund if he or she has not renounced the claim for legitim.[75]

5–44   There is surprisingly little decided authority on the topic of type of advance to be collated although the doctrine is very well established.[76] The general rule is that every provision given inter vivos by the parent to the child must be collated[77] but there are exceptions to this general rule. These exceptions from collation include where the parent has indicated expressly or impliedly that the provision over and above legitim,[78] where the parent has made the provision on his or her deathbed,[79] where the provision is of heritable property,[80] where the payment is in discharge of a parent's natural duty of maintenance and education of his child,[81] and where the provision is part of an onerous contract such as a share in a partnership where the child takes on the liabilities of a partner for the debts of the firm.[82] Thus collation does not include payments by way of remuneration for services which arise out of an onerous contract with the parent and this includes loans

---

[73] *Gilmour's Trustees v Gilmour*, 1922 S.C. 753 at 771–772 disapproving the decision of *Johnston v Cochran* (1829) 7 S. 226 to the contrary.

[74] e.g. as in *Welsh v Welsh* (1878) 5 R. 542. A person who has renounced or exhausted his claim for legitim is known as "forisfamiliated".

[75] See paras 5–58 and 5–59; and *Meston's Succession Opinions*, No.55, p.174.

[76] See the bemused and somewhat despairing remarks by Lord Cooper in *Elliot's Executrix v Elliot*, 1953 S.C. 43.

[77] Erskine, III, ix, 24.

[78] Erskine, III, ix, 25.

[79] Erskine, III, ix, 25.

[80] Erskine, III, ix, 25; *Minto v Kirkpatrick* (1833) 11 S. 632 at 643 per Lord Glenlee. However, advances to allow purchase of a house for example would be collatable.

[81] *Elliot's Executrix v Elliot*, 1953 S.C. 43.

[82] *Minto v Kirkpatrick* (1833) 11 S. 632.

made by the parent.[83] However, payments to the child to permit the child to purchase a house or rent business premises[84] clearly would be included as would payments made to children to allow them to set up a trade,[85] or on the occasion of their marriage.[86]

If a person elects to take a testamentary provision in preference to the legitim, **5–45** he cannot also claim legitim unless there was a partial intestacy, and, if he is not a claimant for legitim, no one can require him to collate any advance made to him.[87]

The onus of proof that a particular transfer was a collatable advance by a parent **5–46** will depend on circumstances.[88] The court can look behind written documents to assess whether an advance was made with assets of the parent or not.[89]

Evasion of legal rights

Before the Succession Act came into force in September 1964 the right to **5–47** legitim could be defeated without the concurrence of the child otherwise entitled thereto if his parents entered into an ante-nuptial marriage contract in which his right was prospectively discharged. This method of defeating a right to legitim was abolished by s.12 of the 1964 Act and it is now true to say of all legal rights, as it was formerly true of the rights other than legitim, that they cannot be defeated without the consent, express or implied, of the person entitled to them.

However, although legal rights cannot be defeated by unilateral action by **5–48** the person whose estate is in question, the practical effects of the legal rights can be evaded. Subject to the doctrine of collation *inter liberos*, the ancestor or spouse is perfectly free to deal with his estate as he sees fit during his lifetime. A person may completely defeat all claims on his estate by transferring the whole of it inter vivos to some third party, either as an outright gift or in return for a liferent. Provided the transfer is genuine and irrevocable, this will leave no estate owned by the deceased at his death on which legal rights can operate.[90] All these transactions may be done with the open and expressed intention of evading legal rights, yet no allegations of fraudulent frustration of legal rights will be entertained.[91]

Alternatively, to take advantage of the fact that there are no legal rights in **5–49** heritage, the moveable part of his estate can be sharply reduced by investing in heritage (including heritable securities). It is true that it is not very convenient to have only heritable assets, as liquidity is then poor. But to the extent that it is suitable in his case, a testator can effectively disinherit his wife and descendants

---

[83] *Webster v Rettie* (1859) 21 D. 915.

[84] *Welsh v Welsh's Trustees* (1878) 5 R. 542.

[85] *Douglas v Douglas* (1876) 4 R. 105.

[86] For an example see *Johnston v Cochran* (1829) 7 S. 226. See also Bell, *Principles*, s.1588.

[87] *Monteith v Monteith's Trustees* (1882) 9 R. 982.

[88] Compare a comment by L. Gifford in *Welsh* (1878) 5 R. 542 at 546 to 547 with *Macphail v Macphail's Trustees* (1906) 13 S.L.T. 879 where the trustees were in fact ordained to lead in the proof.

[89] *Welsh* (1878) 5 R. 542.

[90] For an analysis see *Meston's Succession Opinions*, No.49, p.150 and cases there cited.

[91] *Agnew v Agnew* (1775) Mor. 8210; *Lashley v Hog* (1804) 4 Pat. 581.

by leaving a will (thereby excluding the surviving spouse's prior rights) and by ensuring that the bulk of his estate consists of heritage.

Satisfaction of legal rights

5–50   Unless the amount of a claim for legal rights would be a lesser sum as compared with the amount due under the will, executors will be in safety to act upon a claim by a 16 or 17-year-old. An increased benefit could not be held to be "substantially prejudicial" within the meaning of s.3 of the 1991 Act[92] and entitling the payment of legal rights to be set aside.

5–51   Apart from complete or partial satisfaction of legitim by means of advances which may require to be collated *inter liberos*, legal rights may also be satisfied by testamentary provisions accepted in lieu of the legal rights. Legitim may also be satisfied by provisions in an ante-nuptial marriage contract accepted in place of legitim.[93] The legatee has the choice between the legal right and the testamentary (or ante-nuptial) provision, but if the latter is accepted, the legal right is held to be satisfied thereby.

5–52   In the case of testamentary dispositions to which s.13 of the Succession Act[94] applies, i.e. wills actually executed after the commencement of the Act,[95] this will be wholly a question of approbate and reprobate. No person can both accept and reject the same instrument, and thus no person can accept the legacy in his favour in a will and also claim legal rights in such a manner as to be inconsistent with the testator's intentions for the disposal of his estate. A claim of a legacy does not necessarily bar a spouse or descendant from claiming legal rights in any part of the estate which has fallen into intestacy as can occur when the residue clause of the will is for whatever reason ineffective.[96]

5–53   The general rule is that a legal rights holder will not be deemed to have elected to claim a legacy unless she has been given a copy of the will, informed of the amount of the estate and been advised to obtain independent legal advice.[97] It is of concern that notwithstanding the views expressed in earlier editions of this book and the case law mentioned in the footnotes below (e.g. the *Donaldson* case) some legal practitioners have taken the view that there is no duty on an executor to inform potential legal rights claimants of their entitlement.[98] The implication of such a position would be that the executor would be entitled to leave the lay legal rights claimants in ignorance of their rights, distribute the estate on the basis of a will and hope that no claim was made against him by the claimants during the prescriptive period. It is submitted that such an unjust outcome cannot be the law. Independent legal advice is at the very least desirable where the legal rights holder

---

[92] Age of Legal Capacity (Scotland) Act 1991 (c.50).
[93] See para.S12–02.
[94] Or s.131(4) of the Civil Partnership Act 2004 (c.33).
[95] s.36(3).
[96] *Naismith v Boyes* (1899) 1 F. (HL) 79; *Petrie's Trustees v Manders's Trustee*, 1954 S.C. 430.
[97] *Walker v Orr's Trustees (No.2)*, 1958 S.L.T. 220.
[98] See J. Kerrigan, "Solicitors, Executors and Legal Rights" (2014) 49 S.P.C.L.R. 1.

could be financially prejudiced through the acceptance of the legacy.[99] Acceptance of a legacy can be implied from actings although it has been observed that the evidence must clearly lead to

"a safe implication that the choice was made with fair and free deliberation, and without there being any ignorance of important matters which ought to be known before a decisive course is taken, and also nothing having been done by others tending to mislead".[100]

A ward who is an incapable adult may not make an election without the consent **5–54** of her guardian if such an election is within the guardian's scope of authority.[101] The right of election can pass to executors but the limited right of revocation of an election made by a wife before her husband's death can not.[102] An election may be revoked if it is shown that the beneficiary acted under a false impression as to the relative value of her legal rights and her testamentary provisions, and nothing has followed upon her election which might not easily be undone, so as to restore all parties to the same situation as if the legal rights had been claimed and the legacy rejected.[103] The beneficiary will have to show that she was not in possession of full information about the estate or not given an adequate time for deliberation.[104]

Under the pre-1964 Act law, a claim for legal rights did not automatically **5–55** involve complete forfeiture of testamentary provisions. Unless there was a provision in the testamentary instrument that the provisions thereby made were in full satisfaction of legal rights, or that a claim for legal rights would involve forfeiture of the provisions, the abstruse doctrine of equitable compensation had the effect that the testamentary provision was not irrevocably forfeited by making a claim for legal rights. Instead it was applied in the first instance to restore what was taken from the estate by way of legal rights, and thereafter it remained available to the spouse or child concerned. The cases usually involved a testamentary liferent, in place of which the beneficiary preferred to have an immediate capital sum by way of a claim for legal rights. The action of claiming legal rights does not necessarily accelerate payment of the fee to the fiar unless the will so provides,[105] and hence the balance of the liferented estate continued to produce income. Once this income had accumulated sufficiently to restore to the estate what it had lost in consequence of the claim for legal rights, the fact that complete compensation had been made to the ultimate fiars usually meant that the liferent again became

---

[99] *Stewart v Bruce's Trustees* (1898) 25 R. 965; cf. *Harvie's Executors v Harvie's Trustees*, 1981 S.L.T. (Notes) 136.
[100] *Bell's Trustee v Bell's Trustee*, 1907 S.C. 872 at 877 per Lord Justice-Clerk Macdonald.
[101] Adults with Incapacity (Scotland) Act 2000 (asp 4) s.67(1).
[102] *Edward v Cheyne* (1888) 15 R. (HL) 33 at 34 per Lord Watson.
[103] *Dawson's Trustees v Dawson* (1896) 23 R. 1006.
[104] *Donaldson v Tainsh's Trustees* (1886) 13 R. 967 at 971–972 per Lord Justice-Clerk Moncrieff. *Donaldson* was an action of count reckoning and payment where reduction of the document of election was not sought and beneficiary overcame the document.
[105] *Muirhead v Muirhead* (1890) 17 R. (HL) 45; *Stair Memorial Encyclopaedia: The Laws of Scotland*, Vol.25, paras 953 to 957 but see also the Succession (Scotland) Bill.

available to the beneficiary.[106] However, a clause in the will declaring that its provisions were in full satisfaction of the legatee's legal rights prevented the beneficiary from relying on equitable compensation. Thus even when full compensation had been made over a period of years, the beneficiary could not then resume his liferent. A full satisfaction clause almost invariably appeared in well-drawn wills.

5–56   Section 13 of the Succession Act altered this situation. Even if no full satisfaction clause appears in a testamentary disposition executed after the commencement of the Act, it will take effect as if it contained one, unless there is an express provision to the contrary therein. The result is therefore virtually to abolish the doctrine of equitable compensation in respect of all wills executed after the commencement of the Act. However *Munro's Trustees, Petitioners*[107] holds that there may still be equitable compensation for other non-legal rights-holding beneficiaries adversely affected by the claim for legal rights. In both the 1990 and 2009 Reports on Succession, the Scottish Law Commission recommend a provision to improve on s.13 to eliminate equitable compensation entirely.[108]

5–57   Testators will sometimes prefer a more stringent type of clause under which the consequence of a claim for legal rights is an express forfeiture of all the beneficiary's rights under the will and sometimes also a forfeiture of the benefits destined to the legatee's issue.[109] Such a forfeiture clause is effective according to its terms, but will be narrowly construed. It is however clearly effective to prevent equitable compensation from being made.

Discharge of legal rights

5–58   Legal rights may be expressly discharged by the spouse, civil partner or descendant entitled thereto. Children are capable of granting a discharge from the age of 16 onwards, but as a discharge without full consideration is almost certain to be a prejudicial transaction capable of being set aside by court before the child's 21st birthday, executors would be wise to treat a discharge granted by a 16 or 17-year-old with great caution.[110] Discharge can be done by means of any contract[111] or unilateral undertaking. There is, however, a difference between the effect of a discharge granted during the lifetime of the deceased and of one granted after his death.

5–59   If a discharge is given during the lifetime of the ancestor or spouse from whose estate the rights would have been exigible, the grantor of the discharge is treated as already dead (although not so as to permit the issue of the grantor to claim

---

[106] *Macfarlane's Trustees v Oliver* (1882) 9 R. 1138; *Munro's Trustees, Petitioners*, 1971 S.C. 280.

[107] *Munro's Trustees, Petitioners*, 1971 S.C. 280; 1971 S.L.T. 313.

[108] See Ch.8 paras 8–23 and 8–32.

[109] See *Tindall's Trustees v Tindall*, 1933 S.C. 419, where the forfeiture was sufficient to cut out the claimant's issue. See also *MacNaughton v MacNaughton's Trustees*, 1954 S.C. 312 and *Walker v Orr's Trustees*, 1958 S.L.T. 63.

[110] Age of Legal Capacity (Scotland) Act 1991 ss.1 and 3.

[111] As from the passing of the 1964 Act it is no longer possible for parents to discharge the legal rights of any child of the marriage in an ante-nuptial marriage contract: see 1964 Act s.12 and paras S12–01 and S12–02.

his share by representation). This therefore increases the share of legitim taken by others.[112]

A discharge of legal rights granted after the death of the ancestor or spouse does **5–60** not increase the share taken by other claimants for legal rights but benefits the person entitled to the free estate or the residuary legatee as the case may be.

As an illustration, take the case of a man dying, leaving five children and a **5–61** legitim fund of £5,000. If none of the children has discharged their right to legitim during their father's lifetime, the amount to which any one child is entitled on the father's death is £1,000. This remains the case even if the others accept testamentary provisions in lieu of legitim, or indeed if they should now discharge their claims gratuitously. However, if all the others had discharged their claims before their father's death, the one who had not discharged the right would take the whole legitim fund of £5,000. In *Panmure v Crokat*[113] the discharges were performed by ante-nuptial marriage contract, and the one child not included in the discharge—possibly in error—was held entitled to the whole legitim fund.

Discharges are commonly (and prudently) obtained by executors from persons **5–62** entitled to claim legal rights whether or not the rights are actually claimed. The wording of such a discharge should be drafted carefully or the grantor of the discharge may lose the possibility of claiming legal rights in estate subsequently falling into partial intestacy. The drafter of a discharge is referred to *Melville's Trustees v Melville's Trustees* where the terms of the discharge resulted in such loss and the court advised on the terms of an appropriate discharge.[114]

Prescription and legal rights

Legal rights are exigible from the moveable estate of the deceased. They arise **5–63** upon a spouse, civil partner or child surviving the deceased. They do not arise contemporaneously with any obligation and are not correlative to any obligation. It follows that they are rights relating to property which are extinguished by the negative prescription if no "relevant claim" has been made within a continuous period of 20 years.[115] Time runs from the date the obligation becomes enforceable, which will usually[116] be the date of death.[117] It continues to run during any period during which the legal rights holder was under legal disability.[118]

---

[112] *Hog v Hog* (1791) Mor. 8193; Bell, *Principles*, ss.1581, 1583 and 1590.

[113] *Panmure v Crokat* (1856) 18 D. 703.

[114] *Melville's Trustees v Melville's Trustees*, 1964 S.C. 105 at 112 per Lord President Clyde.

[115] Prescription and Limitation (Scotland) Act 1973 s.8, read with Sch.I para.2(f). The current author respectfully disagrees with his predecessor and *Johnston on Prescription and Limitation* at para.7.06 where it is suggested that s.7 applies.

[116] A legal rights claim upon supervening intestacy caused by the failure of a residue clause becomes enforceable upon the failure of the clause: *Mill's Trustees v Mill's Executors*, 1965 S.C. 384.

[117] *Campbell's Trustees v Campbell's Trustees*, 1950 S.C. 48 applicable by virtue of s.14(1)(e) of the Prescription and Limitation (Scotland) Act 1973.

[118] Prescription and Limitation (Scotland) Act 1973 s.14(1)(b).

CHAPTER 6

TESTATE SUCCESSION AND WILL SUBSTITUTES

6–01 The 1964 Act made only limited alterations to the law affecting succession under a will made by the deceased, but substantial changes have been effected by subsequent legislation. The following is intended to provide a concise account of the law as it now stands and also of the older law which will remain applicable to wills executed when it was in force. The problem of tracing whether a will exists is partly mitigated by the establishment of a National Registry of Wills, which records the location, but not the content, of wills which testators have chosen to register with it.[1]

FORMAL VALIDITY OF WILLS

From August 1, 1995[2]

6–02   The rules for the formal validity of written documents, including wills, were radically changed by the Requirements of Writing (Scotland) Act 1995[3] which came into force on August 1, 1995 and which now restates the whole law of execution of deeds. The 1995 Act has been further altered by the Land Registration etc. (Scotland) Act 2012[4] which, although its relevant provisions are not in force at the time of writing, has introduced the possibility of wills on electronic documents with electronic signatures.[5] Details of the electronic will scheme are beyond the scope of this book although it will no doubt be important in the future. The remainder of this chapter will be concerned with what s.1(2) of the 1995 Act describes as a "traditional document".

6–03   All wills, testamentary trust dispositions and settlements or codicils must be in writing.[6] The writing must comply with s.2 of the 1995 Act which made a radical

---

[1] *http://www.certainty.co.uk* [Accessed April 12, 2015] and Certainty, The Chapel, Chapel Lane, Lapworth, Warwickshire B94 6EU.

[2] Details of the present law of execution of deeds of all types is to be found in Kenneth G.C. Reid, *Requirements of Writing (Scotland) Act 1995*, 2nd edn (Edinburgh: W. Green, 2015); *Halliday's Conveyancing Law and Practice in Scotland*, edited by Iain J.S. Talman, 2nd edn (Edinburgh: W. Green, 1997), paras 3–92 to 3–171 and in G.L. Gretton and Kenneth G.C. Reid, *Conveyancing*, 4th edn (Edinburgh W. Green, 2011), paras 17–01 to 17–27.

[3] (c.7) implementing most of the recommendations of the Scottish Law Commission's *Report on Requirements of Writing* (HMSO, 1988), Scot. Law Com. No.112.

[4] (asp 5).

[5] 1995 Act ss.1(2) and 9B, introduced by the Land Registration etc. (Scotland) Act 2012.

[6] 1995 Act s.1(2)(c).

change in the law by providing that bare validity is achieved merely by the granter subscribing the will without any further formality. Section 2(1) reads:

> "[n]o traditional document required by section 1(2) of this Act shall be valid in respect of the formalities of execution unless it is subscribed by the granter of it . . . but nothing apart from such subscription shall be required for the document to be valid as aforesaid".

Subscription means signature at the end of the last page (excluding any **6–04** annexations).[7] Thus it no longer matters whether the text of the will is in the testator's handwriting and the concept of the holograph will is no longer relevant. It is no longer necessary that there should be witnesses to the signature by the testator. All that is necessary for minimum validity is the signature at the end of the document. The result is that many apparently informal documents will be capable of being treated as wills.

However, although the will achieves validity merely by a signature at the end, **6–05** it does of course remain necessary for the purposes of obtaining confirmation, or in any court proceedings, to establish that the signature is that of the testator.

A presumption that the will was in fact subscribed by the testator arises if, in **6–06** addition to the subscription at the end, the document bears to have been signed by one witness (aged 16 or over) to the testator's subscription and bears to have been signed by the testator somewhere on each separate sheet of the will.[8] The witness should either see the testator subscribing the will or have the signature acknowledged to him by the testator.[9] The presumption can of course be overcome by such matters as proof of forgery, lack of capacity to act as testator or witness, that the witness did not know the testator or either did not see the subscription or have it acknowledged to him.[10] In the absence of any such proof, the witnessed will is regarded as having self-proving status without further procedure and can immediately be put into effect.

While it is inadvisable for a beneficiary to act as a witness to the will, this is not **6–07** in Scotland a ground of invalidity of the will and acting as a witness does not deprive a beneficiary of his rights.

If the will bears to have been subscribed by the testator, but does not qualify for **6–08** the presumption of subscription by him, it is necessary to take court proceedings under s.4 of the Act. If satisfied that the will was genuinely subscribed by the testator, the sheriff will normally order the will to be endorsed with a certificate to that effect, but if the will has already been registered in either the sheriff court books or the Books of Council and Session, a decree will be issued. The evidence will normally be in the form of an affidavit.

---

[7] 1995 Act s.7(1).
[8] 1995 Act ss.3(1)(a) and 3(2).
[9] 1995 Act s.3(7).
[10] 1995 Act s.3(4).

What constitutes a signature?

6–09   Section 7 of the 1995 Act sets out the statutory requirements. A will is signed if it is signed (a) with the full name by which the testator is described in the will; or (b) with a surname preceded by at least one forename or initial or abbreviation or familiar form of a forename; or

> "(c) except for the purposes of section 3(1) to (7) of this Act, with a name (not in accordance with paragraph (a) or (b) above) or description or an initial or mark if it is established that the name, description, initial or mark—
>
> (i)   was his usual method of signing, or his usual method of signing documents or alterations of the type in question; or
> (ii)   was intended by him as his signature of the document in question".

The reference to s.3(1)–(7) merely ensures that such a non-standard signature would not be sufficient to create a presumption of subscription even if there is also a signature of a witness.

6–10   Before the 1995 Act there was a widespread belief that execution of deeds by a mark was not possible in Scotland, even if it was the testator's normal signature. This ignored the fact that early charters were undoubtedly executed by a cross and also that a good many things acceptable as signatures were not legible and were difficult to differentiate from a mark. Indeed in an article on the subject it was suggested that so long as the granter of a deed was not stupid enough to include an express claim that his scrawl was a mark, it would probably be possible to say that it was actually an illegible signature.[11]

6–11   The 1995 Act does, however, now make it clear that a mark can be a valid signature. The important thing is that this is so both if a mark was the normal method of signature and also (even if it was not the normal method) if it was intended as the testator's signature. The word "or" between s.7(2)(c)(i) and (ii) is significant.

6–12   In an opinion by the one of the authors the situation was that a testator was in the last stages of his final illness and had little control of his normal writing hand. He made attempts to sign with that hand, leaving a ragged stroke and rather better attempts at a signature with the other hand. A case could perhaps have been made that these were a signature within the first two categories (even if illegible) but as it was clear that the deceased had intended the penstrokes to be his signature to the will it seemed better to rely on s.7(2)(c)(ii), as at least a mark intended by him to be his signature.

Blind, agraphic or dysgraphic testators

6–13   If a testator is blind or unable to write (i.e. agraphic or dysgraphic) and declares that fact to a "relevant person" the relevant person is entitled to sign the will for the testator in his presence after having read it over to the testator (unless the

---

[11]   M.C. Meston and D. Cusine, "Execution of Deeds by a Mark" (1993) 38 J.L.S. 270; *Meston's Succession Opinions*, No.121, p.399.

testator expressly declares that he does not wish it read over).[12] A witness is preferable, but like other documents it is not necessary for bare validity. There is nothing to stop a blind person from signing the will, but this alternative is available and is probably to be preferred.

The relevant persons who may sign a will for a testator are a solicitor with a **6–14** current practising certificate (although the existence or otherwise of a certificate may be difficult to establish many years later), an advocate, a justice of the peace or a sheriff clerk. If documents are signed outwith Scotland s.1 of the Wills Act 1963 must be complied with.[13]

Informal writings incorporated by reference

The effect of the 1995 Act is that any subscribed informal writing incorporated **6–15** by reference[14] would be valid in its own right without the need for incorporation into another will. It is probable that the 1995 Act requires all such informal writings to be subscribed in accordance with the Act. Given their greater use before the 1995 Act, more detailed consideration is given below.

Execution of wills before August 1, 1995[15]

Oral wills

It was possible to make a purely oral will without any writing, provided the **6–16** words spoken could be vouched by witnesses, but there was a severe practical limitation, in that such an oral will could convey property only up to the value of £100 Scots,[16] which is the equivalent of £8.33 sterling. It was therefore of little practical significance, although an oral legacy of a greater amount was valid up to that sum.

Holograph wills

The holograph will was recognised, and indeed common, in Scotland, although **6–17** not in England. To be effective, a holograph will had to be wholly in the testator's handwriting and subscribed by him. Such a will was valid without the need for any witnesses, although it might be necessary to obtain affidavits to establish that the writing was in fact that of the deceased. If the body of the text was not in the testator's handwriting, it was sufficient if he wrote, in his own handwriting, the words "adopted as holograph" above his signature at the end of the deed.[17] It was

---

[12] 1995 Act s.9(1) and (2).
[13] See paras 7–38 to 7–42.
[14] See paras 6–20 to 6–22.
[15] A detailed account of the law on execution of deeds before the 1995 Act is to be found in *Halliday's Conveyancing Law and Practice in Scotland* (1997), paras 3–01 to 3–91. Where it cannot be ascertained whether a document was executed before or after August 1, 1995, it is presumed that it was executed after that date (s.14(6) of the 1995 Act).
[16] Erskine, III, ix, 7.
[17] In very special circumstances the court might recognise a typed adoption as holograph. *McBeath's Trustees v McBeath*, 1935 S.L.T. 315; cf. *Chisholm v Chisholm*, 1949 S.L.T. 394. Adoption as holograph was rendered wholly superfluous by the 1995 Act.

sufficient for a holograph will to be signed on the last page only, although attested wills had to be signed on each page, and there was (and is) no restriction on the type of surface on which it may be written. A will in the north-east was accepted as valid when it was written on the back of a painting.

Attested wills

6–18   Formal, professionally prepared, wills were invariably attested documents. They were signed on each page by the testator[18] and the testator's signature had to be witnessed on the last page on which there were operative provisions (i.e. not merely the testing clause) by two witnesses. The witnesses had to know the testator, but this requirement was not a great restriction, as a mere introduction could suffice. Though highly desirable it was not actually essential that the witnesses should sign immediately after the testator signed or acknowledged his signature to them.[19] As this implies, it was (and is) not necessary that the witnesses should both be present to see the testator sign, as it is acceptable if the testator acknowledges his signature to them. The acknowledgment may be to both witnesses together, or it may be done separately to each witness. Persons of 16 years of age or older could act as witnesses.[20] In the case of attestations occurring before September 25, 1991, the minimum age was 12 for females and 14 for males.

Notarial execution

6–19   A system of notarial execution was available for a testator who was blind or unable to write.[21] The procedure involved reading over the will to the testator in the presence of witnesses, obtaining the testator's agreement and then a signature on his behalf by one of the list of persons qualified to act. These were law agents (solicitors) whether or not the solicitor had taken out the annual practising certificate, notaries public, justices of the peace or a parish minister of the Church of Scotland acting within his own parish.

Informal writing incorporated by reference

6–20   It was, and remains, common practice to include in formal wills a clause on the following lines:

> "I direct my executors [sic] to give effect to any future writings subscribed by me however informal the same may be provided that in the opinion of my executors they clearly express my intentions."

The purpose of such a clause, commonly referred to as an "informal writings clause" was to allow signed wills to take effect which were neither holograph nor

---

[18] The Conveyancing and Feudal Reform (Scotland) Act 1970 (c.35) s.44 which removed this requirement from other deeds, did not apply to wills.
[19] *Walker v Whitwell*, 1916 S.C. (HL) 75.
[20] Age of Legal Capacity (Scotland) Act 1991 (c.50) ss.1(1)(a) and 9.
[21] Conveyancing (Scotland) Act 1924 (c.27) s.18 and Sch.1.

adopted as holograph.[22] "Writings" in the context of such a clause means writings with testamentary intent.[23] There is nothing in law to prevent the clause from having a wide effect in validating past or future writings.[24] Sometimes the writings to be incorporated are described as "writings under my hand" and this is interpreted as meaning "subscribed".[25] It is the opinion of the executors that is determinative rather than that of the court, subject to the opinion not being wholly unreasonable.[26] The writing must contain legacies.[27]

Giving effect to an informal writing has the effect of incorporating the informal **6–21** document into the incorporating will, with the effect that the two require to be read together.

It is not entirely clear what the situation is if the instruction to incorporate a **6–22** future document does not require the informal document to be subscribed.

REVOCATION OF WILLS

It is one of the fundamental characteristics of a will that the testator is free to **6–23** revoke it and either substitute another will or let the law of intestacy govern the distribution of his estate. The testator may exercise this power of revocation at any moment up to his death. The fairly minimal level of mental capacity which is necessary to permit him to execute a will, equally permits him to revoke any existing will, and there are no considerations of public policy which prevent him from changing his mind and altering his will as often as he wishes.

Although delivery of an inter vivos conveyance or trust deed may put it beyond **6–24** the granter's control and make it irrevocable, delivery of a testamentary document to a beneficiary does not make the will irrevocable.[28] In the case of a will it is normally the death of the testator which is equivalent to delivery of an inter vivos deed as preventing subsequent revocation, and until that moment he has normally complete freedom to revoke.

The freedom to amend or alter is of the essence of a will. Accordingly, a clause **6–25** in a will declaring that the will is to be irrevocable does not bind the testator.[29] Thus, it is often said that a will is ambulatory and speaks from the date of death of the testator. Indeed, it is sometimes erroneously said that a will is deemed to have been made at the moment of the testator's death. This formulation has, however, sometimes caused Parliament to define the date of execution of a will when it is important to distinguish that date from the date of the testator's death.[30]

---

[22] *Wilsone's Trustees v Stirling* (1861) 24 D. 163 at 173–174.

[23] *Lowson v Ford* (1866) 4 M. 631; and *Connell's Trustees v Connell's Trustees* (1886) 13 R. 1175 at 1183.

[24] See e.g. *Macrorie's Executors v McLaren*, 1982 S.L.T. 295 (reversed on a different point 1984 S.L.T. 271).

[25] *Waterson's Trustees v St Giles Boys' Club*, 1943 S.L.T. 295.

[26] *Board of Management for Dundee General Hospitals v Bell's Trustees*, 1952 S.C. (HL) 78.

[27] *Gray's Trustees v Murray*, 1970 S.L.T. (Notes) 3.

[28] *Clark's Executor v Clark*, 1943 S.C. 216; 1943 S.L.T. 266. However, if the deed in question is construed as not being testamentary, delivery would bar revocation: see *Duguid v Caddall's Trustees* (1831) 9 S. 844.

[29] *Dougall's Trustees v Dougall* (1789) Mor. 15949.

[30] 1964 Act s.36(3). WJD, "The date from which a will speaks", 1948 S.L.T. (News) 9.

Contract to make will or not to revoke

6–26   There may be situations in which a testator loses the power to revoke the will. The main situation is where there has been a contract inter vivos. Here the testator has made a valid contract not to revoke his will and thereby has deprived himself of the power to revoke the will so that a purported revocation of the will is ineffective.[31] In the *Paterson* case,[32] Mrs Paterson had entered into a formal minute of agreement with her son binding her to execute a settlement of her whole property in his favour. The minute was in consideration of various payments made to her and her husband. She duly made a will as required by the agreement. When she died it was found that she had subsequently made another will revoking the first one and making a different disposal of the estate. The disappointed son raised an action of reduction of the second will. The action was successful on the ground that the onerous contract entered into by his mother bound her both to make the will in his favour and not to revoke it subsequently. The purported revocation was therefore ineffective. The existence of a contract not to revoke must be proved in the normal way. In the absence of the appropriate proof of constitution of the contract there will be no restraint upon the testator.[33]

6–27   If there is a valid contract not to revoke an existing will, or a contract to make a will in favour of a particular person, the property belongs to the testator during his lifetime. He remains free to use it inter vivos as he wishes, even to the extent of dissipating it entirely so that there is nothing left to be conveyed by the obligatory will.

Mutual wills

6–28   Much of the litigation over alleged contracts not to revoke wills has been in connection with mutual wills. Particularly when the partners to a mutual will are husband and wife, it is frequently alleged that there is a contract between them which prevents the survivor from altering the will.[34] The onus of proof of contract rests upon the person asserting the existence of the contract,[35] and various factors may be taken into account. The uncertainties created by mutual wills are such that they have now lost much of their former popularity and they tend to be treated as separate wills which happen to be on the same piece of paper.[36] If a contract not to alter is desired, it would be better to enter into an express contract to that effect.

---

[31] Stair, III, 8, 28; Erskine, III, 9, 6; Bell, *Principles*, s.1866.

[32] *Paterson v Paterson* (1893) 20 R. 484; followed in *Wheeldon's Executor v Spence's Executrix* [2014] CSOH 69; and see also *De Lathouwer v Anderson*, 2007 S.L.T. 437.

[33] Although proof of a gratuitous promise to make a will in a particular form used to be restricted to the writ or oath of the promiser, *Smith v Oliver*, 1911 S.C. 103, that form of proof was abolished by the 1995 Act.

[34] *Corrance's Trustees v Glen* (1903) 5 F. 777.

[35] *Garioch's Trustees v Garioch's Executors*, 1917 S.C. 404; 1917 1 S.L.T. 197.

[36] *Gibson's Trustees v Gibson* (1877) 4 R. 867.

Revival of wills

In certain circumstances a will which has been revoked can be revived by **6–29** implication where the will causing the revocation, expressly or impliedly, is itself revoked. This is illustrated by the unsatisfactory outcomes in *Bruce's Judicial Factor v Lord Advocate*[37] and *Scott's Judicial Factor v Johnston*[38] to name a few. The Scottish Law Commission has recommended the removal of the rule allowing implied revival of wills. Under cl.28 of the 2009 Report Bill the confused state of the law on the revival of wills is much improved although it is suggested that a will should only be revived by another testamentary writing. A will which has been revoked expressly or impliedly by a later will will no longer be revived by the revocation of the later will.

Express revocation

Express revocation of a will may be carried out either by physical acts of **6–30** cancellation or destruction of the will itself or by a clause of revocation included in a subsequent deed executed with testamentary formalities. It has long been assumed that the more satisfactory of these two methods is the clause of revocation framed in terms such as to cover the deed being revoked, but decisions on the revival of wills cast some doubt on this.[39] The result is a considerable increase in the importance of physical destruction or cancellation of wills.

Revocation by destruction or cancellation

The revocation of a will by destruction or cancellation must be effected both **6–31** *animo et facto*; thus there must be both intention to revoke by destruction and some actual act of destruction. Clearly, if the destruction of the will was accidental, the necessary intention is lacking and the will is not revoked.[40] Similarly, if the testator was insane or otherwise lacked the necessary mental capacity at the time of the destruction of the will, there would not exist the necessary intention to revoke by destruction and the will would not be revoked. Thus in *Laing v Bruce*[41] one of the issues was the state of mind of the testatrix at the time her will disappeared.

The onus of proof of intention is liable to be very important because evidence **6–32** of intention will often be lacking or very thin. In general, it seems that the ordinary rule for proof of facts applies, and thus the onus of proving that acts of destruction were done with intent to revoke lies upon the party founding upon the revocation. In the *Crosbie* case,[42] for example, a testatrix had executed her will in duplicate and the duplicate retained by the testatrix was found in three pieces after her death. The court held that the will was not revoked. This decision was largely

---

[37] *Bruce's Judicial Factor v Lord Advocate*, 1969 S.L.T. 337.
[38] *Scott's Judicial Factor v Johnston*, 1971 S.L.T. (Notes) 41.
[39] *Bruce's Judicial Factor*, 1969 S.C. 296; 1969 S.L.T. 337; *Scott's Judicial Factor*, 1971 S.L.T. (Notes) 41.
[40] *Cunningham v Mouat's Trustees* (1851) 13 D. 1376. The will requires to be re-formed by means of an action of proving the tenor.
[41] *Laing v Bruce* (1838) 1 D. 59.
[42] *Crosbie v Wilson* (1865) 3 M. 870.

based on the absence of proof that the cutting of the will had been carried out by the testatrix but, even if this could have been established, there was also considerable doubt whether it could have been proved to have been done *animo revocandi*. In the *Pattison* case, Lord McLaren expressed this in the first of his four general propositions as follows:

> "on proof that the cancellation was done by the testator himself ... with the intention of revoking the will, the will is to be held revoked; otherwise it is to be treated as a subsisting will".[43]

6–33 The physical acts of destruction or mutilation which revoke a will may take many forms. The obvious actions would be to tear the will into pieces or to burn it. However, it is not necessary that the will be wholly destroyed so long as some positive acts have been performed which are intended by the testator to effect cancellation. Very little by way of physical cancellation will be necessary if the intention of the testator is clear. Thus even a pencil line through a formal deed can suffice, though it has been suggested that writing in pencil is likely to be merely deliberative when written over ink.[44] In the *Nasmyth* case[45] the cancellation consisted of cutting off a seal. Even though the document that remained was *ex facie* probative, being holograph and signed, this was held to amount to revocation. It is sometimes said that this was because the testator had himself prescribed the seal as a formality of execution, but this seems to have been subsidiary to the main point that the mutilation was intended as a symbolic gesture to show that the deed should no longer have effect. In the *Thomson* case[46] very clear evidence of intention, including some holograph writing, indicated that cutting a piece out of a copy of a will should receive effect as a revocation of the part excised. Conversely, if the intention of the testator is less clear, correspondingly stronger evidence of physical cancellation would be necessary to make up the deficiency.

6–34 Acts of destruction or mutilation must he carried out either by the testator himself or at his direction. Obviously acts by third parties have no effect, as otherwise any interested party could cancel the whole or any part of a will merely by running his pen through it. If a will was in the hands of the testator himself, but cannot be found after his death, there arises a presumption that it was destroyed by the testator with intent to revoke.[47] Circumstances may overcome the presumption, but in an action to prove the tenor of a lost will the onus is on the person founding on the will to prove circumstances of loss[48] consistent with its continued validity.[49] If the will was last in the hands of some person other than the testator, for example a solicitor, and cannot be found, there is usually no difficulty in

---

[43] *Pattison's Trustee v University of Edinburgh* (1888) 16 R. 73 at 76.
[44] *Cruickshank's Trustees v Glasgow Magistrates* (1887) 14 R. 603.
[45] *Nasmyth v Hare* (1821) 1 Sh. App. 65.
[46] *Thomson's Trusteess v Bowhill Baptist Church*, 1956 S.C. 217; 1956 S.L.T. 302.
[47] *Clyde v Clyde*, 1958 S.C. 343; *Lauder v Briggs*, 1999 S.C. 453 at 455–456.
[48] The "*casus amissionis*".
[49] *McLernan v Ash*, 2001 G.W.D. 10–374.

proving the tenor of the lost will. The decree granted in such an action will be equivalent to the original will.

Revocation of a will is equally validly effected by destruction at the testator's **6–35** directions as by destruction by the testator himself.[50] This is merely an extension of the proposition that the destruction of the will must be both *animo et facto*. If the intention to revoke exists, it does not matter that someone else acts upon the testator's instructions and tears up the will. The mandate to destroy will not readily be implied.[51] If the agent instructed to destroy the will has not done so at the death of the testator, the act of cancellation is none the less complete[52] on the ground that the testator had done all that was within his power to effect the revocation. The same follows if an intended revocation is frustrated by concealment of the will by an interested party.

Some doubt appears to remain whether the instruction to destroy can properly be **6–36** carried out after the death of the testator,[53] but if the situation in fact is that the instruction to destroy is equivalent to the destruction itself, it should make no difference whether the will is destroyed before or after the testator's death or indeed whether the will is destroyed at all. Undelivered or unauthenticated instructions to destroy a will do not effect revocation,[54] and obviously destruction which is not in fact authorised by the testator is of no effect.

Assuming power to revoke, a will may also be expressly revoked if the testator **6–37** declares the revocation in a subsequent deed executed with testamentary formalities. This subsequent deed need not itself contain alternative provisions for disposal of the estate (in which case total or partial intestacy would usually be the result), but it is essential that it be validly executed as a will. No particular form of words is necessary, provided that an intention to revoke former wills can fairly be deduced from the language used. The onus of proving the revocation of an *ex facie* valid will lies upon the person asserting it.[55]

Problems arising from express written revocations tend to resolve themselves **6–38** into questions as to the interpretation of the language used. If it is intended to revoke all previous wills made by the testator, care has to be taken to ensure that the revocation clause is wide enough to include all of them. For example, in the *Gordon* case[56] the testatrix revoked "two wills . . . both of which are recorded in the Books of Session, Edinburgh", but no such wills were to be found. The only will which was known to have existed was not registered. In the circumstances, including the fact that the onus of proof of revocation rests upon the person founding upon it, the court held that the non-registered will was not revoked. Conversely, if the revocation is only partial, care is required to ensure that the wills or parts of wills to be revoked are accurately described.

---

[50] *Bonthrone v Ireland* (1883) 10 R. 779.
[51] *Cullen's Executor v Elphinstone*, 1948 S.C. 662; 1949 S.L.T. 228.
[52] See *Ferguson v London Missionary Society*, 1919 S.C. 80 at 84 per Lord Sands (obiter).
[53] *Falconer v Stephen* (1849) 11 D. 1338.
[54] *France's Judicial Factor v France's Trustees*, 1916 1 S.L.T. 126.
[55] *Hogg's Executrix v Butcher*, 1947 S.N. 190.
[56] *Gordon's Executor v Macqueen*, 1907 S.C. 373; (1907) 14 S.L.T. 651.

Implied revocation

6–39   A will may be impliedly revoked in whole or in part without any direct expression of the testator's desire to revoke if there is a subsequent validly executed will containing inconsistent provisions. In addition the *conditio si testator sine liberis decesserit* gives an implied presumed power of revocation for the benefit of after-born children.

6–40   In Scots law, a will is not revoked by the subsequent marriage of the testator.[57] However the Scottish Law Commission has recommended that subsequent divorce, dissolution or annulment of a marriage or civil partnership should, unless the will provides otherwise, have the effect of revoking legacies, powers of appointment, and appointments as executor, trustee or guardian in favour of the testator's former spouse or civil partner.[58] This would bring wills into line with special destinations.[59] Following the *2014 Scottish Government Consultation*, the Succession (Scotland) Bill seeks to implement this recommendation by providing that for the purposes of the will the effect of the termination of marriage or civil partnership is to be a deemed predecease of the former spouse or civil partner who is named as the legatee, executor or trustee.

6–41   Where a later will contains provisions inconsistent with an earlier will, but does not expressly revoke it, there is a revocation to the extent of the inconsistency.[60] The courts endeavour to read the documents together as a single will; and while they will go to some lengths to achieve this harmonisation, if the provisions ultimately conflict it will be assumed that the later document contains the later expression of the testator's wishes, and these will prevail over the inconsistent earlier provisions. Thus, if the later will is a universal settlement clearly dealing with the whole of the deceased's estate, the earlier will is necessarily revoked *in toto*. The universality of the subsequent settlement gives it many of the characteristics of an express clause of revocation of the earlier will. In both cases, even if some of the substantive provisions of the two wills would be capable of standing together, the earlier will is wholly set aside.[61] Universality is not necessarily established merely because a will purports on its face to deal with the testator's whole estate. In *Clark's Executor v Clark* a will which left the testator's "whole estate, heritable and moveable" to a society, then left his coin collection to a museum and then expressly cancelled "all Wills previously executed by me" did not revoke a previous holograph testamentary writing which was solely concerned with a bequest of his stamp collection.[62]

6–42   If the subsequent will is not universal, the implied revocation of earlier wills which it effects is only to the extent of the necessary inconsistency between earlier

---

[57] *Westerman's Executor v Schwab* (1905) 8 F. 132.
[58] The *2009 Report on Succession*, recommendation 52.
[59] Family Law (Scotland) Act 2006 (asp 2) s.19; and Civil Partnership Act 2004 (c.33) s.124A now to be re-enacted in the Succession (Scotland) Bill.
[60] But see para.6–104 in relation to cumulative legacies.
[61] *Rutherford's Trustees v Dickie*, 1907 S.C. 1280; 15 S.L.T. 296.
[62] *Clark's Executor v Clark*, 1943 S.C. 216; 1943 S.L.T. 266. The legacy of the coin collection qualified the universality of the earlier bequest and, for a majority of the court (Lord Justice-Clerk Cooper dissenting), the cancellation of all wills previously executed referred to wills which predated the holograph writing.

and later wills.[63] If there can reasonably be found a meaning which permits the apparently conflicting provisions to stand together, then that meaning will be adopted and both the provisions upheld.[64] This has been known to cause some consternation when there have been several home-made wills which do not contain revocation clauses, as it may be that all the bequests have to be paid to the detriment of the residuary beneficiary. The proposed meaning must be a possible interpretation of the testator's wishes and if no reasonable interpretation can reconcile the two provisions, that is if they are necessarily inconsistent, then the later provision must revoke the earlier pro tanto.[65]

If one will is to be impliedly revoked in whole or in part by another, it is because **6–43** the second will is regarded as a later expression of the testator's wishes. It must be established that the second will is in fact a later expression of the testator's intention. If a will is undated, an application can be made to the court for a certificate or decree establishing a presumption as to the date of execution.[66] In the absence of clear evidence of different intent, separate deeds executed or deemed to have been executed on the same day would usually be regarded as parts of the same deed.[67]

The *conditio si testator sine liberis decesserit* is a method of revocation of wills **6–44** by operation of law. The Latin nomenclature is traditional and is very firmly established, but it is rather misleading. Read literally, it suggests that it is a condition of the will that the testator dies without children. In fact it is more complex both as a condition and in relation to the effect of non-compliance with it.

The condition is that if children are born after the date of execution of the will it is **6–45** presumed that the testator did not desire his will to take effect. That presumption can be rebutted only through it being established that (a) he made provision for such post-will children in the will itself; or (b) did not make provision for them in the will by design[68]; or (c) after their birth he affirmed the continuing applicabilty of the will.

The *conditio* is a presumption for the benefit of an after-born child and does not **6–46** involve automatic revocation of the will by the subsequent birth of children. Thus it has been strongly held that only the after-born child himself may seek to found on the *conditio* for the purpose of revocation of the will.[69] If the after-born child chooses not to contest the will, other heirs in intestacy who may have been passed over cannot improve their share of the estate by having the will revoked on this ground and distribution made on the basis of intestacy.

The clearest case for applying the *conditio* and regarding the will as revoked **6–47** would be the original one of the posthumous child. However, it will almost certainly also be applied if the testator dies within a short time of the birth of the child without having had a reasonable opportunity of reviewing the provisions of his will. The mere fact that a long time elapses between the birth of a child and date of the testator's death does not overcome the presumption in favour of

---

[63] *Park's Trustees v Park* (1890) 27 S.L.R. 528.
[64] *Ford's Trustees v Ford*, 1940 S.C. 426; 1940 S.L.T. 362.
[65] *Ford's Trustees*, 1940 S.C. 426.
[66] 1995 Act s.4(2) and (5).
[67] *Wills and Succession*, i, 412.
[68] Erskine, III, viii, 46; and *Elder's Trustees v Elder* (1894) 21 R. 704 at 708.
[69] *Stevenson's Trustees v Stevenson*, 1932 S.C. 657; 1932 S.L.T. 510.

revocation. In *Milligan's Judicial Factor v Milligan*,[70] for example, although ten years had elapsed between the birth of the child and the testator's death, the court held that the will was revoked. Indeed, the opinions in this case suggest that however long a testator may have had to consider whether he wished his will to remain in effect, the court will not accept this by itself as evidence rebutting the presumed intention to revoke.

6–48   In effect the presumption that a will not providing for them is revoked by the subsequent birth of children to the testator has become a very strong one and cases in which the presumption has been overcome are rare.[71] One of the few is *Stuart-Gordon*[72] where, although the testatrix's will made no provision for her child born after it was made, there was evidence that she had been considering the will at the time of the child's birth and that she knew the child was well provided for from other sources. Thus it was held that the testatrix did wish the will to apply and the *conditio* was therefore inapplicable.

6–49   There is a clear concern that testators are unaware of the *conditio* when making their wills, leaving their wills potentially revocable at the instance or on behalf of their children. The Scottish Law Commission has recognised this and recommended that the *conditio* be abolished.[73] Following the *2014 Scottish Government Consultation* in the face of divided opinion over abolition, the Scottish Government decided that "further discussion with stakeholders" was required on the future of the *conditio*.

6–50   Conditional revocation, or dependent relative revocation, may exist in Scots law, although the authority is thin.[74] Under this doctrine a revocation of an existing will would not take effect if an intended replacement will turns out not to have been validly executed. It also appears that wills, when revoked other than by physical destruction, may be revived if the revoking will is itself revoked by some method which does not apply to the original will. This unsatisfactory result may be overturned in future legislation.[75]

ESSENTIAL VALIDITY

Capacity to execute a will

6–51   *Age.* For wills actually executed on or after September 25, 1991, the minimum age of testamentary capacity is 12.[76] Prior to that date, full testamentary capacity was attained on attaining majority at 12 for females and 14 for males.[77]

---

[70] *Milligan's Judicial Factor v Milligan*, 1910 S.C. 58; 1909 2 S.L.T. 338.
[71] *Greenan v Courtney*, 2007 S.L.T. 355 is an example of an unsuccessful attempt at rebuttal.
[72] *Stuart-Gordon v Stuart-Gordon* (1899) 1 F. 1005.
[73] The *2009 Report on Succession*, recommendation 53; and the *1990 Report on Succession*, recommendation 18.
[74] M.C. Meston, "Dependent Relative Revocation in Scots Law", 1977 S.L.T. (News) 77; *France's Judicial Factor v France's Trustees*, 1916 1 S.L.T. 126.
[75] M.C. Meston, "Revival by Revocation of the Revoking Will", 1974 S.L.T. (News) 153; and see para.6–29.
[76] Age of Legal Capacity (Scotland) Act 1991 s.2(2).
[77] *Stevenson v Allans* (1680) Mor. 8949; 1964 Act ss.28 and 38(3).

Incapacity, facility and circumvention. A purported will executed by someone **6–52** incapable of understanding the nature and consequences of the will in question is void on the ground of insanity.[78] Wills executed by someone in the state of mental weakness known as "facility"[79] having been procured by a beneficiary through acts amounting to circumvention,[80] may be set aside by the court. Such acts can amount to the involvement of a beneficiary in fixing the terms of the will or arranging of signature etc. The greater the facility the less is required to prove circumvention. Circumvention may be inferred from circumstances. Medical evidence plays an important role in proof of either incapacity or facility, although lay evidence is also relevant.[81]

Undue influence. Where the deceased was under the influence of a certain indi- **6–53** vidual or individuals and that through (i) fear created by that individual in the deceased, whether intended or not; or (ii) false prejudice created by that individual in the mind of the deceased, a will was executed which favoured the individual in question, that will may be set aside by the court.[82]

Testamentary intent

The deceased must have intended the document to receive immediate effect as **6–54** his will. Mere lists of names and sums of money may prove not to be more than jottings for what is to be included in a future will.[83] Mere instructions to a solicitor are not demonstrative of an intention of immediate effect but of a future intention.[84] An apparently complete will, sufficiently executed, may however contain qualifications which indicate that it was not intended as a will.[85] The courts may however now be more ready to accept an apparently informal writing, such as a letter to a daughter signed merely "Mum", as showing completed testamentary intention.[86] Extrinsic evidence can be looked at to see if there was testamentary intent.[87]

Restrictions on testamentary freedom

Although testators may have a sense of power when disposing of their assets in **6–55** the knowledge that they will not have personal use for the assets at the crucial

---

[78] *Sivewright v Sivewright's Trustees*, 1920 S.C. (HL) 63 at 66 per Lord Atkinson approving Cockburn CJ in the English case *Banks v Goodfellow* (1869–70) L.R. 5 Q.B. 549; *Boyle v Boyle's Executor*, 1999 S.C. 479; the effect of delusions was considered in *Muirden v Garden's Executors*, 1981 S.L.T. (Notes) 9.
[79] i.e. easily imposed upon.
[80] *Clunie v Stirling* (1854) 17 D. 15; *West's Trustee v West*, 1980 S.L.T. 6; *Anderson v Beacon Fellowship*, 1992 S.L.T. 111.
[81] For a recent case see *Smyth v Romanes' Executors* [2014] CSOH 150 where the codicil and will were upheld.
[82] *Weir v Grace* (1899) 2 F. (HL) 30; *Ross v Gosselin's Executors*, 1926 S.C. 325 at 334 per Lord President Clyde; *MacGilvary v Gilmartin*, 1986 S.L.T. 89.
[83] *Colvin v Hutchison* (1885) 12 R. 947; *Jamieson's Executors*, 1982 S.C. 1.
[84] *Stuart v Stuart*, 1942 S.C. 510; cf. *Eadie's Trustees v Lauder*, 1952 S.L.T. (Notes) 15.
[85] *Munro v Coutts* (1813) Dow's App. 437; *Young's Trustees v Henderson*, 1925 S.C. 749.
[86] *Rhodes v Peterson*, 1972 S.L.T. 98.
[87] *Young's Trustees*, 1925 S.C. 749; *Eadie's Trustees*, 1952 S.L.T. (Notes) 15; *MacLaren's Trustees v Mitchell and Brattan*, 1959 S.C. 183.

time and will not be around to face disappointed relatives, there are significant limits on what they can validly do.[88]

6–56   *Legal rights.* The principal restriction upon the freedom of a testator to do as he wishes with his estate is probably the existence of the legal rights of spouses and descendants. These have been discussed above.[89] There will be substantial changes, including the application to the whole estate of the deceased, if and when the proposed new "legal share" is substituted for legal rights in accordance with the proposals of the Scottish Law Commission.[90]

6–57   *Accumulations of income.* Other restrictions upon a testator's freedom include the detailed legislation restricting accumulations of income with the capital for excessive periods.[91] Testators sometimes have the miser's dream of imagining their funds growing after their deaths by the power of compound interest without any expenditure having to be met from it. Spectacular sums can be envisaged if income is added to capital for say 100 years and Mr Peter Thellusson is famous for his scheme which eventually led to a prohibition on others attempting to do the same thing.[92]

No accumulation is permitted beyond one of six periods and all directions for accumulation must fall into one of the six. They are:

(i)   the life of the grantor of the deed;
(ii)   21 years from the death of the grantor;
(iii)   the minority of any person living or *in utero* at the testator's death;
(iv)   the minority of any person who would for the time being, if of full age, be entitled to the income directed to be accumulated;
(v)   21 years from the date of the settlement;
(vi)   the minority of any person living or *in utero* at that date.

The commonest period is probably example (ii), so that an accumulation directed in a will normally ceases exactly 21 years from the death of the testator.[93]

6–58   *Successive liferents.* A testator is prevented from achieving effects similar to those of an entail[94] by creating a series of successive proper or trust liferents. A liferent may be created only in favour of someone alive or *in utero* at the date when the deed creating it came into operation. The draconian sanction is that if anyone born after that date is of full age and becomes entitled to a liferent under the deed, the apparent liferenter becomes the outright fiar and the rights of any fiar nominated in the deed are cancelled.[95] In the case of trust liferents of heritage the

---

[88] M.C. Meston, "The Power of the Will", 1982 Jur. Rev. 172.
[89] See Ch.5.
[90] See paras 8–19 to 8–35.
[91] Trusts (Scotland) Act 1961 (c.57) s.5 as amended by the Law Reform (Miscellaneous Provisions) (Scotland) Act 1966 (c.19) s.6.
[92] *Thellusson v Woodford* [1798] 4 Vesey Jr. 227; aff'd House of Lords 11 Vesey 112.
[93] *Campbell's Trustees v Campbell* (1891) 18 R. 992.
[94] New entails were prohibited from 1914: Entail (Scotland) Act 1914 (4 and 5 Geo. 5 c.43) s.2.
[95] 1968 Act ss.18 and 22(5) in respect of deeds executed on or after November 25, 1968 replacing the Entail Amendment (Scotland) Act 1848 (11 and 12 Vict. c.36) s.48 in respect of proper liferents of heritage and the Trusts (Scotland) Act 1921 (11 and 12 Geo.5 c.58) s.9 and the Entail Amendment (Scotland) Act 1868 (31 and 32 Vict. c.84) s.17 in respect of trust liferents of moveables. Section 47 of the 1848 Act remains in force in respect of trust liferents of heritage: see *Earl of Balfour, Petitioner* [2002] UKHL 42; 2003 S.C. (HL) 1.

apparent liferenter must apply to the Court of Session for a declaration of unfettered ownership. This does not prevent successive liferents in favour of two or more persons alive at the death of the testator.

Repugnancy. This doctrine is not particularly well known, but acts as an impor- **6–59** tant restriction upon the extent to which a testator can impose conditions on the use by the beneficiary of a testamentary gift. It arises when a testator confers an outright gift upon a beneficiary but then proceeds to say that none the less someone else is to look after the property for the beneficiary. Thus where a testator left heritage and bank shares in a trust liferent and fee and directed that at the death of the liferentrix he should like not less than £50 to be left to his sister-in-law, it was held that this desire did not qualify the fee.[96] Similarly where a testator bequeathed his whole estate to his wife and then provided that if she should remarry or die he wished his estate to be divided between his surviving siblings, it was held that the legacy of the whole estate was not qualified by the subsequently expressed wish and no trust was set up.[97]

If a beneficiary under a will is of full age and has a vested, unqualified and inde- **6–60** feasible right of fee (all the conditions being fulfilled) the beneficiary is entitled to have the provision conveyed to him, notwithstanding any direction to trustees to hold the legacy for him until he attains some age later than majority.[98] The direction is repugnant to the right of fee vested in the beneficiary and is of no effect.

Public policy. The courts have developed a somewhat undefined power to **6–61** strike down testamentary provisions, whether conditions of legacies or legacies themselves on the ground of public policy. Thus a condition requiring a wife legatee to move away from her husband was held to be void.[99] A requirement that a child legatee should live apart from his parents while in minority was void.[100] But a condition that the parents of a legatee grand-daughter be living together as man and wife was not *contra bonos mores* and upheld.[101] Given the abolition of the status of illegitimacy from May 4, 2006 (except in relation to titles, honours and dignities), it is questionable whether a condition imposed on or after that date that a legatee was legitimate would be upheld. Most of the cases relating to the legacies themselves which have caught the court's attention have involved what are regarded as excessive memorials by the testator for himself.[102] These have ranged from the statues to be placed in the McCaig tower (commonly known as McCaig's Folly) in Oban via a "massive bronze statue of artistic merit" of a testator in Musselburgh to a permanent exhibition of the testatrix's "valuable art collection" in St Andrews. There is nothing to say that further situations may not be included in future, but obviously this type of power to strike down testamentary provisions must be exercised with considerable care.

---

[96] *Garden's Executor v More*, 1913 S.C. 285.
[97] *Smart v Smart's Trustees*, 1926 S.C. 392; cf. *Cochrane's Executrix v Cochrane*, 1947 S.C. 134.
[98] *Stewart's Trustees v Stewart* (1897) 25 R. 302.
[99] *Williamson v Williamson* (1872) L.R. 12 Eq. 604.
[100] *Grant v Grant* (1898) 25 R. 929.
[101] *Barker v Watson's Trustees*, 1919 S.C. 109.
[102] *McCaig v University of Glasgow*, 1907 S.C. 231; *Aitken's Trustees v Aitken*, 1927 S.C. 374; *Sutherland's Trustee v Verschoyle*, 1968 S.L.T. 43.

6–62   *Expressly unassignable interest in a lease.* Where there is an express prohibition on assignation within the lease the tenant has no power to bequeath his interest, although the tenant's executor may transfer the interest to the "heir" chosen by him despite an express prohibition.[103] However, if the prohibition on assignation is only an implied one, s.29 gives the tenant a right to bequeath his interest to any one of the persons who, if he had died intestate, would be, or would in any circumstances have been, entitled to succeed to his estate under the Act.

CONSTRUCTION OF WILLS

The general approach

6–63   While every will should ideally be so clear that no question of interpreting or construing the terms used will arise, circumstances do change. Difficult questions can then arise over what the testator's meaning was in the words that he used applied to the circumstances at his death. In *Couper's Judicial Factor v Valentine*[104] a testator had made a testamentary provision in favour of "my wife, Mrs Dorothy Couper". He was subsequently divorced a relatively short time before his death but did not alter the will. Was the bequest conditional upon her having the status of his wife at his death—with the name being merely a supplementary description, or was this a gift to the person known as Mrs Dorothy Couper, who happened to be his wife at the time of the will?[105]

6–64   The fundamental rule in establishing the meaning of a will is to read the will, the whole will and in most cases nothing but the will. Many practical problems could be solved by reading the will carefully and then reading it again. The problems might even be avoided if those drafting wills in the first place had read their drafts in the same way. Wills such as one which required the residue to be divided into nine equal parts and then listed the eleven people each of whom were to get one of the shares could then be avoided. Similarly the wife's will which was found (after her death) to have left the residue of her estate to "my wife" might not have caused so much trouble.[106]

6–65   It has been said in the House of Lords that:

> "The primary duty of a court of construction in the interpretation of wills, is to give to each word employed, if it can with propriety receive it, the natural ordinary meaning, which it has in the vocabulary of ordinary life, and not to give to words employed in the vocabulary of ordinary life an artificial, secondary, or technical meaning."[107]

The primary material used to construe a will is to be found solely within the four corners of the will. Only if the terms of the deed appear to be doubtful in their

---

[103] See the commentary on s.16.

[104] *Couper's Judicial Factor v Valentine*, 1976 S.C. 63; cf. *Pirie's Trustees v Pirie*, 1962 S.C. 43.

[105] In the circumstances it was paid to the ex wife; see also *Speaker's Executor v Spicker*, 1969 S.L.T. (Notes) 7; *Stalker's Executors, Petitioners*, 1977 S.L.T. (Notes) 4.

[106] See *Meston's Succession Opinions*, No.77, p.244.

[107] *Young v Robertson* (1862) 4 Macq. 314 at 325.

import will the court be entitled to look to evidence of extraneous circumstances to find the testatrix's intention in using those terms.[108]

Extrinsic evidence is admitted in certain circumstances[109] for example where **6–66** terms of art require to be explained, or legatees or items bequeathed require to be identified. The court is seeking the objective meaning which the testator has expressed, not the subjective intention he may have had nor what disappointed beneficiaries would like to believe he intended. Evidence (after the testator's death) of statements during his lifetime are treated as having little evidential value. Nor are letters of instruction to solicitors[110] or similar documents such as draft wills[111] admissible.

Words will be presumed to have their ordinary meaning unless the contrary is **6–67** shown, e.g. if the testator had written in a code.[112] Technical terms will be presumed to have their technical meaning[113] unless the testator's will shows that he or she used technical words in a non-technical sense.[114] That said, so far as it is reasonably possible a court will always strive to avoid the result that the testator dies intestate with regard to a large portion of his estate.[115] This is seen in different approaches to construction.

One approach is to give as wide as possible a meaning to ordinary terms, partic- **6–68** ularly in home-made wills. Thus a legacy of "all money that I should leave" was construed to cover debts, shares and life assurance[116] and a legacy of "all the money I am possessed of" followed by a list of debts, bank accounts and shares and including in the middle of the list heritable property was construed to include the heritage.[117] Such an approach must be supported by the surrounding circumstances at the time of the will. A phrase used by the testator such as a condition that a legatee is "predeceased by me" may be seen as surplusage.[118]

In carrying out the process of construction the court is entitled to be put in the **6–69** same position as the testator himself occupied and know as far as he did of his estate, his relations with legatees and beneficiaries, and generally the circumstances in which he was making his will.[119] On this basis a court has looked at a title deed and layout of property to ascertain the extent of heritage bequeathed in

---

[108] *Blair v Blair* (1849) 12 D. 97 at 107; and see also *Marley v Rawlings* [2014] 2 W.L.R. 213; [2014] UKSC 2 at [34]–[42] (obiter).

[109] See *Wills and Succession*, i, 373–399; and see *Marley* [2014] 2 W.L.R. 213.

[110] *Blair* (1849) 12 D. 97; but see *Cathcart's Trustees v Bruce*, 1923 S.L.T. 722.

[111] *Wills and Succession*, i, 396.

[112] *Wills and Succession*, i, 376.

[113] *Greig's Trustees v Simpson*, 1918 S.C. 321; *Macdonald's Trustees v Macdonald*, 1974 S.L.T. 87; and see *Stair Memorial Encyclopaedia*, Vol. 25, paras 876–880 where there is useful discussion of the meanings of "family", "issue", "heirs", "next of kin" and "money".

[114] *Borthwick's Trustees v Borthwick*, 1955 S.C. 227 at 230; *Nelson's Trustees v Nelson's Curator Bonis*, 1979 S.L.T. 98.

[115] *Auld's Trustees v Auld*, 1933 S.C. 176 at 179 where Lord Justice-Clerk Alness described the presumption against instestacy as "strong and important". It was followed in *Forsyth v National Kidney Research Fund* [2006] CSIH 35.

[116] *Easson v Thomson's Trustees* (1879) 7 R. 251.

[117] *Ord v Ord*, 1927 S.C. 77; but distinguished in *Lawson's Executor v Lawson*, 1958 S.L.T. (Notes) 38 where the testatrix did not have heritage at the time of her death.

[118] *Elrick's Trustees v Robinson*, 1932 S.C. 448 where intestacy was avoided.

[119] *Dunsmure v Dunsmure* (1879) 7 R. 261 at 264.

a legacy,[120] taken account of a potential beneficiary being incapax at the time of the will[121] and, in a legacy in favour of a spouse, taken account of the absence of any children who would otherwise inherit on intestacy.[122]

6–70   The main situation in which extrinsic evidence will be admitted arises if there is a latent ambiguity in the will. The typical example is the description of a legatee in terms which are capable of being applied to two people without fully describing either or where the legatee has clearly been misdescribed.[123] The Keiller family of Dundee has been a significant contributor to the law in this area.[124] Provided the ambiguity is latent and not obvious on the face of the will extrinsic evidence may be used to determine the true beneficiary. The principle is sometimes put in Latin *"falsa demonstratio non nocet"* (an erroneous description does not injure). There must of course actually be an ambiguity. There was no ambiguity in a bequest of two pubs, although the beneficiary claimed that the testator had intended to include the flats above the pubs.[125] The accurate naming of a legatee creates a strong presumption against any rival who does not possess that name which cannot be overcome except in exceptional circumstances or with cogent evidence.[126]

6–71   Another approach is that where the testator must *necessarily* have intended an interest to be given but where there are no words to give effect to the intention the court can imply or correct words and thus mould the language of the testator to reflect that intention.[127] Each case must be looked at in the context of its own facts but a reference to "heritable estate" has been construed as "heritable and moveable estate"[128]; "article 2" construed as a reference to "article 3",[129] and "or" was construed as "and" in a special destination in a bond.[130]

6–72   Charitable bequests should receive "benignant" interpretations.[131] Thus it was said that where a charitable bequest was capable of two interpretations, one of which would leave it void and the other would make it effectual, the latter must be adopted.[132] Where more than one charitable society claims to be the legatee inaccurately identified by the testator, the court looks to see which had the dominant or leading object coinciding with the description of the testastor.[133]

---

[120] *Donald's Trustees v Donald* (1864) 2 M. 922.

[121] *Nelson's Trustees*, 1979 S.L.T. 98 at 101.

[122] *Simson's Trustees v Simson*, 1922 S.C. 14.

[123] *Macfarlane's Trustees v Henderson* (1878) 6 R. 288 (my brother's "son" construed as my brother's "daughter"); *Yule's Trustees*, 1981 S.L.T. 250 ("child" construed as "grandchild"); *Cathcart's Trustees v Bruce*, 1923 S.L.T. 722 (letter of instruction used to identify parent of child legatees).

[124] *Keiller v Thomson's Trustees* (1824) 3 S. 279 (OE 396) and (1826) 4 S. 730 (OE 724).

[125] *Fortunato's Judicial Factor v Fortunato*, 1981 S.L.T. 277.

[126] *Nasmyth's Trustees v National Society for Prevention of Cruelty to Children*, 1914 S.C. (HL) 76 at 81 and 83.

[127] *Law's Trustees v Gray*, 1921 S.C. 455 at 466 per Lord Mackenzie quoting *Towns v Wentworth* (1858) 11 Moore P.C. 526 at 543 per Lord Kingsdown.

[128] *Clouston's Trustees v Bulloch* (1889) 16 R. 937.

[129] *Reid's Trustees v Reid*, 1929 S.C. 615.

[130] *Bothwells v Earl of Home* (1747) Mor. 16811.

[131] *Magistrates of Dundee v Morris* (1858) 3 Macq. 134 at 155 (HL).

[132] *Bruce v Presbytery of Deer* (1867) 5 M. (HL) 20.

[133] *Sommervail v Edinburgh Bible Society* (1830) 8 S. 370.

Certainty of beneficiaries

If, despite every effort to make sense of the admissible evidence, the benefi- **6–73** ciary of a legacy remains uncertain, the legacy fails from uncertainty.[134]

Accretion

This problem of interpretation arises when a single legacy has been left to two **6–74** or more persons, but one of them has died without having acquired a vested right, normally by predeceasing the testator. Do the others share the whole legacy or does the predeceaser's share fall into residue or intestacy?

If the legacy is left jointly without any words suggesting separate shares, there **6–75** is an implied destination of the predeceaser's share in favour of the surviving legatees by virtue of the doctrine of accretion.[135] In other words the survivors share the legacy. This doctrine of accretion, which is a rule of construction, is based on a combination of the presumed intention of the deceased to avoid intestacy, and not to leave a part of the legacy to someone not named by him. But if a legacy is given to a plurality of persons individually named or sufficiently identified as individuals "equally among them" or "in equal shares" or "share and share alike" or in other language of the same import, the legacy is severed into individual legacies to those legatees, there is no accretion and the survivor is entitled only to his or her own share even if the other share falls into intestacy.[136] There is a further qualification that, if the gift is to a class of persons (the definition of "class" being obscure), the use of such words does not prevent accretion to the survivor.[137] This is because the members of the class may vary before the legacy vests and the testator cannot have known into how many shares the legacy should be divided or indeed whether by the time the class was ascertained, whether the legacy should be divided at all.

While accretion might well accord with the intention of a testator when it deals **6–76** with legacies of corporeal objects, whether heritable or moveable, which cannot readily be divided, it has to be doubted whether it accords with the intention in respect of non-corporeal items such as money, or indeed inspecific legacies of residue to more than one person. The requirement to put in words of severance such as those indicated above to avoid accretion seems excessive and leaves many home-made wills vulnerable to not reflecting the intention of their makers. However, no reform of the law of accretion has been contemplated by the Scottish Law Commission and this underlines the need for a will to be drafted by someone well conversant with the rules of construction.[138]

---

[134] *Meston's Succession Opinions*, No.28, p.78 and No.140, p.462.
[135] *Tulloch v Welsh* (1838) 1 D. 94.
[136] *Paxton's Trustees v Cowie* (1886) 13 R. 1191 as explained in *Cochrane's Trustees v Cochrane*, 1914 S.C. 403.
[137] *Roberts' Trustees v Roberts* (1903) 5 F. 541; *Fraser's Trustees v Fraser*, 1980 S.L.T. 211.
[138] See J. Kerrigan, *Drafting for Succession*, 2nd edn (Edinburgh: W. Green, 2010), paras 11–77 to 11–85.

Conditio si institutus sine liberis decesserit

6–77   This is a rule of construction of wills and applies solely to testamentary writ-ings.[139] Applying the general approach to construction a legacy to a specified person simply fails if that person fails to survive the testator and instead (a) passes to an alternative legatee specified for that eventuality (typically preceded with words such as "failing whom"); or (b) passes to the residuary legatee under a legacy of residue; or (c) falls into instestacy.

6–78   However, the common law has taken the view that where the specified legatee was a child of the testator or was a niece or nephew of the testator,[140] the testator cannot have intended to prefer any of the options (a), (b), or (c) to the descendants of the child, niece or nephew and that his failure to do so was an oversight. This policy is given effect by making the eventualities (a), (b), or (c)[141] conditional on the predeceasing child, niece or nephew not having descendants of their own surviving the testator. Put in Latin, these eventualities under the general approach to construction are presumed to be subject to the *conditio si institutus sine liberis decessiret*. The "*institutus*" is the specified legatee, or the "institute". Given the policy, the specified legatee cannot be a brother or sister of the testator.[142]

6–79   Put another way, if applicable the *conditio* creates a destination-over in favour of the descendants of the specified legatee overriding any express destination or intestacy. Indeed where the legatee survived the testator but before he could acquire a vested right after the testator's death he died, the *conditio* applied to benefit the legatee's descendant in preference to an express destination to an alter-native legatee.[143] For the *conditio* to apply, the legatee must be instituted by the testator. If he has died before the date of the will he will not have been instituted and the *conditio* will not apply.[144] Where the specified legatee was one of a number of legatees for a particular item where but for the *conditio* accretion would apply, the destination over in the *conditio* is restricted to the specified legatee's share assessed at the time of the will, sometimes called the "original share" rather than what the specified legatee would actually have succeeded to had he survived the testator.[145] The Scottish Law Commission has recommended[146] that this unex-pected consequence of the *conditio* applying should be removed in order that the descendants receive the actual share that the specified legatee would have received and this is reflected in the *2014 Scottish Government Consultation*.[147]

6–80   The *conditio* is only a presumption on the basis that the omission of the issue was an oversight, and can be rebutted.[148] The onus is on a challenger to prove that

---

[139] *Spalding v Spalding's Curator ad Litem*, 1963 S.C. 141.
[140] *Bogie's Trustees v Christie* (1882) 9 R. 453 at 456.
[141] *Dixon v Dixon* (1841) 2 Rob. 1, 25 (HL).
[142] *Hall v Hall* (1891) 18 R. 690.
[143] *MacGregor's Trustees v Gray*, 1969 S.L.T. 355.
[144] *McKinnon's Trustees v Brownlie*, 1947 S.C. 27 (a case involving an express conditional institution where the purported institute (primary specified legatee) had died before the date of the will).
[145] *Neville v Shepherd* (1895) 23 R. 351 at 357.
[146] *1990 Report on Succession*, recommendation in para.4.65; *2009 Report on Succession*, recom-mendation 54(4).
[147] Recommendation 54.
[148] *McNab v Brown's Trustees*, 1926 S.C. 387.

this was not so. One way of doing so is to show that the testator made alternative express provision for the person seeking to rely on the *conditio*[149] even if the express provision turned out to be inoperative.[150] Although in exceptional circumstances even such a provision may be unsuccessful in defeating the *conditio*.[151] In the case of specified legatees who are nieces or nephews, a challenger can also establish from the terms of the will that the legacy was made from personal favour rather than because of the family relationship.[152]

In the *2009 Report on Succession* the Scottish Law Commission made recom- **6–81** mendations on the *conditio* which were somewhat unclear. In para.6.29 they recommended the continuation of what was described as

"a rule whereby if a legatee within a certain class dies after the date of the will but before the date of vesting, his or her issue take the legacy unless the will expressly or by implication provides otherwise"

but with the exclusion of its application in favour of the descendants of nieces and nephews and the extension of it to the actual share of the deceased specified legatee (institute). However in para.6.30 they proposed the abolition of the *conditio* and its replacement with new statutory rules reflected in draft cl.33 in the Report. The proposed new statutory provision in draft cl.33 introduces a rule of law favouring the descendants of descendants of the testator only where it is not clear from the terms of the will that the testator intended otherwise. It is provided specifically, that such clarity exists if the will provides expressly that the legacy is bequeathed to the institute and another person and to the survivor of them or bequeathed to the institute whom failing to another person. This would seem to make the new statutory destination-over subject to option (a) outlined above but it would still prevail over implied accretion and, probably, a separate bequest of residue. The new rule would be beneficial in giving this unnecessarily unclear area of law a fresh start and leave it approximating closer to the intention of a testator.

In the Succession (Scotland) Bill the Scottish Government intends to follow the **6–82** suggestion of complete replacement in para.6.30 of the *2014 Scottish Government Consultation*. As yet it has not addressed the possible conflict between the new statutory rules and a separate bequest of residue.

Adopted persons and construction of wills

Adopted persons are defined (s.23(5)) for the purposes of the 1964 Act as **6–83** persons adopted in pursuance of a formal adoption order which has the same meaning as in s.38 of the Adoption (Scotland) Act 1978,[153] whether the order took effect before or after the commencement of the 1964 Act. With effect from September 28, 2009 it includes an adoption order within the meaning of s.28 of the Adoption and Children (Scotland) Act 2007.

---

[149] *Greig v Malcolm* (1835) 13 S. 607.
[150] *Paterson v Paterson*, 1935 S.C. (HL) 7.
[151] *Reid's Trustees v Drew*, 1960 S.C. 46.
[152] *Knox's Executor v Knox*, 1941 S.C. 523 at 541.
[153] (c.28). In force September 1, 1984 (SI 1984/1050).

6–84   The general policy of the 1964 Act was to remove the anomalies of the previous law in relation to adopted persons. The effect of Part IV of the Act is therefore that they are treated for all purposes, whether of succession or of entitlement under an inter vivos deed, as children of the adopter or adopters.[154] This is reinforced by s.39(1) of the Adoption (Scotland) Act 1978 which declares, inter alia, that a child who is the subject of an adoption order is to be treated in law as if he had been born as a legitimate child of the adopter or adopters. Section 24(1) of the 1964 Act specifies the relationship adopted children are to be deemed to have to other children or adopted children of the adopter. The provisions of the Adoption Act 1958 which formerly prevented an adopted child from acquiring any rights of intestate succession or legal rights in the adopter's estate are repealed.[155]

6–85   The details of the reciprocal rights of succession between an adopted child and its adopting parents are considered in the commentary on ss.2 and 24. There are also provisions in the Act relating to the construction of deeds when adopted children exist. Some confusion has existed over the commencement of these provisions in view of the complex relationship between ss.23(2), 23(4) and 36(3).

6–86   Section 23(4) states that nothing in s.23 "shall affect any deed executed . . . before the commencement of this Act". The effect is that wills actually executed[156] before September 10, 1964, have the same meaning as they had then. In other words, references in such wills to "children" or "issue" are presumed not to include adopted children. It is presumed that the testator was aware of the state of the law at the time and that by not mentioning adopted children he intended not to include them. The intention in this, as in other parts of the Act, was to avoid the necessity of disturbing existing arrangements.[157]

6–87   Section 23(2) therefore means that in wills executed on or after September 10, 1964, a general reference to "children" or "issue" will, unless the contrary intention appears, include adopted children. It also means that references to relatives of the adopted child will be determined by reference to the adopting parents rather than the natural parents. The point of the proviso (that for the purposes of s.23(2) a deed taking effect on the death of any person is to be deemed to have been executed on the date of death of that person) is that if a will is executed *after the commencement of the Act* referring to "children", or "issue," and subsequently the testator adopts a child, that child is included. The beginning of s.23(2) refers to references in deeds executed after the making of an adoption order, but the proviso ensures that the will is regarded as being executed at the date of the testator's death and hence after the adoption order, with the consequence that the adopted child is included in the term "children" and the relatives are those by virtue of the adopting rather than natural parents.

6–88   Similarly a deed executed after the commencement of the 1964 Act and taking effect on the death of some person other than the grantor of the deed will be deemed, for the purposes of s.23(2), to have been executed on the date of death of

[154] s.23(1).
[155] 1964 Act s.24(4).
[156] 1964 Act s.36(3).
[157] "Class Terms in the Construction of Deeds" (1969) 14 J.L.S. 204.

that person, and therefore after the adoption of any child who by then had been adopted.

The general policy that an adopted person is to be treated as the child of **6–89** the adopter is specifically applied to the construction of the terms used in wills and of inter vivos deeds disposing of property by s.23(1)(a) and (b). This is subject only to the special transitional provision that if the adopting parent died before September 10, 1964, and the natural parent died on or after August 3, 1966, the child is treated as the child of the natural parent for purposes of succession to that parent.[158]

For so long as it continues to exist it would seem that the *conditio si testator* **6–90** *sine liberis decesserit* would be available to a child adopted after the date of a will for whom no provision is made in it. The proviso to s.23(2) of the Succession Act is only for the purposes of that subsection, which deals with references to children in deeds.

A question was thought to arise whether a bequest to "the issue of any of my **6–91** children who fail to survive me" would include the predeceasing child's adopted child. In the view of the authors, there is no doubt upon the matter. Such an adopted child would be included as "issue". It is, of course, open to a testator to make such provision as he wishes, but if he used a phrase such as that quoted above, the whole purpose of the Act is to ensure that its meaning includes the adopted child. In the vigorous correspondence on this topic[159] the most convincing argument was that presented by Professor Clive at p.182 (January 1981), and this is the view which should be acted upon.

If a person has been adopted more than once, in effect only the last adoption is **6–92** reckoned for the purposes of succession, of establishing relationships and of construction of deeds executed after the last adoption order.[160]

An adoption order may be revoked in various circumstances, e.g. when a child **6–93** who had previously been adopted by his parents is legitimated by virtue of the Legitimation (Scotland) Act 1968. However, s.6 of that Act provides that revocation of an adoption order is not to affect an intestacy which occurred, or a deed which came into operation, before the revocation.

One of the major difficulties preventing the introduction of full rights of succes- **6–94** sion for adopted children at an earlier date was the existence of the rules of primogeniture and preference of males in the succession to heritage. While these rules have now largely disappeared, they are still relevant in the case of titles and some other items to which the Act does not apply.[161] Adopted children have no rights of succession to these items, in so far as included in the estate of the adopter. Accordingly, where the terms of any deed provide that any property or interest in property is to devolve along with a title, honour or dignity, nothing in s.23 of the 1964 Act or in the Children Act 1975 or in the Adoption (Scotland) Act 1978 is to prevent that devolution.[162]

---

[158] Law Reform (Miscellaneous Provisions) (Scotland) Act 1966 s.5.
[159] (1981) J.L.S. (Workshop) pp.159, 165, 172, 182, 191 and 206.
[160] 1964 Act s.24(3).
[161] 1964 Act s.37(1).
[162] 1964 Act s.23(3).

Illegitimate persons in the construction of wills

6–95 At common law there was very serious discrimination against the illegitimate child in the construction of deeds. The rule of construction amounted to a very strong presumption that terms such as "children" or "issue" referred to the legitimate relationship only. This stemmed from the general rule that an illegitimate child is *filius nullius* and the ultimate logic of this rule was well expressed by Lord Watson in *Clarke v Carfin Coal Co*[163] when he said that "at common law the mother is as much as the father, an utter stranger in blood to her child". With this somewhat nonsensical proposition built into the law it is not surprising to find that it could be authoritatively stated[164] that

> "the mere fact that there were no legitimate children answering the description could scarcely be regarded as a sufficient reason for giving to a designative bequest a construction which would admit persons who in law are regarded as strangers".

6–96 In other words, it seemed to be assumed that no testator in his senses would intend to include illegitimate children in the benefits of a bequest to the "children" of a particular person. Thus that construction was avoided unless it was completely impossible to do so—and sometimes even then. For example, in *Mitchell's Trustees v Cables*[165] a testator made a gift to his son "and his lawful children" whom failing to his daughter "and to the whole children procreated or that may yet be procreated of her body". At the date of the will, the daughter had an illegitimate child who was known to and indeed lived with the testator, and one might have thought that the difference in the wording of the two provisions indicated as clearly as humanly possible that the illegitimate child was intended to be a beneficiary. Nonetheless that construction was rejected.

6–97 In the interpretation of deeds executed on or after November 25, 1968, this position was remedied by s.5 of the Law Reform (Miscellaneous Provisions) (Scotland) Act 1968.[166] This provided[167] that in deducing any relationship for the purpose of ascertaining beneficiaries under a deed, the persons concerned are to be taken to be related to each other notwithstanding that the relationship was an illegitimate one only. It is interesting that this part of the 1968 reforms affecting illegitimate children was much wider in scope than the reform of their direct rights of intestate succession. The changed rules of interpretation applied to all deeds benefiting any person, not just to deeds by the parents of an illegitimate child, with the result that the re-enactment and further reform in s.1(2) of the Law Reform (Parent and Child) (Scotland) Act 1986 was of less significance for the construction of wills than in the creation of rights of succession. The rule of

---

[163] *Clarke v Carfin Coal Co* (1891) 18 R. (HL) 63 at 70.
[164] *Wills & Succession*, i, 694.
[165] *Mitchell's Trustees v Cables* (1893) 1 S.L.T. 156.
[166] Deeds exercising a power of appointment are treated as having the date of the deed which created the power: 1968 Act s.5(3).
[167] Until its repeal by the Law Reform (Parent and Child) (Scotland) Act 1986 (c.9).

construction contained in the 1968 Act was already a general one, and the main further change effected in 1986 was to apply the principle of equality to most statutes as well as to private deeds.

The main qualification is that until May 3, 2006, the grantor of the deed was **6–98** entitled to express a contrary intention, probably by using such terms as "lawful children" and such a contrary intention will continue to receive effect.[168] Whether such an entitlement continues with regard to deeds granted on or after May 4, 2006 is not entirely clear but the abolition of actions for declarator of legitimacy or illegitimacy would suggest that it does not. On that date s.21 of the Family Law (Scotland) Act 2006 abolished the status of illegitimacy for all persons whose status is governed by Scots law except that the abolition still does not affect the succession to titles, honours or dignities.[169] However, the provision in the 1968 Act that the new rule of construction did not prevent property from devolving along with a title does not appear in the 1986 Act. Since 1986 it may therefore be that while a title, honour or dignity may pass to the heir at law, property destined along with it in the will may pass to an illegitimate child instead.

Subject to all the same qualifications, s.6 of the 1968 Act also provided that **6–99** illegitimacy was no longer to prevent the operation of *the conditio si testator sine liberis decesserit*, the *conditio si institutus sine liberis decesserit*, or the principle of accretion. Previously a number of cases had established that the children of a predeceasing illegitimate child for whom a testamentary provision had been made could not invoke the *conditio si institutus*.[170] There had been no question of an after-born illegitimate child invoking the *conditio si testator* to set aside a will since it had no ordinary rights of succession to protect, and there was no accretion in a gift to illegitimate children as a class.[171]

Special legacies

A special legacy is a gift of a particular asset which can be identified as a **6–100** specific item of the deceased's estate, as distinguished from a general legacy out of the general assets of the estate, a residuary legacy of what is left after other legacies have been met or the rare demonstrative legacy.[172]

A special legacy has many of the features of an assignation to the legatee. **6–101** However a special legacy is also adeemed (or cancelled) if the object of it is no longer part of the deceased's estate at the time of his death. There is no question of compensation for its value from other sources, and a purely technical decision will be made on whether the object was or was not part of the estate at death.[173] If

---

[168] Law Reform (Parent and Child) (Scotland) Act 1986 s.1(4)(c) repealed by the 2006 Act Sch.3 para.1 but saved in respect of deeds executed before its repeal (The Family Law (Scotland) Act 2006 (Commencement, Transitional Provisions and Savings) Order 2006 (SSI 2006/212) art.9.

[169] 1968 Act s.5(5)(b) and 1986 Act s.9(1)(c).

[170] *Farquharson v Kelly* (1900) 7 S.L.T. 442.

[171] *Wills & Succession*, i, 695.

[172] *Meston's Succession Opinions*, No.19, p.45.

[173] *Anderson v Thomson* (1877) 4 R. 1101; *Ballantyne's Trustees v Ballantyne's Trustees*, 1941 S.C. 35; and *Ogilvie-Forbes' Trustees v Ogilvie-Forbes*, 1955 S.C. 405 at 410–411, 1956 S.L.T. 121 at 124.

missives have been concluded for sale of heritage, but no actual conveyance has yet occurred, the heritage remains part of the seller's estate at the crucial time.[174]

6–102   Because of their "special" nature, special legacies are the last to suffer abatement if the estate is not large enough to meet all the legacies provided by the will. Other types of legacy (residuary, general and demonstrative) may not have funds to meet them, but the special legacy will be effective if the asset remains in the estate at death and the debts of the estate can be satisfied without disposing of it.[175]

Cumulative and substitutional legacies

6–103   It sometimes happens that there are multiple testamentary writings but that none of them revoke previous writings. If the writings include multiple legacies to the same person, the question arises whether the writings should be construed as giving all the legacies to that person or whether only one was intended. The results often cause surprise to those who do not get multiple legacies!

6–104   Everything depends upon a detailed examination of the will. The working principles will be that if the same amount is given twice to the same person in the same deed, the legatee gets only one of the gifts, but that if the same amount is given in different deeds or different amounts are given in the same deed the presumption will be that they are cumulative.[176]

Conditional institution and substitution

6–105   This concerns the effect to be given to destinations-over such as "to A, whom failing to B". In that situation A is called the "institute", i.e. he is the person primarily called or "instituted" as the heir. The question is the position of B and this depends upon the construction to be given to the terms of the will. There are no hard rules about construction; everything depends on a detailed examination of the whole of the will. B may be a "conditional institute" or a "substitute".[177]

6–106   If he is only a conditional institute, the effect is that if A survives the testator he acquires the legacy and B's right permanently disappears. B gets the legacy only if A was alive at the date of the will[178] and predeceases the testator.

6–107   If, however, he is a "substitute", the difference is that even if A does survive to obtain the legacy, B will inherit it after A dies—unless the substitution is defeated by A during his lifetime either by transferring it to someone else or by dealing specifically with it in his will.

6–108   Every substitution includes a conditional institution, but not vice versa. In the construction of a will there is a presumption in favour of substitution when the subjects bequeathed are heritage, but against substitution when the subjects are

---

[174] *Pollock's Trustees v Anderson* (1902) 4 F. 455.
[175] See also paras 3–09 to 3–10.
[176] The classic case is *Royal Infirmary of Edinburgh v Muir's Trustees* (1881) 9 R. 352 at 356. However, the circumstances in *Gillies v Glasgow Royal Infirmary*, 1961 S.L.T. 93 were such that two separate legacies of the same amount in the same deed were treated as cumulative.
[177] *Meston's Succession Opinions*, No.21, p.54.
[178] *McKinnon's Trustees v Brownlie*, 1947 S.C. (HL) 27 at 36.

moveables—moveables would be likely to be difficult to trace once mixed in A's other property, but heritage usually remains identifiable. The Scottish Law Commission in the *2009 Report on Succession* have recommended that a presumption in favour of conditional institution apply regardless of the nature of the subjects bequeathed. This has been reflected in cl.8 of the Succession (Scotland) Bill.

Legal rights

The reader's attention is drawn to the provisions of s.33 of the 1964 Act in **6–109** respect of the interpretation of references to *jus relictae, jus relicti* and legitim or legal rights in all deeds (including wills) executed before the 1964 Act came into force.

RECTIFICATION OF WILLS

It does appear that rectification of a will is possible at common law in certain **6–110** limited circumstances.[179] The requirements and the technique of declarator and reduction have been approved recently by Lord Hodge in the English Supreme Court case *Marley v Rawlings*.[180] Wills are excluded from the general rectification of document provisions in ss.8 and 9 of the Law Reform (Miscellaneous Provisions) (Scotland) Act 1985.[181] The Scottish Government proposes in cl.3 of its Succession (Scotland) Bill that the court (including both the Court of Session and the sheriff court) should be given power to rectify errors in the expression of a will, but only where the will was drawn up by someone other than the testator, and the will as signed did not in fact carry out the testator's instructions. This means that there would have to have been instructions, the existence of which can be proved, which the person preparing the will failed to implement. Applications for rectification would have to be presented within six months of the granting of confirmation to the deceased's estate or of the date of death. Sometimes confirmation is obtained after six months from the date of death and it is unclear whether rectification would still be competent at that stage. It is hoped that this will be clarified.

VESTING OF LEGACIES

It is very important to understand vesting,[182] as the problem arises quite frequently. **6–111** If it is not recognised there is a high probability that an estate will be wound up wrongly. The beneficiary who gets less than his or her entitlement because of your failure to notice the correct answer is likely to be disappointed, and to sue. The

---

[179] *Hudson v St John*, 1977 S.C. 255 at 265 (inter vivos trust rectified).
[180] *Marley v Rawlings* [2014] UKSC 2 at [91]–[93].
[181] (c.73).
[182] See C.R. Henderson, *The Principles of Vesting in the Law of Succession*, 2nd edn (Edinburgh: W. Green, 1938); Robert B.M. Howie, "Vesting" in *Stair Memorial Encyclopaedia*, Vol.25 ("Wills & Succession"); G.L. Gretton, "What is vesting" (1986) J.L.S. 148. See also *Meston's Succession Opinions*, pp.467–499.

beneficiary who obtained funds without genuine right will normally have spent it and be unable to repay the amount received.

6–112   Vesting can arise in two separate situations. The first, and most simple, is that the whole estate of a deceased person vests in the executor for purposes of the administration of the estate when the executor has obtained confirmation from the court.[183] This is the process equivalent to probate in England, but unlike England, a Scottish confirmation includes an inventory of the assets of the deceased to which the executor is confirmed. The assets of the inventory which fall to be administered by Scots law vest in the executor with retrospective effect to the date of death.

6–113   Secondly, regardless of whether an executor has been confirmed, the beneficial right to succeed to a part or the whole of the estate may have vested in the appropriate beneficiaries and it is this beneficial vesting which concerns us here. A beneficial right in this sense is the right to receive a legacy or an intestate share from the estate of a deceased person. Once the beneficiary has a vested right, it is part of his or her estate and he or she can dispose of it by inter vivos or *mortis causa* deed. It is important to realise that a vested right may be obtained long before the beneficiary can get actual possession of it, from an executor, administrator, or trustee, or if abroad, possibly directly. This is where difficulties can arise particularly when a liferent is involved. Renunciation of a liferent may now result in immediate vesting of the fee under the provisions of the Succession (Scotland) Bill.

6–114   Vesting problems are not limited to cases where a liferent is conferred by a will, but they are a common example. A typical example, involved a husband who died in 1980. His will conferred a liferent of his whole estate upon his widow W, who is still alive. The fee of the estate was given to his two children A and B. The widow enjoys the liferent, but child B died in 1985. A seems to think that the whole estate is now his, but B's widow has indicated that she expects to receive one half of the estate when the liferent expires on W's death. It is therefore vital to determine when vesting of the fee occurred. If it occurred in 1980 when father died, B had a vested right at the time of his death, and this passed as part of his estate when B subsequently died. If the estate passed to *his* widow then she is entitled to his half when possession is possible. However if vesting was postponed to the expiry of the liferent, then A does collect the lot.

6–115   The broad principles on which a decision is made on the date of vesting are as follows:

Intention of the testator governs. The basic rule when there is a will is that the intention *expressed* by the testator in the will controls the decision about vesting. Hence a well-drafted will usually includes an express statement about the date of vesting and this will normally (that weasel word) settle the question.

Presumption for early vesting. If there is doubt, the court will favour the interpretation which produces the earlier date of vesting. Vesting of shares in the estate of deceased person cannot take place earlier than the date of his death. Hence the presumption is in favour of vesting *a morte testatoris*.

Shares of an intestate estate vest *a morte* immediately on the death of the intestate. Similarly an ordinary legacy with no qualifications vests immediately.

---

[183] 1964 Act s.14(1) and see the commentary thereon.

Suspensive conditions postpone vesting. A testator may include a condition in his will that a particular legacy is to vest only if some event occurs. If it is uncertain whether the event will ever happen, such a conditional bequest must necessarily postpone vesting until it can be determined whether the event will in fact happen. Most conditions personal to the legatee will tend to be suspensive conditions of this sort, and the commonest form is a survivorship condition or attaining a particular age. If a will is construed as providing that the legatee is to get his legacy only *if* he attains the age of 18 or survives someone else, typically a liferenter, then vesting has to be postponed until it can be established if he will qualify. These are uncertain events, which may never happen. The legatee may die before the event occurs and would not then qualify. Legacies of this sort are therefore said to vest on a "*dies incertus*" and vesting cannot take place before that day becomes certain.

Great care is therefore necessary in drafting clauses referring to survivorship. It must be clear what it is that the legatee has to survive. Many cases occur in which "survivors" are mentioned without making it clear, and there can often be disputes. Another common form of survivorship clause is a gift to A "whom failing" B. It is essential to make it clear when "failure" is to be determined. Is it at the testator's death or at the liferentrix's death?

Payment postponed to a dies certus does *not* postpone vesting. If there is postponement of *payment* until a day which will certainly happen (a *dies certus*), then vesting of the right is not postponed. No one has yet avoided death, and thus the death of a liferenter is an event which will happen sometime, even if it is not known when. Thus in the typical case of a liferent to A and fee to B, B's right to the fee will vest immediately on the testator's death, because the liferenter will die sometime and there is no uncertainty other than as to the date when the fiar will receive the capital of the sum liferented.

So far so good. It is all quite simple. The whole point is that everyone should **6–116** know what he or she does or does not own, and can make provision accordingly. A simple legacy vests immediately. A condition postponing payment until a *dies certus* does not prevent immediate vesting, and the beneficiary could always borrow on the security of the inheritance to come in the future. If there is a suspensive condition, however, there is no vesting until it can be determined whether the condition will be purified and the legatee must just wait to find out whether he gets anything. The problem is that there is a concept of resolutive conditions.

Resolutive conditions do not postpone vesting, but may take it away! The courts **6–117** have introduced in certain cases the concept of vesting subject to defeasance. Even though the whole point of vesting should be to achieve finality and let anyone with a vested right make use of that right even though it has not yet been paid, this doctrine will sometimes allow a court to determine that a right which has vested can be *di*vested or "defeased". Some conditions attached to legacies are held not to be suspensive, but to be resolutive. As such they do not prevent immediate vesting, but if the events specified in the condition do occur, they are "resolutive" of the vesting, and thus bring it to an end. Needless to say this can only be done before the person with the vested right has had a chance to spend the proceeds in the Las Vegas casinos.

6–118   While there is no guarantee that further examples may not emerge, three established cases of vesting subject to defeasance are already known. They all involve liferents and the birth of issue. It is to be hoped that no more do emerge!

6–119   *To A in liferent, A's issue in fee and failing issue of A, then to B in fee.* There is little trace of the doctrine before the case of *Taylor v Gilbert's Trustees*.[184] In that case A had no issue at the time when the testator died and B took a vested right to the fee, but subject to defeasance if A subsequently did have issue.

6–120   *Gift to A with a subsequent direction to hold for A in liferent and his issue in fee.* This is really an example of bad drafting and arises from the case of *Tweeddale's Trustees v Tweeddale*.[185] It begins with an outright gift, but later in the will there appears a provision that it is to be a liferent with the fee to the children. To make sense of both provisions this is treated as an outright gift to A, but subject to the resolutive condition that if he subsequently has issue, his right is reduced to a mere liferent with the fee going to his children. If A never has children, he remains outright owner.

6–121   *To A in liferent and B in fee, but if B predeceases the expiry of the liferent leaving issue, then to the issue in fee.* The main case is *Snell's Trustees v Morrison*.[186] The fiar in such a case takes an immediate vested right to the fee, but subject to defeasance in favour of his issue if he predeceases the liferenter, leaving issue, but only in that event.

WILL SUBSTITUTES

6–122   Various devices are sometimes employed to avoid the necessity of executing a formal will.

Statutory nominations

6–123   These are statutorily authorised for some types of small savings asset, now mainly benefits from friendly societies,[187] but formerly including National Savings investments.[188] They also include shares in, loans to and deposits in a co-operative and community benefit society[189] (formerly industrial and provident society)[190] up to a value of £5,000. Nominations of national savings certificates, deposits in national savings accounts, and national savings stock ceased to be competent on May 1, 1981.[191]

---

[184] *Taylor v Gilbert's Trustees* (1878) 5 R. (HL) 217.
[185] *Tweeddale's Trustees v Tweeddale* (1905) 8 F. 264.
[186] *Snell's Trustees v Morrison* (1877) 4 R. 709.
[187] Friendly Societies Act 1974 (c.46) s.66 as amended by the Civil Partnership Act 2004 Sch.27 para.52.
[188] See, e.g. National Savings Bank Regulations 1972 (SI 1972/764); *Ford's Trustees v Ford*, 1940 S.C. 426 where the nomination of savings certificates prevailed over a codicil; and *Clark's Executors v Macaulay*,1961 S.L.T. 109.
[189] Co-operative and Community Benefit Societies Act 2014 (c.14) s.37.
[190] Industrial and Provident Societies Act 1965 (c.12) s.23, until July 31, 2014 nomination restricted up to a value of £1,500
[191] Savings Certificates Regulations 1991 (SI 1991/1031) Sch.2; National Savings Bank Regulations 1972 reg.33 (as amended); National Savings Stock Regulations 1976 (SI 1976/2012) reg.32 (as amended). Each set of regulations sets out the conditions for the effectiveness of the nominations.

Donatio mortis causa

The *donatio mortis causa* is also accepted in Scots law, and has fewer restric- **6–124** tions than in some other countries. The classic definition was given by Lord President Inglis in *Morris v Riddick*[192] in the following terms:

> "A conveyance . . . so that the property is immediately transferred to the grantee, upon the condition that he shall hold for the grantor so long as he lives, subject to his power of revocation, and failing such revocation, then for the grantee on the death of the grantor."[193]

There must be evidence of an inter vivos transfer to the donee, but the gift is not outright, being subject to a double resolutive condition.[194] The gift reverts to the donor (a) if the donee predeceases the donor; and (b) if the donor revokes the gift. While it is necessary that the gift should have been made in contemplation of death, it is not necessary that the donor should have been in immediate peril of death, and Scots law differs from many others in that if the gift is in fact made in imminent peril of death, it is not automatically revoked if the donor survives the peril that he envisaged at the time. *Donatio mortis causa* is due to be abolished by the Succession (Scotland) Bill.

Special destinations

The main device still used as a will substitute, despite its many dangers, is the **6–125** special destination inserted into the documents of title to certain types of asset, especially, but not restricted to heritable property. By far the most common type of special destination in use is the survivorship destination. For a full description of special destinations the reader is referred to the commentary on s.36(2). Despite what is commonly thought, a survivorship reference in the heading of bank and building society accounts does not amount to a special destination and has of itself no effect upon the succession to the money in the account, because a bank pass-book or its equivalent is not a document of title to the money in the account.[195]

Although capable of being useful if they are understood and are used properly, **6–126** special destinations are a relic of a time when it was not technically possible to make a will disposing of heritage and are liable to produce unintended results.[196] They should certainly be abolished and it is unfortunate that the Scottish Law Commission turned against their abolition.[197]

---

[192] *Morris v Riddick* (1867) 5 M. 1036.
[193] *Morris* (1867) 5 M. 1036; *Aiken's Executors v Aiken*, 1937 S.C. 678, 1937 S.L.T. 414.
[194] *Macpherson's Executrix v Mackay*, 1932 S.C. 505 at 513.
[195] M.C. Meston, "Survivorship Destinations and Bank Accounts" (1996) 1 S.L.P.Q. 315.
[196] M.C. Meston, "Special Destinations" in D.J. Cusine (ed.), *A Scots Conveyancing Miscellany* (Edinburgh: W. Green, 1987), pp.62–65. *Weir v J.M. Hodge & Son*, 1990 S.L.T. 266 illustrates a situation in which the existence of the destination was ignored, leading to an action of damages against the solicitor giving negligent advice.
[197] See Ch.8, paras 8–05 to 8–10.

Chapter 7

INTERNATIONAL PRIVATE LAW

7–01 In the globalised world of the present day individuals have greater freedom to travel, settle, and to acquire assets in a foreign jurisdiction than ever before. It is common for a person to die leaving estate both in Scotland and in another country. For this purpose the three jurisdictions of the UK, namely England and Wales, Northern Ireland and Scotland count as separate countries. The existence of separate jurisdictions or countries within one internationally recognised state is not unique to the UK. In other states, such as the US, individual states also count as separate countries with separate laws of succession. It has never been more important for any person involved in dealing with succession law in Scotland to be conscious of the effect of Scots law on international estates, namely estates lying in more than one country.

7–02 The Scots law of succession can be subdivided into (1) the rules which determine the administrative procedure by which the estate is transferred from the deceased to the person entitled to succeed; and (2) the substantive rules which determine succession to the estate of the deceased, including the rules of international private law (conflict of laws) which determine the law to be applied in determining succession. The effect of s.14(1) of the 1964 Act whereby all estate "falling to be administered by the law of Scotland" vests by confirmation in an executor appointed by a Scottish court underlines the central importance, from a practical point of view, of the rules relating to the administration of estates. In providing for the vesting of the whole estate in an administrator, Scots law has departed conclusively, with the exception of survivorship destinations, from the family of countries whose laws do not require an intermediary in the form of an executor or administrator to enable the transfer of the estate. Countries which do not require an administrator include France, Germany, Poland, Spain and Italy although a testator may choose to appoint an administrator in some of these. In such countries generally, the estate vests in the heirs upon the death of the deceased with a duty on them to settle debts and distribute to any legatees under a will.

7–03 The 1964 Act does not purport to affect or alter the rules of private international law. Section 37(2) expressly preserves the pre-existing law by providing that

> "[n]othing in this Act shall be construed as affecting the operation of any rule of law applicable immediately before the commencement of this Act to the choice of the system of law governing the administration, winding up or distribution of the estate, or part of the estate, of any deceased person".

Scots law on administration of estates

Scots law on the administration of estates applies to all property, moveable or **7–04** heritable, located in Scotland as at the death of the deceased.[1] A Scottish court will not recognise and give effect to the right of either a foreign administrator, foreign legatee or foreign heir on intestacy to ingather estate located in Scotland.[2] The rationale is that the Scottish courts seek to have exclusive control over assets situated in their jurisdiction. It follows from this that apart from certain limited exceptions[3] on the death of any person domiciled anywhere in the world, any estate located in Scotland and belonging to the deceased will be estate "falling to be administered under the law of Scotland" and so will vest in a confirmed executor under s.14(1) of the Act. It follows that location of estate in Scotland is the essential requirement for Scots law to apply to the administration of an estate.

Where the estate comprises corporeal (tangible) property, identification of the **7–05** location of the property at death is fairly straightforward. The only question arises in respect of corporeal moveables such as aircraft and ships which have a place of registration. Does the place of registration prevail over physical location? On the basis of English law it is suggested that the location of property is determined by physical location at death rather than the place of registration.[4]

If the estate comprises incorporeal property, identification of location is more **7–06** difficult. Shares in an incorporated company will be located in the place where they could effectively be dealt with.[5] Typically this requires the place in question to have had a share register into which a transfer could be recorded. While a share register is usually in the country of incorporation it can be located elsewhere and this may result in the shares being situated in a country other than that of incorporation.[6] It is therefore conceivable that shares could be located in Scotland even if the company is not incorporated in Scotland. Ordinary debts owed to the deceased will be located in Scotland only if at the time of his death he could have sued the debtor in Scotland.[7] A non-negotiable promissory note will be located in the place where it is payable by the debtor to the holder.[8] For location of other types of incorporeal property see *Currie on Confirmation*.[9]

If any estate of the deceased was located in Scotland as at the death, prima facie **7–07** s.14(1) of the Act will vest the estate in a Scottish executor upon his confirmation with retrospective effect from the date of death. In certain instances Scottish rules of international private law have recognised the vesting of estate located in

---

[1] *Preston v Melville* (1841) 8 Cl. & F. 1 at 12–13 (HL); (1841) 2 Rob. 88 at 105.
[2] This effect of the EU Succession Regulation has been excluded from the UK, and see para.7–07 below.
[3] See commentary on s.36(2) relating to "estate".
[4] *Dornoch Ltd v Westminster International BV* [2009] EWHC 889 (Admlty); [2009] 1 C.L.C. 645 at [90]–[103] (ship but also applicable to aircraft).
[5] *Brassard v Smith* [1925] A.C. 371 at 376.
[6] *R v Williams* [1942] A.C. 541; and see *Standard Chartered Bank Ltd v Inland Revenue Commissioners* [1978] 1 W.L.R. 1160.
[7] *In re Banque Des Marchands De Moscou (Koupetschensky) (No.2)* [1954] 1 W.L.R. 1108 at 1116.
[8] *Kwok Chi Leung Karl v Commissioner of Estate Duty* [1988] 1 W.L.R. 1035 (PC).
[9] *Currie on Confirmation* (2011), paras 10–61 to 10–63.

Scotland in foreign administrators. Such recognition has been granted in the following instances:

> (A)   executor with a grant of probate or an administrator with letters of administration granted by the High Court or District Probate Registry in England and Wales or the High Court in Northern Ireland, provided that the deceased was domiciled in the country where the probate or letters were granted[10];
>
> (B)   executor or administrator with a grant of probate or letters of administration resealed at Edinburgh Sheriff Court under the Colonial Probates Act 1892[11] which applies to various Commonwealth[12] and Hong Kong Special Administrative Region[13] executors or administrators.

7–08   Otherwise an application for both appointment and confirmation as Scottish executor must be made to enable the property located in Scotland to be transferred to the person succeeding thereto.[14] Under a longstanding rule of Scots international private law, the identity of persons entitled to the office of executor (whether dative or nominate) is determined by the law of domicile of the deceased as ascertained by the Scottish court.[15] This means that where the deceased was domiciled outwith Scotland, the person entitled to be appointed and confirmed as a Scottish executor will be the person entitled to be appointed as an equivalent administrator under the law of domicile of the deceased. Where that law of domicile does not provide for administrators and there is automatic transfer to beneficiaries upon death, the person entitled to be appointed executor-dative and confirmed will be the person entitled to succeed to the Scottish property were it situated in the country of domicile. An affidavit from an expert in the law of domicile as to the person entitled to the office of administrator (failing which to succeed to the property) will require to be submitted with the petition for appointment.[16] The entitlement to administer the Scottish property in such a case will not however guarantee entitlement to succeed to the property under the Scots substantive law of succession (including its rules of international private law) which the executor will have to apply.

7–09   Scots law on the administration of estates does not apply to property located outwith Scotland, even of a deceased with a Scottish domicile at death. This means that a Scottish executor will not by virtue of his Scottish appointment be entitled to ingather property of the deceased located outwith Scotland unless

---

[10]   Administration of Estates Act 1971 (c.25) s.3.

[11]   (55 and 56 Vict. c.6).

[12]   See the list in *Currie on Confirmation* (2011), para.15–03 derived from the Colonial Probates Act Application Orders 1965 (SI 1965/1530) and 1976 (SI 1976/579). Pakistan and India are excluded from the list.

[13]   s.1A of the Colonial Probates Act 1892 introduced by the Hong Kong (Colonial Probates Act) Order 1997 (SI 1997/1572) art.2.

[14]   See the commentary on s.14(1).

[15]   *Anton* (2011), para.23–34; *Marchioness of Hastings v Executors of Marquess of Hastings* (1852) 14 D. 489; and see the cases mentioned in *Currie on Confirmation* (2011), para.2–60.

[16]   See *Currie on Confirmation* (2011), para.2–35; and *Meston's Succession Opinions*, No.76, p.239.

his power to do so is recognised by the country of location.[17] In *Preston v Melville*[18] it was held that the Court of Session had no power to ordain an English administrator to transfer moveable property located in England to a Scottish trustee. This is consistent with s.14(1) of the Act which provides that the estate in the inventory for confirmation vests in the executor only in so far as "falling to be administered under the law of Scotland". While the inventory in a confirmation may include foreign estate, it does not follow automatically that it has vested in the executor. In certain limited instances the title of a Scottish executor is recognised in foreign countries. These limited instances[19] are important, however, and include England and Wales and Northern Ireland[20] but subject to the important proviso that the deceased died domiciled in Scotland.[21] The powers of a Scottish executor in these jurisdictions is equated to that of a local executor or administrator.

Where the deceased was domiciled outwith Scotland and left property both in Scotland and in the country of domicile, the Scottish executor continues to have a duty to distribute estate to beneficiaries resident in the country of domicile and, depending on the law of domicile, he may have a duty to transfer the estate to an administrator in the country of domicile in order to achieve the distribution to the beneficiaries.[22] While such an indirect transfer to beneficiaries may require the transfer of money to allow the administrator of domicile to pay inheritance tax to the state of domicile, a Scottish executor should not use Scottish estate to pay a revenue or taxation claim of a foreign government given that such claims are unenforceable in Scotland.[23] **7–10**

With effect from August 17, 2015 the EU Succession Regulation will provide for recognition by the courts of a member state (with the exception of the UK, Ireland and Denmark) of the decisions in matters of succession given by a court of another member state of the EU or any judicial or other authority or legal professional with competence in the matters of succession which exercise judicial functions or act pursuant to a delegation of power by or under the control of a judicial authority.[24] While it is clear that the effect of the UK opt-out is that it does not alter Scots law in the administration of estates,[25] it is submitted that nevertheless the Regulation does have the effect of allowing UK and Irish court decisions on matters of succession to be recognised by the courts or authorities of other EU member states (apart from Denmark). **7–11**

---

[17] *Scottish National Orchestra Ltd v Thomson's Executor*, 1969 S.L.T. 325 at 327.
[18] *Preston v Melville* (1841) 2 Rob. 88; (1841) 8 Cl. & F. 1 (HL).
[19] Which include countries granting reciprocal rights under the Colonial Probates Act 1892.
[20] All under the Administration of Estates Act 1971 (c.25) ss.1 and 6.
[21] Administration of Estates Act 1971 ss.1(1), 2(2) and 3(1).
[22] *Scottish National Orchestra Ltd*, 1969 S.L.T. 325.
[23] *Scottish National Orchestra Ltd*, 1969 S.L.T. 325 at 330.
[24] EU Succession Regulation arts 39–58.
[25] EU Succession Regulation, preamble, para.(82), e.g. it does not oblige recognition of the effect of the European Certificate of Succession.

Scots substantive international private law

7–12   A Scottish court or executor may require to determine the succession to estate whether situated in Scotland or outwith Scotland. Equally a foreign court or judicial authority or administrator may require to determine succession to estate in its own country where its rules of international private law (choice of law) indicate that Scots law should be applied. Where a Scottish resident owns property located in an EU state where the EU Succession Regulation applies, the Regulation may well require the foreign court or authority to refer to Scots law. In both of these situations the court, authority or administrator may require look to the Scots rules of international private law on succession, before applying the internal (domestic) Scots law of succession.

7–13   The provisions and effect of foreign laws require to be established by expert evidence.[26] In the absence of such expert evidence a Scottish court would apply the presumption that the foreign law is the same as Scots law.[27]

Intestate succession—General

7–14   Under Scots rules of international private law, succession to moveable estate is governed by the *lex domicilii* of the deceased at death whereas succession to immoveable estate is governed by the *lex situs* of the estate in question.[28] This is known as the "scission principle".

7–15   Scots law requires classification of particular items as moveable or immoveable to be performed by the *lex situs* of the property[29] including its rules of international private law if relevant. In particular the outcome need not be identical with the classification as heritable or moveable in Scotland or as real or personal in England. In every case, the classification must be performed so that the appropriate system of law may be applied to determine the succession to the item in question.

7–16   However, while it is clear that this is the present state of Scots international private law, it is by no means so clear that it ought to be the law. Virtually every country in the world has abolished any special rules for the succession to land so that for its own internal purposes no distinction is made between moveable and immoveable property. The distinction is no longer felt to serve a meaningful social purpose, and yet, despite the virtually unanimous international opinion to this effect, Scots law persists with the distinction as if it separated significantly different categories for purposes of choice of law. This can produce bizarre variations in the result in a particular case depending upon where particular items of the estate happen to be situated. Even within the UK, where Northern Ireland, England and Scotland seek to achieve similar results on intestacy but by very different methods, the present rules for the choice of the appropriate system of law

---

[26] e.g. as in *Scottish National Orchestra*, 1969 S.L.T. 325.

[27] *Bonnor v Balfour Kilpatrick Ltd*, 1974 S.L.T. 187.

[28] Erskine, III, ix, 4; and *Wills and Succession*, i, 16.

[29] *Clarke v Newmarsh* (1836) 14 S. 488 at 500; and *Macdonald v Macdonald*, 1932 S.C. (HL) 79 at 84–85 and 86–89; and see paras 7–05 to 7–06 for where estate is situated.

can produce remarkable and quite unjustifiable variations in the amount that a widow will receive depending on the situation of the property.[30]

It is submitted that the law should be reformed so that all property devolves **7–17** according to the law of the deceased's last habitual place of residence and that the role of the *lex situs* should disappear.[31] Given that most fellow EU member states[32] have agreed to adopt the default rule that succession to all property ought to devolve under the law of the state (whether an EU member or not) or territorial unit of a state, where the deceased had his habitual residence at death,[33] it is appropriate that "habitual residence" should be used as the connecting element to determine the law of succession to be applied to the assets of the deceased. The difficulty with common law[34] domicile lies in the artificiality of the domicile of origin acquired at birth from a parent which can apply for persons who abandon any intention of permanent residence. Such persons can hardly have intended that their parents' domicile should decide the law of succession applicable to their international estate. "Habitual residence" has already been used to found jurisdiction in family matters.[35] Indeed, going one stage further, it is submitted that there is no insuperable obstacle to allowing a party to opt out of habitual residence by choosing in a testamentary writing the succession law of any nationality which he possesses at the time of his choice or the time of his death.[36]

If this were carried out, there would, of course, be difficulties in applying rules **7–18** of succession from one country to immoveable property in another country, for rights of a type unknown to the law of the country where the land is situated might have to be catered for and documents of unusual types accepted. However these problems would not be insuperable, and indeed are no more serious than those which already exist, and are already overcome,[37] in our present rules of private international law. The refusal of the UK to adopt the Hague Convention of 1989 on the Law Applicable to the Estates of Deceased Persons and its decision to opt out of the EU Succession Regulation are, it is submitted, no justification for allowing the outdated scission principle to govern the applicable law in

---

[30] See *Morris* (1969) 85 L.Q.R. 339.

[31] In its Consultative Memorandum, *Some Miscellaneous Topics in the Law of Succession* (HMSO, 1986), Scot. Law Com. No.71, the Scottish Law Commission had proposed that both moveables and immoveables should devolve on intestacy according to the law of the last domicile, but made no formal recommendation to this effect in its *1990 Report on Succession* in order to allow the UK Government to consider whether to accede to the draft Convention prepared by the Hague Conference on Private International Law. In its *2009 Report on Succession* the Commission suggested that the matter should be left for consideration with the other UK Law Commissions. No progress has been made since and the proposal has not been included in the *2014 Scottish Government Consultation.*

[32] With the exception of Ireland and Denmark.

[33] EU Succession Regulation arts 21(1) and 36(2).

[34] Now partly statutory: see 2006 Act s.22 and G. Maher, "Reforming Domicile: one step forward (but looking back)", 2006 S.L.T. (News) 149.

[35] Council Regulation (EC) No 2201/2003 concerning jurisdiction and the recognition and enforcement of judgments in matrimonial matters and the matters of parental responsibility, repealing Regulation (EC) No 1347/2000 [2003] OJ L338; Domicile and Matrimonial Proceedings Act 1973 (c.45) ss.7 and 8 as amended.

[36] As suggested in the EU Succession Regulation art.22.

[37] For wills using foreign law terminology: see *Studd v Cook* (1883) 10 R. (HL) 53.

succession. The hope, first expressed in the 4th edition of this book in 1993, that future legislation will effect this reform, remains.

7–19   In the application of the existing rules to the scheme of succession set out in the Succession Act, and in s.29 of the 2006 Act, some points are worth special notice.

Prior rights

7–20   Section 1 provides that inter alia s.8 is to apply to estate "the succession to which falls to be regulated by the law of Scotland". The surviving spouse's prior right under s.8(1)(a)(i) of the 1964 Act to the deceased's interest in the dwelling-house is clearly a right of succession to immoveable property. Thus all houses situated in Scotland are potentially subject to it as the *lex situs*, irrespective of the owner's domicile. For example a wife living apart from her English husband in a house belonging to him in Scotland, would have a prior right to the house on his death. However no house outwith Scotland would be subject to the s.8(1)(a)(i) right as the right would not form part of the foreign *lex situs*.

7–21   In a situation to which s.8(2) applies (i.e. farmhouses and other business premises including a house)[38] a surviving spouse receives a "sum equal to the value of the relevant interest" held by the deceased. It is fairly easy to regard this cash sum as a kind of surrogatum for the immoveable itself, since it is equated with the interest in it which the survivor would otherwise have received. Hence there can be little doubt that this right to a cash sum is also to be treated as a right of succession to an immoveable falling to be governed by the *lex situs*, so that it could be due out of houses situated in but not outwith Scotland, irrespective of the domicile of the owner.

7–22   Is the surviving spouse's right to a fixed sum under s.8(1)(b) where the value of the house is greater than the maximum limit applicable to moveable property? Under s.8(1)(b), where the value of the deceased's "relevant interest" exceeds the maximum limit the survivor is entitled to a sum equal to the maximum limit without any words classifying this sum as a surrogatum for the house itself. An argument can therefore be presented that the right is an interest in moveables, and therefore applicable only to domiciled Scots, and is not due when a house in Scotland is owned by someone domiciled elsewhere. However, the better view would seem to be that the right to the cash sum is a surrogatum in lieu of a share of the house itself. The purpose of the provision is merely to put an upper limit on the benefit to a surviving spouse of the housing right, and in substance it is intended to reflect part of the right to the house, however it may be expressed. Thus it is suggested that if an appropriate house worth more than £473,000 is situated in Scotland, the surviving spouse will be entitled to the cash sum even if the deceased was domiciled outwith Scotland, on the basis that the right is part of the succession to immoveables. That sum could be recovered from a sale of the house. Conversely, the survivor will not be entitled to the cash sum if the house is situated outside Scotland, even if the deceased's domicile was Scottish.[39]

---

[38] See the commentary on s.8.
[39] R.D. Leslie, "Prior Rights in Succession", 1988 S.L.T. (News) 105.

The prior right to furniture and plenishings conferred by s.8(3) appears to be a **7–23** right to moveable estate and thus governed by the *lex domicilii*. The effect of this would be that a deceased domiciled outwith Scotland could have an entitlement to take the furniture and plenishings from the Scottish house. This might seem unlikely although it would be in line with the common law. Is this possible outcome altered by the reference in the statutory arbitration provision in s.8(5) to a deceased who was domiciled furth of (outwith) Scotland? Usually one would not expect Parliament to re-classify furniture and plenishings as heritable on the basis of a dispute resolution provision. In earlier editions of this book it was thought that s.8(5) is ineffective so far as concerns the furniture and plenishings of a deceased person who was domiciled furth of Scotland. However given the purpose of the furniture and plenishings right, namely to allow the spouse to continue to live in the house, it is now submitted that s.8(5) accords with that purpose and indicates that the furniture and plenishings should be treated as heritable property for international private law purposes only.

The prior right under s.9 of the Succession Act requires to be **7–24**

> "borne by, and paid out of, the parts of the intestate estate consisting of heritable and moveable property respectively in proportion to the respective amounts of those parts".[40]

This is the heritable and moveable property remaining after the s.8 rights are satisfied. It is thus part of the Scots law affecting succession to immoveable property (being in effect a charge upon heritage in Scotland) and succession to moveable property.

The result is that if the deceased was domiciled in Scotland, the prior s.9(1) **7–25** right is due from his moveables, wherever situated, and from his immoveable property in Scotland. It is not due from immoveable property situated outside Scotland. However, even if the deceased was domiciled outside Scotland, the fact that the s.9(1) right is part of the Scots law of succession to immoveable property means that the surviving spouse is entitled to £50,000 or to £89,000 as the case may be out of any immoveable property situated in Scotland. The full amount is payable under Scots law to the surviving spouse irrespective of the amount or value of any other estate owned by the deceased, and irrespective of any rights which the surviving spouse may have under any other system.[41] If the deceased was domiciled outwith Scotland the spouse will not be entitled to any part of the sum exigible from moveable property.

Legal rights

Following the Succession Act legal rights in Scots law exist only in the move- **7–26** able estate belonging to the deceased at the time of his death and are classified as rights of succession despite their origin in a form of community of property

---

[40] 1964 Act s.9(3).
[41] M.C. Meston, "Prior Rights in Scottish Heritage" (1967) 12 J.L.S. 401.

between husband and wife. As rules governing succession to moveables they apply only when the deceased was domiciled in Scotland and affect whatever is classed as moveable property under the *lex situs* of that property. Any comparable legal rights provisions in a foreign system of law affecting moveables would be applied in Scotland in the succession to a deceased who was domiciled in that foreign country.

7–27   There are no longer any Scottish legal rights in immoveable property. As succession to immoveables is governed by the *lex situs*, this means that immoveable property situated in Scotland is immune from all legal rights or their equivalents, Scottish or foreign. Immoveable property outwith Scotland will be left to the *lex situs*. When the foreign country has legal rights provisions for immoveable property (and most do), they will apply to such property. Conversely in a country with no such provisions, such as England and Wales, the succession may be governed wholly by the will or intestacy. The limited English discretionary equivalent to legal rights under the Inheritance (Provision for Family and Dependants) Act 1975 applies only in cases where the deceased died domiciled in England and Wales.[42] It cannot therefore be invoked by the dependants of a deceased who dies domiciled in Scotland, but who owned immoveable property in England. The (English) Law Commission has so far rejected proposals for rectification of this.

Family Law (Scotland) Act 2006 s.29 order

7–28   An order under s.29 of the 2006 Act[43] for distribution to a cohabitee from intestate estate can be made only where the deceased was domiciled in Scotland at the time of his or her death.[44] An order can affect either moveable or immoveable property. The scission principle discussed above[45] applies. Accordingly a s.29 order, being part of the *lex domicilii* can cover moveable property anywhere in the world but being part of the *lex situs*, immoveable property only in Scotland. If the deceased was not domiciled in Scotland at his or her death, no inheritance under s.29 can be awarded by the court.

Free estate

7–29   In the distribution of the free estate, the general rules that moveables are governed by the *lex domicilii* of the deceased and immoveables by the *lex situs* of the property operate with full force. The preservation of these rules for this Part of the 1964 Act is reinforced by the provision in s.1(1) that it applies to "estate the succession to which falls to be regulated by the law of Scotland".

The Crown as ultimus haeres

7–30   The property of anyone dying without heirs or testate beneficiaries passes to the Crown as *ultimus haeres*. The estate is received and administered by the Queen's

---

[42] s.1(1).
[43] (asp 2).
[44] 2006 Act s.29(1)(b)(i).
[45] See paras 7–14 and 7–15.

and Lord Treasurer's Remembrancer. There are serious doubts about the theoretical nature of this right of the Crown[46] but in practice the Crown claims the moveable property in Scotland of foreign domiciliaries and does not claim moveable property abroad belonging to Scottish domiciliaries.[47]

Testate succession

The questions of capacity to make a will, of formal validity of the will, of 7–31 essential validity of the will and of construction of the terms used in a will give rise to different considerations of Scots international private law.

Wills may of course set up *mortis causa* trusts and the choice of law provisions 7–32 of the Hague Convention on the Law Applicable to Trusts and on their Recognition which have been incorporated into Scots law by virtue of the Recognition of Trusts Act 1987[48] must also be borne in mind. However art.4 of the Convention provides that it does not apply to preliminary issues relating to the validity of wills or other acts by which assets are transferred to the trustee. It follows that at least in relation to issues of capacity, formal validity and essential validity (other than relating to the validity of bequests in trust), the ordinary rules of international private law apply to wills which set up trusts as much as they do to those that do not.

However it is submitted that in relation to the choice of law for the construction 7–33 and assessment of the validity of bequests in trust, the 1987 Act and Hague Convention should be applied. The choice of law rules in the Hague Convention are applicable to all trusts regardless of whether they might originate from a territory not party to the Convention.[49]

Capacity

In Scotland, capacity to make a will is now attained at the age of 12.[50] Below 7–34 that age, there is no legal capacity to make a will, and other legal systems impose restrictions on different categories of persons. The rule appears to be that capacity to make or revoke a will of moveable estate is referred to the *lex domicilii* of the testator at the date of execution of the will while capacity to make a will dealing with immoveables requires to exist under both the *lex domicilii* and the *lex situs*.[51]

The Scottish Law Commission has recommended that capacity should in all 7–35 cases be referred solely to the *lex domicilii* at the time of making (or revoking) the will.[52] It is hoped that such legislative reform will refer capacity to the internal law of domicile (or preferably habitual residence) thereby excluding the possibility of *renvoi* by the law of domicile or habitual residence back to Scots law (for example on the basis of nationality).

---

[46] *Anton* (2011), para.24–42; *Wills & Succession*, i, 22; *Rutherford v Lord Advocate*, 1932 S.C. 674; *Lord Advocate v Aberdeen University*, 1962 S.L.T. 413.

[47] *Anton* (2011), para.24–43. As between Scotland and England, see Law Reform (Miscellaneous Provisions) (Scotland) Act 1940 (3 and 4 Geo. 6 c.42) s.6.

[48] (c.14)

[49] (c.14) s.1(4)

[50] Age of Legal Capacity (Scotland) Act 1991 (c.50) s.2(2).

[51] *Wills & Succession*, i, 23–24.

[52] *1990 Report on Succession*, recommendation 67; *2009 Report on Succession*, recommendation 45.

7–36   Capacity for this purpose must include loss of capacity through the will being procured by force and fear (duress), facility and circumvention, or undue influence. This is because their effect in relation to a will is to render the will void from the moment of execution, regardless of the situation of the testator or his estate at the date of death.

7–37   Where the validity of a legacy or other provision in a will can be influenced by reference to circumstances existing at the death of the testator, the validity of such a legacy or provision can best be seen as an issue of the essential validity of the will or provisions within it. Thus the question of whether a legacy can be over-ridden by legal rights (forced heirship), should be seen as a question of the essential validity of the legacy as at death rather than a question of whether the testator lacked capacity to make an effective legacy at the time of the will. A testator may have been domiciled in Scotland at the time of his will leaving him unable to escape legal rights in relation to his legacy of Scottish moveable estate. However if by the time of his death his domicile had become English, his legacy may have become effective.

Formal validity

7–38   Formal validity is now governed primarily by the Wills Act 1963.[53] A will is validly executed if it is properly executed according to the internal law of the territory of execution or of the testator's domicile, nationality or habitual residence either at the date of execution or at the date of death.[54] In addition it is validly executed on board a vessel or aircraft if it conforms to the internal law with which a ship or aeroplane is most closely connected having regard to its registration (if any) and any other relevant circumstances.[55] A will dealing only with immoveable property may employ the formalities of the internal rules of the *lex situs* of the immoveable property.[56]

7–39   Applying this to the Scottish solicitor, he or she may therefore use the Scottish formalities whenever (i) a will is executed in Scotland; or (ii) the testator qualifies by reason of domicile, nationality or habitual residence; or (iii) the will deals solely with Scottish immoveables. What he or she must not do is to send a will abroad for signature without advising of the effect of the Wills Act. There are numerous cases in which people with some family connection with Scotland (often an interest in a Scottish trust) seek to make a will dealing only with their Scottish estate although they are no longer domiciled or habitually resident here and are not UK nationals. Unless the will deals solely with Scottish heritage, the solicitor must point out the pre-conditions for a valid execution under the Scottish formalities.

7–40   For EU member states (other than the UK, Ireland and Denmark), formal validity is now[57] governed by the liberal provisions of arts 27 and 83(3) of the EU Succession Regulation one of which is compliance with the law where the will is

---

[53] (c.44).
[54] Wills Act 1963 s.1.
[55] Wills Act 1963 s.2(1)(a).
[56] Wills Act 1963 s.2(1)(b).
[57] From August 17, 2015.

executed. If circumstances require the will to be executed outwith Scotland, the client may not be a UK national, or his or her habitual residence may not be clearly Scotland. The safest route is to advise the client to ensure execution in accordance with the formalities of the territory of execution and to obtain local legal advice on what is involved. Such an approach also has other advantages. First, the formalities of a country of execution can be identified readily after death whereas habitual residence, nationality and domicile may give rise to more dispute. Secondly, most legal systems will accept formal validity under the law of the territory of execution and this can ensure formal validity in other countries also, which may be important for international estates. However, other countries' formalities can be more burdensome than Scottish formalities.

To illustrate the point, where a will sent for signature to Germany when the **7–41** testator was domiciled and resident there, and had German nationality, if executed in accordance with Scottish formalities, it would, but for the testator having also UK nationality, have been invalid.

It seems unlikely that the provisions of the Administration of Justice Act 1982[58] **7–42** will be brought into force. If they are, Scots law will recognise the formal validity of an "international will" which will automatically be accepted as formally valid in all contracting countries of the Washington Convention if it complies with the formalities specified in the Convention (as set out in the Act) irrespective of any contrary requirements in the local law.

Forgery, and thus the absence of a signature, if it is required, prevents the **7–43** formal validity of the will.

Essential validity

This is governed by different considerations, as the content of a will may not be **7–44** valid even if the formalities of execution have been properly observed. Public policy may prevent the full or partial validity of a legacy, for example in the event of forfeiture for homicide or legal rights. Alternatively there may be specific statutory provisions affecting validity such as the Scottish rules prohibiting successive liferents, entails or accumulations. For essential validity of its provisions the law governing the will is the *lex domicilii* at the time of death for moveable property and the *lex situs* for immoveable property.[59]

It is submitted that choice of law in respect of whether a document has testa- **7–45** mentary effect at all, possible revocation of a will (whether by the testator or by operation of law) and the question of the survivorship of a beneficiary would all fall to be considered as issues of essential validity. With regard to revocation, however, there is authority that revocation by operation of law is governed by the domicile of the testator at the time of the alleged revocation.[60] Revocation under

---

[58] (c.53) ss.27, 28, Sch.2 bringing into Scots law the 1973 Washington Convention on Providing a Uniform Law on Form of an International Will.

[59] *Boe v Anderson* (1862) 24 D. 732 (where the *lex domicilii* did not recognise a legacy of a charitable trust); *Brown's Trustees v Gregson*, 1920 S.C. (HL) 87 (where the *lex situs* did not recognise a legacy of immoveable property to be held in trust).

[60] *Westerman v Schwab* (1905) 8 F. 132 (given that a wife no longer acquires her husband's domicile upon marriage, on the facts the wife's *lex domicilii* would have revoked her will).

the *conditio si testator sine liberis decesserit* requires two elements for its application, namely the birth of a child after the will and the exercise after death by or on behalf of the child of the power to revoke that arose with its birth.[61] It is submitted that for the revocation to apply the testator must have been domiciled in Scotland both upon the birth and upon death.

Construction (interpretation)

7–46   Before its effects and essential validity can be assessed a will may require to be construed or interpreted by a Scottish court or executor in order to discover its meaning. Which law does Scots law say should govern the construction of a will? Choice of law for construction of the terms used in wills depends upon the testator's intention.[62] but there is rarely an express statement of intention that a particular law should apply. In the absence of express intentions or of intention clearly inferred from the terms of will[63] there is a presumption that a will of moveable property will be construed according to the law of the domicile as at death[64] and a will of immoveable property by the law of the *situs*.[65] Perhaps under the influence of English law, s.4 of the Wills Act 1963[66] provides that the construction of a will shall not be altered by reason of any change in the testator's domicile after the execution of the will. For a more detailed discussion the reader is referred to the undernoted works.[67]

7–47   Issues such as whether a document has testamentary effect and whether a will has revocable effect involve both construction and essential validity and so both approaches to choice of law may require to be applied to reach an answer.

---

[61] See paras 6–44 to 6–49.

[62] *Mitchell and Baxter v Davies* (1875) 3 R. 208 at 211–212.

[63] In *Mitchell* (1875) 3 R. 208, a will executed in Scotland creating trust fund of a loan secured over heritable property in Scotland to be held by Scottish trustees was found to infer an intention that Scots law apply; and see *Scottish National Orchestra*, 1969 S.L.T. 325 at 328.

[64] *Ommanney v Bingham* (1796) 3 Pat. 448 at 457 (HL); *Smith v Smith* (1891) 18 R. 1036; *McBride's Trustees*, 1952 S.L.T. (Notes) 59; *Anton* (2011), para.24–64 to 24–69; *Meston's Succession Opinions*, No.37, p.106.

[65] *Wills & Succession*, i, 31–32; and see *Studd v Cook* (1880) 8 R. 249; affirmed (1883) 10 R. (HL) 53; *Phipps v Phipps' Trustee*, 1914 1 S.L.T. 239; and *Cripps' Trustees v Cripps*, 1926 S.C. 188.

[66] (c.44).

[67] *Wills & Succession*, i, 30–40; and *Anton* (2011), para.24–67.

CHAPTER 8

THE SCOTTISH LAW COMMISSION'S PROPOSALS
FOR REFORM

The Scottish Law Commission published three consultative memoranda on the **8–01** law of succession in 1986.[1] Following on the comments received in response to the memoranda, the Commission in 1990 published its *Report on Succession*.[2] The *1990 Report on Succession* proposed major changes in the law of intestate succession and a number of reforms in other parts of the law of succession, which, if enacted, would have made valuable improvements in the law. In the 4th edition of this book, in 1993, one of the authors observed:

> "It is not known when the government will find time in the legislative programme for the new Succession Bill, but it is hoped that it will be within the next three or four years and the history of delay before the passing of the 1964 Act referred to in Chapter One will not be repeated with its successor."

By the time of the 5th edition, in 2002, the same sentiment was expressed but "diminishing confidence in view of the lapse of time". Some hope was raised with the Commission revisiting the subject with the publication of a discussion paper in 2007[3] and a further *Report on Succession*[4] in 2009. The delay of 14 years between the Mackintosh Committee Report and the 1964 Act was regarded as scandalous and it is difficult to find any other description for the delay, particularly since the establishment of the Scottish Parliament in 1999 and the 2009 Report. Only at the end of 2014 did the Scottish Government find time for a bill, and that on the "technical aspects" of succession recommended in 2009. Reform of the substantive law of succession continues to be postponed although the *2014 Scottish Government Consultation* does indicate that a further Scottish Government Consultation on reform of the substantive law is in the offing. Perhaps there is light at the end of a long tunnel.

Notwithstanding the subsequent Reports and discussion paper, the detailed **8–02** consideration of the existing law set out in the consultative memoranda remains a valuable resource for finding the existing law. The draft Bill included with

---

[1] *Intestate Succession and Legal Rights* (HMSO, 1986), Scot. Law Com. No.69; *The Making and Revocation of Wills* (HMSO, 1986), Scot. Law Com. No.70; *Some Miscellaneous Topics in the Law of Succession* (HMSO, 1986), Scot. Law Com. No.71.

[2] (HMSO, 1990), Scot. Law Com. No.124.

[3] Scottish Law Commission, *Discussion Paper on Succession* (HMSO, 2007), Scot. Law Com. No.136.

[4] (HMSO, 2009), Scot. Law Com. No.215.

the 1990 Report was the first recommended alternative to ss.1 to 13 of the 1964 Act and it has since been followed by a further draft Bill included in the 2009 Report.

8–03   The aim of this chapter is to set out the broad scheme of the reforms proposed by the Scottish Law Commission in both its 1990 and 2009 Reports on Succession. The focus is on reform of the substantive law of intestacy contained currently in ss.1 to 13 of the 1964 Act, legal rights at common law and s.29 of the 2006 Act. The inadequate proposals in respect of special destinations are also discussed, given their importance. This chapter does not purport to be a detailed analysis of the text of either draft Bill, as the Bill ultimately put before the Scottish Parliament is likely to be in a different form and may well be amended further in the course of its eventual progress through Parliament. However some comment is offered on points where difficulty may arise or where contrary views may be pressed on Parliament.

8–04   The reforms proposed to specific aspects of testate succession and administration of estates are commented on where the existing law is dealt with either in the chapters of this book or in the commentary on the relevant section of the 1964 Act.

Special destinations

8–05   That special destinations can be productive of injustice is something that both authors have seen. The injustice is plain where there is a perfectly valid will postdating the destination which seeks to leave heritage to someone other than the beneficiary (substitute) in the destination. While no surveys of public opinion have been carried out it is reasonable to assume that the public will be unaware that they can make a will in a title deed that might be unalterable and if it is to be altered may require the instruction of a solicitor. That prima facie would appear to be an unacceptable situation. It is made worse by the continuing, but understandable, inability of many within the legal profession to be able to explain to a lay unsophisticated client the circumstances in which and the methods by which a special destination may be evacuated.

8–06   As long ago as 1951 Lord President Cooper observed that it was unfortunate that the device of a special destination originally introduced before 1868 for the purpose of overcoming the prohibition against wills of heritage should still be utilised in circumstances that are more likely to be productive of litigation than any advantage to the parties.[5] In 1996 one of the authors described survivorship destinations as "abominations which ought to be abolished."[6] It has been suggested that even in the absence of abolition conveyancers should not use special destinations[7] but there is little sign that this advice is being heeded. It has been observed that it is tempting to say that those who understand destinations best like them the

---

[5] *Hay's Trustee v Hay's Trustees*, 1951 S.C. 329 at 334.
[6] M.C. Meston, "Survivorship Destinations and Bank Accounts" (1995/6) 1 S.L.P.Q. 315.
[7] D.A. Brand, "Time for special destinations to die?", 2000 S.L.T. (News) 203 at 206.

least.[8] Difficulties caused through their use for inheritance tax planning have been noted.[9] All of this underlines the need for reform.

Until the 1990s destinations were inserted into titles of heritage to husband and **8–07** wife almost as a matter of course. Since then as the Commission observed in its 2009 Report[10] practice has changed in that generally instructions are obtained from clients. The Report claims that the instructions are given only after the effects, advantages and disadvantages have been explained. Given the complexity of destinations and the continuing misunderstanding of what is required to evacuate a destination[11] it has to be seriously doubted whether the average conveyancing solicitor—who is not a succession law specialist—is in a position to or is capable of properly explaining to a lay client what is required to evacuate the survivorship destination that is being contemplated. In a recent article[12] the author of the article, an expert in the area of succession, assumed that the reader was familiar with the difference between a contractual and a non-contractual destination. One has to wonder whether such an assumption is justified for non-succession specialists. In their 2009 Report the Commission appear almost to assume that the clients will understand that their wills will be ineffective in relation to a house with a destination. They conclude:

> "There is therefore a greater expectation now that where the couple agreed to have the succession to their share governed by a survivorship destination it will not be evacuated by either of them in their will."

This appears to assume that couples are advised in general, and wrongly, that survivorship destinations cannot be evacuated by a will even when this is possible.[13] On that basis the Commission recommended no change to the existing law.

What is surprising, and disappointing, is that in recommending no change to the **8–08** existing law the Commission moved away from its own recommendation in 1990[14] that an owner of a *pro indiviso* share of heritage should have power to evacuate a survivorship destination of his share by means of his will regardless of any agreement or undertaking to the contrary.[15] Under the 1990 recommendation it would no longer matter which party provided the money for the purchase, as either would be able to confer a good title to his half either by inter vivos transfer

---

[8] G.L. Gretton, "Death and Debt", 1984 S.L.T. (News) 299.

[9] C. Anderson, "Survivorship Destinations and Section 142 of the Inheritance Tax Act 1984", 2007 S.L.T. (News) 241.

[10] See para.6.64.

[11] See the commentary on s.36(2). In his article noted below John Kerrigan notes that anecdotal evidence exists that parts of the profession have been using "Deeds of Evacuation" which he describes as a problematical practice (albeit in restrospect). One of the authors would corroborate that evidence as to the use of such documents. However, the fact that they were used underlines the continuing lack of understanding of this complex area of law. Clearly the followers of the practice were unaware of *Fleming's Trustee v Fleming*, 2000 S.C. 206.

[12] J. Kerrigan, "Survivorship destinations: the debate continues", 2014 S.L.T. 175.

[13] See commentary at paras S36–10 to S36–16.

[14] *1990 Report on Succession*, recommendation 30(a), para.6.22 and cl.29(3).

[15] However, if there is a contract not to revoke the destination, there could be a claim for damages against the person who has revoked it, based on the contract.

or by will. Even under that recommendation evacuation of the destination by will still required express reference to the destination and a declared intention to revoke it. That was a weakness as it can be easy for a lay person to forget the existence of the destination in the title deed or land certificate. A professional may forget to find out. It is suggested that the requirement in s.30 of the 1964 Act for the will to contain such an express reference should either be omitted altogether or altered to become a requirement to mention the heritable property (rather than the destination) expressly in the will. That would ensure that a clear intention to alter the destination of a share in heritage will not be thwarted by technicality.

8–09   In the 1990 Report all special destinations except the common survivorship destination were to be abolished for deeds executed after the commencement of the new Act.[16] This is not so critical, given their lack of use, although what utility such non-survivorship destinations can have in the modern age other than to cause difficulties to executors[17] is unclear.

8–10   The approach of the Commission to special or survivorship destinations in 2009 was unfortunate and it is hoped that their abolition or at least the reforms proposed in the *1990 Report on Succession* will be pursued by the Scottish Government when they come to consult on reforms to the substantive law of succession. Special destinations were never designed to override wills and their continuing use continues to cause injustice. It is time to move on from 1868.

Intestate succession

8–11   The Commission's proposals would produce a major simplification of the law which is greatly to be welcomed, even if teachers of law will thereby lose a fertile source of knotty examination questions. They will also further increase the preference given to the surviving spouse or civil partner over the deceased's children or other relatives.

8–12   The distinction between heritage and moveables will genuinely disappear, apart from the preservation of the old rules of intestate heritable succession for titles of honour.[18] The estate to be divided on death will be treated as a single cash figure, being the total of the values of all the items of the estate, less the debts. It will not be necessary to keep the values of heritage and moveables separate, and neither will it be necessary to calculate apportionments between them.

8–13   A common feature of both the 1990 and 2009 Reports is the abolition of the present complex method of working through three sets of rules, themselves subdivided, in order to work out the division of an intestate estate. In its place there will be a single Part of the new Act, consisting of four (in the 1990 Report) or ten (in the 2009 Report) sections, which will cover the whole of the rules of intestate succession.

---

[16] cl.29.

[17] Heritage subject to such destinations does not pass automatically to the beneficiary. It vests in the executor under s.18(2) of the 1964 Act.

[18] cl.36(4).

Under both Reports, the surviving spouse will receive a basic slice of the net **8–14** estate up to a certain financial value (the "threshold sum").[19] If there are issue of the intestate, they would be entitled to share only should the estate exceed the threshold sum, when they would be entitled to one half of the surplus over the threshold sum. The remaining half of the surplus would go to the spouse.[20] If there are no issue of the intestate, the surviving spouse would take the whole estate, irrespective of its size, in preference to any other relatives. In the 1990 Report but not in the 2009 Report the spouse would be entitled to require the executor to transfer the matrimonial home as part of his or her share of the estate.[21] The reasoning for the dropping of this proposal was that the size of the threshold sum in the 2009 Report should ensure that the matrimonial home would be covered by the rights of the surviving spouse.

One matter that arises frequently in succession disputes is a conflict between a **8–15** spouse who is a step-parent and the frequently adult issue of the deceased from an earlier marriage who were not brought up by the step-parent. Thus H and W can marry, have two children A and B, then divorce, H re-marries with X and W re-marries with Y. If H dies intestate before X, X will inherit; and if W dies intestate before Y, Y will inherit and the children may end up with nothing at all as the estate from their parents will devolve through the families of X and Y. The Commission cites Professor Norrie's[22] observation that the outcome is not one that can be justified by any principle identified by the Commission other than "the sterile tyranny of simplicity." But it then notes his inability to identify a clear principle for departing from the simple "spouse takes virtually everything rule". It is submitted that the overriding principle of intestacy is that it should represent a "will of the people" while maintaining logic, consistency and avoiding excessive complexity. While no survey has been carried out, it may be surmised that the public may be opposed to children losing out in the scenario set out but also opposed to the second spouse being forced out of the matrimonial home. A clear solution would be to reduce the threshold sum by say a half and to grant a liferent to the spouse upon death over the matrimonial home. To leave a house in liferent to a spouse and the fee to children is a commonly used device to deal with such conflicting interests and there would seem to be no reason why it could not provide a solution to reconcile the competing interests in this case.

If there is no surviving spouse, the proposed order of succession to the whole **8–16** estate would be very like the present rules in s.2 of the 1964 Act for the division of the free estate, except of course that the spouse is not included.[23] However, one significant difference will be that collaterals of the half blood will share equally with collaterals of the full blood instead of being postponed to them as at present.[24]

---

[19] The figure in the 1990 Report was £100,000 representing the value of prior rights at that time (which had fallen behind house prices); that in the 2009 Report was £300,000 representing the value of the prior right in the house at that time. The figure used in the Act, when passed, would be subject to alteration by the Scottish Ministers by statutory instrument.

[20] cl.1(2) of the 1990 Report Bill; cl.2(3) of the 2009 Report Bill.

[21] cl.23 of the 1990 Report Bill.

[22] K. McK. Norrie, "Reforming Succession Law: Intestate Succession" (2008) 12 Edin. L.R. 77.

[23] cl.1(3) of the 1990 Report Bill; cl.6(1) of the 2009 Report Bill.

[24] cl.1(4) of the 1990 Report Bill; cl.6(3) of the 2009 Report Bill.

8–17   Representation will apply on the same basis as in ss.5 and 6 of the 1964 Act[25] and both Bills therefore repeats the error made in 1964 of commencing representation only at the level of the nearest class to the deceased in which a survivor is found. Despite the fact that the Bills state a general principle of representation, this is immediately contradicted and the anomalous variations which arise from the chance of survival of one member of intervening generations will be perpetuated.

8–18   Clause 7 of the 2009 Report Bill is also inconsistent with recommendation 54 in the 2009 Report on representation in legacies to descendants. This inconsistency appears to have been overlooked. In recommendation 54 in the event of a will leaving legacies to children A, B, and C, where A, B and C predecease the testator, and the testator is survived by three children of A, two children of B and one child of C, it is recommended that A's children take A's legacy, B's children B's legacy and C's child C's legacy. If the legacies were one-third shares of the estate A's children would take one-ninth each, B's children would take one-sixth each and A's child would take one-third. This is presumably on the basis that that is what the deceased would have wished. But if there was intestacy and the issue A, B, and C would all have taken a third had they survived, their children would all take one-sixth. This is presumably on the basis that this is what the deceased would have wished. But why would a deceased wish representation *per stirpes* when he makes a will but per capita when he does not? Given that intestacy is in effect a presumed will, there can be no reason why the approach in recommendation 54 should not be applied to intestacy also. It is to be hoped that the Scottish Parliament will recognise and rectify this anomaly and inconsistency.

Legal share and legal rights

8–19   The time-hallowed legal rights of *jus relictae, jus relicti* and legitim, and their various functions, will disappear from the law when the new Act is passed, being expressly abolished. Collation *inter liberos* will disappear along with them. In their place is likely to be[26] a new right, to be called legal share. This will no longer be part of the law of intestate succession[27] and the old authorities on legal rights will no longer be relevant. The *1990 and 2009 Reports on Succession* have different proposals.

8–20   Under the proposals in the 1990 Report the new legal share was to be solely a protection against disinheritance requiring to be claimed by the surviving spouse or issue in general terms within a period of two years from the death of the deceased.[28] This was a clear departure from legal rights which vest on death automatically. However, no consideration was given to executor's duty to provide information to the claimant in sufficient time to allow an informed choice to be made.

---

[25] cll.2 and 3 of the 1990 Report Bill; cll.5 and 7 of the 2009 Report Bill.
[26] The *2009 Report on Succession* also contemplates an option abolishing absolute protection of a deceased's descendants altogether.
[27] Although on the 1990 Report its calculation will depend on the rules of intestate succession.
[28] cl.6 of the 1990 Report Bill.

The protection was to be primarily for the surviving spouse, although the **8–21** Commission did, after some hesitation, recommend that issue should also have protection. With regard to the spouse the Commission took the view that the rationale behind the legal share for a spouse was to recognise his or her "matrimonial property claims". The legal share for the surviving spouse was therefore fixed at a level to ensure a basic protection for such claims. This was to be fixed at 30 per cent of the first £200,000 plus 10 per cent of the excess over £200,000 (this basic level being very roughly the value of prior right to the house at the time of the 1990 Report).

With regard to protection for the issue, the Commission took the view that in the **8–22** absence of a surviving spouse the issue should have the same protection as the spouse. No real reason was given for this but it did have the merit of simplicity. If both spouse and surviving issue survived the deceased, the Commission took the view that in order to avoid excessive interference with testamentary freedom, the issue should receive half of the spouse's entitlement, namely 15 per cent of the first £200,000 and 5 per cent of the excess.[29] In addition the legal share of the issue was to be postponed to the legal share of the spouse in respect of the first £100,000 of the estate.[30] This meant that the spouse would always receive the first £100,000 of the estate and the *Kerr, Petitioner*[31] problem of intestacy being a better means of avoiding the legal rights of issue than testacy would have ceased to exist. The £100,000 appeared to be linked to the guaranteed share of the spouse on intestacy.

The Commission's solution in 1990 to the question of election between legal **8–23** share and testamentary provision was to make it clear that a claim of legal share would involve forfeiture of all other rights of succession in the deceased's estate, the definition of which included property subject to special destinations.[32] In addition the claimant would be deemed to have predeceased the deceased and there were consequential provisions which were to the effect that by virtue of the deemed predecease no estate would vest in the legal share claimant's issue or in any other person who would stand to gain from the claimant.

In addition the Commission suggested a valuable provision in respect of legal **8–24** share which fell to be paid out of agricultural property included in the estate. The executor was to have a discretion to pay the amount of claim due from the agricultural property (with interest only from the date an instalment became due) over a period of 10 years from the date of death in annual instalments, subject to the whole balance becoming due upon a sale of any part of the agricultural property.[33] This is akin to many a provision in partnership deeds where the surviving partners are entitled to opt to pay out to an executor the capital share of a deceased partner over a number of years. Typically the period is five years so it could be said that the Commission was being generous to owners of agricultural property.

By the *2009 Report on Succession*, the views of the Commission had changed. **8–25** The Commission had reverted to the position under legal rights at common law,

---

[29] cl.7 of the 1990 Report Bill.
[30] cl.5(3) of the 1990 Report Bill.
[31] See paras S9–18 to S9–22.
[32] cl.8 of the 1990 Report Bill.
[33] cl.11 of the 1990 Report Bill.

namely that the new legal shares would vest in the beneficiary on death[34] with no claim being required.

8–26   With regard to a surviving spouse, the Commission decided that the 1990 recommendations were too complex and recommended a fixed share of 25 per cent of what the spouse or civil partner would have inherited on intestacy. No real justification is apparent for the figure of 25 per cent other than that it stands in contrast to the 50 per cent used in German law but is lower on account of a proposal for greater rights for the spouse on intestacy than in Germany. That said there was no material opposition to the figure in the course of the consultation. This would mean that, on the basis that the threshold sum for her reserved portion on intestacy was at the level of the existing prior right to the house, if spouse and issue survived her legal share would be £118,250 plus a 12.5 per cent of the excess over £473,000. If she survived without issue of the deceased, she would receive 25 per cent of the whole net estate.

8–27   With regard to protection for the issue, the Commission noted that there remained strong public support for the retention of an equivalent to legitim, especially in the absence of a surviving spouse. There also appeared to be evidence from executry practitioners that most parents do not view the inability to disinherit their children completely as unreasonable. This reaction was opposed to the Commission's view in their Discussion Paper[35] that a fixed legal share for issue should be abolished and replaced by a right for dependant children to apply from the estate where no beneficiary owed them an obligation of aliment. Nevertheless despite the lack of any indication of the sources of support for the abolition of protection for children (other than from part of the Commission and one law lecturer), the Commission noted that respondents were "deeply divided" and that in the light of this and the strength of both arguments the Commission could not recommend one option above the other. They therefore recommended two schemes.

8–28   In the first scheme, on the basis that fixed legal share for issue was to be maintained, the Commission recommended the issue (as a class) should have the fixed share of 25 per cent of what they would have inherited on intestacy. This would provide substantial protection in the absence of a surviving spouse but much less so if a surviving spouse did survive, thus reflecting general public opinion. This is because the legal share of issue on intestacy with a surviving spouse recommended by the Commission would not begin until the threshold limit was reached, which was to be at a minimum of the value of the prior right to the house (currently at £473,000). Thus with a surviving spouse the issue would be entitled to 12.5 per cent of the excess over £473,000. It is fair to say that in the majority of estates where a spouse survived the issue would have no legal share at all.

8–29   It is questionable whether such an outcome would reflect the strong support that appears to exist for issue to have protection against disinheritance. This is particularly acute when one considers the frequently encountered and difficult situation of a spouse who is a step-mother of the children, quite possibly having married the deceased later in life. Currently legal rights offer some protection to

---

[34]   cll.11, 12 and 15 of the 2009 Report Bill.
[35]   Scottish Law Commission, *Discussion Paper on Succession* (HMSO, 2007), Scot. Law Com. No.136.

the children. The de facto removal of all protection of issue against disinheritance where a step-parent has survived the deceased, is something which the Commission do not appear to have considered. It is to be noted that the will does not need to be in favour of the step-parent for the protection to disappear. It is hoped that this matter will be considered by the Scottish Government in their forthcoming consultation and by the Scottish Parliament when it comes to legislate.

Another area where the issue could be prejudiced is through the use of a special **8–30** destination in the title to heritable property or a statutory nomination.[36] This is clearly a testamentary act (albeit not involving a will) and indeed until 1868 it was the only possible testamentary act in respect of heritage. If as seems appropriate legal share is to extend to heritable property there is no reason in principle why property should be excluded merely because it has been transferred to a beneficiary by means of a destination in the title rather than a legacy in the will. The testamentary effect of a special destination has been recognised, properly, by the Commission in the exclusion of property transferred by a special destination from the calculation of the threshold sum due to the surviving spouse on intestacy. It should be recognised also in relation to legal share. In cl.12 of the 2009 Report Bill legal share is conditional on the deceased leaving a will. It should be made conditional on the deceased leaving a will or heritable property with an unevacuated special destination. This would prevent the destinations being a means of avoidance of legal share. The legal share would then become payable from the heritable property subject to the destination under cl.13(1)(d) as it would be from a special legacy.

The 2009 Report does not deal satisfactorily with the question of election **8–31** between legal share and testamentary (or other) provision of the deceased. In particular it does not include a provision equivalent to s.13 of the 1964 Act which implied a condition in every legacy in favour of a spouse or issue that the legacy was in full and final satisfaction of any legal rights in the estate.[37] The provision in cl.13(2) of the 2009 Report Bill is flawed in suggesting that the spouse or issue "elect" to claim legal share when in fact, as with current legal rights, legal share is to vest automatically upon death. It is also flawed in continuing to allow for the possibility of a non-legal rights-holding contingent beneficiary (conditional institute) obtaining a legacy derived from a legacy rejected by the legal rights holder.[38]

Under the current law election of a testamentary provision is a means of extin- **8–32** guishing or satisfying vested legal rights.[39] This is supported by s.13 of the 1964 Act and s.131(4) of the Civil Partnership Act 2004.[40] There is no reason why cl.13(2) cannot be re-drafted to provide for the election of a testamentary provision extinguishing legal share and for the removal of the above flaws. It is hoped that if the otherwise clear scheme for legal share in the 2009 Report is adopted, a suitable cl.13(2) can be adopted perhaps along the following lines, using "B" as the legal share holder:

---

[36] See commentary on s.36(2).
[37] See commentary on s.13 and Ch.5 on legal rights.
[38] See *1990 Report on Succession*, para.3.46; recommendation 14(c) and cl.8.
[39] *Wills & Succession*, i, 135–136, 139.
[40] (c.33).

"Unless, after the death of the deceased, B renounces his entitlement to a legal share, then, in relation to any right of succession in the estate of the deceased other than legal share,

(a) B,
(b) B's issue and
(c) any legatee whose legacy is conditional on B failing to survive the deceased,

are deemed not to have survived the deceased, except in so far as provision to the contrary is made in any will of the deceased."

8–33 The legislation should enable renunciation of legal share either expressly or by implication with implied renunciation including the election to accept a legacy under a will or property under a special destination. Equally there should be provision that B will be deemed to have renounced his or her legal share by implication only after having been given a copy of the will, and the confirmation, having been advised to obtain independent legal advice and having been given a reasonable time to renounce legacies or any special destination.[41]

8–34 In its 2009 Report the Commission sought to address the issue, raised in the 1990 Report, that requiring legal share to be settled out of heritable property could involve the fracturing of agricultural land with undesirable social and economic consequences.[42] This is clearly a laudable aim but the mechanism runs contrary to an executor's duty to be impartial between beneficiaries with conflicting interests. The Report recommends that an executor be given power to apply to the court for an order deferring payment or providing for payment by instalments. An executor acts for all beneficiaries and is not there to act in favour of one beneficiary when their entitlement is challenged by another beneficiary. The standard procedure where there is conflict between beneficiaries is for the executor to invite either beneficiary to raise an action of declarator, failing which to raise an action of multiplepoinding in which parties put in competing claims. The threat of a multiplepoinding is usually effective to force settlement or the raising of an action of declarator or reduction. There is also in some cases a possibility of a petition to the Court of Session for directions or a special case to the Court of Session where the facts are agreed. In this instance, there should be a provision for any legatee or institute in a destination to apply to the court for a time to pay direction in respect of the legal share due from legacy or destination[43] allowing deferment or payment by instalments.

8–35 However, one of the disadvantages of the 2009 proposals as opposed to those of 1990 is the total lack of guidance to the court on the criteria that are to apply in its decision to defer payment or to require instalments. This would be likely to encourage rather than discourage litigation with its consequent cost and risks especially to economically weaker parties, not to mention the consequent delay in winding up the estate. It is suggested that the proposal in the 1990 Report is

---

[41] See paras 5–51 to 5–57 (legal rights).
[42] *2009 Report on Succession*, recommendations 18 and 20(3).
[43] The Debtors (Scotland) Act 1987 (c.18) (as amended) s.1 provides a model.

preferable, with a maximum time limit for payment and including the restriction to agricultural property. However, the court rather than the executor should make the decision in the event of dispute over deferment or the number of instalments.

In its alternative "scheme" for issue, the Commission proposed to abolish guaran- **8–36** teed protection for issue from disinheritance entirely. This scheme appears to have attracted little support but those supporting it appear to have been trenchantly in favour. This alternative proposal is not so much a scheme for inheritance as a scheme for the maintenance of aliment or financial support from certain legacies for a limited period of time. Under this restricted alimentary scheme, children who would be entitled to aliment from the deceased would be entitled to apply to the court within one year of the death for the award of a capital payment (in lump sum or instalments). The capital payment would be met from any part of the estate which was inherited (whether in liferent or fee) by a person not obliged to aliment the child.[44] A legacy to a parent of the child or person who has accepted the child into the family[45] would not be subjected to the scheme at all. Despite the nature of the scheme as one of aliment rather than inheritance there is the somewhat drastic provision that a child claiming under the scheme, presumably without knowledge as to what his award from the court is to be, is deemed to reject any legacy under the will.[46]

The entitlement to apply to the court would be for children under the age of **8–37** 18 years or 18 years to under 25 years who at the time of the death "are" "reasonably and appropriately undergoing instruction at an educational establishment or training for employment or for trade profession or vocation.[47] The definition is vague particularly in relation to training.[48] It is also dependent on whether the instruction or training happened to have begun at the death. An 18-year-old young person about to begin a course or training would be excluded. The capital payment due from the legacies covered would be such as it was "reasonable" to pay out in respect of the period from the death until the time when the deceased's obligation to aliment would have ceased.

It may be doubted whether this alimentary scheme would in practice give rise **8–38** to many awards or extra-judicial settlements by legatees in favour of children. No provision for intimation by the executor to the issue of the right to apply is provided for. The uncertain level of the award, including the provision for the court to have regard to "any" conduct of the child or of another person would provide significant deterrence for the making of claims, particularly given the costs of litigation. For example it would appear that in the assessment of a student child's needs and resources for the calculation of an aliment payment the receipt of payments from a student loan can be taken into account but the repayments not.[49] That seems unfair in a succession context. It would seem to underline the lack of protection for children given by an alimentary approach to matters of succession.

---

[44] cl.18 of the 2009 Report Bill. Clause 18 does not make it clear at what point the legatee must not be alimenting the child for the entitlement to the capital sum to arise.
[45] Except where the child has been "boarded out" by a public authority or voluntary organisation.
[46] cl.20 of the 2009 Report Bill.
[47] cl.18 of the 2009 Report Bill applying Family Law (Scotland) Act 1985 (c.37) s.1(1)(c), (d) and (5).
[48] See Elaine E. Sutherland, "Child and Family Law" in *Stair Memorial Encyclopedia*, Reissue (Edinburgh: Lexis Nexis UK and the Law Society of Scotland, 2004), para.213.
[49] *Park v Park*, 2000 S.L.T (Sh. Ct) 65; and *Watson v McLay* [2002] Fam. L.R. 20.

PART II

SUCCESSION (SCOTLAND) ACT 1964

(c.41)

An Act to assimilate and amend the law of Scotland with respect to the succession to the heritable and moveable property of deceased persons; to amend the law in relation to the legal and other prior rights exigible out of such property, to the administration of deceased persons' estates and other property passing on death, to the capacity of minors to test, and to the presumption of survivorship; to provide for certain testamentary dispositions to be probative; to provide for adopted persons to be treated for certain purposes as children of their adopters; to make new provision as to the financial rights and obligations of the parties on the dissolution of a marriage; and for purposes connected with the matters aforesaid

[June 10, 1964]

INTRODUCTION

When it was passed in 1964 the Succession (Scotland) Act ("the Act") was **S–01** principally a long overdue reform of much of the law of intestate succession in Scotland. However, it also included a number of other reforms to aspects of testate succession and administration of estates. From September 10, 1964 the radically improved position, especially the position of surviving spouses, has been generally accepted, and there is now no trace whatsoever of the case (still being advanced in 1964) for the eldest son to inherit all the heritable (immoveable) property. However, the substantive law of intestacy introduced by the Act is complex and further reform has been necessary for some time. The Scottish Law Commission published its *Report on Succession* in 1990 (Scot. Law Com. No.124); and more recently has followed this up with its *Report on Succession* published in 2009 (Scot. Law Com. No.215).

The Act is not a complete code of the Scots law of succession. Rather it sought **S–02** to amend the common and statutory law elements of the Scots law of succession which existed up to 1964 in various ways. The different aspects of the law being amended are reflected in the division of the Act into a number of Parts. Parts I (ss.1 to 7) and II (ss.8 to 13) deal with alterations to the substantive law of intestate succession. Part III (ss.14 to 22) deals with the law relating to the administration and winding-up of the estates of deceased persons. Part IV (ss.23 and 24) deals with succession by adopted persons. Part V (which has now been repealed) dealt

111

with financial provisions on divorce; and Part VI (ss.29 to 38) dealt with various piecemeal reforms taking in both the substantive law and the administration of estates. Within Part VI is s.36 which provides definitions for various expressions used throughout the Act and which must be looked at in order to understand the meaning of any particular provision, regardless of the Part in which it is found.

S–03   The Act came into force on September 10, 1964 to regulate the succession to the estates of persons dying after midnight on the night of September 9, 1964.[1]

S–04   The increased but limited succession rights of illegitimate children created by Part I of the Law Reform (Miscellaneous Provisions) Scotland) Act 1968[2] came into force in respect of the estates of persons dying on or after November 25, 1968, as did the provisions in Part II of the same Act bringing crofting tenancies within the scope of the Act. Virtual abolition of the status of illegitimacy and the creation of equality in succession for children formerly classed as illegitimate has applied in respect of deaths on or after December 8, 1986[3] and full abolition has applied in respect of wills made on or after May 4, 2006.[4]

S–05   The financial limits of the prior rights of a surviving spouse and, since December 5, 2005 of a civil partner, have been increased periodically. The Succession (Scotland) Act 1973[5] increased these limits and also gave the Secretary of State (now the Scottish Ministers) power to effect further increases by statutory instrument. Details are given in the commentary on s.8.

PARLIAMENTARY DEBATES

Scottish Grand Committee, November 26, 1963; Scottish Standing Committee, December 12, 17 and 19, 1963, January 16, 21, 23, 28 and 30, 1964; HL Vol.256, cols 551, 582, 1043 and 1062; Vol.257, col.352; HC Vol.689, col.1211; Vol.695, col.125.

Part I

Intestate Succession

Assimilation of heritage to moveables for purpose of devolution on intestacy
1.—(1) The whole of the intestate estate of any person dying after the commencement of this Act (so far as it is estate the succession to which falls to be regulated by the law of Scotland) shall devolve, without distinction as between heritable and moveable property, in accordance with—

(a) the provisions of this Part of this Act, and
(b) any enactment or rule of law in force immediately before the commencement of this Act which is not inconsistent with those provisions and which, apart from this section, would apply to that person's moveable intestate estate, if any;

---

[1] Succession (Scotland) Act 1964 s.38(3).
[2] (c.70).
[3] Law Reform (Parent and Child) (Scotland) Act 1986 (c.9).
[4] See para.6–98.
[5] (c.25).

and, subject to section 37 of this Act, any enactment or rule of law in force immediately before the commencement of this Act with respect to the succession to intestate estates shall, in so far as it is inconsistent with the provisions of this Part of this Act, cease to have effect.

[1](2) Nothing in this Part of this Act shall affect legal rights or the prior rights of a surviving spouse or civil partner; and accordingly any reference in this Part of this Act to an intestate estate shall be construed as a reference to so much of the net intestate estate as remains after the satisfaction of those rights, or the proportion thereof properly attributable to the intestate estate.

NOTE

1. As amended by the Civil Partnership Act 2004 (c.33) Sch.28(1) para.1 (effective December 5, 2005).

DEFINITIONS

"estate": s.36(2).
"intestate estate": ss.1(2) and 36(1) and (2). See also s.37(1)(a) and (b).
"legal rights": s.36(1).
"prior rights": s.36(1) and ss.8 and 9.

COMMENTARY

Section 1 deals only with the "intestate estate" which, for the purposes of **S1–01** Part I of the Act, is the free estate remaining after the prior rights of any surviving spouse and the legal rights of spouse and descendants have been satisfied. In relation to that free estate (though not in respect of prior and legal rights) s.1 abolishes the distinction between heritage and moveables. The whole free estate is a single fund for division among those entitled to succeed. The privileged position of the heir-at-law therefore vanished from the law, except in respect of the items (principally titles and coats of arms) excepted from the operation of the Act by s.37.

Assimilation of heritage and moveables

Part of the policy of the Act was to assimilate heritage and moveables for the **S1–02** purposes of succession, and in so far as this was achieved, it was done by s.1. However, the distinction between heritage and moveables was by no means abolished. Although s.10(1) provides that terce and courtesy are no longer exigible from the deceased's heritable estate, s.1(2), as read with the definition of "legal rights" in s.36(1), preserves the common law rule that *jus relicti, jus relictae* and legitim are exigible out of the deceased's moveable estate. Since 1964 the definition of "legal rights" has been expanded to include rights under s.131 of the Civil Partnership Act 2004.

S1–03 Equally the law relating to the incidence of liabilities between heritage and moveables remains unimpaired.[6] The result is that the assimilation of heritage and moveables affects only the free estate after satisfaction of the prior rights of a surviving spouse and of the legal rights of a surviving spouse and descendants. If the free estate consists of heritage to the value of £30,000 and moveables to the value of £50,000 there is simply a fund of £80,000 to be divided up according to the provisions of Part I of the Act.

S1–04 The whole free estate is divided on the principles set out in Part I of the Act (ss.1 to 7) together with such of the previous law of intestate *moveable* succession as is "not inconsistent with" the Act. Among other changes consequential on the partial assimilation of heritage and moveables was the abolition of the doctrine of collation *inter haeredes*. For some time after the Act collation remained relevant in cases where the heir at law succeeded to the tenancy of a croft and had to collate the value of that tenancy in order to share in the moveable estate.[7] However, crofting tenancies, formerly excluded from the operation of the Act, were brought within its scope by Part II of the 1968 Act. Thus the heir at law no longer has, as such, any right of succession to crofts, and collation disappeared in that situation also.

Rights of succession to intestate estate

2.—(1) Subject to the following provisions of this Part of this Act—

(a) **where an intestate is survived by children, they shall have right to the whole of the intestate estate;**

(b) **where an intestate is survived by either of, or both, his parents and is also survived by brothers or sisters, but is not survived by any prior relative, the surviving parent or parents shall have right to one half of the intestate estate and the surviving brothers and sisters to the other half thereof;**

(c) **where an intestate is survived by brothers or sisters, but is not survived by any prior relative, the surviving brothers and sisters shall have right to the whole of the intestate estate;**

(d) **where an intestate is survived by either of, or both, his parents, but is not survived by any prior relative, the surviving parent or parents shall have right to the whole of the intestate estate;**

[1](e) **where an intestate is survived by a husband, wife or civil partner, but is not survived by any prior relative, the surviving spouse or civil partner shall have right to the whole of the intestate estate;**

(f) **where an intestate is survived by uncles or aunts (being brothers or sisters of either parent of the intestate), but is not survived by any prior relative, the surviving uncles and aunts shall have right to the whole of the intestate estate;**

(g) **where an intestate is survived by a grandparent or grandparents (being a parent or parents of either parent of the intestate), but is not survived**

---

[6] s.14(3); and see Ch.3.
[7] M. C. Meston, "Collation of Crofting Tenancies", 1965 S.L.T. (News) 209.

by any prior relative, the surviving grandparent or grandparents shall have right to the whole of the intestate estate;

(h) where an intestate is survived by brothers or sisters of any of his grandparents (being a parent or parents of either parent of the intestate), but is not survived by any prior relative, those surviving brothers and sisters shall have right to the whole of the intestate estate;

(i) where an intestate is not survived by any prior relative, the ancestors of the intestate (being remoter than grandparents) generation by generation successively, without distinction between the paternal and maternal lines, shall have right to the whole of the intestate estate; so however that, failing ancestors of any generation, the brothers and sisters of any of those ancestors shall have right thereto before ancestors of the next more remote generation.

(2) References in the foregoing subsection to brothers or sisters include respectively brothers and sisters of the half blood as well as of the whole blood; and in the said subsection "prior relative", in relation to any class of person mentioned in any paragraph of that subsection, means a person of any other class who, if he had survived the intestate, would have had right to the intestate estate or any of it by virtue of an earlier paragraph of that subsection or by virtue of any such paragraph and section 5 of this Act.

NOTE

1. As amended by the Civil Partnership Act 2004 (c.33) Sch.28(1) para.2(a), (b) (effective December 5, 2005).

DEFINITIONS

"children": include adopted children (ss.23 and 24) and illegitimate children (Law Reform (Parent and Child) (Scotland) Act 1986).
"brothers or sisters": ss.2(2) and 3.
"estate": s.36(2).
"intestate estate": ss.36(1), (2) and 1(2). See also s.37(1)(a) and (b) and note to s.1.
"prior relative": s.2(2).

COMMENTARY

General

Section 2 provides the new statutory order of succession to the free estate **S2–01** whether heritable or moveable. The free estate is the residue of intestate estate (apart from the excepted items specified in s.37 of the Act and heritable property subject to an unevacuated special destination or subject to a power of appointment as provided for in s.36(2)) which remains after any prior rights or legal rights have been deducted[8] and after any payment claimed by and due to any cohabitee of the intestate in terms of s.29 of the Family Law (Scotland) Act 2006.[9] It is unfortunate to say the least that the drafters of the 2006 Act made no attempt to make consequential amendments to the 1964 Act as the uninformed reader of the Act is left blissfully unaware of the existence of potential claims by cohabitees.

S2–02   In other words, if the intestate died survived by neither spouse nor civil partner, nor cohabitee nor issue, these rules apply to the whole estate. It is unclear why this section precedes those dealing with prior and legal rights but it was perhaps intended to highlight at the outset the abolition of the status of the heir at law to heritable property and the practical effect of the assimilation of heritable and moveable property as set out in s.1.

S2–03   The general pattern of the order of succession is similar to the previous law of intestate moveable succession, with the succession opening first to descendants, then to collaterals and then to ascendants, with the qualification that when parents and collaterals both survive, each category takes one-half of the estate. It may still be relevant to refer to the old pre-Act law to fill lacunae in the Act and, accordingly, s.1(1)(b) requires the free intestate estate (heritable and moveable) to be subject to the previous law of intestate moveable succession[10] so far as "not inconsistent with" the particular provisions of Part I of the Act. However, as the existence of a right to succeed is now purely statutory, the common law concept of the "next-of-kin" is no longer relevant in the process of finding the persons entitled to succeed, although it is still relevant in competitions for appointment as executor-dative.

S2–04   The heir or heirs to the free estate are established from the order of the paragraphs of s.2(1) as read with s.5 which allows for representation.[11] The heir under an earlier paragraph takes in preference to those claiming under a later paragraph by virtue of the use of the term "prior relative" as defined in s.2(2). Parents and brothers and sisters have rights under s.2(1)(b) when both categories survive, while brothers and sisters have rights under s.2(1)(c) and parents under s.2 (1)(d). To meet the difficulty in claims under s.2(1)(c) or (d) that parents and brothers and sisters would be their own "prior relatives" by virtue of their rights under s.2(1)(b), the definition in s.2(2) mentions "a person of any *other* class" who would have been entitled under an earlier paragraph.

S2–05   If there is more than one heir bearing the same degree of relationship to the deceased, the means of division of the intestate estate is provided for in s.6.[12]

(1) Descendants

S2–06   The category of descendants must first be considered in determining the order of succession to the free estate, as their right is preferable to that of collaterals, spouse or ascendants. The first provision, contained in s.2(1)(a), is "where an

---

[8] s.1(2).
[9] (asp 2). See the commentary on s.29 of the 2006 Act in Part III of this book.
[10] See Ch.1.
[11] See the commentary on s.5.
[12] See the commentary on s.6.

intestate is survived by children, they shall have right to the whole of the intestate estate". It is to be noticed that the "intestate estate" referred to is defined for the purposes of this Part of the Act by s.1(2). Briefly, it means the free estate after satisfaction of prior rights and legal rights. However, although children take the whole estate left after the spouse's *jus relictae vel relicti* and it is tempting simply to split everything without calculating the children's legitim, it must be remembered that the division of the legitim fund may be unequal if advances have been made to any of the children.[13]

Although s.2(1)(a) refers to "children," it does in fact regulate the whole succes- **S2–07** sion of descendants of the intestate when read in conjunction with the scheme of representation contained in s.5(1) and that of distribution contained in s.6.

Adopted children are now treated as lawful children of the adopter or adopters. **S2–08** The position of adopted children was the final cause of the appointment of the Mackintosh Committee on the Law of Succession, and the provisions of Part IV (ss.23 and 24) of the Act remedy a situation which was a major defect in the previous law of succession. For the purpose of succession to the free estate by descendants on intestacy, the main provisions are contained in s.23(1). So far as here relevant, this provides that

> "[f]or all purposes relating to—
>   (a) the succession to a deceased person (whether testate or intestate), ...
> an adopted person shall be treated as the child of the adopter and not as the child of any other person."

A problem might have arisen over the question of what was encompassed by **S2–09** "succession" and therefore for the purposes of s.23(1) it is provided that "succession to a deceased person" is to be construed as including the distribution of any property in consequence of his death and any claim to prior rights or legal rights out of his estate. A natural parent of the adopted child being "any other person" within the meaning of s.23(1), the child's rights of succession in the estates of its natural parents are cut off and replaced by rights in the estates of the adopting parents.

In one situation, however, cutting off the adopted person's rights in the estates **S2–10** of its natural parents had the unfortunate result that the child had no rights in any estate. If the adopting parents died before the Act came into force on September 10, 1964, and the natural parents then died after the commencement of the Act, the child had no rights in the estate of any parent. To remedy this as far as possible, the Law Reform (Miscellaneous Provisions) (Scotland) Act 1966[14] provided that if the adopting parent died before the commencement of the Act and the natural parent died on or after August 3, 1966, the child is to be treated for the purposes of succession to the estate of that natural parent as the child of the natural parent. However, this is only for the purposes of succession to the natural parent. For all other purposes of succession, the adopted child still falls to be regarded as the

---

[13] See Ch.4.
[14] (c.19) s.5.

child of the adopter. If the child was adopted by two spouses jointly, both the adopting parents must have died prior to September 10, 1964, to bring this transitional provision into effect.[15]

S2–11 *Illegitimate children* were the subject of very limited provisions in the Act itself, but there were radical alterations by the 1968 Act[16] and by the Law Reform (Parent and Child) (Scotland) Act 1986.[17]

S2–12 The Legitimation (Scotland) Act 1968[18] has now been repealed[19] except for the purposes of the determination of any question as to the succession to or devolution of any title, honour or dignity.[20] The effect of the Legitimation Act is that an illegitimate child is always legitimated by the subsequent marriage of his/her parents instead of only if the parents were free to marry at the time of his/her conception as existed under the older common law. Since parents whose marriage did not legitimate their child sometimes adopted the child, the Act made provision for revocation of such adoption orders on the view that legitimation removed the need for them. However, s.6(2) of the 1968 Act (as amended) preserves succession rights in intestacies which occurred before the revocation.

S2–13 The rights of succession of illegitimate children over the duration of the Act can be seen over the following periods:

September 10, 1964 to November 24, 1968. The effect of the original s.4 of the Act — applicable in respect of deaths occurring on or after September 10, 1964, up to and including November 24, 1968 — was to give the illegitimate child a right of succession to the mother's free estate when the mother died intestate and without lawful issue. The child had no right to legitim and was postponed to the prior rights and legal rights (calculated on the basis that the mother was not survived by issue) of the mother's husband. The child had no rights of succession at all if the mother was survived by lawful issue, and could never have rights in the father's intestate estate.

November 25, 1968 to December 7, 1986. The reforms contained in the 1968 Act applied to the estate of any person dying on or after November 25, 1968, up to and including December 7, 1986. The method used was to substitute a new s.4 in the Act 1964.[21] This conferred on the illegitimate child the right to share in the intestate free estate of both parents on a basis of equality with legitimate children. The right to legitim was separately conferred by a new s.10A of the Act as inserted by s.2 of the 1968 Act. The result was that legitimate and illegitimate children were now in a position of formal equality so far as succession to the estates of the parents was concerned. A decree of affiliation and aliment established the paternity of the father for succession purposes unless the contrary was proved.[22]

---

[15] Note, however, that true adoption did not exist in Scotland before 1930 and that informal "adoptions" which took place before that had no effect on the status of the child.

[16] (c.70).

[17] (c.9).

[18] (c.22).

[19] Family Law (Scotland) Act 2006 (asp 2).

[20] The Family Law (Scotland) Act 2006 (Commencement, Transitional Provisions and Savings) Order 2006 (SSI 2006/212) art.11.

[21] 1968 Act (c.70) s.1.

[22] 1968 Act s.11.

The one substantial difference which remained between the succession rights of legitimate and illegitimate children was that the illegitimate child could not represent the predeceasing parent in a succession opening after the parent's death. This was because the scheme of representation established by s.5(1) then permitted "issue" to represent their parents but "issue" was defined as lawful issue, thereby excluding illegitimate children. This was reinforced by the statement in s.4(4) that, except for the specific provisions of s.4 conferring on the child rights in the estates of the parents and the representation provisions of s.5, nothing in Part I of the Act was to be construed as importing any rule of succession through illegitimate relationship. Thus the rights of the illegitimate child in this period were confined to the estates of the persons responsible for his/her birth. The result was that an anomaly whereby an illegitimate grandchild could not represent its predeceasing parent (whether that parent was itself legitimate or illegitimate) in the division of a grandparent's estate, but that a legitimate grandchild could represent the illegitimate parent in the grandparent's estate.

However, if the deceased whose estate was being distributed was more remote **S2–14** than a lineal grandparent, the illegitimate person would not have been entitled to a share if they had survived, so that there could be no representation in such an estate even by a legitimate child.

The effect of the valuable improvements in the lot of the illegitimate child was **S2–15** to implement the Report of the Russell Committee on the *Law of Succession in Relation to Illegitimate Persons*[23] in the light of the views expressed by the Scottish Law Commission in its Memorandum *Reform of the Law Relating to legitimation per subsequens matrimonium*.[24]

December 8, 1986 to May 3, 2006. The Law Reform (Parent and Child) **S2–16** (Scotland) Act 1986[25] enacted a general principle of the legal equality of children by the general statement that:

> "The fact that a person's parents are not or have not been married to one another shall be left out of account in establishing the legal relationship between the person and any other person; and accordingly any such relationship shall have effect as if the parents were or had been married to one another."

In its application to the 1964 Act,[26] this meant that whether or not the parents were married to each other a child will have exactly the same rights of succession to the biological parents and also through them by representation.

May 4, 2006, onwards. In the present law the status of illegitimacy has been virtually abolished.[27] It survives only in respect of succession to titles, honours or dignities.

---

[23] (HMSO, 1966), Cmnd.3051.
[24] (HMSO, 1967), Cmnd.3223.
[25] s.1(1) in force until May 3, 2006.
[26] By virtue of s.36(5).
[27] 1986 Act s.1(1), substituted by s.21 of the 2006 Act and in force from May 4, 2006.

(2) Collaterals (siblings) and nephews and nieces

S2–17   If the category of descendants has been exhausted without finding an heir to the free estate, the category of collaterals, namely siblings, of the deceased is next in the line of succession. Subject to the qualification in s.2(1)(b) of the Act giving the surviving parent or parents of the intestate a right to one-half of the free estate when the deceased is survived both by collaterals and by a parent or parents, the category of collaterals of the deceased must be exhausted before ancestors or a surviving spouse can succeed to the free estate.

S2–18   Assume for the moment that the intestate left no surviving issue, was survived by collaterals, and was predeceased by both parents, so that the right of the collaterals is to the whole of the free intestate estate. The statutory basis for their right to succeed is s.2(1)(c) of the 1964 Act, replacing the previous common law principle that collaterals succeeded next after descendants. Although this paragraph mentions only "brothers or sisters" of the deceased, it must be read along with s.5 (representation by issue) and s.6 (distribution). It is not limited to the case where immediate brothers and sisters of the deceased have survived him.

S2–19   *Collaterals of the half blood.* Giving effect to the recommendations of the Mackintosh Committee, s.2(2) and s.3 of the Act deal with the rights of collaterals of the half blood. Where collaterals have rights of succession, collaterals of the whole blood, having the same mother and the same father as the intestate, are preferred to collaterals of the half blood, sharing only one parent with the intestate. This restates the pre-existing law on the subject, and has the effect that if the intestate is survived by any collaterals of the whole blood, or their descendants by representation,[28] collaterals of the half blood and those claiming through them have no rights of succession at all. Those related by the whole blood take the whole amount of the estate falling to collaterals. Take the following example:

[Father's 1st wife]   =   [Father]   =   [Mother]   =   [Mother's 1st husband]

C   [A]   X   B   D

S2–20   X has died intestate, survived by a full brother, B, and by two half brothers, C and D. In this situation B, the sole surviving collateral of the full blood takes the whole free intestate estate, which, if X left no surviving spouse, is the whole net estate after payment of debts and expenses. C and D, collaterals of the half blood consanguinean and uterine respectively, take no share.

S2–21   If, however, there are no collaterals of the full blood, so that the right of any collaterals of the half blood emerges, s.3 of the 1964 Act made a radical change from the pre-existing law. Collaterals of the half blood now rank "without distinction as between those related to the intestate . . . through their father and those so related through their mother". The words "related through their father" and "related through their mother" were substituted for "consanguinean" and "uterine"

---

[28] 1986 Act s.3 is expressly made subject to the representation provisions of s.5.

in the course of the progress of the Bill through Parliament in the interests of comprehensibility by the layman, but one may wonder whether the same tenderness for the comprehension of the layman might not also have been applied to the rest of the Act. Before the commencement of the Act the half blood consanguinean had full rights of succession, postponed only to the full blood, but the half blood uterine had rights limited in all circumstances to one-half of the moveable estate, and even then postponed to the half blood consanguinean and to the parents of the intestate. Taking the same family as that illustrated above, but this time postulating that both collaterals of the full blood have predeceased, the effect is that C and D share the free intestate estate equally between them as collaterals of the half blood.

Adopted collaterals. Section 24(1) deals with relationships for the purposes of **S2–22** collateral succession between an adopted child and other children or adopted children of the adopter or adopters. It provides that:

"[A]n adopted person shall be deemed to be related to any other person, being the child or the adopted child of the adopter or (in the case of a joint adoption) of either of the adopters—

(a) where he or she was adopted by two spouses jointly and that other person is the child or adopted child of both of them, as a brother or sister of the whole blood;

(b) in any other case, as a brother or sister of the half blood."

The reader is referred to the commentary on s.24.

Illegitimate collaterals

Deaths occurring before December 8, 1986. The position in intestate collat- **S2–23** eral succession remained as before the Act—namely that illegitimate relationship was no relationship at all. Various provisions deeming illegitimate relationship to be the same as legitimate appeared in the 1968 Act, but only for the construction of deeds. Certain similar provisions now appearing in the Act applied only for the purposes of s.6 and that part of s.11 dealing with the division among those beneficially entitled under sections not having the relationship clause. There was no general rule that illegitimate relationship was the same as legitimate relationship[29] and rights of intestate succession existed only between the illegitimate child and its parents, subject to representation of the child by its issue.

Deaths from December 8, 1986. The effect of the Law Reform (Parent and **S2–24** Child) (Scotland) Act 1986[30] was to complete the partial reform begun in 1968. The assimilation of the positions of legitimate and illegitimate children has the result that in the succession to persons who die after the commencement of the 1986 Act a person formerly described as illegitimate has exactly the same rights

---

[29] s.4(4) of the Succession (Scotland) Act 1964 originally provided that, apart from specific sections, nothing in Part 1 of the Act was to be construed as importing any rule of succession through illegitimate relationship.

[30] 1986 Act (c.9) s.1(1); 1964 Act s.36(5).

as he or she would have had if born legitimate. There are now, *de jure*, brothers and sisters who merely existed de facto before, and the normal rights of succession apply fully. This automatically increases the burden on an executor of establishing that he has identified all the relations. In at least some cases of collateral succession, the problem will be mitigated by the fact that the formerly illegitimate person may rank only as a collateral of the half blood and be postponed to the succession rights of collaterals of the full blood.

(3) Collaterals and parents

S2–25   As already noted, parents of the intestate are entitled under s.2(1)(b) to one-half of the free intestate estate when the deceased is not survived by any descendants, but is survived by collaterals and by a parent or parents. The remaining one-half is divided among the collaterals. This is in addition to the right of the parent or parents to succeed to the whole free estate when the category of collaterals has been exhausted. Accordingly, if the intestate is survived by brothers or sisters, or their issue by representation under s.5, and by a parent or parents, one-half of the free estate is divided among the collaterals, and one-half falls to the parent or parents, in both cases according to the rules of division specified in s.6.

S2–26   Although this provision seems very similar to that in the pre-1964 law of moveable succession, it is to be noted that a substantial difference has been made in the position of the mother of the intestate. As part of the general policy of removing discrimination on the ground of sex, the mother is now put upon an equal footing with the father, and shares the one-half falling to parents in this situation equally with the father.[31]

(4) Parents

S2–27   If the categories of descendants and of collaterals of the intestate and collaterals' descendants have been exhausted without finding a survivor, the surviving parent or parents of the intestate are next in the line of succession, and are entitled to the whole of the free intestate estate.[32] This right is separate from their right to share along with collaterals when the intestate is survived both by parents and by collaterals. The division between father and mother is equal by virtue of s.6, they being persons "in the same degree of relationship to the intestate" within the meaning of s.6(a).

Parents of illegitimate children

S2–28   **Deaths prior to December 8, 1986.** In its original form, the Act largely re-enacted earlier legislation by providing rights of succession between the illegitimate child and the mother only. Where an illegitimate person died intestate, and was not survived by lawful issue, or, if the illegitimate person was a woman, by her illegitimate children (or their issue by representation) the surviving mother

---

[31] For the pre-Act situation see Ch.1.
[32] s.2(1)(d).

of the illegitimate person was entitled to the whole of the free intestate estate. Parents of an illegitimate child ranked immediately after descendants, there being no collateral succession.

In the division of the estates of persons dying on or after November 25, 1968, the new right of the illegitimate child to share in the estates of both parents equally with legitimate children was counterbalanced by a right of both parents to succeed to the free estate of the child.[33] Where an illegitimate child died intestate, and was not survived by lawful issue or by an illegitimate child or by lawful issue of such a child, the surviving parent or parents had right to the whole free intestate estate.

The paternity of an illegitimate child might well still be uncertain at the time of death, but there would be no merit in incurring expenditure to prove the paternity of someone who, by definition, had taken no interest in the child till then, in order to present him with a share of the child's estate. It was therefore presumed that an illegitimate person was not survived by his father unless the contrary was shown.[34]

Deaths from December 8, 1986. As the fact that a person's parents were not   **S2–29** married to each other is left out of account[35] both of the biological parents of any person continue to have the full rights of parents in succession, irrespective of any question of legitimacy. The presumption that the father of an illegitimate child had predeceased the child was repealed by the Law Reform (Parent and Child) (Scotland) Act 1986, but there is a protection for executors and trustees. This is achieved by adding to s.7 of the Law Reform (Miscellaneous Provisions) (Scotland) Act 1968 a paragraph (c) entitling a trustee or executor to distribute property without having ascertained that no paternal relative of an illegitimate person exists who is or may be entitled to an interest in the property.

Parents and adopted children. An adopted person being now treated as the   **S2–30** child of the adopter and not as the child of any other person,[36] the right of the natural parents to succeed to the child's estate is cut off. In its place arises a right of the adopting parent or parents to succeed. This is unaffected by the transitional provisions in s.5 of the Law Reform (Miscellaneous Provisions) (Scotland) Act 1966.

(5) Surviving spouse or civil partner

The inclusion of the spouse of the intestate in the list of those entitled to succeed   **S2–31** to the free intestate estate was one of the major changes from the pre-Act law of succession dependent upon blood relationship.[37] As part of the weakening of the emphasis on direct blood relationship and of the improvement of the position of the surviving spouse, the Act made a spouse one of the ordinary heirs in intestacy as well as having prior and legal rights. From December 5, 2005 this category extends to civil partners.[38]

---

[33] 1968 Act s.1.
[34] s.4(3), as substituted by 1968 Act s.1.
[35] 1986 Act s.1(1).
[36] s.23(1).
[37] For the pre-Act situation see Ch.1.
[38] Civil Partnership Act 2004 (c.33) Sch.28(1) para.2(a) and (b).

S2–32   The spouse's right is stated in s.2(1)(e) of the 1964 Act, which allows the surviving spouse to take the free estate in the absence of descendants, parents, or brothers and sisters or their descendants. In other words, the surviving spouse is preferred to uncles and aunts and all remoter ancestors of the intestate, and in the situation where this right arises, the surviving spouse will therefore take the whole net estate after payment of debts, partly by virtue of prior rights, partly by virtue of legal rights and the balance under s.2(1)(e).

S2–33   There is no representation of a spouse under s.2(1)(e)[39] just as there is no representation in respect of his/her prior or legal rights. Thus issue of a predeceasing spouse of the intestate who are not the intestate's issue (i.e. the intestate's step-children) cannot represent their parent so as to claim the free estate in preference to the intestate's uncles and aunts. Even though the principle of blood relationship has been considerably weakened, Parliament still felt that the intestate's own uncles and aunts and remoter ancestors have a better claim than the predeceasing spouse's children by a previous marriage. Admittedly this may give rise to harsh cases where the step-children have been brought up in the intestate's family by the intestate, and find themselves cut off from any share of the estate, but it would be very difficult to frame legislation to cover such cases without including situations where the step-children had no substantial contacts with the intestate. The intestate will have been aware that the step-child is not their child and the remedy is to make a will in their favour.

(6) Ascendants other than parents

S2–34   When an intestate dies without leaving any survivors in the categories of his or her descendants, collaterals, parents or spouse entitled to succeed under the conditions mentioned previously, the succession to the free estate then opens to the ascendants of the intestate other than his parents. The relevant provisions in the 1964 Act are s.2(1)(f), (g), (h) and (i), dealing respectively with uncles and aunts, grandparents, grandparents' collaterals and remoter ancestors. There is also the important provision that representation does now apply at this level of succession.[40]

S2–35   The principle remains that direct lineal ascendants of a given degree form a class nearer in degree to the intestate than the brothers and sisters of these lineal ascendants, and that brothers and sisters of lineal ascendants of one degree (or the issue of such brothers and sisters by representation, i.e. cousins) form a class nearer in degree than lineal ascendants of the next degree. Thus uncles and aunts of the intestate, whether on the paternal side or on the maternal side, succeed in preference to grandparents (s.2(1)(f)). A typical example of the type of situation which arises under these provisions would be as follows:

---

[39] s.5(1).
[40] s.5(1).

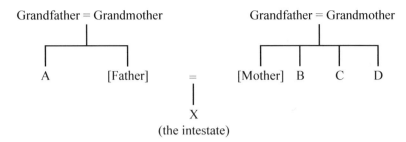

In this case as the father and mother have both predeceased, A, B, C and D, the uncles and aunts of the intestate, divide the free estate equally between them, and the grandparents have no share. It is to be noted that under s.6 the division is equal between all members of the class entitled to succeed. There is no suggestion of a preference for the paternal side over the maternal or vice versa, nor of an equal division between the paternal and maternal families. It is a per capita division between all the surviving persons in the nearest degree of relationship on either side of the house[41] with representation of any predeceasing members of the class.

Only if the uncles and aunts have also predeceased, without leaving issue **S2–36** (i.e. cousins) to represent them, do the grandparents become entitled to succeed.[42] Again, no distinction is made between the paternal and maternal lines. The four grandparents form a class, the surviving members of which share the free estate equally between them when the succession opens at this level.

Failing survivors among the class of grandparents, the brothers and sisters[43] of **S2–37** the grandparents, or their issue by representation, are entitled to the succession.[44] In the absence of any of these, the succession opens to the more remote ancestors of the intestate

> "generation by generation successively, without distinction between the paternal and maternal lines ... so however that, failing ancestors of any generation, the brothers and sisters of any of those ancestors shall have right thereto before ancestors of the next more remote generation".[45]

Illegitimate non-parental ascendants. From the commencement of the Law **S2–38** Reform (Parent and Child) (Scotland) Act 1986[46] illegitimate relationship has been no bar to rights of inheritance. Relationship is traced through illegitimate relatives in exactly the same way as through the legitimate relationship. This further widens the possible area of investigation of relatives, and could lead a solicitor to ask questions embarrassing to his client.[47]

---

[41] 1964 Act s.6(a).
[42] 1964 Act s.2(1)(g).
[43] The full blood and half blood distinction applies here equally as it does for siblings of the intestate and siblings of the intestate's parents.
[44] 1964 Act s.2(1)(h).
[45] 1964 Act s.2(1)(i).
[46] December 8, 1986.
[47] M. C. Meston, "Illegitimacy in Succession" (1986) 31 J.L.S. 358.

S2–39   *Non-parental ascendants of the half blood.* Section 2(2) provides that references to brothers and sisters include references to brothers and sisters of the half blood, while s.3 provides, as has already been noted in the case of brothers and sisters of the intestate himself, that collaterals of a parent or other ancestors of an intestate related by the whole blood exclude collaterals of the half blood, but that in the absence of collaterals of the whole blood, collaterals of the half blood are entitled to the succession without distinction as between the half blood consanguinean and the half blood uterine. Note that the existence of issue of a predeceasing uncle of the full blood will exclude any uncles and aunts of the half blood. In the past it was found that professional searchers had failed to take account of this fact when identifying beneficiaries.

S2–40   Taken together, the principle of infinite search among ancestors specified in s.2(1)(i), the rights of collaterals of the half blood, the removal of the significance of illegitimacy and the availability of representation at all levels, mean that an enormous area of search is opened up when the right of succession appears to open to the remoter ancestors. There may be considerable difficulty in practice in drawing up complete and accurate family trees on both the paternal and maternal sides for possibly several generations back and in tracing all the descendants of every member of the trees. The Mackintosh Committee on the Law of Succession did consider this point, and in para.26 of their report stated that they were much attracted by the principle of limiting succession on intestacy to uncles and aunts and their issue. This was partly because the opening of the succession to maternal relatives should in most cases make further search unnecessary and partly because of the difficulty and expense of further search. However, the Committee made no recommendation as all witnesses to whom they suggested a principle of limitation were strongly against any such idea. The draft Bill which was circulated for comment in 1959 also contained a limitation, the proposal being to exclude relatives more remote than the lineal grandparents, but again objection was taken, mainly on the basis that even if much of the estate might be expended in tracing remoter relatives, this was no justification for increasing the rights of the Crown as *ultimus haeres*. When the Succession Bill was introduced in November 1963, it included a proposal that relatives more remote than lineal grandparents should be excluded from the succession, but the principle of infinite search was restored in Committee in the House of Commons.

S2–41   The English law of intestate succession does contain an exclusion of relatives more remote than grandparents,[48] but it appears now to be accepted in Scotland that an artificial limit on the circle of relations entitled to succeed on intestacy is repugnant to our system of law. We adhere therefore to the longstanding principle that an infinite search must be made following the principles of the version of the parentelic system that we use.

---

[48]   Administration of Estates Act 1925 (15 and 16 Geo 5 c.23) s.46(1)(v), (vi).

(7) The Crown

In the absence of any person entitled to succeed to the free estate of an intestate **S2–42**
by virtue of the specific provisions of Part I of the Act, the right of the Crown to
succeed as *ultimus haeres* is saved by s.7 of the Act: see the commentary on s.7.

Succession of collaterals

**3. Subject to section 5 of this Act, where brothers and sisters of an intestate
or of an ancestor of an intestate (in this section referred to as "collaterals")
have right to the whole, or, in a case to which subsection (1)(b) of the last
foregoing section applies, to a half, of the intestate estate, the collaterals of
the whole blood shall be entitled to succeed thereto in preference to the collaterals of the half blood; but where the collaterals of the half blood have right
as aforesaid they shall rank without distinction as between those related to
the intestate, or, as the case may be, the ancestor, through their father and
those so related through their mother.**

DEFINITIONS

"intestate": s.36(1).
"intestate estate": ss.1(2) and 36(1) and (2). See also s.37(1)(a) and (b).

COMMENTARY

Section 3 applies to collaterals in s.2(1)(b), (c), (f), (h), and (i). It made one of **S3–01**
the changes which were, in 1964, regarded as radical, namely equalisation of the
position of siblings (i.e. "collaterals") of the half blood, whether uterine (through
the mother) or consanguinean (through the father). The whole category of collaterals of the half blood is postponed to the full blood (including their issue by
representation) but if the succession does open to the half blood there is no distinction between those related through the mother and those related through the father.

**4. [*Repealed by the Law Reform (Parent and Child) (Scotland) Act 1986 (c.9)
s.10(2), Sch.2].***

Representation

**5.—[1](1) Subject to section 6 of this Act, where a person who, if he had survived
an intestate, would, by virtue of any of the foregoing provisions of this Part
of this Act, have had right (otherwise than as a parent, spouse or civil partner
of the intestate) to the whole or to any part of the intestate estate has predeceased the intestate, but has left issue who survive the intestate, such issue
shall have the like right to the whole or to that part of the intestate estate as
the said person would have had if he had survived the intestate.**

**(2) The right of any issue entitled to share in an intestate estate by virtue
of the foregoing subsection to be appointed to the office of executor on the
intestate estate shall be postponed to the right thereto of any person who
succeeds to the whole or part of the intestate estate by virtue of the foregoing**

provisions of this Act apart from this section and who applies for appointment to that office.

NOTE

1. As amended by the Civil Partnership Act 2004 (c.33) Sch.28(1) para.3 (effective December 5, 2005).

DEFINITIONS

"intestate estate": ss.1(2) and 36(1) and (2). See also s.37(1)(a) and (b).
"issue": s.36(1).

COMMENTARY

General

S5–01   Being in Part I of the Act, s.5 applies only to the free estate after any legacies, prior and legal rights. There is a full right of representation of anyone other than a parent or spouse of the intestate who would have been entitled to share in the free estate of the intestate had he survived.[49] The exclusion of representation of the intestate's parents is fairly obvious, for in any event the intestate's own collaterals and issue, who would be the representatives of the parents, would normally take before the parents became entitled to any share. It does, however, also ensure that the intestate's collaterals of the half blood cannot represent the predeceasing common parent to the partial exclusion of collaterals of the whole blood. Take, for example, a situation such as the following:

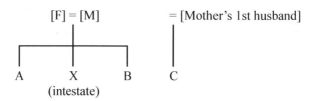

If his mother had survived the intestate, she would have been entitled to one-half of his free estate in preference to A and B under s.2(1)(b). The exclusion of representation of parents means that C, a collateral of the half blood uterine, cannot by representation claim the mother's one-half share of the free estate in a situation where he otherwise has no rights of succession at all.

S5–02   The exclusion of representation of a spouse in respect of his/her rights in the free estate is designed to ensure that step-children of the intestate do not acquire rights of succession in his estate. Step-children have no place at all in intestate succession, but if representation of a spouse had been permitted, they could have come in by the back door to the prejudice of blood relatives such as uncles and aunts and remoter ancestors of the intestate. Strong arguments were presented in

---

[49] s.5(1): applying only to the free estate.

Parliament in debate on the Succession Bill that step-children should have some place in the law of succession, but the attachment to blood relationship as the governing principle, though already weakened, proved too strong to permit this radical change.

Apart from these points, the scheme of representation and division specified in **S5–03** ss.5 and 6 in respect of the free estate is very similar to the separate scheme in s.11 for representation in legitim. As in the case of s.11(1) and (2), s.5(1) might appear to require that division among representatives must always be *per stirpes*, but is stated to be subject to s.6 which specifies the method of division.

The representatives who may take the share of the predeceased heir to the free **S5–04** estate are his descendants. This is the effect of the definition of issue as "issue however remote".[50] Since December 8, 1986, there is no longer any distinction between legitimate and illegitimate children.[51] The former rule that only legitimate issue, however remote, of the predeceaser could represent him now applies only to deaths occurring before December 8, 1986.

Adopted children and representation

The scheme of representation in s.5(1) is in respect of persons entitled to **S5–05** succeed by virtue of the preceding provisions of the Act. The rights of adopted children are specified in s.23(1) in the form that they are to be treated as children of the adopter for all purposes of succession (intestate or testate[52]). Therefore they are entitled to represent their adopting parents in the free estate in which the adopting parents would have been entitled to share by survivance.

Appointment of representative as executor-dative

Subsection (2) is one of the few provisions in the Act dealing with the right to **S5–06** the office of executor. It bears a relationship to the former provision in s.1 of the Intestate Moveable Succession (Scotland) Act 1855[53] and provides that, if there is a competition for office, the right of representatives to the office of executor is postponed to the right of surviving members of the class which they are representing.

Division of intestate estate among those having right thereto
6. If, by virtue of the foregoing provisions of this Part of this Act, there are two or more persons having right among them to the whole, or, in a case to which section 2(1)(b) of this Act relates, to a half, of an intestate estate, then the said estate, or, as the case may be, that half thereof, shall—

(a) if all of those persons are in the same degree of relationship to the intestate, be divided among them equally, and

---

[50] s.36(1).
[51] Law Reform (Parent and Child) (Scotland) Act 1986 s.1(1).
[52] But not in relation to any deed executed before September 10, 1964 (s.23(4)).
[53] (18 and 19 Vict. c.23).

    (b) in any other case, be divided equally into a number of parts equal to the aggregate of—

        (i) those of the said persons who are nearest in degree of relationship to the intestate (in this section referred to as "the nearest surviving relatives") and

        (ii) any other persons who were related to the intestate in that degree, but who have predeceased him leaving issue who survive him;

and, of those parts, one shall be taken by each of the nearest surviving relatives, and one shall be taken per stirpes by the issue of each of the said predeceased persons.

[Words repealed by the Law Reform (Parent and Child) (Scotland) Act 1986 (c.9) s.10(2), Sch.2].

DEFINITION

"intestate estate": ss.1(2) and 36(1) and (2). See also s.37(1)(a) and (b).

COMMENTARY

S6–01   Section 6 is one of the least satisfactory provisions in the Act. It alters the effect of s.5 by substituting special rules for the division of the free estate. The effect can be to produce great variations of succession rights depending upon the accident of the order of deaths. For detailed criticism of the effects of this section see M.C. Meston, "Representation in Succession" (1995) 1 S.L.P.Q. 83, 83–92. It can be said to be contrary to what would be expected by lay persons.

S6–02   Section 6 provides that if all the persons entitled to share in the estate are of the same degree of relationship to the intestate the division is made equally among them per capita.[54] Thus, as in the case of the division of legitim,[55] if the intestate is predeceased by his two children but is survived by four grandchildren, three being issue of one child and one of the other, the division is equal, per capita, into one quarter for each grandchild.

S6–03   If, however, those entitled are not all of the same degree of relationship to the intestate, the division is *per stirpes* at the level of the class nearest to the intestate of which there are surviving members—the "nearest surviving relatives".[56] An example of this is where, in the above example, the intestate is survived by one child but predeceased by the other child with the three surviving grandchildren. The effect of s.6(b) is to divide the estate into two leaving the child with one half but with the other half being taken *per stirpes* by the grandchildren, leaving each with one sixth.

S6–04   On the other hand, if the succession opens to uncles and aunts, it is available to brothers and sisters of both mother and father, and all members of that category

---

[54] s.6(a).
[55] See Ch.5.
[56] s.6(b).

share equally, irrespective of how many are on the paternal side and how many on the maternal side.

If the persons entitled are not all of the same degree of relationship to the **S6–05** deceased, the division is made *per stirpes* at the level of the class nearest to the deceased in which there are members who actually survive. One part is taken by each of the surviving members of that class and one part by the representatives of each predeceasing member who has left issue.

It must be noted that this section (and s.5) apply only to the free estate, and not **S6–06** to prior rights or to legal rights. Similar provision for the division of the legitim fund appears in s.11.

Saving of right of Crown as ultimus haeres

7. Nothing in this Part of this Act shall be held to affect the right of the Crown as *ultimus haeres* to any estate to which no person is entitled by virtue of this Act to succeed.

COMMENTARY

In the absence of any person entitled to succeed to the free estate of an intestate **S7–01** by virtue of the specific provisions of Part I of the Act, the right of the Crown to succeed as *ultimus haeres* is saved by s.7 of the Act. The executor, or anyone holding property for which no valid right of succession can be established, has the duty of transferring it to the Queen's and Lord Treasurer's Remembrancer to be administered on behalf of the Crown. The Queen's and Lord Treasurer's Remembrancer takes possession without the need for confirmation.

The Crown, through the Queen's and Lord Treasurer's Remembrancer, will **S7–02** normally place advertisements in local newspapers to publicise the fact that an estate has fallen to the Crown. If heirs later establish their relationship, the property will be transferred to them. If no heirs come forward, the Crown continues its practice of making grants to persons who have a moral claim on the deceased (as by rendering significant services without payment) or for whom there is evidence to show that the deceased might reasonably have been expected to make provision. Such persons present a Petition for Gift to the Queen's and Lord Treasurer's Remembrancer. At one time the commonest case was that of "relatives" of an illegitimate person who died without issue, but such persons now are treated as full relatives[57] with the result that fewer estates fall to the Crown.

There was a suggestion in Parliament in debate on the Bill that the Common **S7–03** Good fund of the local authority for the area of the deceased's last residence should be substituted for the Crown as *ultimus haeres*, but the principle was not accepted.

---

[57] Law Reform (Miscellaneous Provisions) (Scotland) Act 1968 Part I and the Law Reform (Parent and Child) (Scotland) Act 1986 s.1.

PART II

LEGAL AND OTHER PRIOR RIGHTS IN ESTATES OF DECEASED PERSONS

NOTE

1. See the Finance Act 1985 (c.54) s.84(5) and (6).

Prior rights of surviving spouse, on intestacy, in dwelling house and furniture
8.—[1,2](1) Where a person dies intestate leaving a spouse or civil partner, and the intestate estate includes a relevant interest in a dwelling house mentioned in subsection (4)(a) of this section, the surviving spouse or civil partner shall be entitled, subject to subsection (2B) of this section, to receive out of the intestate estate—

[3,4](a)   where the value of the relevant interest does not exceed £473,000 or such larger amount as may from time to time be fixed by order of the Secretary of State—

> **(i)   if subsection (2) of this section does not apply, the relevant interest;**
> **(ii) if the said subsection (2) applies, a sum equal to the value of the relevant interest;**

[3,4,6](b) in any other case, the sum of £473,000 or such larger amount as may from time to time be fixed by order of the Secretary of State.

(2) This subsection shall apply for the purposes of paragraph (a) of the foregoing subsection if—

(a) the dwelling house forms part only of the subjects comprised in one tenancy or lease under which the intestate was the tenant; or
(b) the dwelling house forms the whole or part of subjects an interest in which is comprised in the intestate estate and which were used by the intestate for carrying on a trade, profession or occupation, and the value of the estate as a whole would be likely to be substantially diminished if the dwelling house were disposed of otherwise than with the assets of the trade, profession or occupation.

[7](2A) Where the tenant of a croft dies intestate leaving a spouse or civil partner or, where he dies leaving no spouse or civil partner, leaving a cohabitant, and the intestate estate includes a relevant interest in a dwelling house mentioned in subsection (4)(b) of this section, the surviving spouse, civil partner or, as the case may be, cohabitant shall be entitled, subject to subsection (2B) of this section, to receive out of the intestate estate—

(a) where the value of the relevant interest does not exceed the amount for the time being fixed by order under subsection (1)(a) of this section, the tenancy of the croft;

(b) in any other case, the sum for the time being fixed by order under subsection (1)(b) of this section.

⁷(2B) If the intestate estate comprises—

(a) a relevant interest in two or more dwelling houses mentioned in subsection (4)(a) of this section, subsection (1) of this section shall have effect only in relation to such one of them as the surviving spouse or civil partner may elect for the purposes of subsection (1) within 6 months after the date of death of the intestate;

(b) a relevant interest in two or more dwelling houses mentioned in subsection (4)(b) of this section, subsection (2A) of this section shall have effect only in relation to such one of them as the surviving spouse, civil partner or cohabitant may elect for the purposes of subsection (2A) within 6 months after that date;

(c) a relevant interest in both—

  (i) one or more dwelling houses mentioned in subsection (4)(a) of this section; and

  (ii) one or more dwelling houses mentioned in subsection (4)(b) of this section,

the surviving spouse or civil partner shall not be entitled to receive both the entitlement under subsection (1) of this section and that under subsection (2A) of this section and must elect within 6 months after that date whether to take the entitlement under the said subsection (1) or under the said subsection (2A).

¹(3) Where a person dies intestate leaving a spouse or civil partner, and the intestate estate includes the furniture and plenishings of a dwelling house to which this section applies (whether or not the dwelling house is comprised in the intestate estate), the surviving spouse or civil partner shall be entitled to receive out of the intestate estate—

^{3, 5}(a) where the value of the furniture and plenishings does not exceed £29,000 or such larger amount as may from time to time be fixed by order of the Secretary of State, the whole thereof;

^{3, 5}(b) in any other case, such part of the furniture and plenishings, to a value not exceeding £29,000 or such larger amount as may from time to time be fixed by order of the Secretary of State, as may be chosen by the surviving spouse or civil partner:

Provided that, if the intestate estate comprises the furniture and plenishings of two or more such dwelling houses, this subsection shall have effect only in relation to the furniture and plenishings of such one of them as the surviving spouse or civil partner may elect for the purposes of this subsection within six months of the date of death of the intestate.

[8](4) The dwelling house is—

(a) in a case mentioned in subsection (1) of this section, any dwelling house in which the surviving spouse or civil partner of the intestate was ordinarily resident at the date of death of the intestate and which did not, at that date, form part of a croft of which the intestate was tenant;

(b) in a case mentioned in subsection (2A) of this section, any dwelling house in which the surviving spouse, civil partner or cohabitant was ordinarily resident at the date of death of the intestate and which, at that date, formed part of a croft of which the intestate was tenant.

(5) Where any question arises as to the value of any furniture or plenishings, or of any interest in a dwelling house, for the purposes of any provision of this section the question shall be determined by arbitration by a single arbiter appointed, in default of agreement, by the sheriff of the county in which the intestate was domiciled at the date of his death or, if that county is uncertain or the intestate was domiciled furth of Scotland, the sheriff of the Lothians and Peebles at Edinburgh.

(6) In this section—

[9](za) "cohabitant" means a person—

(i) who was living with the intestate as if married to him; or

(ii) who was living with the intestate as if in civil partnership with him,

and had been so living for at least 2 years.

(a) "dwelling house" includes a part of a building occupied (at the date of death of the intestate) as a separate dwelling; and any reference to a dwelling house shall be construed as including any garden or portion of ground attached to, and usually occupied with, the dwelling house or otherwise required for the amenity or convenience of the dwelling house;

(b) "furniture and plenishings" includes garden effects, domestic animals, plate, plated articles, linen, china, glass, books, pictures, prints, articles of household use and consumable stores; but does not include any article or animal used at the date of death of the intestate for business purposes, or money or securities for money, or any heirloom;

(c) "heirloom", in relation to an intestate estate, means any article which has associations with the intestate's family of such nature and extent that it ought to pass to some member of that family other than the surviving spouse of the intestate;

(d) "relevant interest", in relation to a dwelling house, means the interest therein of an owner, or the interest therein of a tenant, subject in either case to any heritable debt secured over the interest; and for the purposes

of this definition "tenant" means a tenant under a tenancy or lease (whether of the dwelling house alone or of the dwelling house together with other subjects) which is not a tenancy to which the Rent and Mortgage Interest Restrictions Acts 1920 to 1939 apply.

NOTES

1. As amended by the Civil Partnership Act 2004 (c.33) Sch.28(1) para.4 (effective December 5, 2005).
2. As amended by the Crofting Reform etc. Act 2007 (asp 7) Pt 2 s.14(2) (effective January 28, 2008).
3. As amended by the Succession (Scotland) Act 1973 (c.25) s.1(1)(a).
4. Figure substituted by the Prior Rights of Surviving Spouse and Civil Partner (Scotland) Order 2011 (SSI 2011/436) Sch.1 para.1 (effective February 1, 2012). Earlier values: September 10, 1964 to May 22, 1973— £15,000: May 22, 1973 to July 31, 1981—£30,000; August 1, 1981 to April 30, 1988— £50,000; May 1, 1988 to November 25, 1993—£65,000; November 26, 1993 to April 1, 1999—£110,000; April 2, 1999 to May 31, 2005—£130,000; June 1, 2005 to January 31, 2012—£300,000.
5. Figure substituted by the Prior Rights of Surviving Spouse and Civil Partner (Scotland) Order 2011 (SSI 2011/436) Sch.1 para.1 (effective February 1, 2012). Earlier values: September 10, 1964 to May 22, 1973— £5,000; May 22, 1973 to July 31, 1981—£8,000; August 1, 1981 to April 30, 1988— £10,000; May 1, 1988 to November 25, 1993—£12,000; November 26, 1993 to April 1, 1999—£20,000; April 2, 1999 to May 31, 2005—£22,000; June 1, 2005 to January 31, 2012—£24,000.
6. Words repealed by the Crofting Reform etc. Act 2007 (asp 7) Pt 2 s.14(2)(c) (effective January 28, 2008).
7. Inserted by the Crofting Reform etc. Act 2007 (asp 7) Pt 2 s.14(3) (effective January 28, 2008).
8. Substituted by the Crofting Reform etc. Act 2007 (asp 7) Pt 2 s.14(4) (effective January 28, 2008).
9. Inserted by the Crofting Reform etc. Act 2007 (asp 7) Pt 2 s.14(5) (effective January 28, 2008).

DEFINITIONS

"dwelling house": s.8(6)(a).
"estate": s.36(2).
"furniture and plenishings": s.8(6)(b).
"heirloom": s.8(6)(c).
"intestate": s.36(1).
"intestate estate": s.36(1). See also s.37(1)(a) and (b).
"owner": s.36(1).
"relevant interest": s.8(6)(d).
"Secretary of State": Scotland Act 1998 (c.46) ss.117 and 126(1).
"sheriff": Interpretation Act 1978 s.5 and Sch.1.

COMMENTARY

General

S8–01   Section 8 is probably the most important section in the whole Act, as the "prior right" which it creates was the most important single improvement in the position of a surviving spouse. The general purpose is to ensure that a surviving spouse can live undisturbed in the house which he or she has been occupying, and can retain the furniture and plenishings which he or she wishes to allow him or her to live there. From December 5, 2005 the prior right was extended to civil partners.[58] From January 28, 2008 the prior right was extended to certain cohabitants[59] ordinarily resident in a dwelling house forming part of the crofting tenancy of the deceased.[60] For the sake of convenience, references in this commentary to spouses should be taken to include civil partners and such cohabitants.

S8–02   The surviving spouse's rights to the house and furniture and plenishings under this section are the first items to come out of the deceased spouse's intestate estate. Section 9(6)(a) postpones the second set of prior rights—the monetary provision—to the housing and furniture rights under s.8. Section 10(2) postpones the traditional legal rights, as amended, to both of these prior rights, and s.1(2) postpones the operation of the rules of succession to the free estate to both prior and legal rights. Hence the housing and furniture rights are the first to be considered. The prior rights under ss.8 and 9 apply only on the total or partial intestacy of the deceased. Unlike legal rights, they do not prevail against a contrary will by the deceased. If the intestacy is only partial, prior rights apply only to property which has not been disposed of by will.

S8–03   The prior rights under s.8 comprise (1) the right to the house; and (2) the right to furniture and plenishings.

The right to the house

S8–04   The general substantive right is set out in s.8(1). For a house leased by the deceased under a crofting tenancy the substantive right is set out in s.8(2A). Section 8(1) provides that where the intestate estate includes a "relevant interest" in a dwelling house to which the section applies, the surviving spouse is entitled to receive that interest, if its value does not exceed £473,000. If it does exceed that figure, the surviving spouse is entitled to the sum of £473,000. The concept of a maximum limit on the value of the housing right was intended to meet the difficulties which might arise if very valuable houses or mansions passed to the deceased's widow. At one stage in the Succession Bill's progress through Parliament, it was proposed to give the surviving spouse only the value of the house, and not the ownership (or tenancy) of it, if there were "special circumstances of a historical nature" connected with it. This being so vague as to be

---

[58] Civil Partnership Act 2004 (c.33) Sch.28(1) para.4.

[59] The definition of cohabitant in s.8(6)(za) of the 1964 Act is the same as that in s.25(1) of the 2006 Act but with the additional requirement that the living together should have been for at least two years. See paras F29–04 to F29–10.

[60] Crofting Reform etc. Act 2007 (asp 7) s.14.

probably unworkable, the provision was dropped in favour of a maximum value for the interest which is transferred to the surviving spouse.

For many years the monetary limit under s.8(1) did not keep up with inflation, **S8–05** despite increases in 1973, 1981, 1988, 1993 and 1999.[61] Writing in 2002, one of the authors observed that the original figure of £15,000 in 1964 represented approximately three times the value of a substantial city house purchased by him in that year and that the then current figure of £130,000 was approximately half of the current value of the same house. The intention was that a surviving spouse would be enabled to continue to live undisturbed in the house in which he or she was ordinarily resident before the deceased's death. Given the criticism made of the erosion of fulfilment of that aim, in 2005 and in 2012 there were substantial increases to £300,000 and £473,000 respectively. The effect is that the vast majority of homes should now be covered whether owned wholly by the deceased or not. This accords with the original purpose of prior rights.

If the value of the house is over the limit, or if one of the exceptions stated in **S8–06** s.8(2) applies, the survivor receives a cash payment rather than the house itself. It is not said that this is in lieu of the relevant interest or that it is a *surrogatum* for the interest. Some doubt may therefore exist whether this right falls to be treated as an interest in heritage or as an interest in moveables.[62] The better view, and the only one which makes sense, is that the right falls to be treated as heritable, as being a *surrogatum* for the house itself.

"relevant interest"

It is very important to an understanding of this prior right to observe that it vests **S8–07** in the surviving spouse not the house itself, but the deceased's "relevant interest" in the "dwelling house" both of which are defined in s.8. This is to cope with the various forms of interest which a deceased occupier of a house may have had. The purpose was to ensure that the surviving spouse could obtain the deceased's interest as owner or tenant and could continue to live as before. In contrast to the position with the furniture and plenishings, which must have belonged to the deceased before they can pass as a prior right, it is whatever interest the deceased may have had in the house that vests. The deceased may have been the owner or a tenant, but it is that interest which is transferred. The exception is that any tenancies still subject to the Rent (Scotland) Act 1984 do not pass to the surviving spouse as a prior right, but this is because Rent Act tenancies already have their own code of transmission on the tenant's death[63] as do public sector residential

---

[61] Succession (Scotland) Act 1973 (c.25) s.1; Prior Rights of Surviving Spouse (Scotland) Order 1981 (SI 1981/806); Prior Rights of Surviving Spouse (Scotland) Order 1988 (SI 1988/633); Prior Rights of Surviving Spouse (Scotland) Order 1993 (SI 1993/2690) and Prior Rights of Surviving Spouse (Scotland) Order 1999 (SI 1999/445).

[62] For possible effects of this doubt on the calculation of the legal rights fund and on private international law, see paras 7–21 and 7–22.

[63] Rent (Scotland) Act 1984 (c.58) Schs 1 and 1A. The reference in s.8(6)(d) to the Rent and Mortgage Interest Restrictions Acts 1920 to 1939 is to be read as a reference to the Rent (Scotland) Act 1984 (Rent (Scotland) Act 1971 Sch.19 para.5; and Rent (Scotland) Act 1984 Sch.8 para.2).

tenancies under the Housing (Scotland) Act 2001.[64] It is unclear whether assured tenancies are covered by prior rights or not.[65]

S8–08   "Owner" is defined in s.36 as "the person entitled to receive the rents thereof (other than a tenant)". This embraces the holder of an unregistered disposition in his favour as such a disposition typically includes an assignation of rents.[66] It also includes the transferee under a docket in terms of s.15(2). It is unclear whether the definition would cover a legatee of the house who has not yet received any form of conveyance following the death of the last registered owner.

S8–09   The "relevant interest" of the deceased as defined in s.8(6)(d) is subject to any heritable debt secured over it. In addition to the problem of how much of a debt is heritable when there is also moveable security[67] this means that it is the net value after allowing for the heritable debt which determines whether the limit on value has been reached. The surviving spouse takes the deceased's interest when the value of the interest (and not of the house) does not exceed £473,000.

S8–10   If there is a "mortgage protection" policy on the life of the deceased owner of a house, the surviving spouse commonly assumes that this clears the house of debt and that the whole value is transferred as a prior right, subject to the limit. However, this is incorrect for such a policy is just an ordinary policy of life assurance which pays into the estate a moveable sum which happens to be the amount needed to pay off the heritable debt. It does not alter the fact that, at the moment of death, a heritable debt is secured over the house, and the prior right is to the value subject to the burden of that debt. There is no compensation in the monetary right in s.9 for the presence of a life assurance policy acquired for the purpose of repayment of the heritable debt and attempts to devise a scheme for tying mortgage protection policies directly to the debt so as to cancel the debt at the moment of death have so far failed. This means that any arrangement with a heritable creditor to allow the spouse to continue to reside in the house could depend on the agreement of the intestate deceased's children or other heirs under s.2 who would have entitlement to part of the policy.

"Dwelling house"

S8–11   The dwelling house can be separate dwelling forming part of a larger building. The dwelling house is not limited to the actual structure—the stone and mortar. "Dwelling house" is defined in s.8(6)(a) as including any garden or portion of ground attached to, and usually occupied with, the dwelling house or otherwise required for the amenity or convenience of the house. This would seem to cover not only garden ground physically contiguous to the house but also such things as *pro indiviso* shares in the garden ground in the centre of a square or in a tenement.

S8–12   The Act does not contemplate mobile or temporary residences such as caravans and houseboats as "dwelling houses". This is evident both from s.8(6)(d) which

---

[64] Housing (Scotland) Act 2001 (asp 10) s.22.
[65] Section 31 of the Housing (Scotland) Act 1988 (c.43) provides limited succession rights for spouses, civil partners and cohabitants who hold certain types of assured tenancies, but the interaction with prior rights is unclear.
[66] Now implied in all dispositions: Land Registration (Scotland) Act 1979 (c.33) s.16(3).
[67] See paras 3–11 and 3–12 (Ch.3).

contemplates a relevant interest in a dwelling house being subject to a "heritable debt" and from s.8(6)(a) which contemplates a garden or other ground being attached to the dwelling house. Clearly there cannot be a heritable debt over a moveable property in the form of a houseboat or a mobile caravan. However, not all caravans are equally mobile and some may be fixed with garden ground surrounding them. Whether a caravan is moveable or heritable property will depend on the circumstances.[68]

"Ordinarily resident"

The relevant interest of the deceased must be in any dwelling house in which **S8–13** the surviving spouse of the intestate was ordinarily resident at the date of death of the intestate although the intestate need not have been resident there.

Difficult questions do arise with some regularity over the concept of ordinary **S8–14** residence. In one case spouses had been living in rented accommodation but the husband had concluded missives in January 1977 to purchase a house with entry in March of that year. All formalities were complete when the husband died on the very day of entry. The keys were not collected until a few days later and the widow and children did not move in until some time later. It was therefore clear that the widow was not "ordinarily resident" in the new house at the date of her intestate husband's death, and was thus entitled only to such minimal value as the tenancy had instead of the value of the new house.[69]

It is possible to be ordinarily resident in more than one dwelling house at a time. **S8–15** It may be a rare situation but could arise, for example, if the spouses had town and country houses and used both regularly, keeping two establishments in being. It seems highly unlikely that a holiday cottage would be sufficient to produce an "ordinary" residence of the surviving spouse unless there were evidence of very frequent use as an alternative principal home. To meet the possibility of there being multiple ordinary residences all of which fall into intestacy, the proviso to s.8(2B)(a) ensures that the surviving spouse's right applies to the intestate's interest in only one of the houses in which the survivor was ordinarily resident. When this situation arises, the surviving spouse has an unfettered discretion to choose the house which is to fall under the right with a period of up to six months after the death within which to reach a decision. In the cases when this right of election arises, the surviving spouse will probably be influenced by the capital values, at least if it is a right of ownership that is involved. Unless there is some particular reason for preferring to occupy the less valuable house, the surviving spouse can always opt to take the more valuable, selling it if need be to provide capital for the purchase of a more conveniently located house. This would apply even more strongly if one of the houses was owned and the other merely leased by the deceased spouse. It will be noted, however, that the value of the furniture and plenishings in the two houses need not be a factor, since an entirely separate election is involved in that case.[70]

---

[68] Compare *Redgates Caravan Parks Ltd v Assessor for Ayrshire*, 1973 S.L.T. 52 (heritable) with *Assessor for Angus v Alan*, 1976 S.L.T. (Notes) 54 (moveable).
[69] *Meston's Succession Opinions*, No.64. See also No.65.
[70] s.8(3) proviso.

The Act does not provide for the means by which the election must be made. Given that all estates vest in an executor following confirmation, with retrospective effect to the date of death, it seems clear that the election should be intimated to all of the executors (whether or not confirmed), and if necessary, appointment of an executor, perhaps of the spouse or partner, should be sought at the earliest opportunity. There is no requirement for the election to be made by written notice and this leaves open the possibility of an oral election. However, it is recommended that for the avoidance of all doubt that a written notice of election is intimated.

S8–16   What are the consequences of the right of election not being exercised? On the face of it, s.8(2B) makes the timeous exercise of the election a condition precedent to any entitlement to the prior housing right in s.8(1). This seems drastic given that where the house forms part of, say, a larger agricultural tenancy the Act provides in s.8(1)(a)(ii) that in place of the housing right the spouse is to receive a sum equal to the relevant interest that cannot be readily conveyed to the spouse. Nevertheless, both s.8(2B) and its predecessor, namely the repealed proviso in s.8(1) itself, are clear in their terms and no default position in the event of the election not being made is provided for. This underlines the importance for a surviving spouse to identify at an early stage whether it could be argued that he or she was resident in more than one house in which the intestate had a relevant interest and making the appropriate election timeously.

Exceptions where the surviving spouse or civil partner receives only the value of the house

S8–17   Recognising that, in some circumstances, considerable difficulties might be created by the transfer of the ownership or tenancy of a house to the surviving spouse, two exceptions are stated in s.8(2). In these cases the surviving spouse is entitled to receive the value of the deceased's interest up to the maximum limit, but is not entitled to insist upon a transfer of the interest itself.[71]

S8–18   The first of the exceptions arises under s.8(2)(a) where, although the other conditions are satisfied, the dwelling house forms part only of the subjects comprised in one tenancy or lease under which the intestate was the tenant. A dwelling house for the purposes of s.8 need not be a complete structure in itself. By virtue of s.8(6)(a) the term includes a part of a building occupied (at the date of the death of the intestate) as a separate dwelling. Thus a flat in a large block clearly falls within the definition. If the deceased had a lease of the block of flats, in one of which the survivor was ordinarily resident, the landlord could not reasonably be required to grant a separate lease of that flat to the surviving spouse. Hence the exception applies to a dwelling house forming part of larger subjects tenanted by the deceased and does not arise in cases of ownership. This exception may prove to be of relatively rare occurrence in practice.

S8–19   The second exception is a specialised application of the first which is likely to be of greater importance. It arises in cases of both ownership and tenancy by the

---

[71] s.8(1)(a)(ii).

deceased spouse, and is stated in s.8(2)(b). Again, the surviving spouse is limited to the value of the house in question if it

> "forms the whole or part of subjects an interest in which is comprised in the intestate estate and which were used by the intestate for carrying on a trade, profession or occupation, and the value of the estate as a whole would be likely to be substantially diminished if the dwelling house were disposed of otherwise than with the assets of the trade, profession or occupation".

The typical example of this exception is a farmhouse. Farming qualifies as a **S8–20** "trade, profession or occupation"; the house is part of the subjects used for that trade, etc. and the value of the estate as a whole would undoubtedly be substantially diminished if the farmhouse were not available along with the farming land. If the purchaser cannot have a house from which to run the farm, the amount by which the value of the farm is reduced is likely to be much greater than the value of the house as such, due to the inconvenience to the purchaser. Similar considerations might apply to cases such as that of the doctor's house with surgery attached. In either case, if the whole unit was merely tenanted by the deceased, the house would also come under the first exception in s.8(2)(a), but even if the deceased was the owner, it would seem that the surviving spouse would be entitled only to the value, and not to the ownership, of the deceased's interest in the house. The fall in the value of the whole unit by reason of the absence of the house would be greater than the value of the house itself, qua house, and hence the "value of the estate as a whole would be likely to be substantially diminished" if the house were not disposed of along with the farm or surgery.

The surviving spouse may not regard the cash value of the house or of the **S8–21** tenancy thereof as adequate compensation for loss of the living accommodation, but the general policy that the survivor should not be left without a roof over his or her head gives way in this instance to the general benefit of the estate as a whole.

It is worth remembering that many farms (and surgeries) are owned by partner- **S8–22** ships rather than by individuals. If a farm is owned by a partnership of which the deceased was a partner, his interest is a moveable interest in the partnership. He does not have a direct interest in the individual assets of the partnership, and in particular he would not seem to have any "relevant interest" in the farmhouse unless he has a tenancy agreement with the firm. In the normal case he would be neither owner nor tenant and so would not have a "relevant interest" thereby leaving nothing to pass to his spouse as a prior right under this heading.

Valuation of dwelling houses

The value to be ascertained will presumably be the market value of the **S8–23** deceased's relevant interest, taking into account any heritable debt secured over it,[72] which should mean that in most cases the net value agreed for inheritance tax purposes will be accepted by those concerned.

---

[72] s.8(6)

S8–24   Where any question arises as to the value of the relevant interest of the deceased in the house, for the purpose either of the maximum limit or of the substituted value in cases failing within s.8(2), it is provided by s.8(5) that the question is to be settled by arbitration by a single arbiter (arbitrator). This is a form of statutory arbitration which is governed by s.16 of the Arbitration (Scotland) Act 2010, which at the time of writing has not yet been brought into force. In the absence of s.16 having been brought into force the arbitration is to be governed by the common law. In default of agreement on an arbitrator, he or she is to be appointed by the sheriff[73] of the county in which the intestate was domiciled at the date of death, or if that county is uncertain, or the intestate was domiciled outwith Scotland, by the Sheriff Principal of Lothian and Borders at Edinburgh.

The right to the furniture and plenishings

S8–25   The right to the house would be of little practical use if the surviving spouse had to restock it. The general aim of s.8 is to further the presumed intention of the intestate spouse that the survivor should be enabled to continue to live in the house which he or she previously occupied with as little disturbance as possible. Accordingly, s.8(3) provides that the surviving spouse is entitled to receive the furniture and plenishings so far as part of the intestate estate, of any dwelling house owned by the deceased and occupied by whomsoever as a separate dwelling at the time of his or her death (whether or not the house be part of the intestate estate), subject to a maximum value of £29,000.

S8–26   It will be noted that this excludes furniture being acquired by the deceased on hire purchase. Section 8(3) gives rights to the survivor when "the intestate estate includes the furniture and plenishings". The whole point of a hire purchase agreement being that the articles concerned do not belong to the hirer until fully paid for, furniture on hire purchase is not included in the deceased's estate and does not pass to the surviving spouse under this provision. Subject to any specialties in the terms of the contract, this would presumably also be true even if insurance had been effected to pay off the outstanding debt in the event of the hirer's death. Credit sale agreements do not give rise to this problem as the property in the goods does then pass to the purchaser leaving the seller with only a claim of debt.

The house from which the furniture and plenishings may be taken

S8–27   The right is to furniture and plenishings in the intestate estate from a house in which the surviving spouse was ordinarily resident[74] at the death of the deceased spouse even if the deceased spouse did not have a "relevant interest" in that house. Section 8(3) expressly provides that the right to furniture and plenishings exists whether or not the house is comprised in the intestate estate. The commonest case is that of the wife dying intestate when the house is owned or tenanted by the husband. Here the wife's estate does not include the house, but the husband is entitled to receive as a prior right such of the furniture and plenishings of the house as belonged to the wife, subject always to the £29,000 limit.

---

[73] Now sheriff principal: Sheriff Courts (Scotland) Act 1971 (c.58) s.4(2).
[74] s.8(4).

In cases where the intestate estate comprises the furniture and plenishings of two **S8–28** or more such dwelling houses the surviving spouse is entitled to the furniture and plenishings belonging to the deceased in such one of them as he or she may elect within six months of the death of the intestate.[75] This election is entirely separate from the election under s.8(2B) of a house from two or more in which the survivor was ordinarily resident. It will therefore be possible to take one of the houses with the furniture and plenishings of another. This may be significant where the house not resided in by the survivor or not elected by the survivor has better furniture and plenishings than the house resided in or elected. The existence of the election is significant also on account of the drastic consequences should it not be exercised.

The consequences of the right to elect existing and not being exercised would **S8–29** appear to involve the loss of the furniture and plenishings right as a whole. This is apparent from the terms of the proviso in s.8(3) which in the instance of two or more dwelling houses having intestate furniture and plenishings, makes it a condition precedent to the whole furniture and plenishings right in s.8(3) that timeous election be made by the spouse. Given that the furnishing and plenishing of two or more dwelling houses is by no means uncommon (for example where the second dwelling house is rented out as a furnished let), it is vital that any situations of multiple furnishing by the deceased are identified at the earliest opportunity and the appropriate election made timeously. Given that the s.8(3) right is one to moveable property, furniture and plenishings of a dwelling house outwith Scotland would appear to be covered.

"Furniture and plenishings"

The "furniture and plenishings" which fall under this right are more restric- **S8–30** tively defined than on the first appearance of the Bill. The definition appears in s.8(6)(b), and is not exhaustive of all possibilities, for the term is said to *include* "garden effects, domestic animals, plate, plated articles, linen, china, glass, books, pictures, prints, articles of household use, and consumable stores". It does not include "any article or animal used at the date of death of the intestate for business purposes, or money or securities for money or any heirloom". No mention is made of motorcars although they, with carriages and horses, were included in the version of the Bill which had its first reading in May 1963. One imagines that it might still be possible in rare cases to argue that a car was part of the plenishings of a particular house if it were treated as an appurtenance of the house, e.g. an estate car kept at a country mansion and used solely for ferrying people and their luggage to and from the nearest station. In most cases, however, a car will prove either to have been used for business purposes, or not to be part of the plenishings of the house at all. Professional practice in drawing up inventories of estates would tend to indicate that a car is rarely regarded as part of the plenishings of a house, for cars are usually entered as separate items of estate.

The heirlooms which are not to be treated as part of the furniture and plenish- **S8–31** ings of any particular house are defined as any articles which have associations with the intestate's family of such nature and extent that they ought to pass to

---

[75] s.8(3) proviso.

some member of that family other than the surviving spouse of the intestate.[76] This is a magnificently vague provision which has so far produced little litigation. The type of item envisaged by those who pressed for this provision in Parliament was a regimental trophy, but one wonders whether it could not lead to disputes over grandmother's silver teapot or great-grandmother's best tea dishes.

S8–32   The definition of furniture and plenishings is, of necessity, in fairly general terms, and there is obvious scope for considerable argument over what does and does not fall within it. It is unfortunate, therefore, that the uncertainty and the scope for litigation is further increased by employing this form of definition as "including" certain items. This merely throws one back on the common law concept of what is furniture and plenishing, with a number of specific examples and exceptions pointed out by the Act. Since every item which is held to pass to the surviving spouse under this head automatically reduces the share falling to other persons interested in the succession, there is ample scope for disputes should there be other estate sufficient to satisfy the monetary prior right under s.9. Any family animosities are at their bitterest when an estate is being divided up. An executor would be wise to treat the classification of particular items as furniture and plenishings with considerable caution.

Limit on value

S8–33   Where the value of the furniture and plenishings included in the intestate estate does not exceed £29,000 the surviving spouse is entitled to the whole thereof. If the value is over £29,000, and the excess is not required to meet the prior right under s.9, the executor has the discretion of selecting the items to be covered by this prior right.[77] This limit will be adequate in most estates. Its function is to provide for the possibility that the deceased spouse had extremely valuable paintings hanging on the walls of the house.

S8–34   Disputes as to valuations are to be settled by a single arbiter (arbitrator) under s.8(5), as in the case of valuations of the house.[78] The reference to the intestate being domiciled outwith Scotland is indicative that for the purposes of Scots international private law such furniture and plenishings is to be regarded as heritable property.[79]

Prior right of surviving spouse to financial provision on intestacy
9.—[1,3,6,7](1) Where a person dies intestate and is survived by a husband, wife or civil partner the survivor shall be entitled to receive out of the intestate estate—

[2,3,4](a) if the intestate is survived by issue [. . .] the sum of £50,000 or such larger amount as may from time to time be fixed by order of the Secretary of State, or

[2,3,5](b) if the intestate is not survived by issue [. . .] the sum of £89,000 or such larger amount as may from time to time be fixed by order of the Secretary of State,

---

[76] s.8(6)(c).
[77] See para.S9–25.
[78] See para.S8–24.
[79] See the discussion in para.7–23 (IPL).

together with, in either case, interest at the rate of 7 per cent per annum or, at such rate as may from time to time be fixed by order of the Secretary of State, on such sum from the date of the intestate's death until payment:

Provided that where the surviving spouse or civil partner is entitled to receive a legacy out of the estate of the intestate (other than a legacy of any dwelling house to which the last foregoing section applies or of any furniture and plenishings of any such dwelling house), he or she shall, unless he or she renounces the legacy, be entitled under this subsection to receive only such sum, if any, as remains after deducting from the sum fixed by virtue of para-graph (a) of this subsection or the sum fixed by virtue of paragraph (b) of this subsection, as the case may be, the amount or value of the legacy.

[1](2) Where the intestate estate is less than the amount which the surviving spouse or civil partner is entitled to receive by virtue of subsection (1) of this section the right conferred by the said subsection on the surviving spouse or civil partner shall be satisfied by the transfer to him or her of the whole of the intestate estate.

[1](3) The amount which the surviving spouse or civil partner is entitled to receive by virtue of subsection (1) of this section shall be borne by, and paid out of, the parts of the intestate estate consisting of heritable and moveable property respectively in proportion to the respective amounts of those parts.

[1](4) Where by virtue of subsection (2) of this section a surviving spouse or civil partner has right to the whole of the intestate estate, he or she shall have the right to be appointed executor.

(5) The rights conferred by the Intestate Husband's Estate (Scotland) Acts 1911 to 1959 on a surviving spouse in his or her deceased spouse's estate shall not be exigible out of the estate of any person dying after the commencement of this Act.

(6) For the purposes of this section—

(a) the expression "intestate estate" means so much of the net intestate estate as remains after the satisfaction of any claims under the last foregoing section; and

[1](b) the expression "legacy" includes any payment or benefit to which a surviving spouse or civil partner becomes entitled by virtue of any testa-mentary disposition; and the amount or value of any legacy shall be ascertained as at the date of the intestate's death.

NOTES

1. As amended by the Civil Partnership Act 2004 (c.33) Sch.28(1) para.5 (effec-tive December 5, 2005).
2. Words repealed by the Law Reform (Parent and Child) (Scotland) Act 1986 (c.9) s.10(2), Sch. 2.
3. As amended by the Succession (Scotland) Act 1973 (c.25) s.1(1)(b).
4. Figure substituted by the Prior Rights of Surviving Spouse and Civil Partner (Scotland) Order 2011 (SSI 2011/436) Sch.1 para.1 (effective February 1,

2012). Earlier values: September 10, 1964 to May 22, 1973—£2,500; May 23, 1973 to December 30, 1977—£4,000; December 31, 1977 to July 31, 1981—£8,000 (SI 1977/2110); August 1, 1981 to April 30, 1988—£15,000 (SI 1981/806); May 1, 1988 to November 25, 1993—£21,000; November 26, 1993 to April 1, 1999—£30,000; April 2, 1999 to May 31, 2005—£35,000; June 1, 2005 to January 31, 2012—£42,000.

5. Figure substituted by the Prior Rights of Surviving Spouse and Civil Partner (Scotland) Order 2011 (SSI 2011/436) Sch.1 para.1 (effective February 1, 2012). Earlier values: September 10, 1964 to May 22, 1973— £5,000; May 23, 1973 to December 30, 1977—£8,000; December 31, 1977 to July 31, 1981— £16,000 (SI 1977/2110); August 1, 1981 to April 30, 1988—£25,000 (SI 1981/806); May 1, 1988 to November 25, 1993—£35,000; November 26, 1993 to April 1, 1999—£50,000; April 2, 1999 to May 31, 2005—£58,000; April 2, 1999 to May 31, 2005—£35,000; June 1, 2005 to January 31, 2012—£75,000.

6. As amended by the Interest on Prior Rights (Scotland) Order 1981 (SI 1981/805) art. 2.

7. As amended by the Law Reform (Miscellaneous Provisions) (Scotland) Act 1980 (c.55) s.4(a).

DEFINITIONS

"estate": s.36(2).
"intestate": s.36(1).
"intestate estate": ss.9(6)(a) and 36(1).
"issue": s.36(1).
"legacy": s.9(6)(b).
"testamentary disposition": s.36(1).

COMMENTARY

Monetary prior right under s.9—general

S9–01   Section 9(1) applies where the deceased has died "intestate" which includes partially intestate.[80] It entitles the surviving spouse or civil partner to £50,000 if the deceased was survived by issue, or to £89,000 if the deceased left no issue. This right comes out of the intestate estate left after the housing and furniture and plenishings rights under s.8 have been met[81] and is, therefore, in addition to the right to house, furniture and plenishings.

S9–02   Interest is payable on the £50,000 or £89,000 as the case may be from the date of the intestate's death until payment.[82] Although the Act originally specified a fixed rate of interest (four per cent) the rate is variable by the Secretary of State, and is currently seven per cent per annum.[83]

---

[80]   See commentary on s.36(1) and the definition of "intestate".
[81]   s.9(6)(a).
[82]   s.9(1).
[83]   Interest on Prior Rights (Scotland) Order 1981 (SI 1981/805). From 1964 to 1981 it was 4%.

When the Act came into force in 1964, the surviving spouse's right was **S9–03** restricted to the lower figure only when the deceased was survived by lawful issue. This included adopted children but not illegitimate children. Thus, if a deceased wife was survived only by an illegitimate child, her husband was entitled to a prior right at the higher level even if that entirely defeated the child's claim in the mother's estate. This had also been the case under the corresponding provisions prior to the 1964 Act[84] and still applies in the division of the estates of persons who died on or after September 10, 1964, up to and including November 24, 1968.

However, on November 25, 1968—the commencement of the 1968 Act—the **S9–04** first major improvement of the position of illegitimate children came into force. Illegitimate children were put on the same footing as legitimate children in the succession to both parents (although only in succession directly to the parents). The result is that, since that date the surviving spouse's prior monetary right has been restricted to the lower figure whenever the deceased was survived by children, legitimate or illegitimate.[85] From November 25, 1968, until the Law Reform (Parent and Child) (Scotland) Act 1986[86] came into force on December 8, 1986, the existence of lawful issue, however remote, of a predeceasing child of the intestate also restricted the surviving spouse's right, but illegitimate offspring of a predeceasing child were not taken into account.

This was because the policy was to grant illegitimate children rights of succes- **S9–05** sion in the estates of their parents, but not to permit them to represent their parents in, for example, the division of the estates of their grandparents. When this policy was applied to prior rights, the result was that the existence of an illegitimate child affected the division of the estate of his or her father or mother, but not any other estate. Thus, if the intestate's sole child (legitimate or illegitimate) had predeceased him, only the existence of legitimate offspring of that child reduced the surviving spouse's right.[87]

However, the status of illegitimacy was for practical purposes abolished by the **S9–06** 1986 Act and this has now been confirmed by the 2006 Act.[88] The consequence is that the existence of any issue of the deceased spouse reduces the right of the surviving spouse under s.9 to the lower figure of £50,000.

The children or issue concerned must, of course, be of the deceased spouse but **S9–07** need not be of the surviving spouse. Children of the deceased by a previous marriage or children who would formerly have been classed as illegitimate automatically reduce the surviving spouse's entitlement.

For the situation of posthumous children see Ch.4 of this book. **S9–08**

---

[84] *Osman v Campbell*, 1946 S.C. 204.
[85] 1968 Act (c.70) s.3 and Sch.1, amending s.9(1) of the Act.
[86] (c.9).
[87] s.9(1)(a), as amended, read with the definition of "issue" in s.36(1).
[88] See paras S2–13 to S2–16.

Partial intestacy and the effect of legacies

S9–09 The essential purpose of the monetary right in s.9 was to provide further compensation for a spouse in the situation of total intestacy where there is by definition no bequest in favour of the spouse. Absent the s.9 right, where in such a situation the deceased was survived by children, grandchildren (or great-grandchildren), siblings or parents, the spouse would be left without any interest in the estate other than the housing-related rights in s.8. Section 9 is intended to reflect the provision that a spouse would have made for the other spouse had they made a will.

S9–10 If, however, there is a "testamentary disposition", leaving a "legacy" for the spouse, but some of the estate has fallen into intestacy[89] and thus subject to s.9, the Act provides that account must be taken of the legacy as otherwise the combined effect of the will together with s.9 would be to over-provide for the spouse. The means by which this is achieved is through the granting of the monetary prior right in s.9 under deduction of any unrenounced legacy which the spouse can claim under the will.[90] The exception is where the legacy is of "any dwelling house to which [s.8] applies or any furniture and plenishings of any such dwelling house".[91]

S9–11 The words "any dwelling house to which [s.8] applies" were a reference back to the original wording of s.8(4) which provided:

> "This section applies, in the case of an intestate, to any dwelling house in which the surviving spouse of the intestate was ordinarily resident at the date of death of the intestate".

The re-wording of s.8(4) carried out by s.14(4) of the Crofting Reform etc. Act 2007 took away the words "This section applies" without making any consequential change to the proviso in s.9(1). However, given that in substance both paragraphs (a) and (b) of the re-enacted s.8(4) refer to the dwelling house in which the spouse was ordinarily resident, it can be taken that the exceptions to the deduction of the bequest are a bequest of the house in which the spouse was ordinarily resident at the death of the intestate and a bequest of the furniture and plenishings of that house. This accords with the purpose of s.9 being to give the spouse further monetary provision in addition to her residence and the furniture and plenishings. If she already has the residence under a bequest (rather than under s.8(1)), that should not prejudice her entitlement to the additional monetary provision under s.9.

S9–12 There are also questions (a) whether if the survivor was ordinarily resident in more than one house, he or she may take the s.9 prior right without deduction in respect of legacies of all such houses and the furniture and plenishings of those houses, and (b) whether if the survivor should elect to take intestate furniture and plenishings from a house other than that in which she was ordinarily resident, whether a deduction must be made nevertheless from the s.9 right in respect of a

---

[89] See s.36(1).
[90] s.9(1) proviso.
[91] s.9(1) proviso.

legacy of furniture and plenishings in the house where she was ordinarily resident.

With regard to the first question, to allow a spouse or civil partner to take lega- **S9–13** cies of all houses in which she happened to be ordinarily resident, plus the whole s.9 monetary right would be contrary to the aim of avoiding over-provision. It would result in an unjustified discrimination in relation to the s.9 right between spouses who obtained their residence under s.8(1) and those who obtained their residence under a will. Nevertheless, given that s.9 does not require the making of an election for the purposes of deduction or some other means of selection between the residences, the effect of the proviso is to discriminate in favour of legatees of multiple residences and of the furniture and plenishings in all of them. The effect in such a situation is that there is no deduction in respect of the legacy of any house ordinarily resided in or of the furniture and plenishings in any such house. Clearly there was an error in the drafting of the proviso but neither author has been able see any way around it.

The situation postulated in the second question is likely to be unusual. However, **S9–14** the wording of the proviso is again clear and no deduction falls to be made in respect of the furniture and plenishings in the house of ordinary residence.

If the surviving spouse or civil partner chooses to renounce any legacy affecting **S9–15** the monetary prior right, as might be done if the legacy were of dubious value, and there is no effective residue clause in the will, the full sum may be claimed from the intestate estate.

What falls to be deducted is a "legacy" out of the "estate" of the deceased. **S9–16** Section 9(6)(b) defines a legacy for these purposes as including "any payment or benefit to which a surviving spouse becomes entitled by virtue of any testamentary disposition". The expression "testamentary disposition" may have different meanings in different contexts of the Act.[92] In the context of s.9 it is submitted that "testamentary disposition" can include an inter vivos disposition with a special destination in favour of the surviving spouse as well as provisions in marriage contracts which take effect on death. Given the terms of the scope of "testamentary disposition", special destinations (including survivorship destinations) and marriage contract provisions are deductable as "legacies". Whether donations *mortis causa* are legacies under a "testamentary disposition" is less clear. It is submitted, however, that having regard to the purpose of the proviso to the s.9 monetary right, the definition of "testamentary disposition" in s.9(6)(b) should be construed to include such donations as "legacies".

The valuation of any such legacy is to be made as at the date of the deceased's **S9–17** death.[93]

Estate affected by the s.9 monetary right

Where the amount of the estate available to meet the monetary payments, after **S9–18** deducting the rights under s.8, is less than the specified figures that spouse's s.9

---

[92] See paras S36–28 to S36–29.
[93] s.9(6)(b).

right is held to be satisfied by the transfer to him or her of the whole of the available balance, thereby exhausting the estate.[94] This can give the spouse more than she would receive by way of a will leaving her the whole estate. Consider a man dies intestate leaving a widow and two children. The net value of his estate is £315,000 consisting of a house valued at £250,000, furniture and plenishings thereof valued at £25,000, and net moveable estate of £40,000. The widow's prior right under s.8 gives her the house and furniture and plenishings. Her prior right to a monetary provision under s.9 is to £50,000, there being lawful issue of the deceased spouse. The balance available to meet this right is only £40,000, and hence the widow takes the whole of it in satisfaction of her rights. Thus the whole of the deceased's estate has gone to his widow. The son and daughter have a right to legitim in any moveable estate available after the spouse's prior rights have been met and to any free balance of the estate after *jus relictae* and legitim have been deducted. Here, however, the estate is not large enough to reach the stage of calculating legal rights, let alone dividing up any free balance under the rules in Part I of the Act. Hence the widow takes the whole estate, and the children get nothing.

S9–19   Take, however, exactly the same family with exactly the same items of estate, but postulating that the husband had not taken or received appropriate legal advice and had made a homemade will leaving his whole estate to his wife. Since he has made a will dealing with his whole estate, his widow has no prior rights.[95] There is, therefore, estate from which legitim is exigible, despite the will. The moveable estate amounts to £65,000 (furniture, etc., plus the net moveable estate) and the legitim fund for division between the children is therefore £21,666. The widow receives the remaining £43,334 of the moveable estate and the house by virtue of the will.

S9–20   It is therefore possible, by dying intestate, to achieve an exclusion of the children's right to legitim, although it is not possible to achieve this by express testamentary provision. Indeed the children can be better off when their parent makes a will attempting to cut them out of any share in his estate than when he does nothing at all. At first sight it seemed that there might now be situations in which a solicitor would find himself in the position of advising his client not to make a will. This would have been unsatisfactory, since much depends on the precise value of the estate at the intestate's death and ingenious drafting devices were suggested to achieve the best of both worlds.

S9–21   The simple answer was, however, pointed out by Professor McDonald.[96] If a client seeks to ensure that his widow will receive his whole estate, he should make a will wholly in her favour without a destination over in the event of her failing to take the testamentary gift. If the issue do not claim legitim the will operates whatever the value of the estate. If the issue do claim legitim and the estate is above the limit of value at which intestacy ceases to be more beneficial to the widow than testacy, then the widow takes under the will subject to the legitim. If the issue

---

[94] s.9(2) and (6)(a).
[95] Prior rights come only from the "intestate estate": ss.8(1) and 9(1).
[96] A.J. McDonald, "Succession (Scotland) Act 1964 - I and II" (1965) 10 J.L.S. 4.

claim legitim and the estate is below that critical value (which is rather above the amount that would pass wholly to the widow by prior rights) the widow simply renounces her benefit under the will. This necessarily results in intestacy, there being no other beneficiary under the will and will allow her to claim prior rights.

The question of whether such a renunciation in fact made the deceased **S9–22** an "intestate" for the purpose of s.9 was closely argued in *Kerr, Petitioner*.[97] The decision by the sheriff-substitute, affirmed by the sheriff on appeal, was that intestacy did result, so that the widow became entitled to the whole estate by virtue of her prior rights to the total exclusion of her step-daughter. This result was probably inevitable, for the alternative would have been to postulate the estate falling into a category of neither testacy or intestacy but which merely excluded prior rights. There is nothing to suggest that Parliament intended to create such a category.

Apportioning the s.9 payment between heritage and moveables

Where the amount of the estate available to meet the monetary payment under **S9–23** s.9 is greater than the amount due to the surviving spouse, s.9(3) provides that the amount concerned

> "shall be borne by, and paid out of, the parts of the intestate estate consisting of heritable and moveable property respectively in proportion to the respective amounts of those parts".

Despite the assimilation of heritage and moveables for some purposes of succession, this is necessary because the distinction between heritage and moveables has been kept for the purposes of the legal rights of *jus relicti, jus relictae* and legitim. After the prior rights under ss.8 and 9 have been satisfied, the surviving spouse is entitled to *jus relicti* or *jus relictae* only in the surplus moveables, and issue of the deceased have the right to legitim, also in the surplus moveables. A precise value for moveables must therefore be maintained at the stage of prior rights so that the surplus moveables from which legal rights can be taken may be accurately ascertained.

The proportion of the s.9 prior right payable by heritage and by moveables is **S9–24** the proportion which the net capital value of each bears to the net capital value[98] of the whole estate available to meet the monetary payment. As an example, if the net estate after satisfaction of the housing and plenishing rights under s.8 is £100,000, consisting of heritage to the value of £25,000 and moveables to the value of £75,000, heritage represents one-quarter of the estate and bears one-quarter of the payment to the surviving spouse, i.e. £12,500 or £22,250 as the case may be. Moveables, representing three-quarters of the estate, bear the remaining three-quarters of the s.9 payment. The balance of the moveables is subject to *jus relicti* or *jus relictae*, and to legitim if applicable.

---

[97] *Kerr (Catherine), Petitioner*, 1968 S.L.T. (Sh. Ct) 61 and see the commentary on s.36(1) and (2) and para.S36–26. See also M.C. Meston, "Succession (Scotland) Act 1963" (1968) 13 J.L.S. 192.

[98] After satisfaction of all debts and s.8 claims, and any legacies: ss.9(6)(a) and 36(1).

Making of the s.9 payment

S9–25   The surviving spouse is entitled to insist upon the furniture and plenishings and the deceased's interest in the house being transferred in view of the express terms of the statute. However, for other intestate assets the executor has a discretion whether to realise the asset and distribute the proceeds or to distribute *in specie*.[99] The discretion must be exercised in the interest of the estate as a whole, and if distribution is made *in specie* the executor may distribute equally to the beneficiaries (which will normally be appropriate). However, circumstances may be such that it is appropriate for the executor to be selective and to transfer different assets to individual beneficiaries.[100]

Entitlement to be executor-dative

S9–26   Where the prior rights exhaust the whole intestate estate, s.9(4) provides that the spouse (or civil partner) has the right to be appointed as executor, presumably executor-dative. If there is no appointment by the deceased of an executor-nominate, for example where there is no will at all, an issue has arisen whether s.9(4) gives the spouse an exclusive right to be appointed executor-dative. In the face of commissary practice to that effect, it has been held that s.9(4) does not give the spouse an exclusive right to appointment even if she claims that her prior rights exhaust the whole estate.[101] If there is partial intestacy and an executor-nominate wishing to act, it is submitted that the spouse would be entitled to be appointed executor-dative and then confirmed jointly with the executor-nominate, although such situations would be very unusual. A petition for appointment as executor-dative under the right in s.9 should be made *qua* spouse or civil partner.

Provisions supplementary to ss.8 and 9
[1]9A.—Any order of the Secretary of State, under section 8 or 9 of this Act, fixing an amount or rate—

(a) **shall be made by statutory instrument which shall be subject to annulment in pursuance of a resolution of either House of Parliament; and**
(b) **shall have effect in relation to the estate of any person dying after the coming into force of the order.**

NOTE

1. Inserted by the Law Reform (Miscellaneous Provisions) (Scotland) Act 1980 (c.55) s.4(b).

---

[99] *Cochrane's Executors v Inland Revenue Commissioners*, 1975 S.L.T. 6 where the Lord President stated that the executor was not bound to take directions even from a residuary legatee. See also *Murray's Judicial Factor v Thomas Murray & Sons (Ice Merchants) Ltd*, 1992 S.L.T. 824.
[100] See also the commentary on s.14(1).
[101] *Murray, Petitioner*, 2012 S.L.T. (Sh. Ct) 57; see para.S14–12; and the case commentary by James Inglis, "Murray, Petitioner, 2012 S.L.T. (Sh Ct) 57", 2012 S.L.T. (News) 155.

Abolition of terce and courtesy, and calculation of legal rights

10.—(1) The right of courtesy of a surviving husband in his deceased wife's estate and the right of terce of a surviving wife in her deceased husband's estate shall not be exigible out of the estate of a person dying after the commencement of this Act.

[1](2) The amount of any claim to legal rights out of an estate shall be calculated by reference to so much of the net moveable estate as remains after the satisfaction of any claims thereon under the two last foregoing sections.

NOTE

1. As amended by the Civil Partnership Act 2004 (c.33) Sch.28(1) para.6 (effective December 5, 2005).

DEFINITION

"estate": ss.36(2) and 10(2).

COMMENTARY

The former legal rights of courtesy and terce[102] were abolished for deaths on or after September 10, 1964, but as there was no change to the legal rights of *jus relictae, jus relicti* and legitim, they remain exigible from moveables only. See s.33 for the construction of deeds referring to legal rights. **S10–01**

If the prior rights under ss.8 and 9 exhaust the estate, there will be no estate from which to pay legal rights.[103] **S10–02**

10A. [*Inserted by the Law Reform (Miscellaneous Provisions) (Scotland) Act 1968 (c.70) s.2 in respect of estates of persons dying on or after November 25, 1968, and repealed by the Law Reform (Parent and Child) (Scotland) Act 1986 (c.9) Sch.2.*]

Representation in, and division of, legitim

11.—[1](1) Subject to the next following subsection, where a person (hereinafter in this section referred to as "the deceased") dies predeceased by a child who has left issue who survive the deceased, and the child would, if he had survived the deceased, have been entitled [. . .] to legitim out of the deceased's estate, such issue shall have the like right to *legitim* as the child would have had if he had survived the deceased.

[1](2) If, by virtue of the foregoing subsection or otherwise, there are two or more persons having right among them to *legitim*, then the *legitim* shall—

(a) if all of those persons are in the same degree of relationship to the deceased, be divided among them equally, and

---

[102] See Ch.1.
[103] s.10(2); and see commentary on s.9.

(b) in any other case, be divided equally into a number of parts equal to the aggregate of—

    (i) those of the said persons who are nearest in degree of relationship to the deceased (in this paragraph referred to as "the nearest surviving relatives") and

    (ii) any other persons who were related to the deceased in that degree and who (if they had survived him) would have been entitled to *legitim* out of his estate, but who have predeceased him leaving issue who survive him and are entitled to *legitim* out of his estate;

and, of those parts, one shall be taken by each of the nearest surviving relatives, and one shall be taken *per stirpes* by the issue of each of the said predeceased persons, being issue who are entitled as aforesaid.

[. . .]

(3) Nothing in the last foregoing subsection shall be construed as altering any rule of law as to collation of advances; and where any person is entitled to claim *legitim* out of the estate of a deceased person by virtue of subsection (1) of this section he shall be under the like duty to collate any advances made by the deceased to him, and the proportion appropriate to him of any advances so made to any person through whom he derives such entitlement, as if he had been entitled to claim such *legitim* otherwise than by virtue of the said subsection (1).

[1](4) For the avoidance of doubt it is hereby declared that where any person is entitled by virtue of [. . .] subsection (1) of this section to *legitim* out of the estate of the deceased, and the deceased is not survived by any child, the proportion of the estate due to any surviving spouse in respect of *jus relicti* or *jus relictae* shall be ascertained as if the deceased had been survived by a child.

NOTE

1. Words repealed by the Law Reform (Parent and Child) (Scotland) Act 1986 (c.9) s.10(2), Sch.2.

COMMENTARY

General

S11–01   Until the Act came into force, there was no representation in claims for legitim. Only the surviving immediate children of the deceased qualified, with the result that a single surviving child was entitled to the whole of the legitim fund to the exclusion of the issue of predeceasing children, but also shared with them in the distribution of the dead's part. The introduction of infinite representation means that issue of predeceasing members of the class entitled to legitim will take their parent's share. The rule of division in subsection (2) is the same as that in s.6 and suffers from the same defects, which become particularly obvious when one attempts to calculate "the proportion appropriate to him" of advances to a representative's parent for the purpose of collation (subs.(3)). See the commentary on s.6. For general information on legitim see Ch.5.

Effect on collation inter liberos

Section 11(3) lays down no means of assessment of "the proportion appropriate **S11–02** to [the legal rights holder] of" an advance to his ancestor which the legal rights claimant must collate. This can give rise to severe difficulties if the only persons entitled to legitim are grandchildren, the immediate children having predeceased, for per capita division means that the share of the legitim fund taken by a grandchild is not the same as the share which his parent—to whom an advance was made—would have taken.[104] The grandchild may be entitled to only, say, one-sixth of the legitim fund where his parent might have been entitled to one-half, but the grandchild may still be debited with the whole of the advance made to the parent. Worse, the parent may have dissipated the advance and the grandchild may have received no benefit from it at all. It may be that "the proportion appropriate" should be measured by reference to the benefit from his ancestor's share acquired by the legal rights claimant. This appears to be the equitable solution which it is open for a court to apply. In that event if the claimant received no share from the advance to his ancestor the advance will not be collatable. See also Ch.5 under the heading "Collation *inter liberos*".

Legitim not to be discharged by ante-nuptial marriage contract
12. Nothing in any ante-nuptial contract of marriage executed after the commencement of this Act shall operate so as to exclude, on the occurrence of the death of either party to the marriage, the right of any child of the marriage (or of any issue of his coming in his place by virtue of the last foregoing section) to *legitim* out of the estate of that party unless such child or issue shall elect to accept in lieu of *legitim* the provision made in his favour under the contract.

DEFINITION

"estate": ss.36(2) and 10(2).

COMMENTARY

It was one of the well-known anomalies of the pre-1964 Act law that it was **S12–01** possible by ante-nuptial marriage contract for intending spouses to discharge prospectively the legal rights of any children of the marriage. This could not be done after the marriage but the fact that it was possible at all made a severe dent in the protective function of legal rights for children. The children obviously were not parties to the arrangement, and yet their rights might be discharged for them

---

[104] See M.C. Meston, "Collation of Advances to Ancestors", 1967 S.L.T. (News) 195, and "Letters to the Editor" at 224 and 247.

with very little, or even in some cases no, consideration. For example in *Galloway's Trustees v Fenwick*[105] the marriage contract made a provision for children, but the fact that the father appointed the whole of the provision to one of them did not alter the fact that the right of the others to claim legitim was discharged.[106]

S12–02   Section 12 abolished this anomaly by providing that in relation to an antenuptial marriage contract entered into between the parents and executed[107] after the commencement of the 1964 Act (i.e. on or after September 10, 1964) the right to legitim of a child or of remoter issue cannot be excluded by anything contained in it. Whatever such a marriage contract may provide, the descendant has the election between the provisions in his favour in the marriage contract and his legitim. In other words it is purely a question of satisfaction of legal rights and of approbate and reprobate and no longer one of a prospective discharge of the right to legitim at the instance of third parties. Section 12 applies to any ante-nuptial marriage contract actually executed after the commencement of the 1964 Act. Older ante-nuptial marriage contracts might still come into operation, and an exclusion of the children's legitim contained in such a contract would still be effective.

Equitable compensation

[1]**13. Every testamentary disposition executed after the commencement of this Act by which provision is made in favour of the spouse or of any issue of the testator and which does not contain a declaration that the provision so made is in full and final satisfaction of the right to any share in the testator's estate to which the spouse or the issue, as the case may be, is entitled by virtue of *jus relicti, jus relictae* or *legitim*, shall (unless the disposition contains an express provision to the contrary) have effect as if it contained such a declaration [. . .].**

NOTE

1. Words repealed by the Law Reform (Parent and Child) (Scotland) Act 1986 (c.9) s.10(2), Sch.2.

COMMENTARY

S13–01   In the case of wills actually executed[108] after the commencement of the Act this section removes most of the practical effect of the abstruse doctrine of equitable compensation. In a typical case before the Act, where a testamentary liferent was rejected in favour of a capital sum as the legal right, and vesting of the fee was not thereby accelerated, the income would accumulate. Over a substantial period the accumulated income might amount to enough to restore to the estate what was lost

---

[105] *Galloway's Trustees v Fenwick*, 1943 S.C. 339, 1943 S.L.T. 291.

[106] In *Callander v Callander's Executor*, 1972 S.C. (HL) 70, 1972 S.L.T. 209 the exclusion of legitim by the marriage contract still stood even although the children had assigned all their interests to their father and thus received nothing under the contract.

[107] The date of execution of such a contract is its actual date of execution (s.36(3)).

[108] s.36(3).

by paying out the capital sum. In that case, the liferent again became available to the beneficiary unless there was a clause in the will declaring that its provisions were in full satisfaction of legal rights.

Section 13 now implies such a clause in every will, unless there is an express **S13–02** declaration to the contrary. The result is that in the vast majority of cases, equitable compensation cannot be claimed, but there may still be equitable compensation for other non-legal right holding beneficiaries adversely affected by a claim for legal rights.[109] For that reason the *1990 Report on Succession* recommended reform in relation to the proposed new legal share.[110]

PART III

ADMINISTRATION AND WINDING UP OF ESTATES

Assimilation for purposes of administration, etc., of heritage to moveables

14.—(1) Subject to subsection (3) of this section the enactments and rules of law in force immediately before the commencement of this Act with respect to the administration and winding up of the estate of a deceased person so far as consisting of moveable property shall have effect (as modified by the provisions of this Act) in relation to the whole of the estate without distinction between moveable property and heritable property; and accordingly on the death of any person (whether testate or intestate) every part of his estate (whether consisting of moveable property or heritable property) falling to be administered under the law of Scotland shall, by virtue of confirmation thereto, vest for the purposes of administration in the executor thereby confirmed and shall be administered and disposed of according to law by such executor.

[1](2) Provision shall be made by the Court of Session by act of sederunt made under the enactments mentioned in section 22 of this Act (as extended by that section) for the inclusion in the confirmation of an executor, by reference to an appended inventory or otherwise, of a description, in such form as may be so provided, of any heritable property forming part of the estate.

(3) Nothing in this section shall be taken to alter any rule of law whereby any particular debt of a deceased person falls to be paid out of any particular part of his estate.

NOTE

1. The Administration of Estates Act 1971 s.6 provides:

   "6.—(1) It shall be competent to include in the inventory of the estate of any person who dies domiciled in Scotland any real estate of the deceased situated in England and Wales or Northern Ireland, and accordingly in section 9 of the

---

[109] See Ch.5 under "Satisfaction of Legal Rights".
[110] See Ch.8 at para.8–23.

Confirmation of Executors (Scotland) Act 1858 the word 'personal' wherever it occurs is hereby repealed.

(2) Section 14(2) of the Succession (Scotland) Act 1964 (act of sederunt to provide for description of heritable property) shall apply in relation to such real estate as aforesaid as it applies in relation to heritable property in Scotland".

DEFINITIONS

"estate": s.36(2).

COMMENTARY

General

S14–01   The Act had a profound effect upon the law affecting the administration of estates. The relevant provisions are mainly contained in Part III of the Act (ss.14 to 22) and apply to the administration of the estates of persons dying on or after September 10, 1964.[111] They apply to all estates whether testate or intestate. What follows does not purport to be a full account of the position of executors or of the details of administration of estates, but instead an account of the key features of the appointment and confirmation of executors and their essential duties.[112]

S14–02   Prior to the Act the functions of an executor were confined to the moveable estate of the deceased. In his capacity as executor, he had no concern with the deceased's heritage. Thus while his function was to ingather and distribute moveables after paying moveable debts, the heritage passed directly to the heir at law or legatee without the intervention of a middleman. Section 14 of the Act extended the executor's competence to the whole estate of the deceased, as defined in s.36(2)—other than titles of honour, coats of arms, Scottish secure tenancies and property falling within the provisos to s.36(2).[113] Section 14(1) therefore extended to heritable property all statutory and common law rules relating to the winding up and administration of the moveable estates of deceased persons whether testate or intestate. The general policy was put into effect by s.14(1) and the modification of existing statutes.[114] The executor thus became the key figure in the transfer of any estate of the deceased whether moveable or not, so long as it fell to be administered under Scots law.

Right to the office of executor—executor-nominate

S14–03   The person entitled to the office of executor in preference to all others is the executor-nominated by the deceased. Nothing is said in the Act about those entitled to office as executors-nominate. Accordingly, the position remains that an executor-nominate may be a person expressly or impliedly appointed by the

---

[111] s.37(1)(d).

[112] Full accounts are given in W.A. Wilson and A.G.M. Duncan, *Trusts, Trustees and Executors*, 2nd edn (Edinburgh: W. Green, 1995) and *Currie on Confirmation* (2011).

[113] See commentary on s.36(2).

[114] Sch.2, especially para.3.

deceased[115] or one placed in that position by s.3 of the Executors (Scotland) Act 1900.[116]

The normal, and simplest, case is that of the express appointment of an exec- **S14–04** utor, e.g. "I appoint X to be my executor". Equally, it is practice to treat as executors-nominate any persons on whom the deceased has conferred the powers of an executor, even although he may not have used the term "executor". For example, in *Martin v Ferguson's Trustees*,[117] where the expression used was "I wish my estate to be managed" by specified persons, those persons were to be regarded as executors-nominate.

Constructive appointment as executor-nominate arises under s.3 of the 1900 **S14–05** Act as amended.[118] This provides:

> "Where a testator has not appointed any person to act as his executor, or failing any person so appointed, the testamentary trustees of such testator, original or assumed, or appointed by the Supreme Court or the sheriff court (if any), failing whom any general disponee or universal legatory or resid- uary legatee appointed by such testator, shall be held to be his executor- nominate and entitled to confirmation in that character."

This is a fairly comprehensive coverage of persons whom the deceased might possibly have wished to act as his executor, and it is to be noted that assumed trustees, even if the original trustees have resigned immediately after the assump- tion, are still entitled to confirmation as executors-nominate. Provided that it is clear from the whole tenor of the deceased's will, or from the terms of an appoint- ment of trustees by the court, that there is not intended to be any bar to the persons in question taking up office as executors, they will be entitled to that office in preference to all others whose claim is merely through relationship. For more detail on constructive appointment as executor-nominate under s.3 of the 1900 Act see *Currie on Confirmation*.[119]

Right to the office of executor— executor-dative

It is when the deceased has not appointed executors, either through dying intes- **S14–06** tate or by not making a nomination in his will, or when his executors-nominate or residuary legatees either predecease him or are deemed to predecease him or refuse to take up the office, that an executor-dative is required to be appointed by the court. Equally, a sole executor-nominate can die after taking up office. The rules of preference for the appointment of an executor-dative in such situations are less clear. The only provisions in the Act regulating the right to appointment by the court as executor-dative appear in ss.9(4) and 5(2), and they do not appear

---

[115] See *Currie on Confirmation* (2011), paras 5–01 to 5–47.
[116] (63 and 64 Vict. c.55).
[117] *Martin v Ferguson's Trustees* (1892) 19 R. 474.
[118] (63 and 64 Vict. c.55) s.3, as amended by the Law Reform (Miscellaneous Provisions) (Scotland) Act 1980 (c.55) Sch.2.
[119] *Currie on Confirmation* (2011), paras 5–48 to 5–81 and 5–83 to 5–88.

to cover the whole situation. For s.9(4) see the commentary on s.9.[120] For appointment of executors-dative of persons dying domiciled outwith Scotland see paragraphs 7–07 to 7–08.

S14–07   The other provision in the Act is that in s.5(2). This also bears a relationship to one of the few previous statutory enactments on the subject—namely, the last part of s.1 of the Intestate Moveable Succession (Scotland) Act 1855.[121] That provided that, in a competition for the office of executor, surviving next of kin were to be preferred to the representatives of predeceasing next of kin, who were given a right of succession for the first time by s.1 of the 1855 Act. Section 5(2) provides that the right of representatives to the office of executor is postponed to the right of surviving members of the class, predeceasing members of which they are representing.

S14–08   Leaving aside the exceptional situation of the appointment of an executor-creditor (a type of diligence), any person who is entitled to succeed to the moveables upon intestacy is entitled to be appointed executor-dative.[122] Where more than one person is entitled to be appointed, if those entitled and willing are unable to agree who should be appointed (and there can be more than one appointment[123]), a competition for appointment as executor-dative can arise. In that competition the practice is to follow the order set out in the "Orders to be Observed in the Confirmation of all Testaments" issued in 1666 by the archbishops and bishops with the authority of the Court of Session, notwithstanding the reference to "testaments". The position under the Order was that the next of kin (ascertained according to the common law[124]) were primarily entitled to the office. Failing them, at common law the widow as creditor in respect of her *jus relictae* was entitled to office, followed by other creditors and special legatees. If there was no-one thus entitled and willing to seek appointment, the initial practice was for the procurator fiscal to seek appointment but this has now been replaced by the possibility of the appointment of a judicial factor.[125] Where two persons of the same ranking in the order of appointment seek to be appointed executor-dative the court has no discretion to refuse to appoint any one of them.[126]

S14–09   The various statutory amendments to the common law of intestate moveable succession, particularly the Intestate Moveable Succession (Scotland) Act 1855, had the effect of giving the various new statutory beneficiaries rights to the office of executor postponed to, or along with, the next of kin.[127] For example, the right of succession conferred on a mother by s.4 of the 1855 Act also gave her, by implication, a right to the office of executor-dative *qua* mother,[128] possibly even along with the next of kin if they competed. However, the whole order of preference to the office of executor, as also the order of succession, hinged on the next

---

[120] See para.S9–26.
[121] (18 and 19 Vict. c.23).
[122] Erskine, III, ix, 1; and *Webster v Shiress* (1878) 6 R. 102 at 105.
[123] *Muir* (1876) 4 R. 74.
[124] See Ch.1.
[125] *Wills & Succession*, ii, 861.
[126] *Russo v Russo*, 1998 S.L.T. (Sh. Ct) 32.
[127] *Webster v Shiress* (1878) 6 R. 102.
[128] *Muir* (1876) 4 R. 74.

of kin under the common law rules, followed by the possible additions in respect of statutory beneficiaries.

The Act, however, abolished the common law concept of next of kin for deter- **S14–10** mining the order of the beneficial succession to the estate of a deceased person,[129] replacing it with the statutory list in s.2. A question therefore arose whether the common law concept of the next of kin[130] remained relevant in competitions for the office of executor-dative or whether the Act brought about a new basic concept that the right to be executor depends on the existence of a right of succession under the 1964 Act.

There is no inherent improbability in the existence of a different method of **S14–11** establishing the right to the executorship from that employed in settling the beneficial succession, and it would seem that it is still correct to appoint an executor *qua* next of kin if he falls within the common law category, even though his right of succession may be by a different title under the 1964 Act. There is nothing in the Act to alter the previous rule under which the next of kin had the pre-eminent right. This is fortified by the provisions of Schs 1 and 2 of the Act of Sederunt (Confirmation of Executors) 1964 which continue to provide for decerniture of an executor-dative *qua* next of kin.

On the analogy of the treatment of the purely statutory beneficiaries under the **S14–12** Intestate Moveable Succession (Scotland) Act 1855, those who have a right of succession under the 1964 Act, though not being in the category of next of kin, would seem to be entitled in a competition to be appointed executors together with the next of kin.[131] In a competition it seems doubtful whether the next of kin could be completely ousted by a statutory beneficiary, although there can be cases where the next of kin have no rights of beneficial succession.[132] For example, a deceased might be survived by a spouse and by a paternal uncle. Even if the estate were large enough to leave a surplus after the surviving spouse's prior rights, the free estate after deduction of legal rights would not fall to the uncle, who is the next of kin, but to the surviving spouse under s.2(1)(e). Admittedly, the uncle would be unlikely to seek the office of executor in these circumstances, but it seems very doubtful whether, if he did, his claim could be rejected in favour of that of the spouse. The more probable course would seem to be to make two appointments, one *qua* next of kin and one *qua* surviving spouse. There is a question whether the position would be different if the spouse claimed that her prior rights exhausted the whole estate and sought appointment under s.9(4) but the next of kin took issue with that and sought a co-appointment. It is submitted that the same course, namely a dual appointment, should follow. Nevertheless, this appears to be at odds with commissary practice which at least up to the case of *Murray, Petitioner*[133] was to treat the right of appointment under s.9(4) as an exclusive right. For a critique of this practice and further discussion the reader is referred to *Currie on Confirmation*.[134]

---

[129] s.1(1).
[130] See paras 1–11 to 1–13.
[131] As in *Webster v Shiress* (1878) 6 R. 102.
[132] *Bone v Morrison* (1866) 5 M. 240 at 243–244.
[133] *Murray, Petitioner*, 2012 S.L.T. (Sh. Ct) 57; and see para.S9–26.
[134] *Currie on Confirmation* (2011), paras 6–26 to 6–41.

S14–13   The situation which seems to have arisen most frequently in practice is that of an elderly surviving spouse who is either *incapax* or unwilling to act as executor and an adult child who is willing to act. In these circumstances, if the child was a son it would seem to be perfectly competent to appoint the son executor in his capacity as next of kin. If the estate was not exhausted by the prior rights (assuming that it was intestate), a daughter could confirm in her capacity as a legal rights claimant.

S14–14   Apart from this type of situation, it is probably true that only those who have beneficial rights of succession under the 1964 Act will seek to be appointed executors-dative. The office of executor is usually regarded as a burden rather than as a benefit to be actively sought. But the result would seem to be that those of the statutory beneficiaries who apply and who are also next of kin should be appointed and confirmed in the character of next of kin. Any statutory beneficiary who is not one of the next of kin should be appointed and confirmed in his statutory character. Thus a mother would be confirmed *qua* mother, never being one of the next of kin, while the father would be confirmed *qua* father when there were also brothers and sisters, so that his right of succession was purely statutory, but *qua* next of kin when there were no brothers and sisters. Similarly, when the succession has opened to collaterals of the half blood, there is now no distinction between the half blood consanguincan and the half blood uterine. But only the half blood consanguinean could be next of kin at common law. Hence, if two persons sought appointment as executor, one in each category of collaterals of the half blood, the half blood consanguinean would be confirmed *qua* next of kin but the half blood uterine would be confirmed *qua* brother or sister of the half blood "related through their mother" in the words of s.3. Where two persons of the same ranking in the order of appointment seek to be appointed executor-dative the court has no discretion to refuse to appoint one of them.[135]

S14–15   Anyone who is entitled to be appointed may be appointed without special intimation to other persons having an equal or even a preferable claim to the office. Any applicant to whom an earlier application had not been intimated formally and having the same or an equal right in the order of preference as an existing executor-dative is entitled to be conjoined to the office along with the existing executor-dative.[136] Such an applicant having a right preferable to that of the existing executor-dative is entitled to have the appointment recalled without the need for a reduction.[137]

S14–16   An application for appointment (decerniture) as executor-dative must be made to any sheriff court of the sheriffdom where the deceased died domiciled, and, in the case of persons dying domiciled outwith of Scotland, or without any fixed or known domicile within Scotland but having property in Scotland, to Edinburgh Sheriff Court.[138] For the procedure see *Currie on Confirmation*.[139]

---

[135] *Russo v Russo*, 1998 S.L.T. (Sh. Ct) 32.
[136] *Webster v Shiress* (1878) 6 R. 102.
[137] *Webster v Shiress* (1878) 6 R. 102.
[138] Confirmation of Executors (Scotland) Act 1858 (21 and 22 Vict. c.56) s.3 (as amended) and Act of Sederunt (Commissary Business) 2013 (SSI 2013/291) para.4.
[139] *Currie on Confirmation* (2011), paras 7–09 to 7–58.

Obtaining confirmation

Before obtaining confirmation an executor-dative (but not normally an **S14–17** executor-nominate) must find caution for his administration of the estate.[140] The amount of caution, unless judicially restricted, is the full gross amount of the deceased's estate and is usually provided by means of a bond of caution from an insurance company. There is, however, doubt whether the rules relating to caution serve a useful purpose, at least in certain circumstances. When the executor is also the sole beneficiary there is no need to protect the beneficiary against the possibility that as executor he might defraud himself. The cost of a bond in such circumstances is useless expenditure, and there is now a provision that if an intestate's spouse is executor-dative and is also entitled to the whole estate by virtue of prior rights, there is no requirement to find caution. A serious gap in the protection afforded by bonds of caution arises when items such as civil service gratuities are involved. Such gratuities will not normally be included in the estate confirmed to, and if the executor should fail to account to the beneficiaries for the amount of the gratuity, caution may not protect the true beneficiary.[141]

An application for confirmation must be made to any sheriff court of the sher- **S14–18** iffdom where the deceased died domiciled, and, in the case of persons dying domiciled outwith Scotland, or without any fixed or known domicile within Scotland but having property in Scotland, to Edinburgh Sheriff Court.[142] The application is on a form which contains an inventory of the estate anywhere in the world. For details of the procedure see *Currie on Confirmation*.[143]

As a consequence of the assimilation of heritage and moveables, and of the **S14–19** extension to heritage of the executor's authority, confirmation is granted to the heritage[144] as well as the moveables. Before the Act came into force, an executor, *qua* executor, had authority over moveable estate only and was confirmed only to the moveable estate. He did prepare an inventory which included details of heritage, but that was for taxation purposes. For purposes of confirmation, the inventory was solely of moveable property. A similar situation continues to exist in respect of non-UK property, although additional forms must now be filled in for HM Revenue & Customs.

The executor, unless he is an executor-creditor, must confirm to the whole **S14–20** estate,[145] including agricultural leases and interests therein.[146] The inventory should also include the digital estate of the deceased such as assets held with social media providers such as Facebook.[147] While such estate may be located outwith Scotland,

---

[140] 1823 Act s.2. Executors seeking appointment on the basis of s.9(4) of the 1964 Act are excepted.
[141] See (1967) 12 J.L.S. 258, and the remarkable case of *Harrison v Butters*, 1969 S.L.T. 183 in which a divorced wife represented herself as the widow and obtained confirmation with the backing of a bond of caution. When the true widow appeared, it seems that the caution provided no protection as it would have been void from essential error as to identity.
[142] 1858 Act ss.8 and 3 (as amended) and Act of Sederunt (Commissary Business) 2013 (SSI 2013/291) para.3(3) and Sch.3.
[143] *Currie on Confirmation* (2011), Ch.10.
[144] Except where the heritage is governed by a survivorship destination.
[145] See the definition in s.36(2) and commentary thereon.
[146] *Cormack v McIldowie's Executors*, 1975 S.L.T. 214; *Rotherwick's Trustees v Hope*, 1975 S.L.T. 187.
[147] See I. Sim and B. O'Neill, "Digital Estate", 2013 S.L.T. (News) 97.

the confirmation will at least give the executors title to seek to recover it. If any part of the deceased's estate should prove to have been omitted from the confirmation, or if it has been valued incorrectly, it is necessary for the executor to expede an eik to his confirmation in order to vest the omitted property in him or alter the value in the confirmation. It is only estate to which he has confirmed which vests in the executor. He only requires to account for the value stated in the confirmation.

S14–21   Section 14(2) is consequential to the application of law previously relating to moveable estate to heritable estate. It obliges the Court of Session to exercise its powers under s.22 to specify how heritable property is to be mentioned in an application for confirmation. Pursuant to ss.14(2) and 22, the Act of Sederunt (Confirmation of Executors) 1964 as amended by the Act of Sederunt (Confirmation of Executors Amendment) 1966 provides that the inventory embodied in a confirmation must include such a description of heritage "as will be sufficient to identify the property or interest therein as a separate item in the deceased person's estate". The intention is that something less than a full convey-ancing description will be adequate, so that, for instance, a mere statement of the street name and number would be acceptable. However, a sufficient identification of the heritage is essential for the confirmation to give the executor a title (right) to deal with the heritage.[148] For more guidance on how heritage should be described in the inventory see *Currie on Confirmation*.[149]

Vesting of estate in an executor

S14–22   The effect of confirmation is to vest in the executor every part of the estate set out in the inventory "falling to be administered by the law of Scotland". Whether estate falls to be administered by Scots law depends on whether there is estate situated in Scotland. If there was any estate[150] of the deceased located in Scotland it will fall to be administered by the law of Scotland, regardless of the residence or domicile of the deceased on his or her death. Location of estate is considered in Ch.7.[151] Administration and substantive law must be distinguished. While the estate vesting in an executor is restricted to that located in Scotland, an executor will nevertheless require to take foreign estate into account when deciding on the succession to an estate. The rules which an executor or Scottish court must apply to determining succession to foreign estate are the rules of Scots substantive international private law.[152] The determination of succession under these rules does not of course mean that the decision of a Scottish court will be recognised and enforced in the country where the asset is located. For that to happen, steps must be taken in the country in question under its rules for administration of estates.

S14–23   The effect of vesting differs depending on the nature of the property comprised in the estate which has been confirmed to. The heritage which previously vested directly in the heir at law in cases of intestacy or in a trustee (who might of course

---

[148] See the commentary on s.15(1).
[149] *Currie on Confirmation* (2011), paras 10–77 to 10–83.
[150] See the definition in s.36(2) and commentary thereon.
[151] See paras 7–05 and 7–06.
[152] See Ch.7.

be the executor) if one was appointed, now vests directly in the executor *qua* executor by virtue of confirmation with retrospective effect to the date of death. As such, the executor may exercise all the powers arising from a vested right, including completion of title to heritage.[153]

Duties of an executor

The executor's first duty is to ingather the whole estate of the deceased with due **S14–24** dispatch. The mere nomination, or even judicial appointment, of an executor does not of itself give him the authority to do this unless there are circumstances where steps require to be taken to preserve the estate and it is not possible to obtain confirmation beforehand.[154] This has also been extended to assignation by an unconfirmed executor[155] although it is a condition in both cases that the steps in question, whether the obtaining of a decree or the effectiveness of the assignation, are followed by the confirmation of the executor in question.[156] Otherwise an executor who deals with the estate before confirmation is known as a vitious intromitter, the effect of which at common law can render him personally liable to the creditors (excluding legal rights claimants) of the deceased without regard to the quantum of the estate intromitted with or the quantum of the estate as a whole.[157] Limited relief at common law is available[158] but there has to be some doubt over whether and, if so, to what extent this penal effect of vitious intromission is consistent with art.1 of the First Protocol of the European Convention on Human Rights. Subsequent confirmation prior to the service of a summons or initial writ by the creditor purges the effect of any prior vitious intromission and in the case of intromission by an executor-nominate, or person entitled to be appointed executor-dative, confirmation even after the service will purge provided it is done within one year and one day of the death.[159] If the intromission involves a confirmed executor dealing with an asset not in the inventory and there is service before an eik is obtained, there is a presumption of personal liability.[160]

The second major function of the executor is to use the estate so ingathered to **S14–25** meet the liabilities of the deceased.[161] No change was made in this position by the Act so that, as before, the executor acts independently of both creditors and beneficiaries, and subject to the limitation of his liability to the value of the deceased's estate, he is *eadem persona cum defuncto*. If he discovers, or should

---

[153] *Robertson, Petitioner*, 1978 S.L.T. (Sh. Ct) 30; *Garvie's Trustees v Garvie's Tutors*, 1975 S.L.T. 94. This may possibly mean that the spouse of a single executor could have occupancy rights under the Matrimonial Homes (Family Protection) (Scotland) Act 1981.

[154] *Chalmers' Trustees v Watson* (1860) 22 D. 1060 at 1064.

[155] *Mackay v Mackay*, 1914 S.C. 200. This is important in order to prevent tenancies held by the deceased from being lost: see paras S16–02 and S16–19 to S16–26.

[156] e.g. through the insertion into a decree of a condition that the pursuer obtain confirmation before extracting the decree: *Fyffe v Ferguson* (1842) 4 D. 1482.

[157] Erskine, III, ix, 49.

[158] *Wills & Succession*, ii, 1302; and see *Adam Bros & Co v Campbell* (1854) 16 D. 964.

[159] Erskine, III, ix, 52. Erskine allows the extended purging to "next of kin" a "universal legatee" and "relict". These were persons entitled to be appointed executor-dative but now the entitlement extends to s.2 heirs also.

[160] Erskine, III, ix, 52.

[161] See Ch.3.

have discovered, that the estate is absolutely insolvent, an executor has the duty to petition for sequestration of the estate or the appointment of a judicial factor and to do so within a reasonable period. The sanction is that any intromissions after that date render him liable to the penalties of vitious intromission even although he has obtained confirmation from the court.[162]

S14–26   An executor cannot be compelled to pay any debts (other than privileged debts) before the expiry of a period of six months within which creditors may claim equal ranking.[163] Although the Act does bring both heritage and moveables under his control, it has not entirely assimilated heritage and moveables for the purposes of succession rights. Thus, in order to permit an accurate value to be struck for the moveables subject to legal rights, the executor must still allocate debts between heritage and moveables, and s.14(3) specifically preserves the rules whereby a debt is allocated to a specific part of the estate. The incidence of inheritance tax on heritage and moveables differs from the former rules for estate duty, so that in the absence of expression by the testator to the contrary, a specific legacy of a house does not now bear the burden of the tax applicable to the house if there is other estate available to meet the burden.[164] There is no longer an heir to contrast with the executor, so that the division "as between heir and executor" has now become a division "as between heritage and moveables". Indeed, references in any enactment to "heirs" now include a reference to executors.[165]

S14–27   The third function is to settle any prior or legal rights due from the estate or to obtain from any spouse or descendant entitled to legal rights a discharge of the legal rights or the equivalent in the form of an election in favour of a testamentary provision. Legal rights are a debt of the estate, payable after the settlement of the ordinary debts of the estate and any prior rights and failure to settle any entitlement to legal rights will render the executor personally liable to the legal rights claimant for the amount of legal rights payment.[166] The executor must therefore inform any person entitled to legal rights of their entitlement in general terms and advise them to obtain independent legal advice.[167] If prior rights on intestacy exhaust the whole of the estate there is no need to settle any legal rights as no such claim can arise. See the commentary on ss.8 and 9 on prior rights. See Ch.5 for further commentary on legal rights.

S14–28   Finally, having satisfied the debts, prior (if applicable) and legal rights, the executor is under a duty to distribute the balance of the estate to those entitled to it. This means that the primary responsibility for determining who is entitled to it falls upon the executor, although in the event of uncertainty or a dispute between potential beneficiaries he or she may require claimants to raise an action of declarator of entitlement or present a special case to the Court of Session, failing which he may in the event of a dispute between competing claimants, raise an action of multiplepoinding. There may also be a claim by a cohabitee under s.29 of the 2006 Act. If such a claim is made it is submitted that the executor should,

---

[162] Bankruptcy (Scotland) Act 1985 (c.66) s.8(4).
[163] *Wills & Succession*, ii, 2159.
[164] *Cowie's Trustees, Petitioners*, 1982 S.L.T. 326; Inheritance Tax Act 1984 s.211; and see para.3–17.
[165] Sch.2 para.2(b).
[166] *Earl of Dalhousie v Crokat* (1868) 6 M. 659.
[167] *Donaldson v Tainsh's Trustees* (1886) 13 R. 967 at 972; and see para.5–53.

as executor, maintain neutrality between the claim of the cohabitee and the heirs on intestacy. If he is one of the heirs then any opposition to the claim should be made by him in a personal (individual) capacity and the expenses of it should not be chargeable to the estate as an executor's expense. In the ordinary case, however, the succession will be decided by the executor.

Given that an executor can be personally liable to a beneficiary for wrongful **S14–29** distribution of the estate[168] there is some onus on him, possibly only in the interests of self-protection, to take reasonable and prudent steps to search out beneficiaries. It would be at least advisable for him in an intestacy to investigate the family tree sufficiently to establish that there are no relatives closer to the deceased than those of whose claims he has notice. An executor should also act without undue delay. If the estate contains an interest in a tenancy he should be alert to ensure that the time limits for the transfer of the tenancy to its successor in s.16(3), (4C) and (4D) of the Act are complied with.

However, in view of the practical difficulties which would arise when an illegiti- **S14–30** mate person is, or might be, involved, the 1968 Act[169] gives the executor some protection. Section 7 absolves him of the necessity to establish that there is no illegitimate person who has a right of succession or whose existence would affect rights of succession. In addition, the executor is not required to establish that there is no paternal relative of an illegitimate person.[170] He is exempted from personal liability to any person whose claim depends on illegitimacy if he had no notice of the claim at the time of distribution. The claimant's right is not barred and he may take any steps open to him to recover property from those holding it (which will usually require the executor to make the recovery or lend the claimant his title on the receipt of an indemnity from the claimant), but the executor's personal liability to him is avoided.

If express claims by illegitimate persons (or which depend on the existence of **S14–31** illegitimate persons) are presented to the executor, he will decide on their validity in the usual way, and in cases of doubt will require the claimant to prove his relationship. This proof may now take the form of a declarator of parentage, which gives rise to a general presumption (i.e. one not limited in effect to the parties to the declarator) to the same effect as the declarator.[171]

Similarly, s.24(2) of the Act provides that an executor or trustee may distribute **S14–32** the deceased's estate without ascertaining that no adoption order has been made by virtue of which any person is or may be entitled to an interest therein. An intolerable burden would be placed on an executor if he had to ensure not only that the deceased himself had never adopted a child, but also that his parents, or either of them, or indeed any other relative had never adopted a child. He is therefore freed from liability to any such person of whose claim he had no notice. Similar protection is given in respect of a full gender recognition certificate.[172]

---

[168] *Lamond's Trustees v Croom* (1871) 9 M. 662; *Buttercase and Geddie's Trustees v Geddie* (1897) 24 R. 1128; and see para.S14–33 and s.20, proviso and commentary.
[169] (c.70).
[170] Law Reform (Miscellaneous Provisions) (Scotland) Act 1968 s.7(c) added by the Law Reform (Parent and Child) (Scotland) Act 1986 to replace s.4(3) of the 1964 Act.
[171] Law Reform (Parent and Child) (Scotland) Act 1986 (c.9) ss.7 and 5(3).
[172] Gender Recognition Act 2004 (c.7) s.17.

S14–33   For carrying out his functions, an executor-dative is given by s.20 of the Act all the powers, privileges and immunities of a gratuitous trustee, with the exception of a power to resign or to assume new executors, and is subject to all the restrictions on such a trustee. This includes, for example, the duty to avoid acting as *auctor in rem suam*.[173] Apart from those exceptions, executors-dative have all of the powers, privileges and immunities of a "trustee" in the Trusts (Scotland) Acts 1921 and 1961. This does not, however, exempt an executor-dative from finding caution for his intromissions.[174] Executors-nominate have all of those powers, privileges and immunities unless the contrary be expressed in the deed of appointment.[175] An executor has a duty to account for his intromissions (dealings) with the estate to all beneficiaries (including legal rights claimants) and therefore it is prudent for an executor to keep proper account of his dealings with the estate.

Provisions as to transfer of heritage

15.—[1](1) Section 5(2) of the Conveyancing (Scotland) Act 1924 (which provides that a confirmation which includes a heritable security shall be a valid title to the debt thereby secured) shall have effect as if any reference therein to a heritable security, or to a debt secured by a heritable security, included a reference to any interest in heritable property which has vested in an executor in pursuance of the last foregoing section by virtue of a confirmation:

Provided that a confirmation (other than an implied confirmation within the meaning of the said section 5(2)) shall not be deemed for the purposes of the said section 5(2) to include any such interest unless a description of the property, in accordance with any act of sederunt such as is mentioned in subsection (2) of the last foregoing section, is included or referred to in the confirmation.

[2](2) Where in pursuance of the last foregoing section any heritable property has vested in an executor by virtue of a confirmation, and it is necessary for him in distributing the estate to transfer that property—

(a) to any person in satisfaction of a claim to legal rights or the prior rights of a surviving spouse or civil partner out of the estate, or

(b) to any person entitled to share in the estate by virtue of this Act, or

(c) to any person entitled to take the said property under any testamentary disposition of the deceased,

the executor may effect such transfer by endorsing on the confirmation (or where a certificate of confirmation relating to the property has been issued in pursuance of any act of sederunt, on the certificate) a docket in favour of that person in the form set out in Schedule 1 to this Act, or in a form as nearly as may be to the like effect, and any such docket may be specified as a midcouple

---

[173] *Inglis v Inglis*, 1983 S.L.T. 437.

[174] Unless she has by virtue of her prior rights entitlement to the whole estate (1823 Act s.2, as substituted by the Law Reform (Miscellaneous Provisions) (Scotland) Act 1980 (c.55) s. 5).

[175] 1900 Act s.2.

or link in title in any deduction of title; but this section shall not be construed as prejudicing the competence of any other mode of transfer.

NOTES

1. As amended retrospectively by the Law Reform (Miscellaneous Provisions) (Scotland) Act 1968 (c.70) s.19. The Conveyancing (Scotland) Act 1924 s.5(2) (following the Abolition of Feudal Tenure etc. (Scotland) Act 2000) provides:

   "5.—(2) (a)   When the holder of a heritable security has died, whether with or without a recorded title, and whether testate or intestate, any confirmation in favour of an executor of such deceased which includes such security shall of itself be a valid title to the debt thereby secured, and shall also be a warrant for such executor dealing with such debt and also with such security in terms of the third section of this Act, and also for completing a title to such security in terms of the fourth section of this Act.

   (b) For the purposes of this subsection, "*confirmation*" shall include any probate or letters of administration or other grant of representation to moveable or personal estate of a deceased person issued -

   (a) by any court in England and Wales or Northern Ireland and noting his domicile in England and Wales or Northern Ireland, as the case may be, or
   (b) by any court outwith the United Kingdom and sealed in Scotland under section 2 of the Colonial Probates Act 1892

   and the confirmation thereby implied shall operate in favour of the person or the persons or the survivors or survivor of them to whom such probate, letters of administration or other grant of representation were granted; and "*executor*" shall include such person or persons; and such implied confirmation shall be deemed to include all heritable securities which belonged to the deceased."

2. As amended by the Civil Partnership Act 2004 (c.33) Sch.28(1) para.7 (effective December 5, 2005).

DEFINITIONS

"estate": s.36(2).

COMMENTARY

Effect of heritable property vesting in executor

Section 15(1) sets out the effect of the vesting of heritable property in the **S15–01** executor in terms of s.14(1). It does so through the clumsy device of deeming the words "heritable security" and "debt thereby secured" in s.5(2) of the 1924 Act to mean "any interest in heritable property which has vested in the executor by virtue of confirmation under s.14(1)". Given that s.5(2) applies to deceased holders of unrecorded or unregistered heritable securities it must follow that it applies equally to deceased holders of unrecorded or unregistered titles to heritable property.

The effect of vesting is that the executor is given a "valid title" to the interest held by the deceased in the heritable property. In order for the executor to have such a title to the interest in the heritable property, the inventory submitted in the application for confirmation and therefore the confirmation itself must have a description of the property which is sufficient to identify the property or interest therein as a separate item in the deceased person's estate.[176] For further advice on what is a sufficient description the reader is referred to *Currie on Confirmation*.[177] Such a description is not necessary for the giving of a valid title to foreign executors or administrators who have a deemed confirmation[178] which in s.5(2)(b) of the 1924 Act is referred to as an "implied confirmation".

Completion of title to heritable property

S15–02   However, the valid title given by s.15(1) is incomplete without registration in the Land Register or recording in the Register of Sasines. Section 5(2) of the 1924 Act allows an executor to complete a title *qua* executor to property last registered in the Register of Sasines by means of recording a notice of title under s.4(1) of the 1924 Act in that Register and this has now been extended[179] to registration in the Land Register by means of a notice of title under s.4A of the 1924 Act. Prior to December 8, 2014, s.1(4)(c) of the Land Registration (Scotland) Act 1979 allowed an executor to complete such a title in the Land Register only to property last registered in the Land Register. Section 4A of the 1924 Act allows first registration in the Land Register by means of the said notice of title. This may be of advantage where the executor anticipates holding the heritage as a trustee over a significant period of time.

S15–03   The provisions of the 1964 Act making confirmation the link in the notice of title or subsequent disposition opened up a new stream of title through the executor. It was not immediately obvious what effect this had upon the alternative method of using the deceased's will as the link in title, where there was such a will, and even yet the position is somewhat clouded on certain points. It seems likely that the intention was to make the confirmation the only valid link in title, but this was not in fact done. The position seems to be that in all cases where a will contains a general conveyance to testamentary trustees or executors-nominate, title may be completed or deduced in the registrable deed by using the will as the link. There is, however, grave doubt whether it is competent for a special legatee to whom a direct bequest of heritage is made to complete or deduce his title by use of the will.[180] Difficulties can be avoided by following the recommendation of all the professors and the Law Society of Scotland[181] that the confirmation should be used in preference to the will. It will be noted that use of the confirmation permits

---

[176] s.15(1), proviso; and Act of Sederunt (Confirmation of Executors) 1964 (SI 1964/1143) s.1, as inserted by the Act of Sederunt (Confirmation of Executors Amendment) 1966 (SI 1966/593).

[177] *Currie on Confirmation* (2011), paras 10–77 to 10–83.

[178] See para.7–07.

[179] By the Land Registration etc. (Scotland) Act 2012 (asp 5) s.53.

[180] Opinion of the Professors of Conveyancing (1965) 10 J.L.S. 153 (where the four professors divided equally).

[181] Notes issued by the Law Society (1966) 11 J.L.S. 84.

the use of the simplified docket procedure for transfer and gives the protection of s.17, which would not seem to apply if title is taken through the will.

Transfer of heritable property by docket

Section 15(2) introduced a new procedure, which has proved very popular and **S15–04** effective, permitting an executor to transfer heritage to a beneficiary merely by endorsing a docket on the confirmation—or more usually on a certificate of confirmation relating only to the property in question. The form of the docket is specified in Sch.1. Preferably the signature of the docket should be witnessed in accordance with s.3 of the Requirements of Writing (Scotland) Act 1995 so as to make it presumed to have been signed for evidential purposes and also to allow for registration for preservation in the Books of Council and Session. This is desirable to prevent loss of the document.

The effect of such a docket is to put the beneficiary in the position of being an **S15–05** unregistered owner of the heritage. It is then open for the beneficiary to apply to have his title registered by means of a notice of title under ss.4(1) or 4A of the Conveyancing (Scotland) Act 1924. Such a docket is a valid link in title, in either a notice of title by the beneficiary in favour of himself or in a disposition by the beneficiary in favour of another person. The docketed document cannot be recorded or registered directly into either Land or Sasine Registers. Given that a docket is a transfer to the beneficiary, not merely a statement of who at the deceased's death was entitled to the heritage, it is incompetent to execute a docket in favour of a beneficiary who has died.[182]

Provisions relating to leases

16.—(1) This section applies to any interest, being the interest of a tenant under a lease, which is comprised in the estate of a deceased person and has accordingly vested in the deceased's executor by virtue of section 14 of this Act; and in the following provisions of this section *"interest"* means an interest to which this section applies.

[1,4](2) Subject to subsection (4A), where an interest—

(a) is not the subject of a valid bequest by the deceased, or
(b) is the subject of such a bequest, but the bequest is not accepted by the legatee, or
[2,3](c) being an interest under an agricultural lease, is the subject of such a bequest, but the bequest is declared null and void in pursuance of section 16 of the Act of 1886 or section 11 of the 1991 Act or becomes null and void under section 10 of the Act of 1955,

and there is among the conditions of the lease (whether expressly or by implication) a condition prohibiting assignation of the interest, the executor shall be entitled, subject to subsection (2A) of this section, to transfer the interest.

---

[182] (1966) 11 J.L.S. 36.

[5](2A) Transfer by an executor pursuant to subsection (2) of this section—

(a) *[Repealed by the Crofting Reform (Scotland) Act 2010 (asp 14) Sch.4 para.2(2)(a)(i) (effective October 1, 2011)]*;

[6](b) of an interest under any lease (other than the lease of a croft within the meaning of section 3(1) of the Crofters (Scotland) Act 1993 (c.44)) and which is not a transfer to one of the persons entitled to succeed to the deceased's intestate estate or to claim legal rights or the prior rights of a surviving spouse or civil partner out of the estate, in satisfaction of that person's entitlement or claim, shall require the consent of the landlord.

[1](3) Subject to subsection (4C), if in the case of any interest—

(a) at any time the executor is satisfied that the interest cannot be disposed of according to law and so informs the landlord, or

[1, 6](b)   subject to subsection (3A) the interest is not so disposed of within a period of one year or such longer period as may be fixed by agreement between the landlord and the executor or, failing agreement, by the relevant court on the application of the executor—

   [2](i) in the case of an interest under an agricultural lease which is the subject of a petition to the Land Court under section 16 of the Act of 1886 or an application to that court under section 11 of the 1991 Act, from the date of the determination or withdrawal of the petition or, as the case may be, the application,

      (ia) *[Repealed by the Crofting Reform etc. Act 2007 (asp 7) Sch.2 para.1 (effective January 28, 2008)]*.
      (ib) *[Repealed by the Crofting Reform (Scotland) Act 2010 (asp 14) Sch.4 para.2(2)(b)(ii) (effective October 1, 2011)]*.

   (ii) in any other case, from the date of death of the deceased,

either the landlord or the executor may, on giving notice in accordance with the next following subsection to the other, terminate the lease (in so far as it relates to the interest) notwithstanding any provision therein, or any enactment or rule of law, to the contrary effect.

[7](3A) In the case of an interest in an agricultural lease which is a lease of a croft within the meaning of section 3(1) of the Crofters (Scotland) Act 1993 (c.44), the period for the purposes of subsection (3)(b) is 24 months.

(4) The period of notice given under the last foregoing subsection shall be—

(a) in the case of an agricultural lease, such period as may be agreed, or, failing agreement, a period of not less than one year and not more than two years ending with such term of Whitsunday or Martinmas as may be specified in the notice; and
(b) in the case of any other lease, a period of six months:

Provided that paragraph (b) of this subsection shall be without prejudice to any enactment prescribing a shorter period of notice in relation to the lease in question.

⁸(4A) Where an interest, being an interest under a lease constituting a short limited duration tenancy or a limited duration tenancy–

(a) is not the subject of a valid bequest by the deceased; or
(b) is the subject of such a bequest, but the bequest is not accepted by the legatee; or
(c) is the subject of such a bequest, but the bequest is declared null and void by virtue of section 21 of the 2003 Act,

and there is among the conditions of the lease (whether expressly or by implication) a condition prohibiting assignation of the interest, the executor shall be entitled, notwithstanding that condition, to transfer the interest to a person to whom subsection (4B) below applies; and the executor shall be entitled so to transfer the interest without the consent of the landlord.

⁸(4B) This subsection applies to–

(a) any one of the persons entitled to succeed to the deceased's intestate estate, or to claim legal rights or the prior rights of a surviving spouse out of the estate, in or towards satisfaction of that person's entitlement or claim; or
(b) any other person.

⁸(4C) In the case of any interest under a lease constituting a short limited duration tenancy or a limited duration tenancy–

(a) if at any time the executor is satisfied that the interest cannot be disposed of according to law and so informs the landlord, the executor may terminate the tenancy (in so far as it relates to the interest); and
(b) if the interest is not so disposed of within the period referred to in subsection (4D) below, the lease shall (in so far as it relates to the interest) terminate at the expiry of the period,

notwithstanding any provision in the lease, or any enactment or rule of law, to the contrary effect.

⁸(4D) The period is one year or such longer period as may be fixed by agreement or, failing agreement, by the Land Court on the application of the executor–

(a) in the case of an interest which is the subject of an application to that court by virtue of section 21 of the 2003 Act, from the date of the determination or withdrawal of the application; and
(b) in any other case, from the date of death of the deceased.

⁸(4E) The–

(a) interest may be transferred under subsections (4A) and (4B) above; or

(b) tenancy may be terminated under subsection (4C)(a) above,

only if the transfer, or as the case may be, termination is in the best interests of the deceased's estate.

(5) Subsection (3) of this section shall not prejudice any claim by any party to the lease for compensation or damages in respect of the termination of the lease (or any rights under it) in pursuance of that subsection; but any award of compensation or damages in respect of such termination at the instance of the executor shall be enforceable only against the estate of the deceased and not against the executor personally.

[1](6) Where an interest is an interest under an agricultural lease, and—

[9](a) an application is made under section 3 of the Act of 1931 or section 13 of the Act of 1955 to the Land Court for an order for removal, or

[1,2](b) a reference is made under section 23(2) and (3) of the 1991 Act for the determination of any question which has arisen under section 22(2) (e) of that Act in connection with a notice to quit,

the order or determination shall not be in favour of the landlord, unless [. . .] it is reasonable, having regard to the fact that the interest is vested in the executor in his capacity as executor, that it should be made.

(7) Where an interest is not an interest under an agricultural lease, and the landlord brings an action of removing against the executor in respect of a breach of a condition of the lease, the court shall not grant decree in the action unless it is satisfied that the condition alleged to have been breached is one which it is reasonable to expect the executor to have observed, having regard to the fact that the interest is vested in him in his capacity as an executor.

[1,2,10](8) Where an interest is an interest under an agricultural lease and is the subject of a valid bequest by the deceased, the fact that the interest is vested in the executor under the said section 14 shall not prevent the operation, in relation to the legatee, of paragraphs (a) to (h) of section 16 of the Act of 1886, or, as the case may be, section 11(2) to (8) of the 1991 Act, or, as the case may be, section 21(2) and (3) of the 2003 Act, or, as the case may be, subsections (2) to (7) of section 10of the Act of 1955.

[11](8A) For the purposes of subsection (3)(b) above, the "relevant court" is—

(a) in the case of an interest under a lease constituting a 1991 Act tenancy, the Land Court; and

(b) in any other case, the sheriff,

and an application to the sheriff in any such other case shall be by summary application.

(9) In this section—

[1, 4]"agricultural lease" means a lease of a holding within the meaning of the Small Landholders (Scotland) Act 1886 to 1931, or a lease of a croft within the meaning of section 3(1) of the Crofters (Scotland) Act 1993 (or of any part of a croft if it is a part consisting of a right mentioned in section 3(4)(a) of that Act), or a lease constituting a 1991 Act tenancy, or a lease constituting a short limited duration tenancy or a limited duration tenancy;

"the Act of 1886" means the Crofters Holdings (Scotland) Act 1886;

"the Act of 1931" means the Small Landholders and Agricultural Holdings (Scotland) Act 1931;

[12]"the 1991 Act" means the Agricultural Holdings (Scotland) Act 1991;

[11]"the 2003 Act" means the Agricultural Holdings (Scotland) Act 2003 (asp 11);

[13]"the Act of 1955" means the Crofters (Scotland) Act 1955;

"lease" includes tenancy.

[11]"1991 Act tenancy", "short limited duration tenancy" and "limited duration tenancy" shall be construed in accordance with the 2003 Act.

NOTES

1. As amended by the Agricultural Holdings (Scotland) Act 2003 (asp 11) Sch.1 para.2(1) (effective November 27, 2003).
2. As amended by the Agricultural Holdings (Scotland) Act 1991 (c.55) Sch.11 para.24 (effective September 25, 1991).
3. As amended by the Law Reform (Miscellaneous Provisions) (Scotland) Act 1968 (c.70) s.8, Sch.2 Pt I para.22(a).
4. As amended by the Crofting Reform etc. Act 2007 (asp 7) Pt 2 s.15 (effective January 28, 2008).
5. Inserted by the Crofting Reform etc. Act 2007 (asp 7) Pt 2 s.15(3) (effective January 28, 2008).
6. As amended by the Crofting Reform (Scotland) Act 2010 (asp 14) Sch.4 para.2(2) (effective October 1, 2011).
7. Inserted by the Crofting Reform (Scotland) Act 2010 (asp 14) Sch.4 para.2(2) (c) (effective October 1, 2011).
8. Inserted by the Agricultural Holdings (Scotland) Act 2003 (asp 11) Pt 1 c.2 s.20 (effective November 27, 2003).
9. As amended by the Law Reform (Miscellaneous Provisions) (Scotland) Act 1968 (c.70) s.8, Sch.2 Pt I para.24.
10. As amended by the Law Reform (Miscellaneous Provisions) (Scotland) Act 1968 (c.70), s.8, Sch.2 Pt I para.25.
11. Inserted by the Agricultural Holdings (Scotland) Act 2003 (asp 11) Sch.1 para.2(1) (effective November 27, 2003).
12. Definition substituted by the Agricultural Holdings (Scotland) Act 1991 (c.55) Sch.11 para.24(d)(ii) (effective September 25, 1991).
13. Inserted by the Law Reform (Miscellaneous Provisions) (Scotland) Act 1968 (c.70) s.8, Sch.2 Pt I para.26(b).

DEFINITIONS

"agricultural lease": s.16(9).
"estate": s.36(2).
"interest": s.16(1).
"lease": ss.16(9) and 36(1).
"legal rights": s.36(1).
"limited duration tenancy": s.16(9).
"prior rights": s.36(1).
"short limited duration tenancy": s.16(9).
"the Act of 1886": s.16(9).
"the Act of 1931": s.16(9).
"the Act of 1955": s.16(9).
"the 1991 Act": s.16(9).
"1991 Act tenancy": s.16(9).
"the 2003 Act": s.16(9).

COMMENTARY

Inheritance and transfer of leases

S16–01   The interest of a tenant of land, which comprises his rights and duties *qua* tenant, is heritable property of the tenant, and at common law the default position eventually came to be that the heir at law[183] of the tenant was entitled to succeed to the tenant's interest unless the lease was a "liferent lease" which was expressed to expire on the death of the tenant.[184] There was no need for the property to be let expressly to a tenant "and his heirs" as the heir at law became the new tenant automatically upon the death of the tenant. This default position could be altered by means of (1) a special destination in the lease to someone else; (2) a bequest[185] of an assignable lease to someone else (or a bequest approved by the landlord[186]); or (3) a statutory provision allowing a bequest.[187] Given that the 1964 Act abolished heirs at law and provided for all "estate",[188] including heritable property, to vest in the executor, it was necessary to devise an alternative scheme for the inheritance and transfer of the tenant's interest. Section 16 fulfils this role.

S16–02   It is essential that executors should confirm to and transfer the tenant's interest in any lease.[189] The importance of confirmation was emphasised in *Rotherwick's Trustees v Hope*.[190] The executors had not confirmed to the deceased's lease of a

---

[183] See Ch.1.

[184] J. Rankine, *A Treatise on the Law of Leases in Scotland*, 3rd edn (Edinburgh: W. Green, 1916), pp.160 and 593; confirmed in *Mountain's Trustees v Mountain* [2012] CSIH 73, 2013 S.C. 202 at [32] to [33].

[185] Titles to Land (Consolidation) (Scotland) Act 1868 s.20; and see the Conveyancing (Scotland) Act 1874 ss.27, 46.

[186] *Reid's Trustees v Macpherson*, 1975 S.L.T. 101.

[187] Rankine, *A Treatise on the Law of Leases in Scotland* (1916), p.161.

[188] See commentary on s.36(2).

[189] With the possible exceptions of a residential Scottish secure tenancy under the Housing (Scotland) Act 2001 or a tenancy with an effective special destination.

[190] *Rotherwick's Trustees v Hope*, 1975 S.L.T. 187.

farm. The lease had therefore not vested in them and they therefore did not have the powers of disposal conferred by s.16. As they had not disposed of the lease within one year from the death of the deceased[191] the lease was deemed to have terminated through abandonment by the potential beneficiaries of the disposal[192] and decree of removing was granted. Agricultural and crofting tenancies do have a value which is part of the estate (even if the principles of valuation are not always very clear) and must be confirmed to.[193]

One particular difficulty is that during the period between the death of the tenant **S16–03** and the confirmation of his executor it is unclear in whom the tenant's interest has vested. As there is no longer an heir at law to succeed automatically by default to heritage, this means that a landlord may encounter severe difficulties in attempting to serve a notice to quit during that period, particularly if no executor has yet taken up office. If the tenant dies shortly before a term of Whitsunday or Martinmas, the landlord may be at least delayed in exercising his right to obtain possession by being unable to find someone on whom to serve notice before the term. Various suggestions for methods of coping with this problem have been put forward and the Scottish Law Commission has recommended that any notice to be given under a lease should continue to be addressed to the deceased party to the lease as if he were still alive.[194]

Bequests of leases

Section 16(8) provides that the detailed provisions relating to valid bequests of **S16–04** agricultural leases specified in the Crofters' Holdings (Scotland) Act 1886, the Agricultural Holdings (Scotland) Acts 1991 and 2003 and the Crofters (Scotland) Act 1955, as amended, are to have effect in relation to the legatee (or legatees) notwithstanding that the lease, or the deceased's interest therein, has vested in the executor for purposes of administration. The reference to s.10 of the Crofters (Scotland) Act 1955 must be read as a reference to s.10 of the Crofters (Scotland) Act 1993.[195] The reference in s.16(8) to an interest being the subject of a "valid bequest" must be read as a reference to a bequest that is valid leaving aside the effect of the detailed statutory provisions referred to.

If an executor is faced with a valid bequest[196] of the tenant's interest then he has **S16–05** a power and duty to execute that bequest regardless of s.16. Section 16 also does not apply where there is a valid special destination in the lease itself.[197] This is because the destination prevents the tenant's interest from being part of the "estate" which vests in the executor upon confirmation. A special destination

---

[191] s.16(3)(b).
[192] Rankine, *A Treatise on the Law of Leases in Scotland* (1916), p.161.
[193] In *Inglis v Inglis*, 1983 S.L.T. 437 the assignee of a farm lease was able to obtain a settlement of £35,000 plus a lease of a smaller area from the landlord. This was held to be part of the deceased's estate in a settlement with the other heirs.
[194] Scottish Law Commission, *Report on Recovery of Possession of Heritable Property* (HMSO, 1989), Scot. Law Com. No.118, recommendation 69. This does not appear to have been adopted in the Agricultural Holdings (Scotland) Act 1991. For the similar problem in crofting law, see D.J. MacCuish and D. Flyn, *Crofting Law* (Edinburgh: Butterworths Law, 1992), para.7.05.
[195] Interpretation Act 1978 (c.30) s.17(2)(a).
[196] As to which see s.29 and the commentary thereon.
[197] *Reid's Trustees v Macpherson*, 1975 S.L.T. 101 at 110.

exists where the particular property in the deed is disposed to a particular person (or persons) specifically nominated by the granter, without regard to the normal operation of the law of succession on intestacy.[198] A lease to A "and his heirs" did not contain a special destination to the heir or heirs.

Executor's power to select successor tenant

S16–06   In the absence of a valid bequest of the tenant's interest the executor continues to have a duty to transfer the tenant's interest to an appropriate beneficiary. This duty is important given that a failure to perform it timeously could result in the loss of that interest through the termination of the lease and a claim against the estate. Section 16 provides the executor with the powers to transfer the tenant's interest in the absence of an effective bequest. Section 16(2), (2A) and (4A) provide that where the deceased has not made a valid bequest of his interest, or, such a bequest having been made, it is either not accepted by the legatee[199] or is null and void under certain specified statutory provisions relating to agricultural leases or croft leases, the executor has a power to transfer the tenant's interest to a person selected by him or her even in the face of an express or implied condition in the lease prohibiting assignation. The extent of the executor's power of selection depends on the nature of the lease.

S16–07   Thus for a short limited duration tenancy or a limited duration tenancy under the Agricultural Holdings (Scotland) Act 2003 the executor may transfer the tenant's interest to any one person without the consent of the landlord.[200] The interest may only be transferred if it is "in the best interests of the deceased's estate".[201] It is unfortunate that the validity of such a transfer should have been made conditional on such a vague condition. It is also not made clear how this condition interacts with the implied duties of the executor in selecting the transferee which are discussed below.

S16–08   For a crofting tenancy within the meaning of s.3(1) of the Crofters (Scotland) Act 1993[202] the transfer may be to any one person. A notice of such a transfer must be given by the executor to both the landlord and the Crofting Commission as soon as may be after the transfer.[203] It should also be noted that under s.8(2A) of the 1964 Act it is possible for a spouse or cohabitant to succeed to a crofting tenancy by virtue of her prior rights without requiring selection.

S16–09   For a transfer of any other type of tenant's interest the transfer may be to any person entitled to claim prior rights, legal rights, or the holder of a cohabitant's award under s.29 of the 2006 Act or a right of succession under s.2 without the

---

[198] *Cormack v McIldowie's Executors*, 1975 S.C. 161 at 177, 180, 182.

[199] If the bequest is accepted (even without timeous notification) an intestate transfer is no longer possible: *Coats v Logan*, 1985 S.L.T. 221.

[200] s.16(4A) and (4B). The words "agricultural lease" in s.16(2A) might be seen as including short limited duration or limited duration tenancies by virtue of the definition of "agricultural lease" in s.16(9) but s.16(2), which is linked with s.16(2A), is stated to be "subject to subsection (4A)" which, together with subs.(4B), contain specific provision for short limited duration or limited duration tenancies.

[201] s.16(4E).

[202] (c.44).

[203] Crofters (Scotland) Act 1993 s.11(1).

consent of the landlord or to any person at all with the consent of the landlord. For succession to and transfer of residential tenancies, the reader is referred to the undernoted work.[204]

It was pointed out in debate in the House of Commons that these provisions of s.16 **S16–10** give the executor greater powers over the lease than the deceased himself had. The deceased's power to bequeath at common law as extended by s.29 applies only in the face of an implied prohibition on assignation and is not exercisable in the face of an express prohibition. The executor's power to transfer a lease farming part of the intestate estate transcends both express and implied prohibitions on assignation in the lease. The apparent anomaly can, however, be explained by considering the effect of a prohibition on assignation upon the death of a tenant. Such prohibition used to ensure that the tenant's heir at law[205] would succeed to the tenancy. Succession of the heir at law took place irrespective of any express prohibition on assignation. In consequence of the virtual abolition of the status of heir at law, provision had to be made for an alternative. A landlord could not reasonably be required to accept fragmentation of the tenancy. All heritage now vested in the executor, and therefore it was decided that the executor should have the power to choose the replacement for the "heir at law". Thus, the executor was given power to transfer the lease to a single member of the class entitled to share in the deceased's estate or, for certain specific types of lease, to any single person. This scheme does have the merit that the executor may be able to find a person who is genuinely interested in continuing the tenancy, which was not always the case under the old rules for selection of the heir at law.

In selecting the heir to the tenancy under s.16 an executor has a discretion.[206] **S16–11** That being the case the discretion is not unfettered. First, an executor, whether nominate or dative, is subject to the same limitations and restrictions on his powers as a trustee.[207] In exercising a discretion in selecting a beneficiary a trustee must act in good faith and not act capriciously or wholly unreasonably.[208] If an executor examines all of the candidates and makes an honest selection on the basis of their needs and qualifications such a selection is likely to be beyond any challenge.[209] The ability of a candidate to pay for the tenancy is a factor, given that the tenancy will have a value in the confirmation which will have to be accounted for to those with succession rights to it. This factor is most relevant where the candidate is not an heir on intestacy. If the candidate is an heir on intestacy, the executor can in effect set off the value of an unpaid inheritance against the value of the tenancy. If the candidate requires the consent of the landlord and the landlord is unwilling to give it, that will be a factor.

---

[204] P. Robson, *Residential Tenancies Private and Social Renting in Scotland*, 3rd edn (Edinburgh: W. Green, 2012), Ch.13.

[205] See Ch.1.

[206] But note s.8(2A) of the 1964 Act in relation to spouses or cohabitants of deceased crofting tenants and the provisions as to succession in the Rent (Scotland) Act 1984 and the Housing (Scotland) Act 1988.

[207] Executors (Scotland) Act 1900 s.2 (executors-nominate); 1964 Act s.20 (executors-dative).

[208] See *Mactavish v Reid's Trustees* (1904) 12 S.L.T. 404; and *Train v Buchanan's Trustees*, 1907 S.C. 517.

[209] As suggested in *McPhail v Doulton* (otherwise known as *In re Baden's Deed Trusts*) [1971] A.C. 424 at 449D–E per Lord Wilberforce.

S16–12   In selecting an heir for an interest in an agricultural tenancy or a crofting tenancy, the executor should also bear in mind the provisions of the relevant Agricultural Holdings (Scotland) Act[210] and Crofters (Scotland) Act,[211] whereby the landlord or the Crofting Commission may object to the transfer.

S16–13   Secondly, an executor must avoid acting *in rem suam* whereby his personal interest may conflict with the interests of other beneficiaries, for example, where executors-dative transferred an agricultural tenancy to one of their number.[212] However, if a testator impliedly or expressly authorises (or all of the beneficiaries with an interest authorise) the action *in rem suam* it will not be in breach of fiduciary duty.[213]

S16–14   Thirdly, an executor making a selection for a short limited duration tenancy or limited duration tenancy under the Agricultural Holdings (Scotland) Act 2003 must ensure that the selection is "in the best interests of the deceased's estate".[214] What is to be seen as in the "best interests of the deceased's estate" is not defined. It may be that this includes best financial interests of the estate. If so the executor in making his choice may be required to consider whether and if so the extent of any financial contribution to the estate being offered by a candidate in exchange for his selection.

Transfer of interest and related intimation

S16–15   What is required for a valid "transfer" by the executor in terms of s.16(2) and (4A) or to implement a valid bequest? There are two stages,[215] namely (1) an assignation[216] or, if appropriate, a docket under s.15(2) in favour of the selected transferee or legatee; and (2) intimation by the transferee or legatee of the assignation or docket to the landlord.[217] Intimation of the assignation or the docket completes the transfer. If necessary, for example to meet the statutory time limit for the transfer of the lease, an assignation can be made by an unconfirmed executor and given retroactive effect by the confirmation.[218] Before the 1964 Act the landlord could always find out who was the tenant's heir at law, but he must now be told by the prospective acquirer, transferee or legatee who is to acquire the lease.

S16–16   In the case of an agricultural or crofting tenancy there are additional statutory requirements for intimation to the landlord. In an agricultural tenancy the first

---

[210] Agricultural Holdings (Scotland) Act 1991 s.12 (replacing the Agricultural Holdings (Scotland) Act 1949 s.21); Agricultural Holdings (Scotland) Act 2003 s.22.

[211] Crofters (Scotland) Act 1993 s.58A.

[212] *Inglis v Inglis*, 1983 S.C. 8.

[213] *Sarris v Clark*, 1995 S.L.T. 44.

[214] s.16(4E).

[215] *McGrath v Nelson*, 2011 S.L.T. 107.

[216] For an assignation there must be words giving authority or directions which if fairly carried out will operate a transference together with a present intention to transfer (*Gallemos Ltd (in Receivership) Ltd v Barratt (Falkirk) Ltd*, 1989 S.C. 239 at 246 per Lord Cowie). For whether writing is required, and if so the form necessary, see the 1995 Act. For an example of an informal writing amounting to an assignation of a lease see *Williamson v Fife Special Housing Association* [2006] Hous. L.R. 80 (Lands Tr.).

[217] For methods of intimation see Rankine, *A Treatise on the Law of Leases in Scotland* (1916), pp.181–2.

[218] *Garvie's Trustees v Garvie's Tutors*, 1975 S.L.T. 94 at 97.

step is for the transferee to notify the landlord of the transfer of the tenancy within 21 days of the transfer or where he is prevented by some unavoidable cause from giving such notice within that period,[219] as soon as practicable thereafter. A notice given by the executor rather than the transferee will ordinarily be bad, although in the exceptional circumstance where the notice was given by executors who were also tutors of the transferee its validity was upheld.[220] Thereafter it is up to the landlord to set the procedure of objection in motion by serving a counter-notice within one month. It will be noted that the landlord may have to possess his soul in patience for a very long time, for at least a year may elapse from the death of the tenant before the landlord can find out who the acquirer of the lease is to be.

In the case of a crofting tenancy, s.11(1) of the Crofters (Scotland) Act 1993 **S16–17** requires the executor to, as soon as may be, give notice of the transfer containing particulars of the transferee selected by him to the landlord and at the same time send a copy of the notice to the Crofting Commission.[221]

If the notice is not given within 24 months of "the relevant date"[222] the **S16–18** Commission can give notice that they propose to terminate the tenancy and declare the croft vacant but if they are satisfied that the landlord or executor has already terminated the tenancy under s.16(3) of the 1964 Act, the proposal must lapse.[223]

Time limit for transfer and termination of the lease

Section 16(3), (4), (4C), and (4D) of the 1964 Act provide for termination of the **S16–19** lease, irrespective of its provisions or of any statutory, testamentary or other provisions, either by the executor or by the landlord, if the executor is satisfied that he cannot dispose of the lease to an acquiring beneficiary (whether under s.16 or not) or if he has in fact not disposed of it within the time limit specified.

In the case of a short limited duration tenancy or limited duration tenancy under **S16–20** the Agricultural Holdings (Scotland) Act 2003, if the executor is satisfied that he cannot dispose of the lease he can only terminate the lease if termination is in the best interests of the deceased's estate.[224] The aim is to prevent an executor from concluding too quickly that there is no person interested in taking on the lease, for example in exchange for payment of a consideration to the estate. This suggests that for such a tenancy an executor should be slow to conclude that such a tenancy "cannot" be disposed of within the year after the death of the tenant.

If the executor simply delays in disposal of the lease, it is liable to be lost to the **S16–21** beneficiaries. Only he can initiate disposal of it, but if he fails to do so within the time limit, the lease may be terminated.[225] Beneficiaries must be vigilant to protect

---

[219] Section 22(1) of the Agricultural Holdings (Scotland) Act 2003 provides "(where that [notice within 21 days] is not possible)".
[220] *Garvie's Trustees v Garvie's Tutors*, 1975 S.L.T. 94 at 97.
[221] Crofters (Scotland) Act 1993 s.11(1); and *McGrath v Nelson*, 2011 S.L.T. 107.
[222] See the complex definition in s.11(3) of the Crofters (Scotland) Act 1993 (as amended).
[223] See s.11(4) and (5) of the 1993 Act (as amended).
[224] s.16(4E).
[225] *Sproat v South West Services (Galloway) Ltd* Unreported November 9, 2000 Outer House (T.G. Coutts QC); *Rotherwick's Trustees v Hope*, 1975 S.L.T. 187; *Gifford v Buchanan*, 1983 S.L.T. 613.

their rights, particularly where an executor has not been appointed or not taken up office. Executors who take up office will have to be diligent in ensuring a competent and appropriate disposal of the tenancy so far as possible.

S16–22   The time limit is normally one year from the date of death of the deceased, but in the case of an agricultural lease which is the subject of a petition to the Land Court under s.16 of the Crofters' Holdings (Scotland) Act 1886,[226] an application thereto under s.11 of the Agricultural Holdings (Scotland) Act 1991 or an application thereto under s.21 of the Agricultural Holdings (Scotland) Act 2003, the period of one year runs from the date of the determination or withdrawal of the petition or application. These statutory provisions relate to the situation when the landlord seeks to object to the legatee of a lease as his tenant. The reason for the different trigger for the time limit in the case of such leases is that if the landlord's objection is successful the legacy (bequest) of the interest is null and void and only then does the executor's power to transfer in terms of s.16(2) or (4A) arise. The time limit for crofts is two years from the date of the deceased.[227]

S16–23   The one or two year time limit within which the lease must be transferred may be extended (1) by agreement between the landlord and the executor; or (2) by a relevant court, on the application of the executor. The "relevant court" is in the case of a tenancy under the Agricultural Holdings (Scotland) Act 1991 the Land Court, but in any other tenancy is the sheriff.[228] The application for an extension must be made within the time limit and is not competent after the landlord has given notice of termination.[229] Where the application is to the sheriff it must be made by summary application procedure.[230]

S16–24   "Disposal" for the purposes of the time limit in s.16(3) and (4C) requires either an assignation or docket under s.15(2). Does it also require intimation of the assignation or docket? Section 16(3) and (4C) use the word "disposal" instead of the word "transfer" which is used in s.16(2) and (4A), and this might suggest that intimation, being something done typically by the transferee, is not required for "disposal" by the landlord. On the other hand, s.16(3) and (4C) can be seen as being designed to give relief to the landlord from the uncertainty as to the future of the lease and who his tenant, if any, is to be. If intimation was allowed to be made to a landlord beyond a year after the death, the landlord would be left in uncertainty for a potentially indefinite period. In these circumstances it is suggested that intimation is also required for a "disposal" of the interest to take place in terms of s.16(3) and (4C). This places a special responsibility on the transferee to intimate the transfer to the landlord within the one year time limit. Where the lease is a croft there is an unnecessary distinction between testate and intestate transfers. Where the transfer follows a bequest of a croft the standard

---

[226] Section 16 no longer applies to crofting tenancies falling within the definition of "croft" in s.3 of the Crofters (Scotland) Act 1993 (Crofters (Scotland) Act 1955 (c.21) Sch.6 Pt I).

[227] s.16(3A).

[228] s.16(8A).

[229] *Gifford v Buchanan*, 1983 S.L.T. 613; *Sproat v South West Services (Galloway) Ltd* Unreported November 9, 2000 Outer House.

[230] s.16(8A).

intimation from the transferee[231] is required but where it follows the croft being in intestacy, intimation from the executor is required.[232]

If disposal has not taken place within the time limit either the landlord or the **S16–25** tenant has the power to terminate the lease "in so far as it relates to the interest [of the tenant]". The reason for these words of qualification may not be immediately apparent. However, there may be joint tenants in the lease. An inability or failure to dispose of the interest of the deceased tenant should not result in the termination of the interest of the surviving tenant. This does, however, highlight the potential prejudice to the surviving tenant who, following the death of the deceased, might have to bear the burdens of the lease alone.

Due notice of termination must be given by the landlord or executor. For agricultural **S16–26** leases[233] it is such period as may be agreed or, failing agreement, the familiar period of not less than one year nor more than two years ending with such term of Whitsunday or Martinmas as may be specified in the notice.[234] In the case of any other lease, the period of notice for this purpose is six months, without prejudice to any statutory provision prescribing a shorter period of notice for the lease in question.[235] The period of notice required to terminate a lease of an ordinary dwelling house would normally be substantially less than six months.[236] The notice is akin to a notice of irritancy which terminates the lease on a date other than the ish. If no executor has confirmed to the tenancy by the time of the expiry of the time limits for transfer in s.16(3), (3A) or (4D), the lease will be held to have been abandoned by the executor and it will suffice for the landlord to raise an action of declarator to that effect, given the absence of a confirmed executor on whom a notice of termination could be served.[237]

Claims arising out of termination for non-transfer

The fact that an executor or landlord may terminate a lease does not prejudice **S16–27** any claim by either party to the lease for compensation or damages in respect of the termination.[238] However, to preserve the limitation of the liability of the executor, any award of compensation or damages in respect of a termination by the executor is enforceable only against the estate of the deceased and not against the executor personally.[239]

What claims for "compensation or damages" can have been contemplated by **S16–28** Parliament in s.16(5)? There are a number of possibilities:

---

[231] Prudence suggests that this is in addition to the duty of the legatee to give notice of his acceptance of the legacy to the landlord and the Crofting Commission (for which he may authorise the executor to act as his agent) which must be done within 12 months of the death in terms of s.10(2) of the Crofters (Scotland) Act 1993.

[232] 1993 Act s.11(1).

[233] As defined in s.16(9) to include crofting tenancies.

[234] s.16(4)(a); Whitsunday and Martinmas are May 28th and November 28th respectively (Term and Quarter Days (Scotland) Act 1990 (c.22) s.1).

[235] s.16(4)(b) and proviso.

[236] Typically the period will range from 28 to 40 days before the ish, depending on the duration of the tenancy but in no case less than 28 days (Sheriff Courts (Scotland) Act 1907 (7 Edw.7 c.51) (as amended) ss.37 and 38; and the Rent (Scotland) Act 1984 (c.58) s.112).

[237] *Rotherwick's Trustees v Hope*, 1975 S.L.T. 187.

[238] s.16(5).

[239] s.16(5).

(1)   A claim by a landlord—who is a "party to the lease" in respect of a termination following the executor's failure to dispose of the interest under s.16(3)(b) and deemed abandonment. It must be remembered that the landlord may have a prima facie interest in keeping a lease alive in order to have rental income and if an executor has not transferred the lease timeously, it may be inferred that the landlord is being prejudiced as a result of the executor's failure to implement his duty to dispose and that he should be entitled to damages from the estate if he then is forced to terminate as a result.[240] This would represent a debt of the estate.[241]

(2)   A claim by a surviving co-tenant— who is a "party to the lease" again in respect of a termination following a failure under s.16(3)(b). The co-tenant may have a prima facie interest in the lease being kept alive with a co-tenant who has an obligation to share the burden of paying for the rent, if as is by default the case, the liability is joint and several.[242] It might be argued that there is a claim by the co-tenant for damages against the executor as a result of the notice of termination caused by the executor's failure to dispose.[243]

Termination of the lease for breach by executor

S16–29   The special provisions of s.16(6) and (7) take account of the fact that in considering questions based on breaches of the conditions of a lease a lease is vested in an executor only *qua* executor until its disposal. In the case of agricultural leases (including crofts) the Land Court is not to make an order for removal under s.3 of the Small Landholders and Agricultural Holdings (Scotland) Act 1931 or s.26 of the Crofters (Scotland) Act 1993,[244] and is not to make an order in favour of the landlord in a question under s.22(2)(e) of the Agricultural Holdings (Scotland) Act 1991 unless a court or arbiter is satisfied that it is reasonable, having regard to the fact that the interest is vested in the executor in his capacity as executor, that it should be made.

S16–30   In the case of non-agricultural leases, the court is not to grant decree in an action of removing based on a breach of a condition of the lease unless it is satisfied that the condition alleged to have been breached is one which it is reasonable to expect the executor to have observed, having regard to the fact that the interest is vested in him in his capacity as an executor.

Leases of crofts: special provision relating to the Crofters (Scotland) Act 1993
16A. [Repealed by the Crofting Reform (Scotland) Act 2010 (asp 14) Sch.4
para.2(3) (effective October 1, 2011)].

---

[240]   Before the 1964 Act the executor could be liable in damages (or "liquidated rent") to the landlord if the heir at law refused to take up the lease (*Bethune v Morgan* (1874) 2 R. 186; and *Strathdee v Paterson* (1913) 1 S.L.T. 498).

[241]   See Ch.3.

[242]   Rankine, *A Treatise on the Law of Leases in Scotland* (1916), p.83.

[243]   Similar to the claim in *Burns v Martin* (1887) 14 R. (HL) 20.

[244]   As the reference to s.13 of the Crofters (Scotland) Act 1955 must now be read (Interpretation Act 1978 (c.30) s.17(2)(a)).

DEFINITIONS

"Land Court": s.36(1).

COMMENTARY

It is unclear why s.16A was inserted into the 1964 Act at all given that most of **S16A–01** it deals with the substantive law of succession to an interest in a crofting tenancy rather than the administrative aspects of the transfer of the interest. It may be for that reason that it was repealed by the Crofting Reform (Scotland) Act 2010.

Protection of persons acquiring title
[1]**17. Where any person has in good faith and for value acquired title to any interest in or security over heritable property which has vested in an executor as aforesaid directly or indirectly from—**

(a) the executor, or
(b) a person deriving title directly from the executor,

the title so acquired shall not be challengeable on the ground that the confirmation was reducible or has in fact been reduced, or, in a case falling under paragraph (b) above, that the title should not have been transferred to the person mentioned in that paragraph.

NOTE

1. Saved by the Law Reform (Miscellaneous Provisions) (Scotland) Act 1968 (c.70) s.7.

COMMENTARY

Section 17 provides protection for purchasers of heritage. It will normally mean **S17–01** that there is no need for third party purchasers to investigate the validity of a confirmation. Even if the confirmation was reducible, or has actually been reduced, the title obtained from the executor or a beneficiary by a purchaser in good faith and for value is not challengeable on that ground.

It is conceivable that a will appointing the executor could be reduced for forgery **S17–02** or other grounds of reduction some time after the executor had disposed of heritage from the estate. In such circumstances the confirmation would be rendered reducible or could be reduced but s.17 would prevent such a step from prejudicing purchasers of heritable property. Another example is where, some time after the disposal of heritage, an heir or beneficiary ("a person deriving title directly from the executor") is convicted of the unlawful killing of the deceased and is disqualified from succeeding to the heritage. A purchaser of heritage from the disqualified killer in good faith as to the seller's innocence is thus protected from prejudice. It is submitted that as a matter of principle a "person deriving title directly from the executor" includes the executor in his personal capacity.

The protection of s.17 does not protect the ownership of purchasers of moveable property or legatees or donees of either heritable or moveable property. The Succession (Scotland) Bill proposes the re-enactment of s.17 and its extension to purchasers of moveable property.[245]

Provisions as to entails and special destinations

¹18.—(1) *[Repealed by the Abolition of Feudal Tenure etc. (Scotland) Act 2000 (asp 5) Sch.13(1) para.1 (effective November 28, 2004)].*

(2) On the death of a person entitled to any heritable property subject to a special destination in favour of some other person, being a destination which the deceased could not competently have, or in fact has not, evacuated by testamentary disposition or otherwise, the property shall, if the executor of the deceased is confirmed thereto, vest in the executor for the purpose of enabling it to be conveyed to the person next entitled thereto under the destination (if such conveyance is necessary) and for that purpose only.

(3) Section 14(2) of this Act shall apply in relation to property to which this section refers as it applies to property to which the said section 14(2) refers.

(4) Sections 15 and 17 of this Act shall apply to property which has vested in an executor by virtue of this section as they apply to property which has vested in an executor by virtue of section 14 of this Act, as if the person next entitled to the first mentioned property were a person entitled to share in the estate of the deceased.

NOTE

1. See the Inheritance Tax Act 1984 (c.51) s.209(1).

DEFINITIONS

"testamentary disposition": s.36(1).

COMMENTARY

S18–01 Supplementary provisions about the effect of confirmation in estates including entailed property and special destinations appear in s.18(1) and (2). Despite the prohibition on the creation of new entails which existed since 1914,[246] there were apparently about 1,000 entails still in existence in Scotland in 1964, justifying special provisions. Section 18(1) provided that, on the death of an heir of entail in possession, the entailed property, though not regarded as part of the deceased's estate, nevertheless vested by confirmation in the executor in order that it might be conveyed to the person next entitled to it under the entail. The vesting in the executor was for that purpose only and, apparently, if no such conveyance to the next person entitled was necessary, there is no vesting in the executor at all. All property in Scotland was disentailed on November 28, 2004 and s.18(1) was repealed.[247]

---

[245] Implementing recommendation 72 of the *2009 Report on Succession.*
[246] Entail (Scotland) Act 1914 (4 and 5 Geo. 5 c.43) s.2.
[247] Abolition of Feudal Tenure etc. (Scotland) Act 2000 (asp 5) s.50.

Section 18(2) makes very similar provisions in respect of heritage subject to an **S18–02** unrevoked (unevacuated) special destination.[248] Such heritage is not part of the "estate" of the deceased in terms of s.36(2)[249] and does not vest in an executor under s.14(1). In most cases special destinations take the form of a survivorship destination where the surviving heir in terms of the destination ("the heir of provision") already has a *pro indiviso* title. In such cases the *pro indiviso* title of the deceased transfers automatically to the survivor without the need for any further procedure.[250] Given that an heir of provision in an unevacuated survivorship destination does not require a title, s.18(2) does not apply to property with such a destination and a purported confirmation to such property would be ineffective.

However, in other cases of special destination the heir of provision called in the **S18–03** destination requires to have a title formally conferred on him, and the function of s.18(2) is to permit a limited vesting in the executor to enable him to grant that title. Thus it is only when the heir of provision (or his successor) requires a title that the executor can and should confirm to heritage with a special destination. The confirmation in the executor is solely for the purpose of conveyance to the person next entitled to it, if such conveyance is necessary. The heir of provision, whether under a survivorship or other special destination, remains liable for the debts of the deceased.[251]

Sections 14(2), 15, and 17 apply to heritage vesting in the executor under **S18–04** s.18(2) as they apply to heritage vesting under s.14(1) and the reader is referred to the commentary on those sections.

Estate Duty
19. *[Repealed by the Finance Act 1975 (c.7) Sch.13.]*

Executor-dative to have powers of a trustee
20. An executor-dative appointed to administer the estate of a deceased person shall have in his administration of such estate the whole powers, privileges and immunities, and be subject to the same obligations, limitations and restrictions, which gratuitous trustees have, or are subject to, under any enactment or under common law, and the Trusts (Scotland) Acts 1921 and 1961 shall have effect as if any reference therein to a trustee included a reference to such an executor-dative:

Provided that nothing in this section shall exempt an executor-dative from finding caution for his intromissions or confer upon him any power to resign or to assume new trustees.

DEFINITIONS

"estate": s.36(2).

---

[248] See commentary on s.36(2).
[249] See commentary on s.36(2).
[250] *Bisset v Walker*, Faculty Collection 26.11.1799; McDonald (1965) 10 J.L.S. at 73.
[251] See commentary on s.36(2).

COMMENTARY

S20–01   This is an important provision which goes beyond its title. It places executors-dative largely, but not wholly, on the same footing as executors-nominate, namely as gratuitous trustees under not merely the common law but also the Trusts (Scotland) Acts 1921 and 1961. It grants important powers and immunities to executors-dative such as the right to seek relief from personal liability for wrongful distribution and other breaches of trust.[252] It lays to rest any practical debate over whether executors-dative are covered by the general law relating to trustees. Section 20 is modelled on s.2 of the 1900 Act[253] but includes a proviso applicable to executors-dative which does not apply to executors-nominate.

S20–02   The proviso is in two parts. First, executors-dative[254] are required to find caution for their intromissions whereas trustees are not. This is because trustees, or at least the initial trustees, are selected by the truster for their trustworthiness and therefore no caution is thought to be required. In contrast, executors-dative are not selected on any such basis[255] and therefore the policy of the common law, preserved by the proviso to s.20, is that caution is to be obtained.

S20–03   Secondly, the proviso excludes from executors-dative a trustee's power to resign or to assume new trustees. The restriction on resignation originates from the appointment having been made by the court. The restriction on assumption has the same origin and is linked to the need to find caution. If an executor-dative were to have the unrestricted power to assume new executors or trustees, this would allow the estate to be administered by executors who had not been appointed by the testator nor had found caution, which is contrary to the policy of the common law.

Evidence as to holograph wills in commissary proceedings
21.—(1) Notwithstanding any rule of law or practice to the contrary, confirmation of an executor to property disposed of in a holograph testamentary disposition shall not be granted unless the court is satisfied by evidence consisting at least of an affidavit by each of two persons that the writing and signature of the disposition are in the handwriting of the testator.

[1](2) This section shall not apply to a testamentary document executed after the commencement of the Requirements of Writing (Scotland) Act 1995.

NOTE

1. Inserted by the Requirements of Writing (Scotland) Act 1995 (c.7) Sch.4(2) para.38 (effective August 1, 1995).

DEFINITIONS

"testamentary disposition": s.36(2).

---

[252] Trusts (Scotland) Act 1921 (11 and 12 Geo. 5 c.58) ss.3, 32.
[253] (63 and 64 Vict. c.55).
[254] Other than a spouse or civil partner appointed by virtue of s.9(4) of the 1964 Act (1823 Act s.2 construed in accordance with s.3(1) of the Human Rights Act 1998 (c.42)).
[255] For selection of executors-dative see paras S14–06 to S14–15.

COMMENTARY

Section 21 applies only to wills executed before August 1, 1995 being the date **S21–01** of commencement of the 1995 Act. For wills executed on or after that date s.21 has been replaced by s.21A to take account of the abolition of holograph wills by the 1995 Act. The rationale behind s.21 remains in relation to s.21A and the reader is referred to the commentary on s.21A.

Evidence as to testamentary documents in commissary proceedings
[1]21A. Confirmation of an executor to property disposed of in a testamentary document executed after the commencement of the Requirements of Writing (Scotland) Act 1995 shall not be granted unless the formal validity of the document is governed—

[2](a) by Scots law and the document is presumed under section 3 or 9D of that Act to have been subscribed or under section 9C or 9D (or by virtue of section 9E(1)) of that Act to have been authenticated by the granter so disposing of that property; or
(b) by a law other than Scots law and the court is satisfied that the document is formally valid according to the law governing such validity.

NOTES

1. Inserted by the Requirements of Writing (Scotland) Act 1995 (c.7) Sch.4(2) para.39 (effective August 1, 1995).
2. As amended by the Land Registration etc. (Scotland) Act 2012 (asp 5) Sch.5 para.14 (effective December 8, 2014).

DEFINITIONS

"testamentary disposition": s.36(2).

COMMENTARY

An application for confirmation requires to state whether the applicant is **S21A–01** applying as executor-nominate or executor-dative. The latter requires to obtain caution for intromissions while the former does not. At common law an applicant for confirmation as executor-nominate was entitled to rely on a holograph will as evidence of his appointment without any further proof of its execution by the testator.[256] This was consistent with confirmation being administrative in nature and as such not requiring any proof of the validity of any will by which the estate required to be distributed.[257] Therefore confirmation could be granted even when the signature of the testator was in dispute. There was no real advantage in the probativity of an attested (witnessed) will over a holograph will. With the extension of confirmation to heritage, the view was taken that the common law position was too open

[256] *Wills & Succession*, ii, 877; and *Cranston* (1890) 17 R. 410.
[257] See *Hamilton v Hardie* (1888) 16 R. 192 at 197–198 and *MacHardy v Steele* (1902) 4 F. 765.

to abuse and s.21 was enacted to provide some comfort to the court and beneficiaries that confirmation would be granted to an executor only if there was prima
facie evidence corroborating the signature of the testator on a holograph will.

S21A–02   Accordingly s.21 was enacted to prevent the court from granting confirmation
for administration by a holograph will unless the application was accompanied by
at least an affidavit by each of two persons deponing (testifying) to a notary public
that the writing and signature of the disposition are in the handwriting of the
testator. This process was and remains known as "setting up the will". A "holograph testamentary disposition" was a will in the handwriting of the testator and
signed by him or her but could also include a typed will with the signature
preceded by the words "adopted as holograph".[258]

S21A–03   The Requirements of Writing (Scotland) Act 1995 abolished the special status
of holograph wills and the validity of a will required merely the subscription of
the testator. In order to maintain the limited protection of s.21, s.21A was enacted
to prevent confirmation being granted to allow distribution under a will (the
formal validity of which is governed by Scots law) other than a will either
witnessed under the procedure in s.3 of the 1995 Act or "set up" under the procedure in s.4 of the 1995 Act.[259]

S21A–04   If the formal validity of the will is governed by a law other than Scots law the
court must be satisfied that the document is formally valid according to the law
governing such validity.[260] Section 21A does not specify what must be done for
the court to be satisfied as to the formal validity of a will under a foreign law.

S21A–05   The Land Registration etc. (Scotland) Act 2012[261] introduced the possibility of
electronic wills into the 1995 Act.[262] Accordingly, s.21A has been amended to allow
for an authentication procedure for the electronic signatures of such documents. At
the time of writing the provisions on electronic wills have not been brought into force.

Court of Session may regulate procedure in commissary proceedings
[1]**22.—(1) The powers exercisable by the Court of Session by act of sederunt
under section 18 of the Confirmation of Executors (Scotland) Act 1858, section
16 of the Sheriff Courts and Legal Officers (Scotland) Act 1927 and section 34
of the Administration of Justice (Scotland) Act 1933 (which empower the
court to regulate inter alia procedure in proceedings in the sheriff court and
in proceedings for the confirmation of executors) shall include power to regulate the procedure to be followed, and to prescribe the form and content of
any petition, writ or other document to be used, in connection with the confirmation of executors in cases where, by virtue of this Act, heritable property
devolves upon the executor.**

**(2) Without prejudice to the generality of the powers conferred on the
court by the said sections and by this section, the power conferred by the said**

---

[258] *Gavine's Trustees v Lee* (1883) 10 R. 448 (where the words followed the signature); distinguished
in *Harvey v Smith* (1904) 6 F. 511.
[259] See Act of Sederunt (Requirements of Writing) 1996 (SI 1996/1534).
[260] See paras 7–38 to 7–42.
[261] (asp 5).
[262] Requirements of Writing (Scotland) Act 1995 ss.9C, 9D and 9E.

section 34 to modify, amend or repeal by act of sederunt enactments relating to certain matters shall include power so to modify, amend or repeal any enactment relating to the procedure to be followed in proceedings for the confirmation of executors in such cases as aforesaid.

(3) *[Repealed by the Law Reform (Miscellaneous Provisions)(Scotland) Act 1966 (c.19) Sch. Pt I].*

(4) *[Repealed by the Finance Act 1975 (c.7) ss.52(2), 59, Sch.13 Pt I].*

NOTE

1. See the Act of Sederunt (Confirmation of Executors) (SI 1964/1143) and the Act of Sederunt (Edictal Citations, Commissary Petitions and Petitions of Service) (SI 1971/1165).

PART IV

ADOPTED PERSONS

Adopted person to be treated for purposes of succession etc. as child of adopter
23.—(1) For all purposes relating to—

(a) the succession to a deceased person (whether testate or intestate), and
(b) the disposal of property by virtue of any *inter vivos* deed,

an adopted person shall be treated as the child of the adopter and not as the child of any other person.

In this subsection and in the following provisions of this Part of this Act any reference to succession to a deceased person shall be construed as including a reference to the distribution of any property in consequence of the death of the deceased person and any claim to legal rights or the prior rights of a surviving spouse out of his estate.

(2) In any deed whereby property is conveyed or under which a succession arises, being a deed executed after the making of an adoption order, unless the contrary intention appears, any reference (whether express or implied)—

(a) to the child or children of the adopter shall be construed as, or as including, a reference to the adopted person;
(b) to the child or children of the adopted person's natural parents or either of them shall be construed as not being, or as not including, a reference to the adopted person; and
(c) to a person related to the adopted person in any particular degree shall be construed as a reference to the person who would be related to him in that degree if he were the child of the adopter and were not the child of any other person:

Provided that for the purposes of this subsection a deed containing a provision taking effect on the death of any person shall be deemed to have been executed on the date of death of that person.

[1,2](3) Where the terms of any deed provide that any property or interest in property shall devolve along with a title, honour or dignity, nothing in this [section or in the Children Act 1975 or in the Adoption (Scotland) Act 1978 or in the Adoption and Children (Scotland) Act 2007 (asp 4) shall prevent that property or interest from so devolving.

(4) Nothing in this section shall affect any deed executed, or the devolution of any property on, or in consequence of, the death of a person who dies, before the commencement of this Act.

(5) In this Part of this Act the expression—

[3]"adoption order"

(a) has the same meaning as in section 38 of the Adoption (Scotland) Act 1978 (whether the order took effect before or after the commencement of this Act); and

(b) includes an adoption order within the meaning of section 28(1) of the Adoption and Children (Scotland) Act 2007 (asp 4); and

[4]"adopted" means adopted in pursuance of an adoption order.

NOTES

1. As amended by the Adoption (Scotland) Act 1978 (c.28) s.66, Sch.3 para.4.
2. As amended by the Adoption and Children (Scotland) Act 2007 (asp 4) Sch.2 para.1(2)(a) (effective September 28, 2009).
3. Existing text renumbered as s.23(5)(a) and s.23(5)(b) inserted by the Adoption and Children (Scotland) Act 2007 (asp 4) Sch.2 para.1(2)(b) (effective September 28, 2009).
4. Definition substituted by the Adoption (Scotland) Act 1978 (c.28) s.66, Sch.3 para.4.

DEFINITIONS

"adoption order": s.23(5); and the Adoption (Scotland) Act 1978 s.38.
"deed": s.36(1).
"estate": s.36(2).
"legal rights": s.36(1).
"prior rights": s.36(1).
"testamentary disposition": s.36(1).

COMMENTARY

S23–01   The anomalously unfair lack of provision for adopted children prior to the 1964 Act was one of the prime reasons for the appointment of the Mackintosh

Committee on the Law of Succession. Adopted children had no rights in the succession to their adopting parents and retained any rights which they had in the estates of their biological parents.

Section 23 altered this not merely in relation to succession but also in relation **S23–02** to any document "conveying property" even if it took effect inter vivos (during the lifetime of the granter). Adopted children are now treated as children of the adopter or adopters and not as children of any other person. They have full rights of succession, including legal rights, to the adopting parents and lose all rights in the estates of the natural parents. A child or children of the adopter include those adopted by various, but not all, overseas adoptions. This is the effect of the broad definition of "adoption order" in s.38 of the Adoption (Scotland) Act 1978.[263] In addition, the definition in s.23(5) includes adoption orders made before or after the commencement of the 1964 Act.[264]

Section 23(1) is the governing part of s.23. Section 23(2) is designed to deal **S23–03** with the question of whether a granter of a deed or a testator, in the knowledge of the Act and the existence of an adoption order, intended that references in the will or other deed to a natural relationship be construed as including relationships arising from the adoption and that is its only effect.[265] This was expressed in a case where it was argued that references in a deed made before the making of an adoption order could not be construed as referring to adopted children. The court found that s.23(2) could not cut down the scope of s.23(1) and that the adopted children had to be treated as children of the truster's son even though the provision in favour of the children of the truster's son predated the adoption orders.

The one major exception to the scope of s.23 is succession to titles, honours and **S23–04** dignities. These are not affected by the Act (s.37(1)(a)) and therefore no right of succession to titles, etc. was conferred on adopted children by the Act. If a deed prescribes that property is to devolve along with a title, nothing in the adoption legislation prevents that (s.23(3)).

Provisions supplementary to s.23

[1]**24.—(1) For the purposes of the law regulating the succession to any property and for the purposes of the construction of any such deed as is mentioned in the last foregoing section, an adopted person shall be deemed to be related to any other person, being the child or the adopted child of the adopter or (in the case of a joint adoption) of either of the adopters,**

(a) **where he or she was adopted by two spouses jointly and that other person is the child or adopted child of both of them, as a brother or sister of the whole blood;**
(b) **in any other case, as a brother or sister of the half blood.**

---

[263] See, e.g. *Salvesen's Trustees, Petitioners*, 1993 S.C. 14; 1993 S.L.T. 1327.
[264] *Salvesen's Trustees, Petitioners*, 1993 S.C. 14 at 18; 1993 S.L.T. 1327 at 1330.
[265] *Salvesen's Trustees, Petitioners*, 1993 S.C. 14 at 21; 1993 S.L.T. 1327 at 1332.

[2, 3](1A) Where, in relation to any purpose specified in section 23(1) of this Act, any right is conferred or any obligation is imposed, whether by operation of law or under any deed coming into operation after the commencement of the Children Act 1975 , by reference to the relative seniority of the members of a class of persons, then [. . .],

(a) any member of that class who is an adopted person shall rank as if he had been born on the date of his adoption, and

(b) if two or more members of the class are adopted persons whose dates of adoption are the same, they shall rank as between themselves in accordance with their respective times of birth.

(2) Notwithstanding anything in the last foregoing section, a trustee or an executor may distribute any property for the distribution of which he is responsible without having ascertained that no adoption order has been made by virtue of which any person is or may be entitled to any interest therein, and shall not be liable to any such person of whose claim he has not had notice at the time of the distribution; but (without prejudice to section 17 of this Act) nothing in this subsection shall affect any right of any such person to recover the property, or any property representing it, from any person who may have received it.

(3) Where an adoption order is made in respect of a person who has been previously adopted, the previous adoption shall be disregarded for the purposes of the last foregoing section in relation to the devolution of any property on the death of any person dying after the date of the subsequent adoption order, and in relation to any deed executed after that date whereby property is conveyed or under which a succession arises.

(4) *[Repealed by the Adoption (Scotland) Act 1978 (c.28) s.66, Sch. 4].*

NOTES

1. Saved by the Legitimation (Scotland) Act 1968 (c.22) ss.2(6), 6(2).
2. Inserted by the Children Act 1975 (c.72) s.8(10), Sch.2 para.5(3).
3. Words repealed by the Family Law (Scotland) Act 2006 (Consequential Modifications) Order 2006 (SSI 2006/384) art.2 (effective June 30, 2006).

COMMENTARY

S24–01   The effect of s.24(1) is that if a childless couple adopt a child and subsequently have a child of their own, these two children are, for the purposes of succession, related to each other as brothers or sisters of the full blood. Equally, a couple's second adopted child is for this purpose a brother or sister of the full blood to the first. But if either party to a marriage had a child by a previous marriage, or had adopted a child before the current marriage, such child or adopted child would be a collateral of the half blood to any child or adopted child of the present marriage.

S24–02   Certain odd consequences emerge from the provisions of s.24(1). An adopted child can be related as a brother or sister of the full blood to any other person only if he or she has been adopted by two spouses jointly and that other person is the child or adopted child of both of them.[266] In any other case the adopted child is related to any other child or adopted child of the adopter or adopters as a brother or sister of the half blood.[267] This means, for example, that if an unmarried woman gives birth to twins and without marrying subsequently adopts them these children are related to each other as collaterals of the half blood for the purposes of succession. They cannot be collaterals of the full blood as they do not fall within the provisions of s.24(1)(a) requiring adoption by two spouses jointly. If the mother of the twins subsequently marries someone other than the natural father of the children, and there is a child or adopted child of that marriage, the twins and the subsequent child are all collaterals of the half blood. One twin has no better rights of succession in the other's estate than has the child or adopted child of the subsequent marriage. Until the 1986 Act came into force it is true that one illegitimate twin was not regarded in law as being in any way related to the other, so that neither had any rights of succession at all in the other's estate without the adoption. However, since 1986, the effect of an adoption by their mother would be to reduce their rights in each other's estate from that of a collateral of the full blood to only half blood status, which might have to be shared with others.

Any question of seniority between collaterals who include an adopted child is resolved by s.24(1A), added by the Children Act 1975. Briefly, an adopted child ranks in seniority as if born on the date of adoption, while two children adopted on the same day take seniority *inter se* according to their actual time of birth. **S24–03**

PART V

FINANCIAL PROVISION ON DIVORCE

25.–27. *[Repealed by the Divorce (Scotland) Act 1976 (c.39) Sch.2].*

PART VI

MISCELLANEOUS AND SUPPLEMENTARY

Power of minor to test on heritage
28. *[Repealed by the Age of Legal Capacity (Scotland) Act 1991 (c.50) Sch.2 (effective September 25, 1991)].*

Right of tenant to bequeath interest under lease
29.—(1) A bequest by a tenant of his interest under a tenancy or lease to any one of the persons who, if the tenant had died intestate, would be, or would in any circumstances have been, entitled to succeed to his intestate estate by virtue of this Act shall not be treated as invalid by reason only that there is among the conditions of the tenancy or lease an implied condition prohibiting assignation.

---

[266] s.24(1)(a).
[267] s.24(1)(b).

[1, 2, 3](2) **This section shall not prejudice the operation of section 16 of the Crofters Holdings (Scotland) Act 1886 or section 11 of the Agricultural Holdings (Scotland) Act 1991 or section 21 of the Agricultural Holdings (Scotland) Act 2003 (asp 11) (which relate to bequests in the case of agricultural leases) or of section 10 of the Crofters (Scotland) Act 1955 (which makes similar provisions in relation to Crofts.)**

NOTES

1. As amended by the Law Reform (Miscellaneous Provisions) (Scotland) Act 1968 (c.70) s.8, Sch.2 Pt I para.27.
2. As amended by the Agricultural Holdings (Scotland) Act 1991 (c.55) Sch.11 para.25 (effective September 25, 1991).
3. As amended by the Agricultural Holdings (Scotland) Act 2003 (asp 11) Sch.1 para.2(2) (effective November 27, 2003).

DEFINITIONS

"estate": s.36(2).
"intestate estate": ss.36(1), (2) and 1(2). See also s.37(1)(a) and (b) and note to s.1.
"tenancy": s.36(1).

COMMENTARY

S29–01   Where a lease is assignable the tenant is at common law entitled to bequeath his interest in the lease to a chosen legatee. The interest can be bequeathed in a legacy of residue.[268] Whether it is bequeathed in any other legacy will depend on the wording of the legacy.[269] A valid bequest had the effect of making the legatee the successor to the tenant's interest in place of the heir at law. At common law, if the lease was not assignable, the landlord could object to the legatee or acquiesce in it. If he objected, the heir at law was entitled to claim the tenant's interest if he chose.

S29–02   The default rule at common law is that leases are not assignable[270] although there are major exceptions to this such as for leases of urban subjects where the use of buildings is the principal object of the lease. Where there was a doubt whether a lease was assignable at common law the only way in which the tenant could ensure that the lease pass to a person other than his heir at law was through having a special destination inserted into the lease. That, however, could be impossible to alter.

S29–03   The effect of s.29 is to allow a tenant to bequeath his interest, in the face of objection from the landlord, where the lease is not assignable at common law. In assessing the validity of a tenant's bequest of a lease, the focus is thus placed on whether there is an express prohibition of assignation within the lease itself (which in practice commonly exists) or in statutory conditions applicable to the

---

[268] *Gardner v Curran*, 2008 S.L.T. (Sh. Ct) 105.
[269] See Rankine, *A Treatise on the Law of Leases in Scotland* (1916), pp.162 to 164.
[270] See Rankine, *A Treatise on the Law of Leases in Scotland* (1916), p.172.

lease[271] whether there is an objection to the bequest under the various specific provisions referred to in s.29(2). The need for a special destination disappears unless there is such an express prohibition of assignation.

If a landlord expresses a valid objection to the legatee, given the disappearance **S29–04** of the heir at law, the executor has power to select the heir to the tenant's interest under s.16(2) of the Act.

Effect of testamentary dispositions on special destinations
30. A testamentary disposition executed after the commencement of this Act shall not have effect so as to evacuate a special destination (being a destination which could competently be evacuated by the testamentary disposition) unless it contains a specific reference to the destination and a declared intention on the part of the testator to evacuate it.

DEFINITIONS

"testamentary disposition": s.36(1).

COMMENTARY

This brief section is particularly important. Despite its importance, however, it **S30–01** is frequently ignored. Special destinations are an abominable relic of the law and ought to be abolished, but while they exist their functions and effects cannot be ignored. If their nature is understood, they can be used sensibly but far too many cases have arisen in which it would appear that they have either not been understood or merely ignored.[272] For a detailed discussion of special destinations see the commentary on s.36(2).

If power to revoke does exist,[273] this section makes it clear that it cannot be **S30–02** revoked by implication. There must be a specific reference in the will to the destination and a declared intention on the part of the testator to revoke it.[274] While s.30 provides a clear test for how a destination could be evacuated, it is a high requirement for evacuation. In practice, this, combined with the uncertainty as to whether there is a power to evacuate by means of a will at all, has meant that s.30 has contributed to difficulty in evacuation.

Presumption of survivorship in respect of claims to property
31.—[1](1) Where two persons have died in circumstances indicating that they died simultaneously or rendering it uncertain which, if either, of them survived the other, then, for all purposes affecting title or succession to property or claims to legal rights or the prior rights of a surviving spouse or civil partner,

---

[271] e.g. Rent (Scotland) Act 1984 (c.58) s.17(2); but not the Housing (Scotland) Act 1988 s.23(1) which imposes an implied term prohibiting assignation without the consent of the landlord.

[272] For an example of professional negligence in this respect see *Weir v J.M. Hodge & Son*, 1990 S.L.T. 266.

[273] See para.S36–11.

[274] *Stirling's Trustees v Stirling*, 1977 S.C. 139, 1977 S.L.T. 229.

(a) **where the persons were husband and wife or civil partners to each other, it shall be presumed that neither survived the other; and**

(b) **in any other case, it shall be presumed that the younger person survived the elder unless the next following subsection applies.**

(2) If, in a case to which paragraph (*b*) of the foregoing subsection would (apart from this subsection) apply, the elder person has left a testamentary disposition containing a provision, however expressed, in favour of the younger if he survives the elder and, failing the younger, in favour of a third person, and the younger person has died intestate, then it shall be presumed for the purposes of that provision that the elder person survived the younger.

NOTE

1. As amended by the Civil Partnership Act 2004 (c.33) Sch.28(1) para.9.

DEFINITIONS

"intestate": s.36(1).
"legal rights": s.36(1).
"prior rights": s.36(1).
"testamentary disposition": s.36(1).

COMMENTARY

Death and survivorship

S31–01   The deceased whose estate is in question must be proved to have died and any person claiming or who is claimed to be a beneficiary must be affirmatively proved to have survived him or her.[275] The onus of proof lies on the person relying on the death or survivorship, and the consequence of failure of proof is the failure of that person's claim on the estate.

S31–02   Death certificates are sufficient, though not conclusive, evidence of the death, and an action is available under the Presumption of Death (Scotland) Act 1977[276] for fixing the date of death in cases of missing persons who are thought to have died or have not been known to be alive for a period of at least seven years. The action is available only in respect of missing persons who had either a common law Scots domicile when last known to be alive or had a habitual residence in Scotland throughout the period of one year ending with the date of last knowledge. It is also available only to spouses and civil partners of the missing person. The 1977 Act also makes provision for the recall or variation of the decree, presumably because evidence not previously before the court indicates that on a balance of probabilities any element of the decree that was granted was in error.

---

[275] See paras 4–01 and 4–02.
[276] (c.27), as amended by the Civil Partnership Act 2004 (c.33) Sch.28(4) para.45(2) and (3); and the Marriage and Civil Partnership (Scotland) Act 2014 (asp 5) Sch.1 para.2.

In addition, where a court outwith Scotland in a country where the missing **S31–03** person was domiciled or habitually resident on the last date of known life, issues a decree that the person has died or is presumed to have died, such a decree is sufficient evidence of the facts declared in it for the purposes of a Scottish court.[277] This means that while the decree may prove the death, a Scottish court is not bound by it if there is evidence rebutting any element of the foreign decree.

Common calamities

The 1964 Act effected a very valuable change in establishing survivorship. **S31–04** Section 31 deals with situations where

> "two persons have died in circumstances indicating that they died simultaneously or rendering it uncertain which, if either of them, survived the other".

Such circumstances are frequently called a "common calamity", although that label appears nowhere in the Act. For the sake of convenience such circumstances are described as "common calamity circumstances" in this commentary.

For s.31 to apply, the "circumstances" must either (a) indicate "simultaneous **S31–05** death" of two persons; or (b) "render it uncertain which, if either, survived the other". Such circumstances will include, typically, calamities during travel such as car or aircraft crashes or explosions in general or natural disasters. However, they are not restricted to such incidents. All that is necessary is that the circumstances of death must render it uncertain which, if either, survived the other.

If such circumstances exist, s.31(1) creates presumptions of survivorship based **S31–06** on marriage and age. If there is proof on the balance of probabilities[278] that in those common calamity circumstances one person survived the other, effect is given to that order of death.[279] It is only if there is no such proof of survivorship that the presumptions in s.31(1) are conclusive.

The general rule in s.31(1)(b) is that, where two persons have died in common **S31–07** calamity circumstances, the younger is presumed to have survived the elder for all purposes of succession.[280]

However, in two particular cases, different presumptions apply. First, where the **S31–08** persons concerned are spouses or civil partners, s.31(1)(a) states a positive presumption that neither survived the other. The different treatment for spouses and civil partners is intended to avoid a situation in which the estate of the elder spouse or partner would pass to the younger by virtue of the presumption and then to the younger spouse's relatives to the exclusion of the elder spouse's relatives. For example, if a childless couple perished in a car crash (or died in independent

---

[277] Presumption of Death (Scotland) Act 1977 s.10.

[278] *Lamb v Lord Advocate*, 1976 S.C.110.

[279] In *Lamb v Lord Advocate*, 1976 S.C.110 it was held that if there was proof of survivorship, s.31(1) did not apply. It is suggested, respectfully, that in the circumstances of *Lamb* (a house fire), s.31(1) did apply but that the presumption that the neither spouse survived the other was rebutted by the evidence assessed on a balance of probabilities.

[280] s.31(1)(b). Note that it is not necessary to attempt to prove exactly simultaneous death. It is sufficient to establish that it is uncertain which survived the other.

incidents) without proof of survivorship, the husband's estate might pass out of his family and into his wife's family or vice-versa. It was felt in Parliament that this would be likely to be contrary to the wishes of the deceased, and thus the presumption in this case is that neither survived the other. The effect is that in common calamity circumstances, in considering succession to the estate of the spouse or civil partner, it is taken that the other spouse or partner predeceased.

S31–09 However, if one spouse has made a will in favour of the other with an alternative provision in the event of the other "predeceasing", the legacy will still fail if both perish in a common calamity. The statutory presumption that the other "did not survive" is not deemed to mean "predecease" for the purposes of a condition in a will using that term. Hence the essential precondition of the alternative provision cannot be shown to exist and it cannot take effect. It might have been better to direct the logically impossible presumption that each predeceased the other. The common practice of making testamentary provisions for a spouse conditional upon that spouse surviving for a specified period avoids the problem.

S31–10 The other special case where a different presumption of survivorship applies is the somewhat complicated one specified in s.31(2). Where two persons other than husband and wife have perished in common calamity circumstances the presumption would normally be that the younger survived the elder. But, if the elder has left a testamentary disposition containing a provision in favour of the younger, and failing the younger, in favour of a third party, and if the younger has died intestate, then it is presumed for the purposes of that destination that the elder person survived the younger. The effect is that the elder's property will go to the nominated third person. Without such a provision, in spite of the known wishes of the elder person as specified in the destination, the property so bequeathed would have passed via the younger to those who would be entitled to succeed on the intestacy of the younger person.

S31–11 The drafting of s.31(2) is not beyond criticism, even if one accepts the need for this exception to the usual presumption of survivorship. The younger person must die "intestate" before the reversed presumption applies. This is defined in s.36(1) as "leaving undisposed of by testamentary disposition the whole or any part of" one's estate. Thus one dies "intestate" if any part of one's estate is effectively undisposed of.[281] Thus, in the situation envisaged in s.31(2), even if the younger person has made explicit provision in his will for the property which he expects to pass to him on the elder person's death, he has died "intestate" within the meaning of s.31(2) if he has failed to dispose of any other item of his estate. The younger person being "intestate", the presumption for the purpose of the destination would be that the elder survived him, and the property would pass to the third party nominated in the destination. Only if he had also made a testamentary disposition of every item of his estate would the younger person avoid being "intestate". One might have thought that, if this exception to the usual presumption of survivorship is necessary (which seems doubtful), it would have applied whether or not the younger person made a will, or alternatively only in cases where he was intestate as to the property subject to the destination. To make it apply in cases only where he is intestate as to any part of his estate seems to be a defect in drafting.

---

[281] See paras S36–21 to S36–22.

The Scottish Law Commission has recommended the removal of the presump- **S31–12** tions based on age and their replacement by a rule of law applicable to all circumstances where two persons die simultaneously or in circumstances where it is "uncertain" who survived whom, namely that neither is to be treated as surviving the other.[282] This has been included in the Succession (Scotland) Bill. In its effect on intestacy such a rule may have the effect of recreating the outcome at common law as exemplified in the Clydebank blitz case *Drummond's Judicial Factor v Her Majesty's Advocate.*[283] In that case there was a married couple and two children. The wife owned war savings certificates. All four perished in the air attack. The order of death was unknown. The wife died intestate. She had no other relatives. Her husband might have claimed the certificates under his prior right or her children might have claimed as her next of kin. The husband's siblings sought to inherit the certificates as next of kin of either the deceased husband or the deceased children. The court held that as they could not establish that either the husband or any child had survived the deceased, they could have no claim as next of kin and preferred the Crown. Under s.31 the brothers/sister-in-law could have inherited but if the recommendation is followed the Crown will gain. Clearly the proposed reform puts a premium on survivance by a spouse, civil partner or some blood relative. While s.31 is not perfect it is not entirely clear that this would be in line with public expectation. On any view it is hoped that in the light of the arguments which arose over the word "uncertain" in s.31, a formulation such as "the order of death cannot be established on a balance of probabilities" will be adopted in any provision replacing s.31.

For purposes of Inheritance Tax, persons dying in a common calamity without **S31–13** proof of survivorship are deemed to die at the same instant.[284]

Certain testamentary dispositions to be formally valid
[1]**32.—(1) For the purpose of any question arising as to entitlement, by virtue of a testamentary disposition, to any relevant property or to any interest therein, the disposition shall be treated as valid in respect of the formalities of execution.**

(2) Subsection (1) above is without prejudice to any right to challenge the validity of the testamentary disposition on the ground of forgery or on any other ground of essential invalidity.

(3) In this section "relevant property" means property disposed of in the testamentary disposition in respect of which—

(a) confirmation has been granted; or
(b) probate, letters of administration or other grant of representation—

---

[282] *2009 Report on Succession* recommendation 57 and cl.35 of the 2009 Report Bill.
[283] *Drummond's Judicial Factor v Her Majesty's Advocate*, 1944 S.C. 298.
[284] Inheritance Tax Act 1984 (c.51) s.4(2). This presumption avoids the risk of duplicated taxation, and is also the general rule adopted by some countries, e.g. Germany (Verschollenheitsgesetz §11) for all cases of common calamities.

(i) has been issued, and has noted the domicile of the deceased to be, in England and Wales or Northern Ireland; or

(ii) has been issued outwith the United Kingdom and had been sealed in Scotland under section 2 of the Colonial Probates Act 1892.

NOTE

1. Substituted by the Requirements of Writing (Scotland) Act 1995 (c.7) Sch.4(2) para.40 (effective August 1, 1995).

DEFINITIONS

"relevant property": s.32(3).
"testamentary disposition": s.36(1).

COMMENTARY

S32–01   The purpose of s.32 is somewhat obscure. The current wording was inserted by the 1995 Act.[285] It replaced the original wording which in subs.(1) provided that a testamentary disposition which was not probative but in respect of which confirmation had been granted would be treated as probative. "Probativity" meant simply that the document could be founded on in court proceedings without requiring an appropriate witness to give oral evidence as to its authenticity. A document that was "probative" was presumed to be valid and authentic but no more.

S32–02   The 1995 Act abolished the concept of "probativity" for documents executed after it came into force and therefore the original s.32 required to be altered. However, the new wording did not make reference to the new form of probativity introduced by ss.3 and 4 of the 1995 Act. Instead it went further and deemed the testamentary document "valid" as a matter of law in respect of the formalities of execution, other than the genuineness of any signature.

S32–03   The possible effect of the new and current wording of s.32 is to impose res judicata on beneficiaries in respect of the formalities of a testamentary disposition where any part of the estate disposed therein has been either confirmed to or where the designated probate, letters of administration or other grant of representation have been issued or issued and re-sealed. That in turn protects the confirmed executor in respect of any claim arising out of wrongful distribution on the basis of a will with incomplete formalities which was incorporated into the confirmation. It is unclear whether s.32 imposes res judicata in respect of the formalities of testamentary dispositions which may be discovered after confirmation but which dispose of estate already confirmed to. The answer depends on the construction of the words "property disposed of in the testamentary disposition in respect of which (a) confirmation has been granted" where they appear in s.32(3). It is submitted that a purposive construction should be applied. The apparent purpose of s.32 is to allow confirmation to put an end to disputes over formalities of execution. Since confirmation is only concerned with formalities of execution by virtue of the documentary requirements of ss.21 and

---

[285] (c.7).

21A, s.32 cannot have been intended to cover documents which happen not to have been lodged with the application for confirmation. It follows that in s.32(3) the words "in respect of which confirmation has been granted" should be interpreted as relating to both the property and the testamentary disposition.

Construction of existing deeds

¹33.—²(1) **Subject to subsection (2) of this section, any reference in any deed taking effect after the commencement of this Act to *jus relicti, jus relictae* or legitim shall be construed as a reference to the right to *jus relicti, jus relictae* or legitim, as the case may be, as modified by Part II of this Act; and any reference in any such deed to courtesy or terce shall be of no effect.**

³(2) **Any reference to legal rights in a marriage contract made before the commencement of this Act and taking effect in consequence of a decree of divorce granted in an action commenced after the commencement of this Act shall be construed as a reference to any right which the husband or the wife, as the case may be, might obtain by virtue of the provisions of section 26 of this Act or section 5 of the Divorce (Scotland) Act 1976 or section 29 of the Matrimonial and Family Proceedings Act 1984 or section 8 of the Family Law (Scotland) Act 1985.**

NOTES

1. As amended by the Law Reform (Miscellaneous Provisions) (Scotland) Act 1968 (c.70) Sch.1, in respect of the estate of any person dying on or after November 25, 1968.
2. As amended by the Law Reform (Parent and Child) (Scotland) Act 1986 (c.9) Sch.1 para.7(1) and Sch.2 (effective December 8, 1986).
3. As amended by the Divorce (Scotland) Act 1976 (c.39) Sch.1 para.2, the Matrimonial and Family Proceedings Act 1984 (c.42) Sch.1 para.6 and the Family Law (Scotland) Act 1985 (c.37) Sch.1 para.4.

DEFINITIONS

"deed": s.36(1).
"legal rights": s.36(1).

COMMENTARY

Section 33(1) is a provision consequential on the extension of legitim in terms **S33–01** of s.11, its subordination to prior rights in terms of s.10(2) and the abolition of courtesy and terce in terms of s.10(1).

Section 25 reformed the old rule that legal rights were due on divorce as if **S33–02** the guilty spouse had died. It substituted a new discretionary system, subsequently much amended in separate legislation.[286] Section 33(2) is a provision

---

[286] s.25, repealed and replaced by the Divorce (Scotland) Act 1976 (c.39) Sch.2 and ss.5 and 6. The basis of the present law is the Family Law (Scotland) Act 1985 (c.37).

consequential on s.25 and the new provisions in the legislation mentioned in s.33(2). Thus references to legal rights in marriage contracts which were entered into before September 10, 1964, but which take effect on divorce granted in an action commenced on or after that date are now to be construed as references to rights which the spouse might obtain under the new schemes of financial provision on divorce.[287] Any reference to legal rights in a pre-1964 marriage contract tended to take the form of a renunciation of them by the parties. The result is that such a clause will be treated as a renunciation of any claim for financial provision on divorce. It may also exclude the right to seek a variation of the marriage contract on divorce.[288] The traditional legal rights no longer have any function in dealing with the financial consequences of divorce.

Modification of enactments and repeals

34.—(1) Subject to the provisions of section 37 of this Act, the enactments mentioned in Schedule 2 to this Act shall have effect subject to the modifications specified in that Schedule, being modifications consequential on the provisions of this Act.

(2) [*Repealed by the Statute Law (Repeals) Act 1974 (c.22) Sch. Pt XI*].

COMMENTARY

S34–01   Schedule 2 makes both general modifications to all pieces of legislation and specific modifications of specific pieces of legislation. The general modifications involve the construction (interpretation) of references in legislation to "heir-at-law", "heir" and references in legislation relating to the confirmation of executors or administration of moveable estates of deceased persons to "moveable or personal property or estate of a deceased person".

S34–02   The new constructions are designed to reflect the replacement of heirs-at-law for succession purposes with prior rights and s.2 rights and for administrative purposes with executors, and the extension of confirmation and the function of executors to the whole of the estate and not merely the moveable estate. In addition references to terce and courtesy are to be of no effect.

Transfer of certain jurisdiction to Sheriff of Chancery

35.—(1) If at any time it appears to the Secretary of State expedient to do so he may by order transfer to the Sheriff of Chancery the jurisdiction of any other sheriff in relation to the service of heirs.

(2) An order made under this section may contain such consequential provisions as appears to the Secretary of State to be necessary, including provisions for the consequential repeal or consequential modification of any enactment relating to the matters dealt with in the order.

(3) Any order made under this section shall be made by statutory instrument.

---

[287] See the Divorce (Scotland) Act 1976 s.5; Matrimonial and Family Proceedings Act 1984 (c.42) s.29.
[288] *Thomson v Thomson*, 1982 S.L.T. 521.

DEFINITIONS

"Secretary of State": Scotland Act 1998 (c.46) ss.117 and 126(1).

COMMENTARY

The Sheriff of Chancery (Transfer of Jurisdiction) Order 1971[289] has been made **S35–01** under the power in s.35. It had the effect of transferring to the Sheriff of Chancery the jurisdiction of every other sheriff in relation to the service of heirs. It also provided that any reference in any legislation or other document making a reference to a sheriff of a county in relation to the service of heirs should be construed as a reference to the Sheriff of Chancery. The Sheriff of Chancery is the Sheriff Principal of Lothian and Borders.[290]

For the reformed procedure which has replaced service of heirs[291] see ss.26A **S35–02** and 26B of the Titles to Land Consolidation (Scotland) Act 1868[292] and the Chancery Procedure Rules 2006.[293] Section 26C of the 1868 Act provides that any reference in legislation or any deed to a decree of service of heirs (however expressed) shall be taken to include a reference to the declarator granted under ss.26A or 26B of the 1868 Act.

Interpretation
36.—(1) In this Act the following expressions shall, unless the context otherwise requires, have the meanings hereby respectively assigned to them, that is to say—

"deed" includes any disposition, contract, instrument or writing, whether inter vivos or mortis causa;

"an intestate" means a person who has died leaving undisposed of by testamentary disposition the whole or any part of his estate, and "intestate" shall be construed accordingly;

"intestate estate", in relation to an intestate, means (subject to sections 1(2) and 9(6)(a) of this Act) so much of his estate as is undisposed of by testamentary disposition;

[1]"issue" means [. . .] issue however remote;

"Land Court" means the Scottish Land Court;

"lease" and "tenancy" include sub-lease and sub-tenancy, and tenant shall be construed accordingly;

[2]"legal rights" means *jus relicti, jus relictae*, legitim and rights under section 131 of the Civil Partnership Act 2004;

"net estate" and "net intestate estate" mean respectively so much of an estate or an intestate estate as remains after provision for the satisfaction of estate duty and other liabilities of the estate having priority over

---

[289] Sheriff of Chancery (Transfer of Jurisdiction) Order 1971 (SI 1971/743).
[290] In accordance with the Administration of Justice (Scotland) Act 1933 s.31(1).
[291] Abolition of Feudal Tenure etc. (Scotland) Act 2000 (asp 5) Sch.12 para.8(11).
[292] As inserted by the Abolition of Feudal Tenure etc. (Scotland) Act 2000 s.68.
[293] Act of Sederunt (Chancery Procedure Rules) 2006 (SSI 2006/292).

legal rights, the prior rights of a surviving spouse and rights of succession, or, as the case may be, the proportion thereof properly attributable to the intestate estate;

"owner" in relation to any heritable property means the person entitled to receive the rents thereof (other than rents under a sub-lease or sub-tenancy);

[3]"prior rights" , in relation to a surviving spouse or civil partner, means the rights conferred by sections 8 and 9 of this Act;

"testamentary disposition", in relation to a deceased, includes any deed taking effect on his death whereby any part of his estate is disposed of or under which a succession thereto arises.

(2) Any reference in this Act to the estate of a deceased person shall, unless the context otherwise requires, be construed as a reference to the whole estate, whether heritable or moveable, or partly heritable and partly moveable, belonging to the deceased at the time of his death or over which the deceased had a power of appointment and, where the deceased immediately before his death held the interest of a tenant under a tenancy or lease which was not expressed to expire on his death, includes that interest:

Provided that—

(a) where any heritable property belonging to a deceased person at the date of his death is subject to a special destination in favour of any person, the property shall not be treated for the purposes of this Act as part of the estate of the deceased unless the destination is one which could competently be, and has in fact been, evacuated by the deceased by testamentary disposition or otherwise; and in that case the property shall be treated for the purposes of this Act as if it were part of the deceased's estate on which he has tested; and

(b) where any heritable property over which a deceased person had a power of appointment has not been disposed of in exercise of that power and is in those circumstances subject to a power of appointment by some other person, that property shall not be treated for the purposes of this Act as part of the estate of the deceased.

(3) Without prejudice to the proviso to section 23(2) of this Act, references in this Act to the date of execution of a testamentary disposition shall be construed as references to the date on which the disposition was actually executed and not to the date of death of the testator.

(4) References in this Act to any enactment shall, except where the context otherwise requires, be construed as references to that enactment as amended by or under any other enactment, including this Act.

[4](5) Section 1(1) (legal equality of children) of the Law Reform (Parent and Child) (Scotland) Act 1986 shall apply to this Act; and any reference (however expressed) in this Act to a relative shall be construed accordingly.

NOTES

1. Word repealed by the Law Reform (Parent and Child) (Scotland) Act 1986 (c.9) s.10(2), Sch. 2.
2. As amended by the Civil Partnership Act 2004 (c.33) Pt 3 c.6 s.131(5) (effective December 5, 2005).
3. As amended by the Civil Partnership Act 2004 (c.33) Sch.28(1) para.10 (effective December 5, 2005).
4. Inserted by the Law Reform (Parent and Child) (Scotland) Act 1986 (c.9) s.10(1), Sch.1 para.7(2).

DEFINITIONS

"deed": s.36(1).
"estate": s.36(2).
"estate duty": Inheritance Tax Act 1984 (c.51) Sch.6 para.1 and the Finance Act 1986 (c.41).
"intestate": s.36(1).
"intestate estate": s.36(1).
"legal rights": s.36(1).
"prior rights": s.36(1).
"testamentary disposition": s.36(1).

COMMENTARY

The interpretation section is critical for a proper understanding of the **S36–01** provisions of the Act. Given its importance this commentary will begin will a consideration of the concept of "estate" as it is defined in s.36(2) and used in the Act. It will then consider the definitions in s.36(1).

Section 36(2)—"estate of a deceased person"

General

Considerable care must be taken over the terms of this definition which is **S36–02** central to the whole scheme of the Act, including intestate succession and the administration of estates. Section 36(2) provides that the estate of a deceased person comprises the whole estate (a) belonging to the deceased at the time of his death, subject to one exception; and (b) over which the deceased held a power of appointment, subject to one exception. "Whole" estate means that it includes moveable and heritable, corporeal and incorporeal property. Rights held by or vested in the deceased will, for the purposes of the Act, be incorporeal estate belonging to him or her. "Belonging" to the deceased must mean owned by or vested in the deceased. Heritable property in which the deceased had an unregistered right (e.g. as a recipient of a delivered disposition in his favour) will "belong" to the deceased and thus be part of his estate.[294] The interest of a tenant other than

---

[294] Erskine, II, ii, 5.

one expressed to expire on his death, will be part of his estate except where it was a public sector residential tenancy under the Housing (Scotland) Act 2001.[295] Leases cannot, however, be included in the deceased's estate if they are "liferent leases" expiring on his death.[296] A right vested in the deceased contrasts with a *spes successionis* which is not a vested right.[297] As McLaren observes:

> "A *spes successionis* or contingent right may be assigned but the assignment will be operative only in case the right becomes vested."[298]

Given that vesting in an executor operates as a statutory assignation (assignment) as at the death of the deceased, if on his death the deceased held a mere *spes successionis*, the vesting cannot be operative to transfer the *spes* to the executor.

Special destinations—general

S36–03   The first exception to inclusion within the concept of the deceased's "estate" is that heritage subject to a special destination in favour of a third party is not part of the deceased's estate unless the deceased could and did evacuate that destination. The second exception provides that if heritage over which the deceased held a power of appointment has not been disposed of under that power, and it is in those circumstances subject to a power of appointment by some other person, it is not to be treated as part of the deceased's estate.

S36–04   In certain circumstances incorporeal moveable property (e.g. bonds and shares) can also be held subject to a destination.[299] Not being heritable property, such property continues to fall within the definition of "estate" which is used in the Act. It will therefore still fall to be confirmed to and will vest in the executor for onward transmission, unless the destination has been evacuated. However, the provision commonly found in bank accounts or deposit receipts that they are payable to "A or B or to the survivor" has no testamentary effect[300] and is not an effective destination. See also M.C. Meston, "Survivorship Destinations and Bank Accounts" [1996] 1 S.L.P.Q. 315.

S36–05   Where a bank account is held in joint names there is a presumption that the account holders named own an equal portion of the monies held as at the death of one of them.[301] As with all presumptions it may be rebutted with satisfactory extraneous evidence.[302]

---

[295] (asp 10) which provides in s.22 that such a tenancy "passes by operation of law" to a "qualified person" set out in Sch.3. Section 22 operates in effect like a statutory special destination and prevents the tenancy from vesting in an executor.

[296] *Cormack v McIldowie's Executors*, 1975 S.C. 161 at 171 and 182 approving this passage in the 2nd edition of this book; and *Mountain's Trustees v Mountain* [2012] CSIH 73, 2013 S.C. 202 at [34].

[297] *Reid v Morrison* (1893) 20 R. 510 at 512.

[298] *Wills & Succession*, ii, 843.

[299] *Connell's Trustees v Connell's Trustees* (1886) 13 R. 1175.

[300] *Connell's Trustees v Connell's Trustees* (1886) 13 R. 1175; and *Dinwoodie's Executrix v Carruthers' Executor* (1895) 25 R. 234.

[301] *Trotter v Spence* (1885) 22 S.L.R. 353 at 355–356; the obiter remarks in *Allan's Executor v Union Bank of Scotland*, 1909 S.C. 206 at 211 to the effect that "no inference can be drawn from the terms in which the money is deposited as to the ownership of the money" must be read subject to the position in default of satisfactory evidence as set out in *Trotter*.

[302] As in *Forrest-Hamilton's Trustee v Forrest Hamilton*, 1970 S.L.T. 338.

There are examples of incorporeal moveable property ceasing to be part of the **S36–06** estate upon the death of the deceased. Typically this is where the right (or interest) in question had become subject to a contractual[303] or statutory nomination in favour of a third party nominee. Whether a nomination has the effect of taking the right out of the estate of the deceased upon death depends on the terms of the contract under which it is permitted.

Special destinations in heritable property

Section 36(2) expressly excludes heritable property subject to an unrevoked **S36–07** special destination from being included in the deceased's "estate" for the purposes of the Act. It is therefore incompetent for the deceased's executor to confirm to it (unless a conveyance by the executor to the heir under the destination is necessary to transfer title[304]), although it will still be part of the estate liable to meet the debts of the deceased, including taxation.[305] For that reason such heritable property should not be included in the application for confirmation but it will require to be mentioned in the HM Revenue and Customs forms which form either an inheritance tax return or account and where the destination is a survivorship destination, in any form relating to "joint property".

Special destinations are a means of regulating succession principally to heritable **S36–08** property which originate from the period before 1868 when it was not competent to bequeath heritable property by means of a will or *mortis causa* trust disposition and settlement. Instead, one of the means of disinheriting the heir-at-law was through the owner of the heritable property arranging for the insertion into his title of a substitute owner upon his death known as an "heir of provision". If this was done, then upon the death of the owner the heir of provision could acquire the property through service as heir of provision which decree could then be recorded in the Register of Sasines or, after the Conveyancing (Scotland) Acts 1874 and 1924, by means of a notice of title recorded in the Register of Sasines. These procedures were unnecessary if the heir of provision already had a recorded title to the property in question, as in a destination to a survivor of two or more *pro indiviso* owners (vassals or feuars).[306] This remains the law. Such destinations to the survivor of two or more *pro indiviso* owners, known as "survivorship destinations", remain the most common form of special destination. The adjective "special" indicates that there is a destination to specified heirs or a class of heirs contained in the title to the property (heritable or moveable) as opposed to a destination-over in a will or a general settlement either in an inter vivos deed or in a will. The heir or heirs must be specific or "special" and a destination to the disponee's "disponees" or to the "heirs and assignees" of a tenant will not be a special destination.[307]

---

[303] *Campbell v Campbell*, 1917 1 S.L.T. 339.
[304] See s.18(2).
[305] See Ch.3.
[306] *Bisset v Walker*, Faculty Collection 26.11.1799.
[307] *Webster's Trustees v Webster* (1876) 4 R. 101; and *Cormack v McIldowie's Executors*, 1975 S.C. 161, 1975 S.L.T. 214.

S36–09   The commonest example of a survivorship destination is in a title in favour of a husband and wife and "the survivor". In this case registration of the disposition in a property register confers on each a one-half *pro indiviso* share of the heritage (unless a different share is expressed) *and* a right to inherit the other's share. In effect the survivorship destination makes each *pro indiviso* owner a substitute owner in respect of the share of the other *pro indiviso* owner upon the prior death of that other owner.

S36–10   Whether this share of the other *pro indiviso* owner forms part of his estate for the purposes of the Act depends upon two factors. One is whether there was power to evacuate (revoke) the destination. The other is whether, even assuming the power to exist, evacuation has in fact occurred. Special factors apply where two of the *pro indiviso* owners with the destination were married (or civil partners) during their ownership with the destination and thereafter divorced or had their marriage annulled.

S36–11   Evacuation can take place by means of either a testamentary (*mortis causa*) or lifetime (inter vivos) document. In the absence of express contractual provisions (which can be contained within the disposition itself[308]), the existence of a power to evacuate by testamentary deed is normally dependent on the source of the finance used in the purchase of the property. If the price was provided at least to a significant extent by both disponees and this is narrated in the disposition, the destination is a contractual arrangement which neither has power to evacuate[309] by testamentary document without the consent of the other. Equally, if the property was funded by one of the disponees only, then while he has power to evacuate the destination of his share in favour of the other disponees they do not have power to evacuate the destinations of their shares at all whether they be in his favour or in favour of their co-donees[310] without his consent. While it appears that in assessing the source of funding and whether the power to evacuate has been excluded in a contractual arrangement the court is restricted to looking at the terms of the disposition,[311] in a case where the parties agreed in court proceedings that the narration in the disposition was inaccurate the court found that it was entitled to disregard the narration.[312] The power to evacuate could be granted by the funding disponee giving his consent to the evacuaton in the testamentary document which seeks to carry it out.[313] In the absence of power to revoke, any purported evacuation of a destination by means of a testamentary document is totally ineffective.

S36–12   However, if the power exists, the question of whether evacuation has occurred so as to bring the property into the "estate" of the deceased has been simplified by s.30 of the Act. Briefly, only if the testamentary document contains an express reference to the destination and a declared intention to evacuate it will there be

---

[308] But virtually never are.

[309] *Perrett's Trustee v Perrett*, 1909 S.C. 522; *Gordon-Rogers v Thomson's Executors*, 1988 S.C. 145; *Smith v Mackintosh*, 1988 S.C. 453.

[310] *Brown's Trustees v Brown*, 1943 S.C. 488. In *Brown* the report does not record the narration of the funding in the disposition but the court followed *Chalmers' Trustees v Thomson's Executor*, 1923 S.C. 271 where there is no indication that the funding was narrated in the disposition.

[311] *Gordon-Rogers v Thomson's Executors*, 1988 S.C. 145.

[312] *Hay's Trustee v Hay's Trustees*, 1951 S.C. 329.

[313] The consent could be endorsed onto the will.

evacuation.[314] The old practice of including in the will a general reference to destinations without specifying them, and which is still sometimes encountered, is not effective.

Any *pro indiviso* owner of heritage subject to a survivorship destination has **S36–13** power to evacuate the destination of his share by means of an alienation of the share inter vivos to a third party who acquires a registered title to that share.[315] However, in that situation the share will have ceased to be part of his estate on his death.

An inter vivos alienation by one *pro indiviso* owner to the other, while effective **S36–14** to evacuate the destination in the disponer's title will be ineffective to evacuate the destination in the disponee's title. In that situation the disponer would remain an heir of provision (in the destination of the disponee's share). Therefore, in order for both *pro indiviso* owners to evacuate their destinations, it is necessary for each to grant a disposition of their share to the other or for both to grant a disposition to one of them or to themselves without the insertion of the survivorship destination and to register that disposition.[316] This is the most reliable method of evacuation of a survivorship destination. An unregistered inter vivos document such as an act and warrant of a trustee in sequestration is insufficient to evacuate a special destination.[317]

One of the authors has seen documents entitled "Evacuation of Special **S36–15** Destination" containing an agreement by the *pro indiviso* owners that the destinations should be evacuated. Such a document cannot suffice on its own. At most it can provide power for the owners to evacuate through wills as described above or perhaps form the basis for an obligation to co-operate in the granting and registration of an inter vivos disposition. In neither instance had either of these courses been followed and the destinations remained effective.

Aside from the general rules for evacuation of special destinations, s.19 of the **S36–16** 2006 Act[318] provides that where spouses own heritable property *pro indiviso* with a survivorship destination in each other's favour and there is subsequently a divorce or annulment of the marriage before either should die, the heir under the destination is deemed to have predeceased the deceased owner. The deemed predecease would presumably have the effect of preventing the property from being "subject to a special destination in favour of any person" and leaving it as part of the deceased's "estate" for the purpose of the Act. Why the effect of divorce or annulment could not have been expressed as an evacuation is unclear.

Where the destination is in moveable property such as Scottish shares or **S36–17** bonds[319] the principles relating to evacuation are largely the same as for heritable property. In relation to the power to evacuate, given the format of shares, both modern and in former times, it may be unrealistic to restrict the court to looking at a share certificate or a bond in standard form for evidence of a contractual

---

[314] See paras S30–01 and S30–02.
[315] *Steele v Caldwell*, 1979 S.L.T. 228; and *Smith v Mackintosh*, 1988 S.C. 453.
[316] In *Povey v Povey's Executor*, 2014 S.L.T. 643 such a disposition was executed but not registered and was thus ineffective to evacuate.
[317] *Fleming's Trustee v Fleming*, 2000 S.C. 206.
[318] (asp 2).
[319] See para.S36–04.

arrangement or evidence of donation to an heir.[320] With regard to evacuation, if done through a *mortis causa* document, s.30 will have to be complied with. Evacuation inter vivos may be more difficult given that to alter the title of incorporeal property the agreement of the debtor as well as both *pro indiviso* creditors (holders) will be required. For reasons which are again unclear, s.19 of the 2006 Act does not apply to destinations in moveable property.

S36–18   The heir of provision remains liable for the debts of the deceased[321] (heritable or moveable as appropriate), and an executor is entitled to ensure that an heir in a survivorship destination is not unjustifiably excluded from sharing in the liability for debts of the deceased which extends potentially up to the value of the heritable property inherited under the destination.

Powers of appointment

S36–19   For the purposes of the Act, the general proposition in s.36(2) is that the "estate" of a deceased person includes property over which he had a power of appointment. Taken literally this could mean that (apart from the situation in the proviso) where the deceased had a power of appointment, whether general or special, whether or not he exercised it and indeed whether or not the property concerned belonged to him, the deceased's family could claim rights of beneficial succession in it. The prospect of the widow acquiring prior rights out of property which her husband did not own would have been a startling one. However, this provision appears in fact to be a purely administrative one giving the executor power to obtain a title to the property for the purpose of conveying to those beneficially interested by virtue of the appointment or of the deed creating the power. In addition rights of succession under the Act to property not belonging to the deceased donee of the power can be seen as excluded in the following way.

S36–20   The case where the deceased was owner of the property would arise where the power was completely general or where he was given a full liferent with an unqualified power of disposal.[322] No greater problem arises in applying the Act to this type of property than to any other property which he owned. However, if the deceased had no right of fee in the property over which he had the power of appointment—e.g. if either the liferent or the power was qualified in some way— then it will be found that the various rights of succession in the Act are set out in such a way as not to apply to such property.

S36–21   The surviving spouse's prior rights under ss.8 and 9 come out of the intestate estate of the deceased. Similarly, the provisions of Part I for succession to the free estate apply solely to the intestate estate. If the deceased exercised the power of appointment, he was not intestate *quoad* the property subject to the power. However, even if he did not exercise the power, the property is still not part of his "intestate estate" as that phrase is defined in s.36(1), because it has been disposed of by "testamentary disposition" within the meaning of the same section. The

---

[320] There was no such restriction in *Dennis v Aitchison*, 1923 S.C. 819, aff'd 1924 S.C. (HL) 122.
[321] *Fleming's Trustee v Fleming*, 2000 S.C. 206; and see in general Ch.3.
[322] *MacKenzie's Trustees v Kilmarnock's Trustees* (1908) 16 S.L.T. 676; 1909 S.C. 472; *Ewing's Trustees v Ewing*, 1909 1 S.L.T. 104; 1909 S.C. 409.

definition there given is not limited to deeds by the deceased and includes "any deed taking effect on his death whereby any part of his estate is disposed of". If he failed to exercise his power of appointment, the deed by which the power was created takes effect on his death and disposes of part of his "estate". Hence property subject to an unexercised power would nevertheless still not be part of the intestate estate for the purposes of prior rights or the free estate.

So far as legal rights are concerned, s.10(2) provides that they are to be calculated **S36–22** by reference to so much of the net moveable estate as remains after satisfaction of prior rights. "Net estate" is defined as so much of an estate as remains after

> "estate duty[323] and other liabilities of the estate having priority over legal rights, the prior rights of a surviving spouse and rights of succession".

It would seem that one of the liabilities of the estate having this priority would arise from the duty to transfer property which the deceased did not own to those who have a vested right to it.

Hence one is left again with the proposition that property subject to a power **S36–23** of appointment by the deceased is part of the deceased's "estate" solely for the purpose of completion of title.

Section 36(1)—"an intestate" and "intestate estate"

Taking these expressions together, "an intestate" means a person who has died **S36–24** leaving "intestate estate" in terms of the general definition of that latter expression.

The general definition of "intestate estate" is so much of the "estate" of the **S36–25** deceased that he has left undisposed of by "testamentary disposition." Heritable property subject to an unevacuated special destination or over which the deceased had a power of appointment is excluded from "intestate estate" by virtue of it not being part of the "estate".[324] Property subject to statutory nominations and possibly nominations contractually binding on the deceased are excluded from "intestate estate" by virtue of having been disposed of by "testamentary disposition".[325]

"Undisposed of" means effectively undisposed of. Thus where there was a will **S36–26** with a legacy of the entire estate which was rejected by the legatee, it was held that the testamentary writing had not made an effective disposal of the estate.[326] The effect was that the deceased was an intestate and the whole of his estate fell into intestacy and subject to prior rights. Equally if any legacy of less than the entire estate is rejected by a legatee and there is no effective legacy of residue, the effect will be to render the whole estate an "intestate estate" and the deceased owner an "intestate" for the purposes of the Act.[327]

---

[323] Includes Capital Transfer Tax ("CTT") and Inheritance Tax ("IHT"). Inheritance Tax Act 1984 (c.51) Sch.6 para.1 and Finance Act 1986 (c.41) s.100(1)(b).

[324] See paras S36–03 to S36–23.

[325] See paras S36–33 to S36–36.

[326] *Kerr, Petitioner*, 1968 S.L.T. (Sh. Ct) 61 at 63 per Sheriff Principal A.G. Walker QC; and see the commentary on "testamentary disposition" below.

[327] *Munro's Trustees, Petitioners*, 1971 S.C. 280 at 291–292 per Lord Fraser (approving *Kerr, Petitioner*, 1968 S.L.T. (Sh. Ct) 61).

S36–27   Aside from its general meaning, "intestate estate" can have more specific meanings in specific parts of the Act. Thus in s.9 of the Act, it means so much of the intestate estate (in its general meaning) as remains after the satisfaction of the prior rights in s.8 (s.9(6)(a)). And, in Part I of the Act (ss.1 to 7), "intestate estate" means so much of the intestate estate as remains after the satisfaction of all prior and legal rights (s.1(2)).

Section 36(1)—"net estate" and "net intestate estate"

S36–28   The general meaning of "net estate" or "net intestate estate" in the Act is so much of the estate or intestate estate after provision for the satisfaction of all "estate duty"[328] and all other liabilities of the estate having priority over prior rights, legal rights, or s.2 rights to the intestate estate. These other liabilities will be the debts of the deceased.[329]

Section 36(1)—"issue"

S36–29   Issue is defined as "issue however remote". This begs the meaning of "issue". The expression is commonly used in wills. It has been held to mean direct descendants of every degree *per stirpes* unless the context requires a more limited construction.[330] It will cover descendants through adoption.[331]

Section 36(1)—"legal rights"

S36–30   See Ch.5 and the commentary on ss.10–13.

Section 36(1)—"owner"

S36–31   See the commentary on s.8.[332]

Section 36(1)—"prior rights"

S36–32   See the commentary on ss.8 and 9.

Section 36(1)—"testamentary disposition"

S36–33   The definition of the important expression "testamentary disposition" is broad. Section 36(1) provides that it

> "includes any deed taking effect on [the death of the deceased] whereby any part of his estate is disposed of or under which a succession thereto arises."

---

[328] See fn.327, above.
[329] See Ch.3.
[330] *Stewart's Trustees v Whitelaw*, 1926 S.C. 701; and see opinion No.10 in *Meston's Succession Opinions*.
[331] ss.23(1) and 24(1); and see the commentary thereon.
[332] para.S8–08.

The word "deed" is itself defined to include "any disposition, contract, instrument or writing, whether *inter vivos* or *mortis causa*."[333] The word "contract" indicates that an inter vivos "deed" need not be in writing. Rather what is critical is that upon his death the "deed" takes effect to dispose of any part of his estate.

The key to the meaning of "testamentary disposition" lies in the effectiveness **S36–34** of the deed occurring upon the death of the deceased. It follows that the expression "testamentary disposition" has a broad meaning which extends beyond what would normally be regarded as testamentary writings such as wills or codicils. It is broad enough to include deeds of appointment. It was suggested in earlier editions of this book that the expression could cover dispositions containing a special destination. On the face of it the definition of "testamentary disposition" in s.36(1) might be capable of covering such deeds. However, the context in which that expression is used may require a more restricted meaning. Thus in s.30 Parliament clearly contemplated that a "testamentary disposition" would be executed by a testator, and therefore for the purpose of s.30 the expression must mean a document with a testator, namely a will. The position with donations *mortis causa* is less clear given that they dispose of the property before death and death merely renders them irrevocable by the donor (assuming that they have not been revoked by the predecease of the donee). Whether the expression covers such "deeds" will depend on the context in which it is used in the Act.

The importance of the expression lies in the fact that if a person dies leaving any **S36–35** of his estate "undisposed of" by "testamentary disposition", he is deemed to be an intestate and the estate which is so undisposed is deemed "intestate estate" opening it up to prior rights, a potential cohabitee's claim and s.2 rights. In *Kerr, Petitioner*[334] a person died leaving a wife and child with a will of the whole of his estate to his wife and his wife rejected her legacy. The question arose whether he had died "intestate" thus entitling the wife to prior rights under s.9. That in turn depended on whether he had died leaving undisposed of by testamentary disposition any part of his estate, that is to say undisposed of by a deed taking effect on his death whereby any part of his estate was disposed of or under which a right of succession arose. It was argued for the child that the will took effect on his death and thereby disposed of the estate prior to the wife's rejection of the legacy. The difficulty for the argument was in explaining what was to happen to the residue of the estate after the child and wife took their legal rights. On the argument it was said not to fall into intestacy, yet the wife had rejected the legacy. As the Sheriff Principal A.G. Walker QC observed:

"The effect of the definition of 'intestate' in s.36(1) of the 1964 Act is, in my opinion that there is intestacy where there is no will at all, and also where there is a will which becomes wholly or partly inoperable. It is not possible, moreover, in my opinion, for a deceased person to leave estate which is neither testate nor intestate, but which falls into some third category applicable to estate, which although not intestate, must be distributed as if it were intestate estate. The attempt to introduce such an additional category would,

---

[333] s.36(1).
[334] *Kerr, Petitioner*, 1968 S.L.T. (Sh. Ct) 61.

if successful, inevitably lead to confusion. In my opinion estate which is not in fact disposed of by testamentary disposition must necessarily be intestate estate, with the result that s.9(1) . . . applies to it."[335]

Section 36(3)—"date of execution of a testamentary disposition"

S36–36 Section 36(3) provides that references to the date of execution of a testamentary disposition are to be understood as references to its date of actual execution rather than the death of the testator. This is without prejudice to s.23(2) which provides in general terms that where a deed relates to an adopted person and includes a provision to take effect on the death of any person, the deed is deemed to have been executed on the death of that person.

S36–37 Statutory nominations[336] would be seen as covered by the expression thereby preventing assets covered by such nominations from being intestate estate.[337] Whether nomination of benefits by the holder of a life assurance policy or similar contract has the effect of disposing of part of his estate upon death or gives rise to a right of succession (and being a "testamentary disposition") will depend on the terms of the contract in question.[338]

Section 36(4)—References to "enactment"

S36–38 Section 36(4) provides for the avoidance of doubt that references in the Act to any legislation means not merely the legislation as it stood at the time of enactment of the Act but also as subsequently amended. This is a useful provision.

Section 36(5)—Applicability of abolition of illegitimacy

S36–39 Section 1(4) of the Law Reform (Parent and Child) (Scotland) Act 1986[339] (as originally enacted) required the effect of its s.1(1) which deemed illegitimacy legitimacy, on previous enactments to be expressly incorporated into such enactments. The 1964 Act was one of these and s.36(5) was inserted therein.

Exclusion of certain matters from operation of Act
37.—[1, 2](1) Save as otherwise expressly provided, nothing in this Act or (as respects paragraph (a) of this subsection) in the Children Act 1975 or the Adoption (Scotland) Act 1978 or the Adoption and Children (Scotland) Act 2007 (asp 4) shall—

(a) apply to any title, coat of arms, honour or dignity transmissible on the death of the holder thereof or affect the succession thereto or the devolution thereof;

---

[335] *Kerr, Petitioner*, 1968 S.L.T. (Sh. Ct) 61 at 63.
[336] See para.6–123.
[337] Confirming the outcome of *Gill v Gill*, 1938 S.C. 65.
[338] *Young v Waterson*, 1918 S.C. 9 (where the nomination was construed as not taking the benefits out of the estate but giving the nominee merely an administrative right to be paid the benefits and where the Inner House doubted the Outer House decision in *Campbell v Campbell*, 1917 1 S.L.T. 339).
[339] (c.9).

(b) *[Repealed by the Law Reform (Miscellaneous Provisions) (Scotland) Act 1968 (c.70) ss.8, 22(3), Sch.2 Pt I para.28, Sch.3].*

(c) affect any right on the part of a surviving spouse to claim from the representatives of his or her deceased spouse payment of aliment out of the estate of that spouse;

(d) affect the administration, winding up or distribution of or the making up of title to any part of the estate of any person who died before the commencement of this Act or the rights of succession to such an estate or any claim for legal rights or terce or courtesy or any rights arising under the Intestate Husband's Estate (Scotland) Acts 1911 to 1959 out of such an estate or the right to take any legal proceedings with respect to any such matters;

(e) affect any claim for legal rights arising out of an action of divorce commenced before the commencement of this Act;

and in relation to the matters aforesaid the law in force immediately before the commencement of this Act shall continue to have effect as if this Act had not passed.

(2) Nothing in this Act shall be construed as affecting the operation of any rule of law applicable immediately before the commencement of this Act to the choice of the system of law governing the administration, winding up or distribution of the estate, or any part of the estate, of any deceased person.

NOTES

1. As amended by the Adoption(Scotland) Act 1978 (c.28) s.66, Sch.3 para.5.
2. As amended by the Adoption and Children (Scotland) Act 2007 (asp 4) Sch.2 para.1(3) (effective September 28, 2009).

DEFINITIONS

"estate": s.36(2).
"legal rights": s.36(1).

COMMENTARY

Peerages excluded from the Act

Under s.37(1)(a), nothing in the Act applies to any title, coat of arms, honour or **S37–01** dignity transmissible on the death of the holder thereof or affects the succession thereto or the devolution thereof. This has the result, for example, that succession to peerages is still governed by the principles of primogeniture and preference for males. It also means that adopted and illegitimate children, whose rights of succession are conferred by the Act, cannot succeed to them.[340] Legitimated

---

[340] The extension of the rights of illegitimate children by the Law Reform (Miscellaneous Provisions) (Scotland) Act 1968 took the form of inserting the provisions into the 1964 Act, while the further liberalisation in the separate Law Reform (Parent and Child) (Scotland) Act 1986 contains in s.9(1) (c) an express exemption of succession to titles, etc.

children can, however, succeed to titles. This was always true of those legitimated at common law, while those whose legitimation depends upon the Legitimation (Scotland) Act 1968[341] have rights independent of the 1964 Act. The Legitimation (Scotland) Act 1968 continues in force for titles etc. despite the amendments to s.1 of the 1986 Act introduced by the 2006 Act.[342]

Crofting tenancies

S37–02   Originally crofting tenancies were excluded from the scope of the Act by s.37(1)(b) and had special rules of succession giving the primary right to the tenancy (and its value) to the heir at law. However, by virtue of the 1968 Act, the exclusion was repealed. Now, a crofting tenancy is just another item of heritable estate to be dealt with like any other. It has a value, whatever difficulties there may be in ascertaining it, and that value may now have to be divided among those beneficially interested in the estate, although only one person can be the new tenant. This may lead to competition for the office of executor, as the executor controls the transmission of the tenancy.[343]

Choice of law

S37–03   Section 37(2) preserved the rules of international private law in existence prior to the Act coming into force. For further information on these see Ch.7.

Citation, extent and commencement
38.—(1) This Act may be cited as the Succession (Scotland) Act 1964.
     (2) This Act shall extend to Scotland only.
     (3) This Act shall come into operation on the expiration of the period of three months beginning with the date on which it is passed.

COMMENTARY

Section 38(2)—Application in Scotland

S38–01   Section 38(2) makes it clear that the Act applies only in Scotland as part of Scots law.

Section 38(3)—Commencement

S38–02   The Act received the Royal Assent on June 10, 1964. The effect of s.38(3) was to bring it into force for persons dying after midnight from September 9 to September 10, 1964. The commencement of amendments to the various provisions of the Act are indicated in the commentary on the provision in question.

---

[341] (c.22).
[342] The Family Law (Scotland) Act 2006 (Commencement, Transitional Provisions and Savings) Order 2006 (SSI 2006/212) art.11.
[343] MacCuish and Flyn, *Crofting Law* (1990), para.7.05.

SCHEDULES

SCHEDULE 1

Section 15

[1]FORM OF DOCKET

I AB, being by virtue of the within confirmation [*or certificate of confirmation*] the executor on the estate of the deceased CD so far as specified in the confirmation [*or certificate or inventory attached hereto*] hereby nominate EF [*designed*] as the person entitled—

(a) **in [part] satisfaction of his claim to prior rights, as a surviving spouse, on the death of the deceased,**

(b) **in [part] satisfaction of his claim to legal rights on the death of the deceased,**

(c) **in [part] satisfaction of his share in the said estate,**

(d) **in [part] implement of a trust disposition and settlement, [*or will, or as the case may be*] of the deceased dated and registered in the Books of Council and Session**

to the following item of estate, that it to say, [*short description*] being number of the items of the estate specified in the said confirmation [*or certificate or inventory*].

 Testing clause*

*Note—Subscription of the document by the granter of it will be sufficient for the document to be formally valid, but witnessing of it may be necessary or desirable for other purposes (see the Requirements of Writing (Scotland) Act 1995).

NOTE

1. As amended by the Requirements of Writing (Scotland) Act 1995 (c.7) Sch.4 para.41 (effective August 1, 1995: s.15(2)).

SCHEDULE 2

Section 34

MODIFICATION OF ENACTMENTS

GENERAL MODIFICATIONS

[1]1. Subject to the specific modifications made by the following provisions of this Schedule, references in any enactment to the heir-at-law of a deceased

person in relation to any heritable property shall be construed as references to the persons who by virtue of this Act are entitled to succeed to such property on intestacy.

NOTE

1. As amended by the Law Reform (Miscellaneous Provisions) (Scotland) Act 1968 (c.70) ss.8, 22(3), Sch.2 Pt I para.29, Sch.3.

2. Subject as aforesaid references in general terms in any enactment to the heirs of a deceased person shall include—

(a) **the persons entitled by virtue of this Act to succeed on intestacy to any part of the estate of the deceased; and**
(b) **so far as is necessary for the purposes of Part III of this Act, the executor of the deceased.**

3. References in any enactment relating to the confirmation of executors or the administration of the moveable estates of deceased persons to the moveable or personal property or estate of a deceased person shall, except where the context otherwise requires, be construed as references to the whole estate of the deceased person.
    4. References in any enactment (other than in this Act) to courtesy or terce shall be of no effect.

NOTE

See the Registration of Leases (Scotland) Act 1857 ss.8, 9 and Schs C, F; Titles to Land Consolidation (Scotland) Act 1868 s.20; Conveyancing (Scotland) Act 1924 ss.32, 33.

PART III

FAMILY LAW (SCOTLAND) ACT 2006

(asp 2)

An Act of the Scottish Parliament to amend the law in relation to marriage, divorce and the jurisdiction of the courts in certain consistorial actions; . . . to make provision conferring rights in relation to property, succession and claims in damages for persons living, or having lived, together as if husband and wife or civil partners; . . . and for connected purposes.
[January 20, 2006]

Application to court by survivor for provision on intestacy
²29.—(1) This section applies where—

(a) a cohabitant (the "deceased") dies intestate; and
(b) immediately before the death the deceased was—

    (i) domiciled in Scotland; and
    (ii) cohabiting with another cohabitant (the "survivor").

(2) Subject to subsection (4), on the application of the survivor, the court may—

(a) after having regard to the matters mentioned in subsection (3), make an order—

    (i) for payment to the survivor out of the deceased's net intestate estate of a capital sum of such amount as may be specified in the order;
    (ii) for transfer to the survivor of such property (whether heritable or moveable) from that estate as may be so specified;

(b) make such interim order as it thinks fit.

(3) Those matters are—

(a) the size and nature of the deceased's net intestate estate;
(b) any benefit received, or to be received, by the survivor—

(i) on, or in consequence of, the deceased's death; and

(ii) from somewhere other than the deceased's net intestate estate;

(c) the nature and extent of any other rights against, or claims on, the deceased's net intestate estate; and

(d) any other matter the court considers appropriate.

(4) An order or interim order under subsection (2) shall not have the effect of awarding to the survivor an amount which would exceed the amount to which the survivor would have been entitled had the survivor been the spouse or civil partner of the deceased.

(5) An application under this section may be made to—

(a) the Court of Session;

(b) a sheriff in the sheriffdom in which the deceased was habitually resident at the date of death;

(c) if at the date of death it is uncertain in which sheriffdom the deceased was habitually resident, the sheriff at Edinburgh.

[1](6) Subject to section 29A, any application under this section shall be made before the expiry of the period of 6 months beginning with the day on which the deceased died.

(7) In making an order under paragraph (a)(i) of subsection (2), the court may specify that the capital sum shall be payable—

(a) on such date as may be specified;

(b) in instalments.

(8) In making an order under paragraph (a)(ii) of subsection (2), the court may specify that the transfer shall be effective on such date as may be specified.

(9) If the court makes an order in accordance with subsection (7), it may, on an application by any party having an interest, vary the date or method of payment of the capital sum.

(10) In this section—

"intestate" shall be construed in accordance with section 36(1) of the Succession (Scotland) Act 1964 (c.41);

"legal rights" has the meaning given by section 36(1) of the Succession (Scotland) Act 1964 (c.41);

"net intestate estate" means so much of the intestate estate as remains after provision for the satisfaction of—

(a) inheritance tax;

(b) other liabilities of the estate having priority over legal rights and the prior rights of a surviving spouse or surviving civil partner; and

(c) the legal rights, and the prior rights, of any surviving spouse or surviving civil partner; and

"prior rights" has the meaning given by section 36(1) of the Succession (Scotland) Act 1964 (c.41).

NOTES

1. As amended by the Cross-Border Mediation (Scotland) Regulations 2011 (SSI 2011/234) reg.9(3) (effective April 6, 2011).

2. Section 25 of the Family Law (Scotland) Act 2006, provides:

"25.—(1) In sections 26 to 29 "cohabitant" means either member of a couple consisting of –

(a) a man and a woman who are (or were) living together as if they were husband and wife; or

(b) two persons of the same sex who are (or were) living together as if they were civil partners.

(2) In determining for the purposes of any of sections 26 to 29 whether a person ("A") is a cohabitant of another person ("B") the court shall have regard to –

(a) the length of the period during which A and B have been living together (or lived together);

(b) the nature of their relationship during that period; and

(c) the nature and extent of any financial arrangements subsisting, or which subsisted, during that period.

(3) In subsection (2) . . . "court" means Court of Session or sheriff."

DEFINITIONS

"cohabitant": 2006 Act s.25.
"estate": s.36(2).
"intestate": 2006 Act s.29(1); 1964 Act s.36(1).
"legal rights": 2006 Act s.29(10); 1964 Act s.36(1).
"net intestate estate": 2006 Act s.29(10); see also 1964 Act s.36(1).
"prior rights": 2006 Act s.29(10); 1964 Act s.36(1); see ss.8 and 9 of the 1964 Act.

COMMENTARY

General

Society in Scotland has changed greatly since 1964 and indeed by 1990 cohabi- **F29–01**
tation of couples outside marriage had become sufficiently widespread for the
Scottish Law Commission to issue a discussion paper covering, among other

matters, the granting of rights of succession to cohabitants.[1] This resulted in the publication of a Report[2] which recommended[3] in 1992 that a surviving cohabitant should not be given automatic rights of intestate succession or legal rights but should be allowed to apply to the court for an award out of the estate. As Lord Hope observed in *Gow v Grant*[4]:

> "There was a respectable body of opinion that it would be unwise to impose marriage-like consequences on couples who had deliberately chosen not to marry".

Flexibility of relationship was to be matched by flexibility of entitlement. In any event the Law Commission observed that there was no clear pattern of public and legal opinion on the extent of succession rights that cohabitants should have. Perhaps this reflects the many different circumstances covered by cohabitation, even within the definition that has come to be used in the 2006 Act. The need for cohabitants to apply to the court reflects the fact that cohabitants continue not to have rights of succession vesting on death.

F29–02   It is also important to be aware that provisions for cohabitants were introduced in the context of the allowance of claims for financial provision in the event of inter vivos separation. Claims for such financial provision were introduced by s.28 of the 2006 Act. However, that provision requires the taking into account of whether and if so, to what extent, the defender in the claim has derived economic advantage from the claimant's contributions and whether the claimant has suffered economic disadvantage in the interests of the defender or any child of the former couple or accepted by them as their child. Such matters are not mentioned in s.29 and their omission may be significant.

Intestacy

F29–03   Section 29 affects only intestate estates,[5] although in its *2009 Report on Succession* the Scottish Law Commission recommended that it should be extended to testate estates.[6]

Cohabitant

F29–04   The right to apply is restricted to the surviving[7] "cohabitant" of an intestate deceased with whom the deceased was cohabiting immediately before his death.[8]

---

[1] Scottish Law Commission, *Discussion Paper on The Effects of Cohabitation in Private Law* (HMSO, 1990), Scot. Law Com. No.86; and see in general K. Malcolm, F. Kendall and D. Kellas, *Cohabitation*, 2nd edn (Edinburgh: W Green, 2011), especially para.1–01.
[2] Scottish Law Commission, *Report on Family Law* (HMSO, 1992), Scot. Law Com. No.135.
[3] Recommendation 83
[4] *Gow v Grant* [2012] UKSC 29 at [4]; 2013 S.C. (U.K.S.C.) 1 at 4 (an inter vivos separation case).
[5] 2006 Act s.29(1)(a); 1964 Act s.36(1) and see para.S36–21.
[6] For a critique of this see J. Kerrigan, "Testamentary Freedom Revisited—Further erosion?", 2012 S.L.T. (News) 29.
[7] See Ch.4.
[8] 2006 Act s.29(1).

"Cohabitant" is defined in s.25 of the 2006 Act.[9] The critical feature of that definition is in s.25(1), namely that an individual must be a member of a couple in which he or she "lives together" with another individual "as if" they were "husband and wife" or "civil partners". In order to assist the court s.25(2) provides that in deciding whether a person is a "cohabitant", the court must have regard to:

(a)   the length of period during which the two individuals have lived together;

(b)   the nature of their relationship during the period of living together;

(c)   the nature and extent of any financial arrangements which subsisted during that period.

The basic definition or definitions similar to it with immaterial differences occur **F29–05** in other legislation both English and Scottish. One example is in legislation dealing with succession to residential tenancies.[10] An early use of the definition was in social security legislation. In that context it was said,

"... it is not sufficient to establish that a man and woman are living together as husband and wife, to show that they are living in the same household. If there is the fact that they are living together in the same household, that may raise the question whether they are living together as man and wife; but in each case it is necessary to go on and ascertain in so far as this is possible, the manner in which and why they are living together in the same household ...".[11]

It was observed, further, that:

"What Parliament had in mind was ... that where a couple live together as husband and wife, they shall not be in any different position whether they are married or not; and once one has established a relationship between the couple which is properly regarded as one between husband and wife in fact, then [the definition is satisfied] and of course thereafter it will continue to apply until that relationship ceases. Once one has established the relationship to exist then it is much easier to show that it continues and it may well be that although many of the features of living together between husband and wife have ceased, perhaps because of advancing years or for other reasons, the [definition] will still continue to apply. This would be the position even though a court would come to a different conclusion as to whether the [definition] applied, if at the outset all that existed was that state of affairs."[12]

---

[9]   See the Notes to s.29 above.
[10]   e.g. Housing (Scotland) Act 1988 (c.43) s.31(4); Rent (Scotland) Act 1984 (c.58) Sch.1A para.2(2) as introduced by the 1988 Act (c.43).
[11]   *Crake v Supplementary Benefits Commission* [1982] 1 All E.R. 498 at 502d per Woolf J.
[12]   *Crake v Supplementary Benefits Commission* [1982] 1 All E.R. 498 at 502g–h.

F29–06   It will be apparent from this that the applicant under s.29 must establish first that he became a cohabitant of the deceased in terms of the definition and secondly that this status continued up to immediately before his death. It may be easier to demonstrate continuation of the status than the commencement of the status. Thus where due to relationship breakdown a man moved out of the commonly owned house leaving his belongings in the house, and for four months up to the relevant date continued to receive his mail at the house and stayed at the house on occasion socialising with the other individual, sleeping once with her between his departure and the relevant date, it was held that the individuals were still "living together as husband and wife" within the definition in s.25(1).[13] While such facts could hardly have been sufficient to create cohabitation over the four months up to the relevant date, they still allowed the definition to be satisfied up to the relevant date.

F29–07   In order to establish the status of cohabitant, the basic requirement is that he and the deceased have "lived together". This requires that the two individuals be sharing the same household.[14] Where they merely spent time in each others' respective properties, this was not enough to be seen as "living together".[15] Mere occupation of the same premises, sleeping in different rooms and not sharing meals or household expenditure, for example, where rent or mortgage payments are paid separately, may not amount to sharing the same household and living together.

F29–08   Next the applicant must establish that reasons for living together to allow the court to find as an objective fact that they lived as if they were a married couple or civil partners. This excludes various other reasons for living together. A man living with a woman to assist her recovery from an accident was not living with her as husband and wife.[16] It is under this head that the statutory factors in s.25(2) come into play. They are not exclusive.[17] The court may look at other factors which tend to indicate whether the reason for living together was to live as a married couple. This involves a consideration of the characteristics of marriage and whether they are present to such an extent that marriage can be said to be present despite no formal ceremony having taken place. Other factors have been suggested to include: (1) the length of time during which the parties lived together, (2) the amount and nature of the time the parties spent together, (3) whether they lived under the same roof in the same household, (4) whether they slept together, (5) whether they had sexual intercourse, (6) whether they ate together, (7) whether they had a social life together, (8) whether they supported each other, talked to and were affectionate to each other, (9) outward appearances, (10) their financial arrangements, whether they shared resources, household and child-care tasks,

---

[13] *MB v JB* Unreported September 5, 2014 Edinburgh Sheriff Court, Sheriff Principal Stephen.
[14] *Crake v Supplementary Benefits Commission* [1982] 1 All E.R. 498 at 502d.
[15] *Williamson v Picken, Black and Others* Unreported October 29, 2010 Edinburgh Sheriff Court, Sheriff Jarvie.
[16] *Crake v Supplementary Benefits Commission* [1982] 1 All E.R. 498.
[17] *Garrad v Inglis* Unreported November 19, 2013 Edinburgh Sheriff Court, Sheriff Morrison QC at [8]. This case is available at *http://www.scotcourts.gov.uk/search-judgments/judgment?id=e43a 87a6-8980-69d2-b500-ff0000d74aa7* [Accessed April 14, 2015]..

(11) the intentions of each party and whether any of them were communicated to the other party, and (12) physical separation.[18]

One of the features of marriage and civil partnership is that they involve a mutual **F29–09** lifelong commitment of the couple. If that is absent it must be doubted that the living together was as a married couple or civil partners. The mutual intentions behind the living together as demonstrated by conduct are therefore of great importance.[19] Hence, in a recent residential tenancy succession case, *Amicus Horizon Ltd v Estate of Judy Mabbott and Brand*[20] where the couple lived together and had a child, but the deceased wished to preserve her independence because of bad previous relationships, the court concluded that they did not live together as husband and wife and this was upheld by the England and Wales Court of Appeal. In *Amicus* the court approved the following indicia[21] of a marriage and made the following observations although it was noted that given the complexity and variance of human relationships it could not necessarily be regarded as comprehensive:

"(a) Have the parties openly set up home together ?

(b) Is the relationship an emotional one of mutual lifetime commitment rather than simply one of convenience, friendship, companionship or the living together of lovers?

(c) Is the relationship one which has been presented to the outside world openly and unequivocally so that society considers it to be of permanent intent—the words 'till death us do part' being apposite? and

(d) Do the parties have a common life together, both domestically (in relation to the household) and externally (in relation to family and friends)?

The above indicia (which may overlap) must principally be objectively assessed by reference to what the outside world can see (albeit that the domestic aspect may not be viewable without visitors) and the indicia at (b) must also be assessed by reference to the viewpoint of the parties themselves, so far as that can be ascertained on evidence. In that regard the relationship of the spouse does have some subjective element to it, but accompanying its subjectivity there must be express or implied communication of one party to the other by way of a demonstration of a lifetime emotional commitment. Whilst the length of time which the relationship has been in existence is irrelevant to the above indicia, it may sometimes corroborate them or even, in appropriate cases, be of sufficient length to satisfy a court that they are satisfied that the relationship of spouse exists."

The English court did not have to apply the statutory factors in s.25(2) which always require the length of time of the living together to be taken into account.

---

[18] *Garrad v Inglis* Unreported November 19, 2013 Edinburgh Sheriff Court at [9] per Sheriff Morrison QC.

[19] *City of Westminster v Peart* (1992) 24 H.L.R. 389 at 398.

[20] *Amicus Horizon Ltd v Estate of Judy Mabbott and Brand* [2012] EWCA Civ 895; [2012] H.L.R. 42.

[21] Taken from *Nutting v Southern Housing Group* [2004] EWHC 2982; [2005] H.L.R. 25.

In other respects it is submitted that they form a good guide for the application of the s.25(1) definition. There is no statutory minimum period for living together in order for an individual to qualify as a "cohabitant". However, the length of time of cohabitation is a factor that has to be taken into account in assessing whether the "as if husband or wife/civil partner" test is satisfied[22] and one would expect it to be taken into account in determining the quantum of any award to be made.[23]

F29–10   Finally, it must be shown that the applicant continued to be a cohabitant of the deceased immediately before the death.[24] Death during a temporary separation of weeks or even a few months for work or leisure purposes or in the event of illness would not prevent the individuals from being seen as living together but ultimately each case must be considered on its own facts. As has been noted, some of the features which allowed the status to be acquired may be lost without loss of the status, but there must come a point when the relationship is over and cohabitation is lost. The nature of the any cohabitation within the definition which existed before the alleged cessation may be a factor which casts light on whether the definition has ceased to be satisfied.[25] Each case will depend on its own facts. Cases which deal with cessation of cohabitation for the purposes of establishing a date for the valuation of matrimonial property on divorce under the Family Law (Scotland) Act 1985 may be instructive if the circumstances are sufficiently similar.

The estate subject to a s.29 award

F29–11   Not only does the deceased require to die intestate[26] but, in addition, any award made by the court is restricted to the intestate estate which remains after satisfaction of inheritance tax, ordinary debts, prior rights and legal rights of both spouse or civil partner and issue.[27] The description of the estate available for a s.29 award as "net intestate estate" should not be confused with the different (and broader) meaning of those words for the purpose of the 1964 Act.[28] However, it is submitted that a common feature of the expressions in both Acts is that property that has passed under a special destination is not included in "net intestate estate".

F29–12   As an award under s.29 is part of the law of succession, and whether estate situated abroad is available for and governed by s.29 depends on Scots international private law.[29] If the deceased left a spouse or civil partner residing in a house partly or wholly owned by him, then began to cohabit but had not yet achieved divorce or dissolution before his death, there may, in the absence of a will, be little

---

[22] 2006 Act s.25(2)(a).

[23] 2006 Act s.29(3)(d).

[24] 2006 Act s.29(1)(b).

[25] *Bain v Bain* [2008] CSOH 95; [2008] Fam. L.R. 81 at [10]. See, e.g. *Banks v Banks* [2005] Fam. L.R. 116 at [34] and [36].

[26] 2006 Act s.29(1)(a); and see commentary on s.36(1) of the 1964 Act at para.S36–21.

[27] This is the effect of the definitions in s.29(1) of the 2006 Act and s.36(1) of the 1964 Act.

[28] See commentary on s.36(1) at para.S36–23.

[29] *Kerr v Mangan* [2014] CSIH 69; 2014 S.L.T. 866; and see Ch.7 (international private law).

left for the surviving cohabitant.[30] The surviving children of the deceased will have their legal rights in preference to the surviving cohabitant, leaving the balance of intestate estate subject to a potential competition between the children with their vested rights as heirs under s.2 of the 1964 Act[31] and the surviving cohabitant with his or her application under s.29. Before making a s.29 award the court will require to make a finding as to the extent of the "net intestate estate" for the purposes of s.29 and this will involve consideration of whether any debts are due by the deceased to the cohabitant.[32] It should also require consideration of the quantum of other debts (including the administrative expenses of executors) and any prior or legal rights which may be due.

Quantification of capital sum or moveable or heritable property

Quantification of any award is perhaps the most difficult aspect of s.29. The **F29–13** only express guidance is that award of the sum or moveable or heritable property cannot exceed the amount to which the applicant would have been entitled had he or she been married to or in civil partnership with the deceased.[33] In short the cohabitant cannot end up better off through the cohabitation than if he or she had married the deceased or entered into civil partnership. As was observed (obiter) in a recent case,

> "the court's discretion is so unfettered as to make it extraordinarily difficult, if not impossible, to predict accurately what may be the outcome, at first instance of an application".[34]

This is a quite undesirable state of affairs for both cohabitants and s.2 heirs.

While it is nowhere stated in the legislation it is submitted that the general prin- **F29–14** ciples of succession law should guide the court in determining the quantification of the sum, if any. The overriding principle is that the estate should be distributed in accordance with the intentions of the deceased. In this the starting point must be the "statutory and common law will" of the deceased which is comprised in the law of intestacy.[35] An individual is deemed to know or at least accept the law of intestacy to guide the distribution of his estate. As such the succession of his or her heirs under s.2 of the 1964 Act is part of his presumed intention. Essentially the unenviable task of the court in exercising its discretion under s.29(2) is to discover to what extent, if any, the deceased can be said to have intended that his cohabitant be preferred to his heirs. This helps to explain why the factors in s.28 relating to payments on the cessation of cohabitation inter vivos[36] were *not*

---

[30] See the commentary on ss.8 and 9 (prior rights) and Ch.5 (legal rights).
[31] See the commentary on s.2.
[32] *Fulwood v O'Halloran* Unreported January 6, 2014 Glasgow Sheriff Court, Sheriff I.H.L. Miller at [57].
[33] 2006 Act s.29(4).
[34] *Kerr v Mangan* [2014] CSIH 69 at [18] per Lady Smith; 2014 S.L.T. 866 at 870 to 871.
[35] See Erskine, III, viii, 2 where Erskine describes a legal heir as deriving right from the "presumed will" of the deceased.
[36] e.g. economic advantage and disadvantage in s.28(3) and (9).

included in s.29. It explains why the award cannot exceed the succession of a spouse. The deceased could not possibly have intended such an excessive award.

F29–15 It must be borne in mind that the deceased could have provided for the cohabitant through the making of a will. Essentially the question for the court is, to what extent, if at all, did the deceased intend the cohabitant to benefit nevertheless from his estate and thereby rebutting his presumed intent to follow intestacy? Fairness to the cohabitant should play a secondary role to the intention of the deceased. In effect the court must decide what, if any, legacy the deceased intended to make in favour of the cohabitant, but for whatever reason did not achieve.

F29–16 In answering that question the court is directed to have regard to:

    (a)   the size and nature of the estate available for a claim;

    (b)   any benefit received or to be received by the claimant in consequence of the deceased's death from another source;

    (c)   the nature and extent of the competing rights (of the heirs) on the intestate estate; and

    (d)   any other matter the court considers appropriate.[37]

F29–17 With regard to factor (a), it is difficult to see how the size of the available estate can cast any light on the deceased's intentions. Perhaps the larger the estate, the more likely it is that the deceased intended that the cohabitant should benefit. The nature of the estate is more material. Monies in a joint account might be seen as intended for the cohabitant, particularly if there is a survivorship provision. If the estate comprised monetary assets, the nature of the estate would appear to be broadly neutral as a factor. Household items or personal belongings of the deceased which may have no connection with the competing heirs but which have a connection with the cohabitant might point towards an intent to favour the cohabitant. Conversely, if there are items which may have passed to the deceased from an ancestor such as family heirlooms, there may be little to rebut the presumption of succession by heirs who are the deceased's children or siblings. It cannot be assumed that such personal belongings will have been handed over in satisfaction of legal rights.[38]

F29–18 Greater difficulty arises over heritable property which remains available for a s.29 award. If there is heritable property which is owned in equal one half *pro indiviso* shares to which both cohabitants have contributed financially, and in which they resided, then that may infer an intention that the claimant inherit the deceased's share. Equally if there is any evidence at all that that the deceased expressed an intention, for example orally, or through some other representation that the cohabitant take his share on death, that would be a weighty factor for the claimant.[39] Clearly there would have to be specific averments of the circumstances being relied on. If the couple had children residing with them then that might be an additional factor for the claimant in respect of a claim to the half

---

[37] 2006 Act s.29(3).
[38] See para.5–44.
[39] It might be covered by factor (d).

share. If the house had been acquired solely by the deceased and funded solely with his own money then, in the absence of any indication of an intention to benefit the claimant, matters become more problematic. If the house had been inherited then that would tend to support it remaining within the family rather than going to the cohabitant, unless the heir was a distant relative or the deceased had poor relationships with the heir.

With regard to factor (b), what is contemplated is a contractual or trust entitle- **F29–19** ment of the claimant which has been triggered by the death of the deceased or the effect of a survivorship destination in heritable property owned jointly by the couple. Entitlement to a legacy in a partial intestacy situation would also be covered. The more that the claimant receives from other sources the less likely it is that the deceased can have intended to disrupt his presumed intention in favour of the heirs. A lump sum death benefit to the claimant from the deceased's pension of almost £125,000 together with a consequent annual pension for the cohabitant of £9,500 valued at nearly £300,000 were held to be the critical factor for the refusal of a claim in its entirety in the context of available estate of about £190,000.[40] However, in another case a lump sum pension of £25,451 still allowed the court to award transfer of a house with a net value of £120,000, furniture and plenishings and a cash sum of £34,000 from available estate of about £305,000.[41]

Factor (c) is somewhat opaque. It is not immediately apparent what other **F29–20** "rights against" or "claims on" the deceased's net intestate estate are. It will not cover, for example, claims for payment of debts owed by the deceased to the cohabitant before the death. This is because such rights or claims are against the gross intestate estate rather than the net intestate estate. Rather factor (c) appears to be directed to where in the pecking order in s.2 of the 1964 Act the competing heir falls. In other words the familial distance (through blood or adoption) of the heir from the deceased is a relevant factor which must be considered by the court. The higher up the s.2 order the competing heir is, the less likely the deceased can be thought to have intended to favour the cohabitant at his expense. Thus it may be less likely that the deceased would have wished to prefer the cohabitant at the expense of his children but more likely that he would have wished to prefer the cohabitant at the expense of his parents, uncles or aunts. From the point of view of the cohabitant the further down the s.2 order the heir falls, the stronger it is for him, and vice-versa. It is unclear what is meant by the "extent" of the heirs' competing right, since clearly that competing right will cover the whole net intestate estate (as defined). However, it may be that if the heir concedes part of the available estate in favour of the cohabitant and seeks to retain only the balance of estate, the consequent inheritance of the cohabitant may be seen as a sufficient reflection of any intention the deceased may have had to benefit the cohabitant. The same effect can be achieved by the cohabitant moderating the extent of his claim to less than the maximum.

---

[40] *Savage v Purches*, 2009 S.L.T. (Sh. Ct) 36; 2009 Fam. L.R. 6 at [16] per Sheriff P.A. Arthurson QC.
[41] *Windram, Applicant* [2009] Fam. L.R. 157 (Sheriff J.M. Scott QC).

F29–21　Factor (d) is entirely open textured. The difficulty is that the legislation sets out no clear purpose against which the appropriateness of such other factors is to be assessed. It is submitted that a factor is relevant in so far as it might indicate that the deceased intended to benefit his cohabitant at the expense of his heir or heirs. This is consistent with the general principle of succession law, namely that effect should be given to the intention of the deceased so far as possible.

F29–22　The application of this principle to factor (d) and s.29(2)(a) as a whole, renders irrelevant or otiose the issue of whether the purpose of s.29 was to avoid hardship for the cohabitant or to enable the payment of a sum akin to that which would be payable by the deceased upon separation inter vivos and whether these two purposes require to be "balanced". The latter purpose might be supported in the context of s.29 within the 2006 Act and its proximity to ss.26 to 28 which govern separation. But there are two difficulties with this. First, Parliament has not included the same factors in s.29 as it included in s.28 for inter vivos separations. Secondly, the nature and extent of the heirs' interests are irrelevant to an inter vivos separation.

F29–23　In practice the courts have applied a "just and equitable"[42] or "fair balance"[43] approach incorporating elements of both purposes. On this basis factor (d) has been held to include questions of economic advantage and disadvantage accrued during the cohabitation,[44] the length of the cohabitation,[45] the lack of sharing in financial affairs such as the absence of a joint bank account,[46] the cohabitee lacking a bank account and being wholly dependent on the deceased's account,[47] the discussion of marriage shortly before death with it being probable that marriage was prevented by the death,[48] in a 24 year cohabitation with two children the claimant's foregoing of the opportunity to become financially independent on account of looking after them.[49] The leaving of a significant value of estate to child heirs is a factor that has been taken into account.[50] The existence of debts due to the cohabitant by the deceased has been held to be relevant but it is submitted that this could lead to double counting[51] and, notwithstanding the broad terms of factor (d), cannot be correct. A court has rejected the cohabitant's notional entitlement under prior and legal rights were he a spouse or civil partner as irrelevant.[52]

---

[42] *Fulwood v O'Halloran* Unreported January 6, 2014 Glasgow Sheriff Court, Sheriff I.H.L. Miller at [37]

[43] *Windram, Applicant* [2009] Fam. L.R. 157 at [13].

[44] *Fulwood v O'Halloran* Unreported January 6, 2014 Glasgow Sheriff Court, Sheriff I.H.L. Miller at [39]; and *Windram, Applicant* [2009] Fam. L.R. 157 at [14] and [15].

[45] *Savage v Purches*, 2009 S.L.T. (Sh. Ct) 36 at [16] (2 years 6 months seen as "short" in comparison to previous 15 year cohabitation by deceased with a previous cohabitant).

[46] *Savage v Purches*, 2009 S.L.T. (Sh. Ct) 36 at [16].

[47] *Windram, Applicant* [2009] Fam. L.R. 157 at [14].

[48] *Windram, Applicant* [2009] Fam. L.R. 157 at [14].

[49] *Windram, Applicant* [2009] Fam. L.R. 157 at [15].

[50] *Windram, Applicant* [2009] Fam. L.R. 157 at [18].

[51] Leading to the cohabitant being paid by the estate as both creditor and s.29 claimant.

[52] *Fulwood v O'Halloran* Unreported January 6, 2014 Glasgow Sheriff Court, Sheriff I.H.L. Miller at [58].

It is submitted that the only matters that should be taken into account are ones **F29–24** which tend to show that the deceased intended to benefit the cohabitant at the expense of his heir(s). Unfortunately the courts have not been invited to focus on the intention of the deceased, which it is submitted is the correct approach. On that basis the "just and equitable" or "fair balance" approaches should not be followed. Rather the task for the court should involve an objective assessment of the subjective intention of the deceased as to benefiting the cohabitant at the expense of his heir(s). Questions of past economic advantage and disadvantage and whether the cohabitant gave up financial independence to look after children are, it is submitted, of no relevance for the purposes of s.29(3) in the absence of objective indication that the deceased intended to redress any such matter in favour of the cohabitant. Equally the mere absence of a joint bank account does not shed much light on the deceased's intentions.

However, the discussion of marriage shortly before death might suggest that **F29–25** the deceased intended the cohabitant to inherit. In such a situation the cohabitant's notional entitlement under prior and legal rights were he a spouse or civil partner should not be irrelevant.[53] The weight to be given to notional prior and legal rights entitlement will, however, vary for each case. The longer and more established the cohabitation and the more intimate the relationship over a longer period, the easier it is to infer that the deceased intended to benefit his cohabitant as if he or she was a spouse or civil partner, particularly if the competing heirs are not the children, or possibly siblings with whom the deceased enjoyed a close relationship. Evidence of a refusal of the deceased to marry, would be a factor suggesting an intention not to benefit the deceased, at least to anything like the full exclusion of his heirs.

The existence of children of the deceased and cohabitant is unlikely to indicate **F29–26** any intention of the deceased to disinherit them in favour of the cohabitant. However, the existence of children of the deceased from a previous relationship prior to the cohabitation in question might suggest that the deceased would not have wished to disinherit them, at least to any material extent.

Having considered all of factors (a) to (d), the court must weigh them up and **F29–27** reach a decision as to quantification and identification of any legacy which the deceased would have wished to make in favour of the cohabitant. This will inevitably be an imprecise task but the court must do what it can. The award in favour of the cohabitant can include specific items of moveable or heritable property as well as a monetary award.

The application to the court—Time limit and jurisdiction

An application must be made to the appropriate court before the expiry of six **F29–28** months beginning with the date of death.[54] The tight time limit appears to be to avoid delays in the executor's winding up of the estate: he cannot wind up the estate while there is still a possibility of a claim and ordinary creditors have six

---

[53] cf. *Fulwood v O'Halloran* Unreported January 6, 2014 Glasgow Sheriff Court, Sheriff I.H.L. Miller at [58].

[54] 2006 Act s.29(6).

months after death to come forward with their claims.[55] There is no provision for the extension of this time limit[56] except in the specified circumstances of mediation set out in s.29A of the 2006 Act. In principle such a time limit is desirable although it can cause some practical difficulties with procedure which are discussed below.

F29–29   Jurisdiction to decide the claim lies with the Court of Session or with a sheriff court in the sheriffdom in which the deceased was habitually resident at death or, where it is "uncertain" where he was habitually resident, at Edinburgh Sheriff Court.[57] This link to habitual residence rather than domicile is welcome given international acceptance of that criterion as a connecting factor and also in that it will be readily ascertainable by the applicant as an ex-cohabitant, free of the technicalities of common law domicile. What may be less welcome is that confirmation is granted on the basis of common law domicile of the deceased. While an applicant may check with the commissary courts of the sheriffdom of domicile to see if confirmation has been granted (or even possibly lodge a caveat in respect of an application for confirmation), he might have to make his application to a different court if the deceased was habitually resident in a different sheriffdom.

F29–30   "Habitual residence" is a residence where a person has a habit of residing. Whether the deceased was habitually resident in a sheriffdom is a question of fact. The Scottish dicta which provide various glosses on the meaning of "habitual residence" are summarised in *Chebotareva v King's Executrix*[58] where, on the facts, habitual residence in the sheriffdom of application was not established. While that case was decided on the deceased not having spent an appreciable amount of time in the sheriffdom, there is no minimum time limit for a habit of residing in the sheriffdom in question to be developed.

The application to the court—Procedure

F29–31   The Rules of the Court of Session have provided that the claim under s.29 must be made by summons.[59] On an analogy with the Court of Session, a sheriff court claim requires to be made by an ordinary action commenced with an initial writ.[60] The executor, whether appointed as executor-nominate, executor-dative[61] or confirmed in either capacity requires to be called as a defender.[62] In addition, in the Court of Session the summons must seek a warrant for intimation to all of the s.2 heirs who would otherwise be entitled to the estate available under s.29.[63] This

---

[55] See para.S4–26.
[56] *Simpson v Downie*, 2013 S.L.T. 178; [2012] CSIH 74 (a s.28 case where it was held that the time limits for both s.28 and s.29 affected the competency of the actions and that failure to plead incompetency due to time bar did not validate the action).
[57] 2006 Act s.29(5).
[58] *Chebotareva v King's Executrix* [2008] Fam. L.R. 66 (Stirling Sheriff Court) per Sheriff Ward.
[59] RCS r.49.1(q); and see Note 14.1.2 of *Green's Annotated Rules of the Court of Session* (Edinburgh: W. Green, 2014).
[60] Sheriff Courts (Scotland) Act 1907 (7 Edw.7 c.51) as amended, First Schedule, OCR r.33B.2(1)(b).
[61] See the commentary on s.14(1) at paras S14–06 to S14–16.
[62] RCS r.49.90; OCR r.33B.2(2)(a).
[63] RCS r.49.8(1)(n).

applies equally to the sheriff court initial writ.[64] If there are no known heirs, the Lord Advocate should be called as representing the Queen's and Lord Treasurer's Remembrancer on behalf of the Crown as *ultimus haeres*. Where the identity or address of any heir is not known and cannot be ascertained the cohabitant must aver that fact and what steps have been taken to discover the identity or address of that person.[65] This may lead to the need for service by newspaper advertisement.

Where with the six months closing in no executor has been confirmed, the estate is *haereditas jacens* (lying estate). In such a situation the summons or initial writ should seek decree *cognitionis causa tantum*. A decree *cognitionis causa tantum*[66] would enable the court to order payment from the estate which the claimant could enforce through appointment and confirmation as an executor creditor. **F29–32**

The summons or initial writ should contain a warrant for intimation on the heirs and be accompanied by a notice of intimation to them in the appropriate statutory form.[67] Where an heir is under the age of 16 years and is a child of the cohabitant a curator ad litem may require to be appointed to represent his or her interests. **F29–33**

The initial writ or summons should contain averments which are sufficiently specific to enable the defender and the court to calculate with reasonable accuracy how the award claimed is to be reached.[68] These averments will have to address the matters of the gross estate, the debts of the deceased, any prior rights, any legal rights and the net intestate estate for the purposes of s.29. A cohabitant should be entitled to see the confirmation in order to allow him to make these averments. If an executor has not yet confirmed by the deadline for making the application this should be averred and steps taken to have one confirmed.[69] **F29–34**

If the application is opposed, an heir must lodge a minute opposing the application. Thereafter ordinary cause procedure applies. **F29–35**

Interim order of the court

Section 29(2)(b) allows the court to make such interim order as it thinks fit. An interim order could in theory involve a provisional payment to the cohabitant or a protective order designed to preserve the estate pending the final decision on the application. **F29–36**

The difficulty with the former type of order is that any such payment may be difficult to recover by the executor should the final decision go against the cohabitant. It is not a type of order that is made lightly. It is of note that in a personal injuries action the court will not make an interim order for the payment of damages unless the court is satisfied (1) that the pursuer will almost certainly succeed on the question of liability, and (2) the defender is insured, is a public authority or is a person "whose means and resources are such as to enable him to make the **F29–37**

---

[64] OCR r.33B.2(2)(b).
[65] OCR r.33B.2(3); RCS r.49.4.
[66] An example was in *Kerr v Mangan*, 2013 S.L.T. (Sh. Ct) 102 at first instance before the decision was reversed on appeal.
[67] RCS r.49.8(1)(n); and OCR r.33B.2(2)(b).
[68] *Fulwood v O'Halloran* Unreported January 6, 2014 Glasgow Sheriff Court, Sheriff I.H.L. Miller at [44].
[69] See paras S14–03 to S14–16.

interim payment", and (3) the payment will not exceed a reasonable proportion of the damages which are likely to be recovered.[70] This could serve as a guide in relation to interim orders for payment. While therefore there might be circumstances where an interim order of payment might be appropriate, such as where the deceased's intentions to benefit the cohabitant were clear (e.g. where he died in an accident having instructed a will to be prepared in her favour), and the heirs were of substantial means, it is suggested that these will be rare.

F29–38   It is therefore more likely that an interim order will be of the latter type, namely an order of interim interdict to preserve the estate pending the final decision on the application. This could include an interim interdict to allow the cohabitant to remain resident in any dwellinghouse which he is claiming. Whichever type of order is sought, it will have to be sought in the summons or initial writ in the usual way.

Final decree of the court

F29–39   Section 29(7) allows the court to provide for payment of a capital sum by instalments on specified dates. Section 29(9) allows presumably the executor to seek a variation of the dates for payment of the capital sum and the quantum of instalments. Section 29(8) provides for the court to specify the date upon which a transfer of any specific moveable or heritable property which it orders is to become "effective". It is not clear what is meant by "effectiveness" in this context. On any view one would expect the court in such a situation to specify a date for the delivery of the moveable property or documents of title to it and to specify a date for the delivery of the disposition of heritable property and ancillary documents to allow a good title to be registered by the cohabitant.

F29–40   If an interim order has been made under s.29(2)(b) one would expect the final decree of the court to deal with the interim order by either recalling it or making it permanent.

Extension of time limits for applications under sections 28 and 29: cross-border mediation

[1]**29A.**—(1) This section applies to the calculation of—

(a) the one year period for the purposes of section 28(8) in relation to a relevant cross-border dispute; and
(b) the 6 month period for the purposes of section 29(6) in relation to a relevant cross-border dispute.

(2) A period referred to in subsection (1) is extended where it would, apart from this subsection, expire—

(a) in the 8 weeks after the date that a mediation in relation to the dispute ends;

---

[70] See, e.g. RCS r.43.11; OCR r.36.9.

(b) on the date that a mediation in relation to the dispute ends; or

(c) after the date when all of the parties to the dispute agree to participate in a mediation in relation to the dispute but before the date that such mediation ends.

(3) Where subsection (2) applies, the period is extended so that it expires on the date falling 8 weeks after the date on which the mediation ends.

(4) For the purposes of this section, mediation in relation to a relevant cross-border dispute ends when any of the following occurs—

(a) all of the parties reach an agreement in resolution of the dispute;

(b) all of the parties agree to end the mediation;

(c) a party withdraws from the mediation, which is the date on which—

　　(i) a party informs all of the other parties of that party's withdrawal,

　　(ii) in the case of a mediation involving 2 parties, 14 days expire after a request made by one party to the other party for confirmation of whether the other party has withdrawn, if the other party does not respond in that period, or

　　(iii) in the case of a mediation involving more than 2 parties, a party informs all of the remaining parties that the party received no response in the 14 days after a request to another party for confirmation of whether the other party had withdrawn; or

(d) a period of 14 days expires after the date on which the mediator's tenure ends (by reason of death, resignation or otherwise), if a replacement mediator has not been appointed.

(5) In this section—

　　"the Directive" means Directive 2008/52/EC of the European Parliament and of the Council of 21st May 2008 on certain aspects of mediation in civil and commercial matters;

　　"mediation" and "mediator" have the meanings given by Article 3 of the Directive; and

　　"relevant cross-border dispute" means a cross-border dispute within the meaning given by Article 2 of the Directive which is about—

　　(a) a sum which a court may order to be paid under section 28(2);

　　(b) a sum which a court may order to be paid under section 29(2); or

　　(c) property which a court may order to be transferred under section 29(2).

NOTE

1. Inserted by the Cross-Border Mediation (Scotland) Regulations 2011 (SSI 2011/234) reg.9(4) (effective April 6, 2011).

DEFINITIONS

"cross-border dispute": Directive 2008/52/EC of the European Parliament and of the Council of 21 May 2008 on certain aspects of mediation in civil and commercial matters art.2.
"Directive": 2006 Act s.29A(5).
"mediation": Directive 2008/52/EC of the European Parliament and of the Council of 21 May 2008 on certain aspects of mediation in civil and commercial matters art.3.
"mediator": Directive 2008/52/EC of the European Parliament and of the Council of 21 May 2008 on certain aspects of mediation in civil and commercial matters art.3.
"relevant cross-border dispute": 2006 Act s.29A(5).

COMMENTARY

F29A–01 It is clearly desirable for claims under s.29 to be settled without the need for expensive and protracted litigation. In that respect mediation can allow claims to be settled which otherwise might require to be litigated (or, with the agreement of the parties, arbitrated). The purpose of s.29A is to provide more time to allow cross-border disputes over s.29 claims to be settled by way of mediation. It is necessary because parties cannot agree to waive the time limit in s.29 for claims to be brought before a court. It originates from a much broader EU Directive but is useful nevertheless. It is perhaps a pity that s.29A has not been extended to all claims where parties have agreed to use mediation after the dispute has arisen.

F29A–02 Article 2 of the EU Directive defines a "cross-border dispute" as follows:

> "1. For the purposes of this Directive a cross-border dispute shall be one in which at least one of the parties is domiciled or habitually resident in a Member State other than that of any other party on the date on which:
>
> (a) the parties agree to use mediation after the dispute has arisen;
> (b) mediation is ordered by a court;
> (c) an obligation to use mediation arises under national law; or
> (d) for the purposes of Article 5 an invitation is made to the parties.
>
> 2. Notwithstanding paragraph 1, for the purposes of Articles 7 and 8 a cross-border dispute shall also be one in which judicial proceedings or arbitration following mediation between the parties are initiated in a Member State other than that in which the parties were domiciled or habitually resident on the date referred to in paragraph 1(a), (b) or (c).
>
> 3. For the purposes of paragraphs 1 and 2, domicile shall be determined in accordance with Articles 59 and 60 of Regulation (EC) No 44/2001."

The reference to an invitation for the purposes of art.5 is a reference to the court inviting parties to mediate.

F29A–03 Article 3 of the Directive defines "mediation" and "mediator" as follows:

"(a) 'Mediation' means a structured process, however named or referred to, whereby two or more parties to a dispute attempt by themselves, on a voluntary basis, to reach an agreement on the settlement of their dispute with the assistance of a mediator. This process may be initiated by the parties or suggested or ordered by a court or prescribed by the law of a Member State.

It includes mediation conducted by a judge who is not responsible for any judicial proceedings concerning the dispute in question. It excludes attempts made by the court or the judge seised to settle a dispute in the course of judicial proceedings concerning the dispute in question.

(b) 'Mediator' means any third person who is asked to conduct a mediation in an effective, impartial and competent way, regardless of the denomination or profession of that third person in the Member State concerned and of the way in which the third person has been appointed or requested to conduct the mediation."

RULES OF DIVISION, ACCORDING TO THE LAW OF SCOTLAND, OF THE ESTATE OF A PERSON WHO HAD DIED INTESTATE ON OR AFTER SEPTEMBER 10, 1964

NOTE

Figures applicable to person dying on or after February 1, 2012. For earlier figures see notes to ss.8 and 9 of the 1964 Act.

References to a section are to that section of the 1964 Act. References to spouses include civil partners. There being three different sets of rules, any or all of which may be called into play in a given succession, those applied are indicated against each entry by the following abbreviations:

PR—Prior rights to a house, furniture and a monetary provision under ss.8 and 9.

LR—Legal rights of *jus relicti, jus relictae* and legitim under common law as amended by the 1964 Act and other statutes.

FE—Succession to the free estate, heritable and moveable, under ss.1 to 7 of the 1964 Act calculated after deduction of any award made following a claim under s.29 of the 2006 Act.

The reader is also referred to the Notes at the end of the table and for further detail to the commentary on the relevant sections of the Act and, in relation to legal rights, to Ch.5.

I. SUCCESSION BY A SURVIVING SPOUSE

If the person dies, leaving	Rules applicable	The estate is divided thus
1. Spouse only.	PR LR FE	Whole to spouse. Comprising (1) prior right under s. 8 to deceased's interest in the house in which surviving spouse was ordinarily resident (maximum £473,000), and to the deceased's interest in the furniture and plenishings of that house (maximum £29,000); (2) prior right under s. 9 to £89,000; (3) *jus relicti* or *jus*

		relictae (1/2) from balance of moveables, and (4) whole free estate under s.2(1)(e).
2. Spouse and the deceased's child whether by marriage to the surviving spouse or not, and whether legitimate or not.	PR LR FE	Spouse has (1) prior right under s. 8 to deceased's interest in the house in which the surviving spouse was ordinarily resident (maximum £473,000) and to the deceased's interest in the furniture and plenishings of that house (maximum £29,000); (2) if net balance of the estate is less than £50,000, prior right under s.9 to whole balance; if balance is over £50,000, prior right to £50,000 therefrom, taken rateably from heritage and moveables; and (3) legal right of *jus relicti* or *jus relictae* to one-third of the moveable estate remaining after the prior rights under ss.8 and 9 have been met. Child (or children equally among them) receive the whole remainder of the estate, comprising (a) legitim—a further one-third of the moveable estate remaining after the spouse's prior rights under ss.8 and 9, and (b) free estate—the remaining one-third of the moveables plus the heritage not required for prior rights.
3. Spouse and that spouse's children by marriage to deceased and prior marriages.	PR LR FE	Spouse entitled to rights as in No.2. Remainder (legitim and free estate as above) to deceased's children equally.
4. Spouse and children and issue of predeceasing children.	PR LR FE	Spouse entitled to rights as in No.2. Remainder (legitim and free estate) to surviving children per capita and issue of predeceasing children *per stirpes*.
5. Spouse and grandchild or grandchildren.	PR LR FE	Spouse entitled to rights as in No.2. Remainder (legitim and free estate) to grandchild or among grandchildren equally.
6. Spouse and remoter issue.	PR LR FE	Spouse entitled to rights as in No.2. Remainder (legitim and free estate) to members of the nearest class of issue of which there are survivors, per capita, and to issue of predeceasing members of that class, *per stirpes*.

7. Spouse and brothers and sisters. (See note 3 at end).	PR LR FE	Spouse has (1) prior right under s. 8 to deceased's interest in the house in which the surviving spouse was ordinarily resident (maximum £473,000) and to the deceased's interest in the furniture and plenishing of that house (maximum £29,000); (2) If the net balance of the estate is less than £89,000, prior right under s. 9 to the whole balance: if the balance is over £89,000, prior right to £89,000 therefrom, rateably from heritage and moveables, and (3) legal right of *jus relicti* or *jus relictae* to one-half of the moveable estate remaining after the prior rights under ss.8 and 9 have been met. Brothers and sisters share the whole remainder of the estate equally between them as free estate.
8. Spouse and brothers and sisters and/or issue of predeceasing brothers and sisters.	PR LR FE	Spouse entitled to rights as in No.7. Remainder to surviving brothers and sisters per capita and issue of predeceasing brothers and sisters *per stirpes*. If all brothers and sisters have predeceased, and there is issue of some or all of them, the remainder to members of the nearest class of issue of which there are survivors, per capita, and to issue of predeceasing members of that class, *per stirpes*.
9. Spouse and parent or parents, and brothers and sisters and/or issue of predeceasing brothers and sisters.	PR LR FE	Spouse entitled to rights as in No.7. Remainder, one-half to surviving parent or to both parents equally between them, and one-half to brothers and sisters equally (or to their issue on principles noted in No.8).
10. Spouse and parent or parents.	PR LR FE	Spouse entitled to rights as in No.7. Remainder to surviving parent or to both parents equally between them.
11. Spouse and uncles and aunts (or issue thereof) and/or grandparents or remoter ancestors.	PR LR FE	Whole to spouse (as in No.1).

II. SUCCESSION BY DESCENDANTS

If the person dies, leaving	Rules applicable	The estate is divided thus
12. Children only.	LR FE	Whole estate to children equally. (One-half of moveable estate as legitim, noting that the division of legitim may be unequal if advances have been made. Whole balance of estate as free estate.)
13. Children and issue of predeceasing children.	LR FE	Whole estate to surviving children per capita and issue of predeceasing children *per stirpes*. (Legitim and free estate as in No.12.)
14. Grandchildren.	LR FE	Whole estate (being legitim and free estate as in No.12) to grandchildren equally.
15. Remoter issue.	LR FE	Whole estate (being legitim and free estate as in No.12) to members of the nearest class of issue of which there are survivors, per capita, and to issue of predeceasing members of that class, *per stirpes*.
16. Issue and spouse.	PR LR FE	See Nos 2 to 6.
17. Issue and collaterals.	LR FE	Whole to issue as in Nos 12 to 15.
18. Issue and ascendents.	LR FE	Whole to issue as in Nos 12 to 15.

III. SUCCESSION BY COLLATERALS

If the person dies, leaving	Rules applicable	The estate is divided thus
19. Brothers and sisters.	FE	Whole estate equally among them.
20. Brothers and sisters and nephews and nieces, being issue of predeceasing brothers and sisters.	FE	Whole estate to brothers and sisters per capita and nephews and nieces *per stirpes*.
21. Nephews and nieces.	FE	Whole estate equally among them.

22. Remoter issue of brothers and sisters.	FE	Whole estate to members of the nearest class of issue of which there are survivors, per capita, and to issue of predeceasing members of that class, *per stirpes*.
23. Brothers and sisters (or their issue) and issue of the intestate.	LR FE	Brothers and sisters (or their issue) are excluded: whole to issue. (See No.17 and Nos 12–15.)
24. Brothers and sisters (or their issue) and spouse.	PR LR FE	See Nos 7 and 8.
25. Brothers and sisters (or their issue), spouse and parent or parents.	PR LR FE	See No.9.
26. Brothers and sisters and parent or parents.	FE	One-half of the estate to brothers and sisters equally; one-half to surviving parent or to both parents equally.
27. Brothers and sisters, nephews and nieces, and parent or parents.	FE	One-half of the estate to brothers and sisters per capita and nephews and nieces *per stirpes*; one-half to surviving parent or to both parents equally.
28. Remoter issue of brothers and sisters, and parent or parents.	FE	One-half of the estate to members of the nearest class of issue of brothers and sisters of which there are survivors, per capita, and to issue of predeceasing members of that class, *per stirpes*; one-half to surviving parent or to both parents equally.
29. Brothers and sisters (or their issue), and uncles and aunts or remoter ascendants.	FE	Whole estate to brothers and sisters or their issue, the division being to members of the class nearest to the intestate of which there are survivors, per capita, and to issue of predeceasing members of that class, *per stirpes*.
30. Brothers and sisters, full blood, and brothers and sisters of half blood (consanguinean and uterine).	FE	Whole estate to brothers and sisters of full blood equally among them.

31. Brothers and sisters of half blood (consanguinean and uterine).	FE	Whole estate equally among them, with no distinction between consanguinean and uterine.
32. Brothers and sisters of half blood (consanguinean and uterine), and/or issue of same.	FE	As for full blood. See Nos 19 to 22.
33. Brothers and sisters of half blood (consanguinean and uterine), spouse and other relations of intestate.	PR LR FE	As for full blood. See Nos 23 to 29.

IV. SUCCESSION BY ASCENDANTS

If the person dies, leaving	*Rules applicable*	*The estate is divided thus*
34. Father only.	FE	Whole estate to father.
35. Mother only.	FE	Whole estate to mother.
36. Father and mother.	FE	Whole estate equally between father and mother.
37. Parent or parents, uncles and aunts (paternal and maternal) and their descendants.	FE	Whole estate to the surviving parent or to both parents equally as in Nos 34 to 36.
38. Parent or parents and grandparents (paternal and maternal) or remoter ancestors.	FE	Whole estate to the surviving parent or to both parents equally as in Nos 34 to 36.
39. Paternal and maternal uncles and aunts, and issue of predeceasing uncles and aunts.	FE	Whole estate to uncles and aunts (paternal and maternal) per capita and to cousins *per stirpes.*
40. Cousins only (on paternal or	FE	Whole estate to cousins (paternal or maternal) or their issue, the division being

maternal sides), or their issue.		to members of the class nearest to the intestate of which there are survivors, per capita, and to issue of predeceasing members of that class, *per stirpes*.
41. Paternal and maternal uncles and aunts, or their issue and paternal and maternal grandparents or remoter ancestors.	FE	Whole estate to uncles and aunts (paternal and maternal) per capita and to cousins *per stirpes*.
42. Paternal and maternal grandparents, great uncles and great aunts.	FE	Whole estate to grandparents (paternal and maternal) equally among them.
43. Paternal and maternal great uncles and great aunts (or issue of such) and great grandparents or remoter ancestors (or issue of collaterals of such).	FE	Whole estate to great uncles and great aunts (paternal and maternal) or their issue, the division being to members of the class nearest to the intestate of which there are survivors, per capita, and to issue of predeceasing members of that class, *per stirpes*.
44. Great grandparents or remoter ancestors and issue of collaterals of such.	FE	Infinite search, with division on the principles illustrated in Nos 34 to 43; lineal ancestors on paternal or maternal sides succeeding before their collaterals and division among such collaterals and their issue being to members of the class nearest to the intestate of which there are survivors, per capita, and to issue of predeceasing members of that class, *per stirpes*.
45. Parent or parents and spouse.	PR LR FE	See No.10.
46. Remoter ascendants and spouse.	PR LR FE	See No.11.
47. Ascendants and issue of intestate.	LR FE	See No.18 and Nos 12 to 15.

48. Parent or parents and collaterals.	FE	See Nos 26 to 28.
49. Remoter ascendants and collaterals.	FE	See No.29.

V. CROWN

If the person dies, leaving	Rules applicable	The estate is divided thus
50. No other successor.	FE	Whole to Crown as *ultimus haeres*.

NOTES

1. *Estate affected*

This table applies to the whole of the intestate estate, both heritable and moveable, of a deceased person so far as it is estate the succession to which falls to be regulated by the law of Scotland. There are, however, certain specialties:

(a) *Tenancies of crofts.* Crofting tenancies were originally excluded from the operation of the Act, but in respect of the estates of persons dying on or after November 25, 1968, they now fall to be dealt with under the Act;

(b) *Titles, coats of arms, etc.* The 1964 Act does not apply to the succession to any title, coat of arms, honour or dignity transmissible on the death of the holder thereof. Accordingly these items fall to be regulated by the pre-existing law (s.37(1)(a)).

2. *International private law*

Briefly, this table applies to the devolution of the moveable estate of persons who die domiciled in Scotland and to the devolution of all immoveable property in Scotland, whatever the domicile of the deceased. The pre-existing rules for choice of law are preserved by s.37(2).

EXAMPLES OF THE DIVISION OF INTESTATE ESTATES

Some simplified examples are given of the division of typical estates to illustrate points which arise in practice. The figures of value may be dated but the principles and technique of calculation still apply. Unless otherwise stated, the values shown are the net values of the estate after taxation, payment of debts and expenses of administration. In addition the examples are worked out as if the distribution of the estate occurred on the day of death, so that no account is taken of the interest payable on prior and legal rights from the date of death until payment, nor of any income arising after the date of death. The distinction between heritage and moveables is preserved where it is still relevant, i.e. in prior and legal rights. It is assumed that there is no cohabitee award under s.29 of the 2006 Act.

X is the intestate. Square brackets indicate that the person concerned predeceased the intestate. The deceased was domiciled in Scotland and all the assets are situated in Scotland.

Example 1. Surviving spouse's prior rights exhaust the estate.

Family   [X] = W

```
      ┌───┴───┐
      S       D
```

Estate (Net values after debts, etc.)

	Heritage £	Moveables £
Deceased's house (widow ordinarily resident therein)	250,000	
Furniture and plenishings thereof		20,000
Other moveable estate		40,000
	250,000	60,000

(1) Prior rights (s.8)
Widow—house (she being ordinarily resident and value being under or at £473,000)   250,000

Widow—its furniture and plenishings
  (subject to £29,000 limit on value)   20,000

                                 Balance   _____   _____
                                             40,000

	Heritage £	Moveables £

(2) Prior rights (s.9)
Widow—preferential right to £50,000
  (there being issue of the deceased),
  if so much is available   40,000
Balance   —   —

The estate is not large enough for there to be a surplus after the spouse's prior rights and thus the widow takes the whole estate and the children receive nothing. Their rights are postponed to those of the deceased's spouse (s.9(2)). If there had been a will in favour of the widow, there would have been no prior rights and the children would have been entitled to legitim of one-third of the total moveable estate, but if there was no destination-over of the gift to the wife, she might have been able to create an intestacy by renouncing her benefit under the will (*Kerr, Petitioner*, 1968 S.L.T. (Sh. Ct) 61).

Example 2. All rules of intestate succession operate.

Family   [X] = W

```
        |
   ┌────┴────┐
   S         D
```

Estate

	Heritage £	Moveables £
Deceased's house (widow ordinarily resident)	150,000	
Furniture and plenishings thereof		15,000
Holiday house	25,000	
Other estate (bank a/cs; shares, etc.)		110,000
Gross estate	175,000	125,000
Less Debts		
Loan secured over matrimonial home	20,000	
Suppliers' accounts		10,000
Net estate	155,000	115,000

(1) Prior rights s.8
Widow—deceased's interest in house
(value £130,000 after heritable debt:
   s.(8)(6)(d))   130,000
Widow—furniture and plenishings   .   15,000

Net after s.8	25,000	100,000

(2) Prior rights s.9
Widow—right to £50,000, rateably
   from heritage and moveables.
Total estate available 125,000.
Of which heritage is 1/5 and bears 1/5   10,000
Of which moveables are 4/5 and bear 4/5   40,000

Net after prior rights	15,000	60,000

(3) Legal rights
Widow—*jus relictae* (1/3rd
of moveables)   20,000
Children—legitim 1/3
moveables   20,000

                                      40,000

Net after legal rights	15,000	20,000

(4) Free estate
Heritage and moveables
   assimilated   35,000
S receives 1/2 (s.2)   17,500
D receives 1/2 (s.2)   17,500   35,000

                                    £

Scheme of division
Widow
   Prior rights   £
   s.8(1)   130,000
   s.8(3)   15,000
   s.9   50,000

                        195,000
jus relictae   20,000   215,000

Son

Legitim	10,000	
Free estate (s.2)	17,500	27,500

Daughter

Legitim	10,000	
Free estate	17,500	27,500
		270,000

Example 3. Same family as in example 2 but with foreign assets.

Family   [X] = W

     S   D

The deceased was domiciled in Scotland. The matrimonial home, the furniture and plenishings and the holiday cottage in Scotland are the same as in example 2. There is a villa in Spain owned by the deceased and the moveable estate of £110,000 includes a yacht moored in Spanish waters near the villa. Hence the estate is as follows:

Deceased's house (widow ordinarily resident)	150,000
Furniture and plenishings thereof	15,000
Holiday house in Scotland.	25,000
Spanish villa	30,000
Yacht in Spain	10,000
Other estate (bank a/cs; shares, etc.)	100,000
Gross estate	330,000

Less debts

Loan secured over matrimonial home	20,000	
Suppliers' accounts	10,000	30,000
	Net estate	300,000

It is assumed that the villa in Spain is classified as immoveable by Spanish law (the *lex situs*). Hence the rights of inheritance to it are governed by Spanish law, not Scots law. Section 37(2) of the Act expressly preserves the previous rules about choice of law. Thus the Spanish villa is not taken into account for the purposes of the 1964 Act. Evidence of the devolution of the villa under Spanish law is required and any equivalent of legal rights in the villa are those determined by Spanish law—as also are the procedural requirements for completion of title.

It is also assumed that Spanish law would classify the yacht which is physically in Spanish waters as moveable in the international sense. Thus the yacht forms part of the deceased's moveable estate governed by Scots law as the *lex domicilii*.

The result is that the estate distributed according to Scots law is exactly the same as in Example 2 with the same result. The net heritable estate is still £155,000 and the net moveable estate is still £115,000. The villa devolves according to Spanish law and even if this should result in the whole or any part of the villa being transferred to the widow, that fact has no effect upon the amount or value of the prior and legal rights under Scots law. She would be entitled to both.

Example 4. Advances and collation *inter liberos* when there is representation in legitim (see also Ch.5).

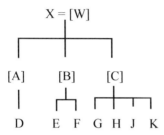

The intestate has died, predeceased by his spouse and all three of his children, but is survived by seven grandchildren, in families of one, two and four respectively. All seven have chosen legitim. During his lifetime, X had made an advance of £3,000 to A. The legitim fund derived from the estate owned by X at the date of his death amounts to £18,000. Although only £18,000 is available for distribution as legitim at the date of death, the total after collation *inter liberos* is £21,000.

The existence of collation demonstrates that the right to legitim is not necessarily co-extensive with the right to share in the free estate and that it is not appropriate to lump together the legitim fund and the free estate and then to divide the total.

If A had survived his father, he would have been entitled to 1/3 of £21,000 = £7,000 less the £3,000 advance, i.e. £4,000 and this might have passed down to his only child D.

As A has predeceased his father, along with all the other children of X, the effect of s.11(2) is that there is not true representation by division into thirds, one part going to each of the families of A, B and C. Instead there is equal division into 1/7 shares among the seven grandchildren, although D would have been entitled to 1/3 of the fund if any of A, B or C had survived their father X.

In these circumstances, D is entitled to only 1/7 of the combined fund of legitim plus advance (£21,000), i.e. £3,000. However, as a condition of that entitlement, s.11(3) requires him to collate "the proportion appropriate to him" of any advances to his ancestor A. The advance to A was of exactly the amount to which D would be entitled from the combined fund. If the "appropriate" proportion which D must collate is the whole of the advance (as seems likely despite the unfairness) then D receives nothing, although he would have received £4,000 if his father had not been inconsiderate enough to die before the grandfather.

Example 5. Heritable securities in the calculation of legal rights.

[H] = X

S   D

X dies intestate leaving a net estate consisting of a debt of £35,000 due to her, secured by a standard security and also moveable assets worth £35,000, making a total of £70,000. There being no house or furniture owned by the intestate, her husband is entitled to a s.9 prior right of £50,000 plus *jus relicti* of one-third of the remaining moveables.

The heritable security is heritable for the purposes of *jus relicti* and legitim, but is moveable for all other purposes of succession. This leaves the executor with an insoluble problem when allocating funds to meet the husband's prior right, as his possible courses of action lead to different total shares for the husband. The problem lies in s.117 of the 1868 Act (as amended).[1] Two possible courses of action may be envisaged.

I. *The heritable security is allocated wholly to the prior right*
   Prior right s.9 (the whole security along with some of the
   moveables is allocated to this
   right, and there remains £20,000 of moveables)   £50,000
   Jus relicti (1/3 of remaining moveables)   £6,666

                                        Total for husband   £56,666

II. *Moveables other than the security allocated to the prior right*
    Prior right s.9 (the moveables other than the security
    are allocated to this right, and there remains the
    heritably secured debt of £35,000)   £35,000
    Jus relicti (secured debt heritable and not subject to
    legal rights)   —

                                        Total for husband   £35,000

---

[1] See para.5–24.

III. *Heritable security and other moveables allocated equally   to prior right*

	Heritable security £	Other moveables £	Husband £
	35,000	35,000	
Prior right s.9 apportioned equally	25,000	25,000	50,000
	10,000	10,000	
Jus relicti		3,333	3,333
	Total for husband		£53,333

Situation I gives the husband £56,666, Situation II gives him only £35,000 and Situation III gives him £53,333. The executor has a discretion in deciding how much of the secured debt to allocate to bear the s.9 prior right. Although the choice lies in the discretion of the executor, it is suggested that it would be a perverse exercise of the discretion to allocate none of the heritable security to the s.9 right. The most equitable answer seems to be the third course, by allowing the prior right to be borne by the heritable security and the other moveables in the proportions the security and the other moveables bear to the whole estate.

Example 6. Partial intestacy.

X has died, survived by his wife and his mother, but predeceased by his only child and by his father. His estate (net of debts) consisted of the matrimonial home in which W is ordinarily resident, valued at £150,000; the furniture and plenishings of that house, valued at £30,000 and other moveable estate of £200,000.

X's will leaves the house, furniture and plenishings and a legacy of £50,000 to his wife, and the residue to his son, with no alternative provision. The result is a partial intestacy of the residue amounting to:

		150,000
Prior rights		
s.8 No house or furniture etc. included in intestate estate.	—	
s.9 Widow entitled to	89,000	
less legacy (s.9(1) proviso))	50,000	39,000
		111,000

Note: The fact that the values of the testamentary gifts of the house, furniture and plenishings are greater than the *maxima* which would have applied if they had been part of the intestate estate is of no consequence. The proviso to s.9(1) states that no deduction is made from the widow's right under s.9 in respect of a legacy of "any" house to which s.8 applies or of "any" furniture, etc. of such a house. It is not limited to the maximum values specified in s.8.

Legal rights
Widow's *jus relictae*—One half 55,500

55,500

Free estate
Whole to deceased's mother (s.2(1)(d)) 55,500

—

INDEX

valuation of property, 5–35
wills
  construction, 6–109
  testamentary freedom, 6–56
Legal share
generally, 8–19 to 8–35
"Legitim"
see also **Legal rights**
ante-nuptial marriage contracts, S12–01 to
  S12–02
assimilation of heritage and moveables,
  S1–02
construction of existing deeds, S33–01
construction of wills, 6–109
division, S6–02
generally, 5–08 to 5–09
intestate succession pre-1964 Act, 1–06 to
  1–09
legal rights
  collation *inter liberos*, 5–36 to 5–46
  discharge, 5–59
  evasion, 5–47
  generally, 5–08 to 5–09
  introduction, 5–01
  persons entitled, 5–13 to 5–18
  reform proposals, 8–19
  satisfaction, 5–51
posthumous children, 4–05
prior rights to financial provision, S9–18 to
  S9–21
representation, S11–01 to S11–02
Legitimation, S2–12, S37–01
peerages, 6–98, S37–01
Liabilities of estate
See **Debts**
Life policies
legal rights, 5–58
Securities for debts of the estate, 3–11 to
  3–12
Liferents
equitable compensation, S13–01
essential validity of wills, 6–58
leases, S16–01
legal rights
  evasion, 5–48
  satisfaction, 5–55
successive, 6–58
vesting of legacies, 6–113 to 6–121

Mackintosh Committee
adopted children, S2–08, S23–01
generally, 2–03
persons entitled to legal rights, 5–15
Marriage
See also **Divorce, Annulment**
revocation of wills, 6–40
revocation of survivorship destinations,
  4–22
Marriage contracts, ante nuptial
legal rights and, 5–51
legal rights before the 1964 Act, 1–10

Mental capacity
revocation of wills, 6–23, 6.31
Missing persons
survivorship
  generally, S31–02 to S31–03
  succession pre 1964 Act, 1–29 to 1–30
Monetary prior right
adopted children, and, S9–03
amount, S9–01
apportionment of payment between heritage
  and moveables, S9–23 to S9–24
estate affected, S9–18 to S9–22
executor-dative, and, S9–26
general, S9–01 to S9–08
illegitimate children, S9–03 to S9–06
interest, and, S9–02
legacies, and, S9–09 to S9–17
making payment, S9–25
supplementary provisions, S9A
Moral claim
Crown as *ultimus haeres*, S7–02
Mortgage protection policy
prior rights to dwelling house, and, S8–10
Mothers
abolition of old regime, and, 2–12
construction of wills
  illegitimate persons, 6–95
intestate succession pre 1964 Act
  heritage, 1–23
  moveables, 1–16 to 1–17
mutual wills, 6–28
prior right to financial provision, S9–05
residue of estate
  adopted children, S2–30
  collaterals, and, S2–25 to S2–26
  generally, S2–27
  illegitimate children, of, S2–28 to S2–29
revocation of wills, 6–26
right to office of executor, S14–09
unusual debts, 3–14
Mourning allowance
debts, 3–15
Moveable property
abolition of certain rights, S10–01 to
  S10–02
assimilation with moveables, S1–01 to
  S1–04
conversion to and from heritage, 5–29 to
  5–31
intestate succession pre 1964 Act
  collation *inter haeredes*, 1–24 to 1–26
  common law rules, 1–11 to 1–18
  fragmentation of approach, 1–04
  introduction, 1–03
  legal rights, 1–06 to 1–10
  representation of pre–deceasing heir, 1–19
  statutory preference, 1–05
legal rights, 5–28
special destinations, 5–32
Mutual wills
revocation of wills, 6–28